# Democracy, Governance, and Economic Performance

# Democracy, Governance, and Economic Performance

Theory and Evidence

Yi Feng

The MIT Press
Cambridge, Massachusetts
London, England

This book was set in Palatino on 3B2 by Asco Typesetters, Hong Kong, and was printed and bound in the United States of America.

Library of Congress Cataloging-in-Publication Data

Feng, Yi, 1956–
  Democracy, governance, and economic performance : theory and evidence / Yi Feng.
      p.    cm.
  Includes bibliographical references and index.
  ISBN 0-262-06235-6 (hc. : alk. paper)
  1. Democracy—Economic aspects. 2. Economic development—Political aspects.
3. Political science—Economic aspects. I. Title.
JC423 .F395 2003
338.9—dc21                                                        2002038677

10 9 8 7 6 5 4 3 2 1

For Katherine Qibing, Thomas, and Alex, with love

# Contents

# Preface

This book is about political institutions and economic performance. Recent years have witnessed a surge of literature on political and economic development, with the relationship between political systems and economic performance constituting an important component. Rising interest in this topic is a result of two grand trends that have, over the previous two decades, fundamentally altered how billions of people live and work: political democratization and economic liberalization. Beginning in the early 1990s, economists, political scientists, and sociologists have made this area of study one of the most dynamic and fruitful in the social sciences. It will remain one of the most important research topics—if not the single most important topic—in the field of international and comparative political economy for many years to come. The need to study the relationship between these two types of development is imperative, requiring explication and elaboration.

The purpose of this book is to investigate the circumstances under which democracy plays a crucial role in economic growth and development. In the exploration of this connection, other major facets of political life, such as government capacity and political stability, are examined. The interaction of the political and economic systems is perhaps the most basic fact of the world in which we are living.

I was motivated to write this book by a desire to bring together political analysis and economic approaches. I believe that economic activities are fundamentally human affairs and are therefore subject to the influence of political institutions that may inhibit or advance optimal production and consumption under the assumptions of neoclassical economics. When I set out to study the political economy of growth and development, I found that a new perspective was warranted. In a typical study of economic growth, political scientists tend to leave important details concerning economic conditions out of their consideration, whereas economists tend not to spend much time on a systematic explanation of political regimes. As Buchanan and Wagner lament, "The criteria for good [economic] theory are necessarily related to the political institutions of the society.... This necessary linkage or interdependence between the basic political structure of a society and the economic theory of policy has never been properly recognized by economists, despite its elementary logic and its overwhelming empirical appearance" (1977, 4–5).

Combining theoretical exposition with data analysis and case studies, this book emphasizes the conceptualization and operationalization of problems, subjecting theoretically driven implications to hypothesis testing. Each substantive chapter deals with the relationship between political systems and a particular aspect of economic performance or social development, such as economic growth, inflation, private investment, human capital, income distribution, economic freedom, and demographic trends. Ultimately, the fundamental relationships between political life and economic pursuits can be identified and examined through a systematic and integrative analysis.

The genesis of this book can be traced back to 1992, when I started teaching International Political Economy at the University of California, Riverside. Political and economic development was a recurrent issue surfacing throughout the class meetings. My interest in the subject was stimulated by the growing nexus between polities and economies in everyday life and by the increasing interdisciplinary collaboration among economics, political science, and sociology in academic pursuit. How is economic development defined and measured? How is democracy conceptualized and operationalized? Does democracy lead to higher or lower growth rates of an economy? Does economic development cause transitions to democracy? Are political democracy and political stability related? Do they have any consequences on growth or vice versa? What are their impacts on investment, education, inflation, economic freedom, and income equality? Answers to these questions require careful theoretical elaboration predicated on various assumptions, well-designed cross-country multivariate statistical investigation, and in-depth historical and country-specific case analysis.

Elements of the book began in my lecture notes, followed by the publication of over 50 articles on the political economy of economic development in political science and economics journals and as book chapters. Some chapters were adapted from earlier journal articles, while most were written for the purpose of presenting an organic whole of political and economic development. While I have published on the political economy of growth and development in the regions of sub-Sahara Africa (Feng 1996), Latin America (Feng 1995, Feng and Hsiang 1998), and Pacific Asia (Feng 2000a; Feng, Gizelis, and Lee 2002; Feng, Hsiang, and Lee 2002), this book intends to provide a *general* framework for theorizing about political economy of development and testing the related hypotheses.

As I wrote each chapter, imaginary readers, comprising both my colleagues from political science and economics and my past and future students, remained in the back of my mind. My hope is that this book will serve as useful complementary reading for courses in international political economy, international relations, comparative politics, economic growth, development economics, and studies of democracy and social development.

# Acknowledgments

In the long process of writing, I have accumulated untold intellectual and material debts to many people and institutions. I first want to thank two exceptional scholars for the inspiration of ideas in this book. I have learned from Bruce Bueno de Mesquita the importance of modeling individuals or coalitions engaging in strategic choices and interactions to shape the outcome of an event. I have also benefited from intellectual exchanges with Jacek Kugler, who is convinced that all actors, political or economic, are constrained by institutions and structures. Their ideas have influenced my research and thinking.

I am grateful to my students at Claremont Graduate University. They have used various segments from this book as a textual framework for further explorations. Their comments and critiques have improved the quality of the book and its applicability in the classroom. The transdisciplinary environment at the School of Politics and Economics of Claremont Graduate University particularly nurtures research of this kind.

I am very appreciative of research grants from the National Science Foundation, the Lincoln Foundation, the John Randolph Haynes and Dora Haynes Foundation, the Fletcher Jones Faculty Research Fellowship, and the Freeman Program in Asian Political Economy at the Claremont Colleges. My thanks also go to the Hoover Institution on War, Revolution, and Peace, at Stanford University, for the Edward Teller National Fellowship.

During many long hours of writing, I have benefited tremendously from exchanges of ideas with a great many of the finest scholars, including Thomas E. Borcherding, Shawn Bowler, Bruce Bueno de Mesquita, Baizhu Chen, Arthur T. Denzau, Larry Diamond, Mark J. Gasiorowski, John F. Helliwell, Robert W. Jackman,

Phillip Keefer, Jacek Kugler, Michael S. Lewis-Beck, Dean E. McHenry Jr., William H. Moore III, James D. Morrow, Paul Peretz, David Sanders, Randolph M. Siverson, Lewis W. Snider, Thomas D. Willett, and Paul J. Zak. Their comments and critique have sharpened my mind, clarified my thinking, and improved this work. Contributions made by Antonio C. Hsiang, Margaret Huckeba, Jae-Hoon Lee, Piyawat Sivaraks, and Aaron Williams to discussions on Indonesia, South Korea, and Thailand are also gratefully acknowledged.

I am indebted to Arthur S. Banks, Patricia Dillon, Mark J. Gasiorowski, Ted Robert Gurr, Philip Keefer, William H. Moore III, Robert Summers, Mark Wolkenfeld, Holger C. Wolf, and Frank Wykoff for making various data sets available for this study. I am grateful to panel participants at the annual meetings of the American Political Science Association, the International Studies Association, and the Public Choice Society, where the pristine forms of various components of this book have been presented. Brian Efird, Marie Besancon, Emily Acevedo, and Janina Enriquez have assisted in data collection. Kristin Johnson, Brinton Anderson-McGill, Sara Fisher, Steve Hellerman, and Michael Toner have proved invaluable with their prompt and efficient editorial assistance in preparing the manuscript. Sandra Seymour and Gwen Williams have provided indispensable logistic support.

I thank two anonymous reviewers for their insightful comments and excellent suggestions, which have helped improve the organization and presentation of the book. I am indebted to Mr. John S. Covell, Senior Editor at the MIT Press, whose deep commitment to the advancement of the social sciences will be a life-long stimulus to my career. I also thank Alan Thwaits and the rest of the production team at the MIT Press for their first-rate execution. *Earth Lights*, the cover image with its rich connotations for this book, was made available by NASA.

Some material was adapted from articles I published previously. I thank Cambridge University Press for permission to adapt part of "Democracy, Stability, and Economic Growth" (*British Journal of Political Science* 27: 397–418), Blackwell Publishers for permission to adapt part of "Political Institutions and Private Investment: A Study of Developing Countries" (*International Studies Quarterly* 45: 271–294), Elsevier Science for permission to adapt part of "Some Political Determinants of Economic Growth: Theory and Empirical

Implications" (coauthored with Baizhu Chen, *European Journal of Political Economy* 12: 609–627), and Taylor & Francis for permission to adapt "Democracy, Political Stability and Economic Performance" (*Encyclopedia of Political Economy*, 186–188) and "Democracy and Economic Growth" (*Routledge Encyclopedia of International Political Economy*, 299–304).

I dedicate this book to my wife, Katherine Qibing, and my sons, Thomas and Alex.

# Democracy, Governance, and Economic Performance

# 1    Introduction

## 1.1  Background

Scholarly work on political, social, and economic development has grown rapidly in recent years; economists, political scientists, and sociologists have made this area of research one of the most dynamic and fruitful in the social sciences. This book systematically incorporates principles of political science and economics into a single research agenda in order to seek an understanding of the interplay between politics and economics. Specifically, the book focuses on the political determinants of economic performance. A primary topic throughout is whether or not democracy or political freedom contributes to quality of life by providing a useful and constructive political infrastructure.

This book systematically studies three major dimensions of a political system—political freedom, political stability, and policy certainty—and relates them to economic development. These dimensions constitute the political foundation of economic management and affect not only economic growth, but also the economic determinants of growth, such as inflation, investment, human capital, income inequality, property rights, and population growth. The book studies both the direct and indirect effects on economic growth of the political institutions examined herein. Of the three variables, the role played by democracy or political freedom in growth is the most controversial. Democracy has been both lauded as a vehicle for happiness and prosperity, and blamed for hampering capital formation and the long-term growth of nations. On one side of the debate lies the characteristic viewpoint of less developed countries, where poverty is rampant: "The poverty and hunger are not the result of a scarcity of food. The world is awash with food. But they are the result of scarcity of democracy" (Carmen 1996, 94). Scholars, in contrast, often voice concerns about the pitfalls that democracy presents to economic development. For instance, in the development literature, one encounters the concept of "antagonistic growth," which refers to a situation where democratic governments face the possibly untenable problem of resolving conflicting claims of vested interests while concurrently pursuing sustainable paths for growth (Foxley, MacPherson, and O'Donnell 1986).[1]

Some scholars tend to base theoretical arguments on a simple relationship between democracy and development (for example, the two conflicting perspectives noted above), but by doing so, they ignore complex relationships that belong within the focus of this book. Their theoretical efforts argue for and against the direct effect of democracy on growth. However, we also need to carefully examine the *indirect* effects of democracy on growth through reduction of political instability, promotion of private investment, improvement in human capital, correction of income inequality, protection of property rights, and facilitation of demographic transitions.[2] As a result, this book aims at studying the complex relationships between politics and growth by examining both direct and indirect effects. It formalizes and tests the effects of democracy on growth and subsequently studies the potential indirect effects of democracy on the factors that affect economic growth. Those variables include political stability, inflation, investment, education, income distribution, property rights, and population growth.

The controversy regarding the effect of democracy on economic development and growth stems from using entirely different assumptions to buttress the final claims. A theoretical impasse will ensue if we cling to these assumptions without first examining the circumstances by which some of these assumptions are closer to the truth than others. Breakthroughs in the evaluation of these claims must start with empirical evidence stipulated or implied by general theory.

Hyland raises three qualities of democracy against which this form of government should be evaluated:

The robust conception of democracy as effective political equality grounded in an informed understanding of public affairs will have to be evaluated as a political ideal from three perspectives. Firstly, as Schumpeter says, it is a method for arriving at political decisions.... Secondly, however, we need to take into account the more general impact that the operation of democratic procedures might be expected to have on the quality of life of people living in a community of political equals. Thirdly, we need to take seriously the possibility that the complexity of human actions and institutions that constitute democracy in action have constitutive features that are intrinsically worthwhile, independent of any consequences whether direct or indirect. (1995, 164)

The second feature of democracy noted by Hyland constitutes the groundwork on which the theorization and empirical testing of this book are carried out. In this book, democracy is not evaluated on the basis of its intrinsic normative value. Rather, it is examined for its general effects on the major aspects of people's substantive livelihoods. These aspects are realized via political and economic processes and include political stability, economic growth, inflation, physical capital formation, human capital accumulation, income equality, the protection of property rights, and demographic transitions. Furthermore, it is the *degree* or *level* of democracy or political freedom (rather than the qualitative state of democracy) that is studied as the independent variable here. I am interested in whether or not political freedom or a high degree of democracy improves life through promoting economic growth, reducing income inequality, and improving education.

## 1.2   A Basic Puzzle

Some countries grow fast, while others grow slowly. Academics and policy makers have long been puzzled by the coexistence of the uneven and erratic growth trajectories of some less-developed countries and the rapid and sustained growth paths of other formerly less-developed countries. The discrepancy in economic growth among various countries has become a tantalizing research target for scholars.

For instance, the economic miracles produced in some Pacific Asian countries have been stellar. Despite the 1997 financial crisis that plagued the region, these countries still outperformed most developing nations. Following Balassa (1991), who compares eight Pacific Asian economies with Latin American countries at similar levels of development, I compare real GDP per capita in Indonesia, South Korea, Malaysia, the Philippines, Taiwan, and Thailand to a larger comparison group and with a more precise measure than Balassa.[3] I exclude Singapore and Hong Kong, as they both are city-economies and their performance tends to be dominated by their financial sectors. The inclusion of these two high fliers would have made the Pacific Asian group look even better.

Figures 1.1 through 1.4 are based on the real-GDP-per-capita data from *The Penn World Table* (version 6), compiled by Summers and Heston (2001), who adjust national income levels according to purchasing-power parity and thus overcome the complications caused by using foreign-currency exchange rates.[4] They demonstrate long-run economic growth trends in those countries.

Economic growth in this book is indicated by the average annual growth rate of real gross domestic product (GDP) per capita, as defined in *The Penn World Table*. There are three real-GDP-per-capita measures in the data: RGDP, CGDP, and RGDPCH. RGDP is real GDP per capita, based on 1985 price levels. It is suitable for studies that involve relatively "short" time series close to 1985. CGDP is current-year real GDP per capita and is ideal for cross-country, single-year analysis. RGDPCH is real GDP per capita that uses a price chain index with the base year changed from year to year. Of the three, this book focuses on RGDPCH, which is adjusted both annually to capture price changes and cross-sectionally to reflect purchasing-power parity. By design, it is the best indicator of long-run economic growth.

Figure 1.1 presents the growth paths of the selected Pacific Asian countries for the period of 1960 through 1998. In general, this group of countries follows a growth pattern characterized by overall increases and a lack or absence of reversals until 1997, when a major financial crisis hit the region. South Korea and Taiwan are the two economies that stand out in long-run economic growth. Their GDP per capita levels started below the levels of the Philippines and Malaysia in 1960. At that time Taiwan's GDP per capita was 1,466 international dollars, and South Korea's was 1,474, compared to 2,090 for the Philippines and 2,134 for Malaysia. Toward the end of the 1960s, the real per capita GDP levels in South Korea, Taiwan, and Malaysia began to mirror each other until 1984, when Malaysia's GDP per capita dropped. Taiwan also withstood the 1997 financial crisis relatively well. Thailand's population-adjusted GDP level had been below those of the three countries named above, but since 1987 has moved significantly higher than those of Indonesia and the Philippines. From 1960 to 1998 the growth leaders in this region were Taiwan (6.7%) and South Korea (6.1%), followed by Thailand (4.5%), Indonesia (4.1%), Malaysia (3.7%), and the Philippines (1.3%). The

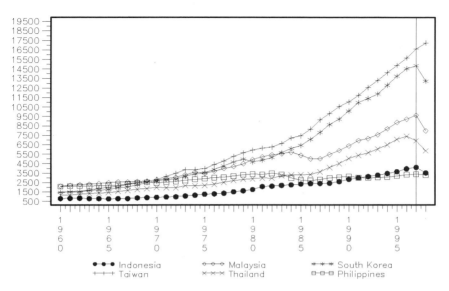

**Figure 1.1**
Real GDP per capita of selected Pacific Asian economies

numbers in parentheses are the average annual growth rates of real GDP per capita from 1960 to 1998.

Countries being compared fall into three groups: Latin America, sub-Saharan Africa, and the G-7 nations. For Latin American and sub-Saharan countries, they have to satisfy two selection criteria: they are among the largest economies in the region in 1960 below the 2,600 international dollar mark in Summers and Heston's data, a level under which the six Pacific Asian economies started at 1960, and their population exceeded one million. Only nine Latin American countries qualify: Bolivia, Brazil, Colombia, Dominican Republic, Ecuador, Guatemala, Honduras, Panama, and Paraguay. From sub-Sahara, ten countries enter my selection: Angola, Cameroon, Central African Republic, Côte d'Ivoire, Ghana, Mozambique, Niger, Senegal, Zambia, and Zimbabwe.

Compared to the Pacific Asian countries' smooth and almost monotonously increasing growth trend, most of these Latin American countries show a growth pattern of relative flatness and even decline (figure 1.2). During the 1980s, also known as the lost decade, they encountered substantial negative growth. From 1975 to 1982, Latin America's long-term debt increased from $45.2 billion to $176.4

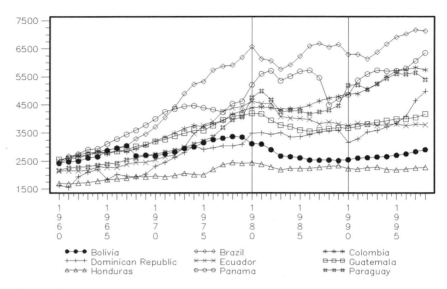

**Figure 1.2**
Real GDP per capita of selected Latin American economies

billion. Including short-term loans and IMF credits, the total debt in 1982 was $333 billion. The financial bankruptcy in Latin America led to huge budget deficits and entrenched inflation.[5] Over the years examined, only two countries in this group grew well: the Dominican Republic, whose GDP per capita increased at an average annual rate of 3.2%, and Brazil, whose annual growth averaged 2.9%. The laggards were Bolivia (0.5%) and Honduras (0.8%). Even if we include the Asian financial crisis period, the average growth rate of real GDP per capita at the international price level was 4.4% for the six Pacific Asian countries and regions, but only 2.0% for the nine Latin American countries.

Similar statistics were calculated for the ten sub-Saharan African economies that were at a comparable level to the six Asian economies in 1960. Their income per capita was comparable to that of East Asia in 1960, ranging from 1,606 for Ghana to 2,447 for Angola, in terms of international prices. As figure 1.3 demonstrates, the growth rates in the ten African countries have been neither strong nor stable. The sizeable reductions in Angola's and Zambia's economies are staggering. Within a few years of 1973 in Angola and 1974 in Zambia, the two countries' national wealth was halved. Only three

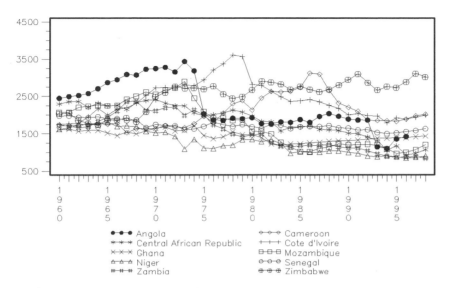

**Figure 1.3**
Real GDP per capita of selected sub-Saharan economies

economies—Cameroon, Côte d'Ivoire, and Zimbabwe—had a positive average annual growth rate, with Zimbabwe's at 1.2%, far ahead of second-place Cameroon (0.67%) and third-place Côte d'Ivoire (0.56%). The average annual growth rates for the rest were negative. The Central African Republic, Ghana, Mozambique, Niger, Senegal, and Zambia all had a higher level of real GDP per capita in 1960 than in 1998. In the data Angola ended 1996 with per capita GDP of 1,419, which is significantly lower than its level in 1960: 2,447. The average growth rate for the 10 countries over the period of 1960 through 1998 was about −0.5%. Whereas Latin American countries lost a decade, many sub-Saharan countries are likely to lose half a century, if not more.

In general, the growth trends in these African countries look similar to those of the nine Latin American countries. There are two common features of the growth trajectories for these two groups of nations: their growth rates have been low, and many of these countries have frequently experienced negative growth. While the former phenomenon may imply some systemic factors that prevent countries from growing fast, the latter shows that development in some of these countries has been unstable and unsustainable.

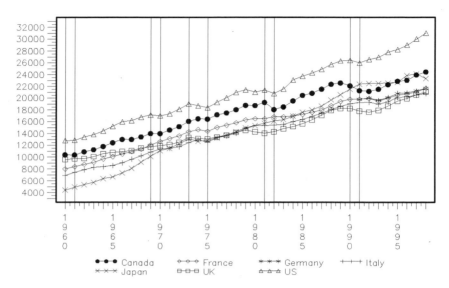

**Figure 1.4**
Real GDP per capita of the G-7 economies

Finally, figure 1.4 depicts the growth pattern of the richest nations in the world: Canada, France, Germany, Italy, Japan, the United Kingdom, and the United States. The seven economies show a smoothly ascending growth pattern, which is qualitatively similar to that of the Pacific Asian countries. The average growth rate for this group over the period of 1960 through 1998 is 2.8%. The United States and Canada led the group. The four European countries evince a high degree of homogeneity in the growth trajectories of their real GDP per capita, which in combination with their homogenous domestic economic institutions, has been conducive to their economic integration, culminating in the European Union (Feng and Genna 2003).

The reference lines in figure 1.4 signify five economic recessions in the United States from 1960 to 1998: those recessions were during 1960–1961, 1969–1970, 1973–1975, 1981–1982, and 1990–1991. In addition to the five recessions in this period, there was also a short recession in 1980. As I am finishing this book, the United States' economy is still suffering from a recession that started in 2000. On Monday, July 22, 2002, the Dow Jones Industrial Average

(DJIA) fell to its first close below 8,000 since October 1998, down from its record high of 11,722.98 on January 14, 2000. The Nasdaq and S&P 500 dropped to their lowest closes since May 1997. As will be made clear in chapter 2, however, the focus of this book is long-run economic growth, rather than cyclical economic symptoms. Figure 1.4 shows that the United States and the others have recovered from each recession and subsequently increased their wealth to much higher levels.

Why do the G-7 and the six Pacific Asian countries have similar growth patterns? Why are the growth experiences of the nine Latin American and ten African nations so alike? Why did Zimbabwe perform well relative to other countries in the sub-Saharan group? Do politics and policy play a role in determining growth rates? Scholars who argue for democracy will show that an increase in political freedom feeds back to sustainable long-run growth in Taiwan and South Korea, the two countries that eventually became full democracies in the 1990s. People who argue against democracy will point at the Philippines, which has gained ground regarding political freedom but continued to lose its economic battles.

We have observed some regional regularity in the figures above. While growth has been generally stable in Pacific Asia and the G-7 countries, it has vacillated wildly in many sub-Saharan and Latin American countries. Why do these regional patterns form? What regional factors act behind the economic growth curves? Are these factors affecting Latin American countries and sub-Saharan countries in the same manner? Most important, can those regional patterns be generalized and explained by a theory of economic growth? This book intends to provide answers to these debates and questions. As we will see, the regional similarities are related to the political and economic regularities.

## 1.3   An Analytical Structure

The objective of this book is to examine political factors that differentiate a country's growth history from the patterns of other countries. The long-run growth rate of a country is determined by politics, as well as economic behavior and demographic trends. On the one hand, given a nation's propensity to consume (and thus to save) and its demographic structures involving fertility and mortality rates, a targeted level of development will be set and eventually met, if everything else is kept constant. Political institutions have the potential for relaxing the constraints imposed on economic and demographic structures and, consequently, raising the development level, which would otherwise have been determined by economic and demographic elements alone.

Barro (1997) has provided a framework for the determination of growth. In his model, $g = f(y, y^*)$, where $g$ is the growth rate of per capita output (e.g., gross domestic product), $y$ is the current level of per capita output, and $y^*$ is the steady-state level of per capita output. At the steady-state level, the level of output per worker still increases because of exogenous labor-augmenting technological innovations, though the output per unit of effective labor will remain constant.[6] In such an economy, output, investment, and population grow at the same rate. Given the steady-state level of output $y^*$, an increase in output decreases the growth rate of future output because of diminishing returns (i.e., $\partial g / \partial y < 0$). Given the current output level $y$, an increase in the eventual equilibrium level of output $y^*$ will increase the growth rate of output (i.e., $\partial g / \partial y^* > 0$).

The first proposition implies that rich countries will grow more slowly than poor countries, and thus gives rise to the convergence hypothesis.[7] According to the convergence hypothesis, the nine Latin American countries and ten sub-Saharan countries should grow at a rate similar to the six Pacific Asian countries, and all those countries should grow faster than the G-7 countries. Actually, only the Pacific Asian group (except the Philippines) was able to attain a growth rate higher than the average growth of the G-7 countries. There is no evidence or weak evidence for the growth patterns predicted by the neoclassical economic theory of growth based on the diminishing-returns principle, and this consequently forces us to look at the second proposition.

The steady-state level of output is determined by economic, social, cultural, demographic, and political structures. It depends on savings and consumption patterns, fertility, life expectancy, and (last but not least) political determinants such as political stability, democracy, and policy certainty. For a society with a propensity toward consumption and an aversion to savings (e.g., as the result of a national prevalence of a culturally informed value system), the steady-state level of output is lower than that of a nation that saves and invests a lot, with everything else held constant. In addition to economic and demographic factors, output at the steady-state level is determined by political and social institutions. For instance, "tax rates, the extent of distortions of markets and business decisions, maintenance of the rule of law and property rights, and the degree of political freedom" (Barro 1997, 8) may all affect growth.

In general, an improvement in political conditions will lead to faster and sustained growth; however, due to diminishing returns, this politically generated growth eventually will be slowed to a rate mainly determined by exogenous technological innovations. In this scenario of politically enhanced growth, the effects of political institutions on growth may persist over a long period of time (Barro 1997). For example, when a nation increases its level of economic freedom from a minimal to a maximal level as the result of political change, tremendous room will be created for long-run economic growth. Under such circumstances, the role played by politics has to be crucial in influencing economic performance.

This book seriously considers the argument that political institutions matter in growth. While it espouses the principles of the New Institutional Economics (e.g., North 1990, Furubotn and Richter 1997), its focus is on the general political conditions for economic performance, rather than specific economic relations informed by transaction costs, property rights, contracts, and voting games.

Using individual rationality constrained by politics as the foundation for explaining economic behavior (Bates 2001), the book begins with an exposition of a mathematical model of expected utility in order to incorporate political considerations into the economic decision-making process. The theoretical results indicate that the growth of any economy is embedded in political institutions that set the political parameters for economic as well as social development. As North aptly points out, "It is the incentive structure imbedded in the institutional/organizational structure of economies that has to be a key to unraveling the puzzle of uneven and erratic growth" (North 1996a, 3).

As political institutions are at the very center of this book's investigation, they need to be defined here. North makes a distinction between institutions and organizations:

Institutions are the rules of the game—both formal rules and informal constraints (conventions, norms of behavior and self-imposed codes of conducts)—and their enforcement characteristics. Together, they define the way the game is played....

Organizations are the players. They are made up of groups of individuals held together by some common objectives. Economic organizations are firms, trade unions, cooperatives, etc.; political organizations are political parties, legislatures, regulatory bodies, vocational training centers. (North 1996b, 342, 356)

This book emphasizes institutions defined as such, as it examines the systematic characteristics related to political organizations. These characteristics may be guided by some norms (such as liberal democracy in the case of political freedom, or capitalism in the case of economic freedom), or they may be institutionalized behavior (such as political stability and policy certainty).[8] Political and economic freedom, as well as liberal democracy, clearly have normative values and represent rules, whereas coups d'état and revolutions, when achieving a status of relative regularity in a country, belong to institutionalized political behavior. Therefore, the phrase "political institutions" in this book has specific meaning and connotations. In particular, it refers to political freedom, political stability, and policy certainty, the definitions of which will all become clear in the following chapters.

It is not the purpose of this project to examine whether the Ministry of Trade and Industry has designed a feasible industrial policy, or whether a specific policy has worked well under the guidance of a certain government. Rather, the focus will be on the general rules and behavior of the political system. While a great deal of research has been carried out to investigate the economic dimensions of the problem (e.g., trade, finance, and investment), the attention given to the effect of political institutions on economic growth is far from adequate. Additionally, some research on the political economy of growth in less developed countries has tended to focus on the effects of specific government policies on the economy, rather than examine the overall relationship between political systems and growth.[9]

In contrast, this work is devoted to a study of the general patterns of political regimes and economic growth in a cross-national setting. Of all broad features of political institutions, the particular focus here is on three such features: the type of political system (e.g., the degree of political freedom), political stability (e.g., the likelihood of unconstitutional government change), and policy certainty (e.g., the intensity of political opposition). As this book will demonstrate, the three political aspects, although related, are distinct from one another. In terms of their relationships to economic growth, there are two major implications. First, no single political dimension alone can determine growth; second, in addition to their direct impact on growth, these political aspects also affect growth through their influence on other variables that are themselves either detrimental or conducive to growth. Such factors include inflation, investment, human capital, income inequality, property rights, and population growth.

## 1.4  Outline of the Book

This book studies the direct and indirect effects of political institutions on economic growth. Chapter 2 provides a theoretical foundation for the book by formalizing the effects of political institutions on economic growth. The propositions from the model show that political freedom, political stability, and policy certainty—the three main facets of political institutions that constitute the basic political environment for economic growth and socioeconomic development—all condition and constrain an individual's economic decision to invest in reproducible capital in the marketplace.

Chapter 3 introduces measurements of the variables that will be used to test various propositions and hypotheses in the book. In particular, it reviews or develops the measures of the three key political variables identified in the mathematical model of chapter 2, namely, political freedom, political stability, and policy certainty. The chapter examines the reliability of various indices of political freedom and constructs the variables for political stability and policy certainty.

On the basis of the theoretical model in chapter 2 and the measurements in chapter 3, chapter 4 first tests the implications of the model so far developed—i.e., the effects on economic growth of political freedom, political stability, and policy certainty—controlling the variables that have been argued as economic determinants of growth: initial level of development, inflation, investment, education, property rights, and population growth.

The following chapters investigate the indirect effects of democracy on growth through the channels of those other variables studied in chapter 4, i.e., political instability, inflation, investment, education, income distribution, property rights, and population growth. For instance, political freedom may indirectly promote economic growth by reducing income inequality or by building a public educational system. Chapter 5 investigates the impact of democracy on political stability, an important channel through which democracy promotes long-run growth. It is the first step in this book to show that democracy promotes economic growth in a complex way. Chapter 6 studies the effects of political institutions on inflation. While inflation is found in general to have a negative effect on growth, it is important to find out how political institutions affect inflation, so that the effects of political institutions on long-run growth can be better understood. Chapter 7 studies the effects of political institutions on private investment, arguing that political freedom, policy certainty, and political stability all affect the individual's decision to invest in the asset market. Chapter 8 investigates the relationship between the state and education. It focuses on the effect of political freedom on both years of and higher education. While controlling for political stability, I argue that a democratic political system with strong political capacity is the key to success in accumulating human capital. Chapter 9 revisits the issue of democracy and income equality, focusing upon the effect of democracy on the reduction of income inequality, a topic studied by numerous political scientists and sociologists in the 1970s and 1980s. Benefiting from a tremendous improvement in the quantity and quality of income distribution data, as well as data on political institutions, this chapter evaluates various models regarding the relationship between a democratic political system and the level of income inequality. Chapter 10 uses the Granger-causality procedure to examine the association between political freedom and economic freedom. The purpose of the statistical design is to find out whether political freedom increases economic freedom, thus improving the conditions for long-run growth. Chapter 11 analyzes the effects of political institutions on population growth, which is one of the most important determinants of long-run economic growth. This chapter is one of the very few works that link politics to growth through the demographic structure. Chapter 12 concludes the book by reviewing the major results in this research and suggesting policy implications.

# 2        The Fundamental Political Environment for Economic Growth

*It is the incentive structure imbedded in the institutional/organizational structure of economies that has to be a key to unraveling the puzzle of uneven and erratic growth.*

Douglass C. North

The preceding chapter posed the question of why certain countries grow faster than others and posited political institutions as significant in the growth trajectory of a nation. In this chapter, section 2.1 will discuss three main features of political institutions in the context of their respective impacts on, and their creation of the basic environment for, economic growth and socioeconomic development. Section 2.2 discusses the implications of the theoretical model in section 2.1, arguing that an individual's economic decisions are rationally conditioned by his assessment of the political environs for the marketplace. In particular, economic growth—a function of accumulation of reproducible capital—will increase or decrease as a function of three political variables: political freedom, political stability, and policy certainty.

To illustrate the potential effects of the three variables, section 2.3 offers some casual observations and case studies investigating different patterns of economic growth in developing countries. This section also demonstrates the offsetting effects of these variables under certain conditions. While none of the three variables is a sufficient condition for growth, all together they play critical roles in lifting countries out of poverty. The last section of the chapter discusses the policy implications of the political-economy model of economic growth.

## 2.1   The Basic Model

This section elaborates on a model that identifies some fundamental political conditions for economic growth.[1] The model incorporates political factors into an endogenous growth model and derives the effects of political repression, political stability, and policy certainty on long-run economic growth.[2] While it is based on some simplifying assumptions, the theoretical results the model derives have general significance regarding political institutions and economic development.

The model considers an economy without population growth where individuals live for two periods and have the same preferences. Assume that a representative individual born in period $t-1$ maximizes the following time-separable utility function:

$$V_t = u(c_{t-1}) + \frac{1}{1+\rho} E_t u(d_t) \qquad [1]$$

In [1], $c$ is the individual's consumption when young, $d$ is the individual's consumption when old, $t$ the time period, $\rho$ the measure of time preference, and $E$ the expectation operator. For simplicity of calculation, the intratemporal utility function is assumed to have constant elasticity:

$$u(c_{t-1}) = \frac{1}{1-\sigma} c_{t-1}^{1-\sigma} \quad \text{and} \quad u(d_t) = \frac{1}{1-\sigma} d_t^{1-\sigma} \qquad [2]$$

Here $0 < \sigma < 1$ measures the elasticity of intertemporal substitution. Such a utility form satisfies the concave function characterized by the diminishing utility in consumption. It also simplifies the mathematical calculation when derivatives are taken.

The budget constraint when the individual is young is

$$c_{t-1} + k_t = y_{t-1}, \qquad [3]$$

where $y_{t-1}$ is the individual's income when young and $k_t$ is the accumulation of reproducible capital, including human capital. Obviously in this model, income levels determine the amounts of consumption and investment. One important innovation of the theory of reproducible capital is how an individual allocates his time over various activities in the current period affects his productivity in the future period (Arrow 1962, Romer 1986, Lucas 1988).

Also, since $k$ is the composite of physical and human capital, it creates a knowledge spill-over on the basic skills of the new generation. Income when young is defined as

$$y_{t-1} = w_{t-1}k_{t-1} = y_{t-1}, \qquad [4]$$

where $w$ is an exogenous endowment of "basic skills." It measures personal productivity in utilizing the total capital accumulated, as wage-earning potential varies from person to person with the same level of reproducible capital. Since $k$ can be considered the average accumulation of reproducible capital in the economy, equation [4] implies that the reproducible capital accumulated by the previous generation is a positive externality on the income of the new generation. The higher the average capital accumulated, the higher the income for the new generation, with the endowment of basic skills kept constant.

So far, we have an economic model of consumption and investment. A person decides how much to consume currently and invest for consumption in the future, conditioned by his income, while how much he earns depends on his idiosyncratic capacity and the existing reproducible capital.

Next, political factors are embedded into the model according to economic factors and considerations. Any economy functions within some sort of political framework, and consequently it is impossible for an economic agent to be impervious to the political structure surrounding the economy. Of all the political factors, the model identifies three as fundamentally important. First, we start with a political regime that exists during the first period of the economic agent's life. If this regime remains in power in the second period, with a probability of $\pi$, the budget constraint of the individual when old is

$$d_t = r_t(1 - \tau)k_t, \qquad \tau < 1, \qquad [5]$$

where $r_t$ is the exogenous rate of return, and $\tau$ is the social cost imposed by the government.[3] Therefore, $(1 - \tau)$ measures how well an individual can appropriate the returns on his physical and human capital investment, given the political constraints.[4] In a broad sense, $\tau$ captures the idea of how a government runs an economy. The government may be repressive, expropriating the gains of the marketplace and stifling productivity. The totalitarian government in the Soviet Union or China under Mao belongs to the extremely repressive category. Or the government may be conducive to the market by establishing rules that protect growth-enhancing incentives. For instance, the government may pass laws and take actions to protect property rights. The government may also provide public goods, such as national defense, communications networks, transportation infrastructure, research, and education, all of which lead to increased private investment. Note that when government policy has a positive effect on the incentive of the economic agent to invest, $\tau$ takes a negative value, which will augment the investment returns to the individual, when the exogenous rate $r$ is kept constant. When government policy takes a toll on the economic activities, $\tau$ takes a positive value between zero and one.[5] As a result, the total returns to the individual will decrease, compared to the benchmark of no government, which is $d_t = r_t k_t$. The variable $\tau$ reflects the fundamental characteristics of a political system. For the sake of argument, it is called political repression, the reverse of which is *political freedom*, one of the three principal political variables in this book.

*Political stability* is another political variable to be placed in the model. Since the probability that the current government will extend its rule for the second period is only $\pi$, the probability that the current regime will be replaced at period $t$ must be $1 - \pi$. If the current government can maintain its rule in the future, then we can expect policy continuation. Investors will not be surprised by any significant policy change. In this simplified model, I assume that each political regime is identified with a particular set of policies, and that those policies do not change fundamentally. If the policies do undergo radical change, that is equivalent to a political regime change. One example is the policy change from Mao's Cultural Revolution to Deng's economic reform. While both periods were under the reign of the Communist Party of China, they were guided by different political and policy agendas. Therefore, the political regime changed for the two historical periods. The variable $\pi$ captures the longevity of the current government; it is another name for political stability in this book.

Also, assume that once the new political regime is installed, there is a probability of 50% that the new regime will be more repressive than the current one by $\Delta\tau$ (and logically a probability of 50% that it will be less repressive by $\Delta\tau$). According to Alesina, Özler, Roubini, and Swagel (1996), it can be reasonably assumed that regime change produces uncertainty when a large sample of cases is examined. In a mathematical model, a 50% probability best captures the uncertainty brought about by regime change.

Thus the budget constraint of the old generation when a new political regime is installed is

$$d_t = r_t(1 - \tau + \Delta\tau)k_t, \quad \text{with } p = \frac{1}{2}, \tag{6}$$

$$d_t = r_t(1 - \tau - \Delta\tau)k_t, \quad \text{with } p = \frac{1}{2}, \tag{7}$$

where $\Delta\tau$ measures the difference in political and social cost imposed by the new and old regimes. In this simplified model, the specification of the incremental change of repression can be viewed as a special case of a random-walk process, in which the innovations of repression take only two discrete values with equal probability. Again, the idea is to capture political uncertainty caused by regime change. The 50% probability is based on the assumption that the policy of the new political regime is untested and, once the new regime is installed, it is equally likely to be either more or less repressive than the current regime by $\Delta\tau$. Here $\Delta\tau$ gives us the third political variable, which I call *policy uncertainty*, the reverse of which is *policy certainty*. If $\Delta\tau$ equals zero, then there will not be any policy difference between the current and future political regimes. In other words, policy certainty is the highest when $\Delta\tau$ equals zero.

With the three political variables in place, the individual's problem is to maximize equation [1], subject to constraints [2] to [7]. That is:

$$\text{Max}_{c_{t-1},k_t} \, u(c_{t-1}) + \frac{1}{1+\rho} E_t u(d_t) \tag{8}$$

Setting the marginal utility from consumption in $t - 1$ equal to the marginal utility from consumption in $t$,

$$c_{t-1}^{-\sigma} = \frac{1}{1+\rho} \left( \pi(r_t(1 - \tau))^{1-\sigma} \right.$$

$$\left. + \left( \frac{1-\pi}{2} \right) \left( (r_t(1 - \tau + \Delta\tau))^{1-\sigma} + (r_t(1 - \tau - \Delta\tau))^{1-\sigma} \right) k_t^{-\sigma} \tag{9}$$

Dividing both sides of [9] by $k_t^{-\sigma}$ and substituting $w_{t-1}k_{t-1} - k_t$ for $c_{t-1}$,

$$\left(\frac{k_t}{w_{t-1}k_{t-1} - k_t}\right)^{\sigma}$$

$$= (1+\rho)^{-1}\left(\pi(1-\tau)^{1-\sigma} + \frac{1-\pi}{2}((1-\tau+\Delta\tau)^{1-\sigma} + (1-\tau-\Delta\tau)^{1-\sigma})\right)r_t^{1-\sigma}$$

[10]

Defining $g = \dfrac{k_t}{k_{t-1}}$ and denoting

$$\beta(\pi, \tau, \Delta\tau) = \pi(1-\tau)^{1-\sigma}$$

$$+ \left(\frac{1-\pi}{2}\right)((1-\tau+\Delta\tau)^{1-\sigma} + (1-\tau-\Delta\tau)^{1-\sigma}),$$    [11]

we have

$$g = w_{t-1}(1 + (1+\rho)^{1/\sigma}r_t^{1-1/\sigma}\beta^{-1/\sigma})^{-1}.$$    [12]

Evidently, $\beta$ and $g$ are monotonically increasing or decreasing.[6]

LEMMAS   (i) $\partial\beta/\partial\pi > 0$,   (ii) $\partial\beta/\partial\Delta\tau < 0$,   (iii) $\partial\beta/\partial\tau < 0$.

*Proof*   (i) Equation [11] implies that

$$\frac{\partial\beta}{\partial\pi} = (1-\tau)^{1-\sigma} - \frac{1}{2}((1-\tau+\Delta\tau)^{1-\sigma} + (1-\tau-\Delta\tau)^{1-\sigma}) > 0.$$    [13]

Since $(1-\tau)^{1-\sigma}$ is a concave function of $(1-\tau)$, it follows that $(1-\tau)^{1-\sigma}$ is larger than the average value of $(1-\tau+\Delta\tau)^{1-\sigma}$ and $(1-\tau-\Delta\tau)^{1-\sigma}$. So we have $\partial\beta/\partial\pi > 0$.

(ii) Take the first order derivative of Equation [11] with respect to $\Delta\tau$, we have

$$\frac{\partial\beta}{\partial\Delta\tau} = \underbrace{\frac{1-\pi}{2}}_{+}\underbrace{(1-\sigma)}_{+}\underbrace{((1-\tau+\Delta\tau)^{-\sigma} - (1-\tau-\Delta\tau)^{-\sigma})}_{-} < 0$$    [14]

(iii) Taking the first-order derivative of equation [11] with respect to $\tau$, we have

$$\frac{\partial\beta}{\partial\tau} = \underbrace{(\sigma-1)}_{-}\left[\underbrace{\pi(1-\tau)^{-\sigma}}_{+} + \underbrace{\frac{1}{2}(1-\pi)}_{+}\underbrace{((1-\tau+\Delta\tau)^{-\sigma} + (1-\tau-\Delta\tau)^{-\sigma})}_{+}\right] < 0.$$

[15]

Q.E.D.

The lemmas yield the following propositions:

(i)   $\dfrac{\partial g}{\partial \pi} > 0$

(ii)  $\dfrac{\partial g}{\partial (\Delta \tau)} < 0$

(iii) $\dfrac{\partial g}{\partial \tau} < 0$

Therefore, we can draw the following theoretical conclusions: *ceteris paribus*, first, the lower the probability of the survival of the current regime or the higher the level of political instability, the lower the growth rate; second, the more polarized the policy positions between opposing parties or the higher the degree of policy uncertainty, the lower the growth rate; third, the more repressive the government or the lower the level of political freedom, the lower the growth rate.

## 2.2   A Theoretical Discussion

"Economic development occurs when persons form capital and invest, making present sacrifices in order to reap future gains" (Bates 2001, 101). This chapter derives the direct linkage between three political variables and capital formation. These political variables represent three fundamental dimensions of a political system. The variable $\pi$ stands for political stability, as it conceptualizes the probability of the current political regime remaining in place. The variable $\tau$ indicates the political and social cost imposed by this regime on the economy. The term $\Delta \tau$ is the difference between the current regime and the potential future regime in terms of their respective political and social costs to the economy. Notice that, according to the model, what is emphasized here is the margin, rather than the direction, of the policy shift between the current and future governments. While the future regime's policy could be more or less repressive than that of the current regime, political uncertainty ensues from concern that the market has not tested the policy formulated by a drastically different government to be installed in the future.

Evaluating the political environment is an essential part of an investor's reasoning process when he makes a decision regarding investment and consumption. Particularly, he is concerned about the likelihood of the current regime being replaced in the future, that is, how large $\pi$ is. Associated with the probability of regime change is the degree of policy deviation by the new government in the future from the current government ($\Delta\tau$). Finally, political freedom ($-\tau$) that favors investment under the current government is also a concern. The following paragraphs detail each of these propositions.

The probability of political regime change, no matter how small, always exists. According to the model, an individual born in the current period is assumed to be uncertain of the policy, and its implications, that would be generated by a new government, if installed. Associated with the probability of a new government replacing the current one is the notion that the policy of the future government is not tested or experienced by the marketplace. Given that the investor is risk averse, he would prefer to wait rather than risk his investment today, particularly if there is a large probability that the current government will be superseded by a new one. Radical political change involving different regimes particularly adds to the uncertainty of investment decision making, thus reducing capital inflow and economic growth. As we will find in chapter 7, investment requires a stable political environment. Though it is dramatic to say that one can make money in any policy environment as long as it remains unchanged, there is a lot of truth in this adage: investors appreciate consistent public policy, which comes more easily if the government does not change. Of course, some countries have experienced military coups without concurrent or subsequent changes to the economic system or the policies installed by the previous government. Economic growth should not be seriously affected as a result. I will examine this case in chapter 4.

The theoretical model specifies government change as a prototype of fundamental government change. Such change is often the result of a military coup d'état. The process of power transfer as a result of a democratic election sometimes also engenders uncertainty. For instance, the presidential election in the United States in 2000 will forever serve as a classic example in American politics courses as an extremely tight election. Ex ante, this close political race did create uncertainty that was not welcomed by the market. Nonetheless, such uncertainty paled compared to a military coup d'état somewhere else. The United States Constitution was intact, no matter who won the critical 25 electoral votes of Florida. After November 7, 2000, the campaign battle between the Democrats and Republicans erupted into a series of battles in courts. Nonetheless, a military takeover in the United States was inconceivable. On the contrary, the differences between the two parties were resolved according to the laws of the state and the federation.

Thus, the theoretical model and subsequent empirical discussion in this chapter focus on fundamental political change, rather than constitutional government change. While the former occurs outside the constitutional framework, thus creating political uncertainty, the latter represents policy adjustment, usually as a consequence of political elections. In a simultaneous-equation model of political stability, democracy, and growth, Feng (1997a) distinguishes between irregular government change, major regular government change, and minor regular government change. Irregular government change is defined as the change in the chief executive of the nation outside the constitutional framework, including forced removal by military coups d'état or revolutions. Major regular government change is a power transfer that happens under the constitution and involves a change in the governing party. Minor regular government change is a power transfer that complies with the constitution while the same party remains in power. By comparison, Alesina, Özler, Roubini, and Swagel (1996) focus on major government changes, which include all unconstitutional government transfers and major constitutional government changes, assuming that the two kinds of change have similar effects on growth. However, it can be contended that it is the extraconstitutional change (such as military coup d'état), rather than regular government change (which represents mere policy adjustments instead of any fundamental change in the political system) that has a pronounced negative consequence on economic growth.

The effects of five kinds of political actions on growth are compared in Feng and Chen (1996); these are coups d'état, revolutions, riots, strikes, and assassinations. Political instability shows a pattern in terms of levels of significance: the most violent or the most extensive political actions (that is, coups and revolutions) tend to be significant, while less violent or less extensive political actions (namely riots, strikes, and assassinations) tend to be less significant. The results of standardized coefficient estimates are consistent with the above analysis.[7] As the best organized and the most violent political actions, coups d'état and revolutions have the largest negative effect on growth. Riots have a greater negative effect on the economy than assassinations and strikes, and finally, assassinations lead strikes in the degree of adverse impact on economic growth. This pattern is consistent with the theoretical argument that a higher level of political instability is associated with a lower level of economic growth.

As previously stated, investors appreciate consistent public policy, which is better guaranteed if the government does not change. Consequently, if political change in the future implies an improvement in political conditions in favor of investment, an investor will prefer to hold his money for the future. If political change in the future implies an increase in the cost of investment, he will still not invest. In both cases, even though political change implies different policy outcomes, the current economic decision is the same, namely, a reduction in investment, which leads to slow or negative growth rates.

However, the investor would discount the effect of regime change on growth if policy certainty were high, that is, if the difference between the current and future regimes were negligible. In this chapter, policy certainty is defined as the absence or lack of disagreement over public policy between the government and its opponents. The opposite concept is policy polarization, which means change from the current social policy or deviation from the current level of government repression by a new government in the future. Policy certainty therefore captures the extent to which the new and old regimes differ in their basic political orientation of running an economy or organizing a government.[8]

If the future government is perceived to be very different from the current government in its policy—thus implying a high level of uncertainty caused by a potentially large policy shift from the current government—the investor will prefer liquidizing or consuming assets today, rather than making a commitment to long-term investment. Notice that this model emphasizes the margin, rather than the direction, of the policy shift from the current government to the future one. The fundamental difference between the current regime and its political adversary implies that the future policy change may be huge. This potentially drastic change deters the investor from leaving too much capital in the market. For better or worse, given that he is risk-averse, he will prefer to hold off investing and instead adopt a waiting policy. By reducing capital inflow and economic growth, radical political change that involves different regimes adds particularly to the uncertainty of investment decision making. However, if policy certainty is high, then investors will be comfortable in making long-term investment decisions, everything else being constant. As in the case of political stability, investors prefer certainty to uncertainty regarding the future policy orientation of the government.

One example of policy uncertainty can be found in the case of Peru. The deterioration of the Peruvian economy has been associated with the rise of revolutionary movements that seek to not only topple the nation's political system but to replace the capitalist economic infrastructure with the preindustrial relationships envisioned by Maoist doctrine. These movements have deeply and adversely affected economic growth in Peru, discouraging foreign and domestic private investment. The hostage crisis of December 17, 1996, illustrated the deep political divide in the Peruvian society when Leftist Tupac Amaru Revolutionary Movement rebels seized over 400 hostages from a birthday celebration party in honor of the Japanese emperor at the Japanese embassy in Lima, including top ranking government and military officials, business dignitaries, celebrities, and about 20 ambassadors. The rebels demanded that the government release hundreds of their jailed comrades and an about-face change in the government economic policy from favoring foreign investors to a preindustrial economic structure.[9]

Finally, political and social costs imposed by a government imply that some sorts of governments expropriate social wealth, while others promote it. It seems to beg the question here to ask which type of political regime—civilian, military, democracy, or autocracy—is the most suitable to provide growth-enhancing public-sector products. While the effects on growth of political instability and policy certainty are derived mathematically, the effect of government repression or political freedom has to be assumed. As is shown later, democracy or political freedom has a positive effect on growth, mostly through other variables that are conducive to growth. That is where the main controversy over the role played by democracy in economic growth is likely to arise.[10] In this work, I maintain that political freedom or liberal democracy provides a political foundation for long-run economic development. Such a political system not only is inherently stable, but also provides an opportunity to make policy adjustments that fine-tune the economy, and to increase investment incentives. I also argue that political freedom reduces uncertainty in the marketplace and promotes factors that are conducive to economic growth. Furthermore, I put to rigorous statistical examination the idea that political freedom or liberal democracy is good for the economy.

Large $\tau$, in our interpretation a low level of freedom, will decrease the economic agent's incentive to invest, thus reducing economic growth. In contrast to political stability and policy certainty, where the relevancy lies in the future, freedom is a current choice. Originating in the current government's political and economic orientation, it stands for policies that depress private investment (Özler and Rodrik 1992). The government may adopt a policy from a set of options (ranging from highest to lowest political, economic, and social freedoms) that exert impacts on the economic agent's investment decisions. Examples of government repression affecting investment and growth are property-rights infringement, lack of patent protection, abuse or misuse of resources to satisfy interest groups, government corruption, and violations of human and civil rights.

The government may also initiate and provide public goods such as national defense, infrastructure, education, a framework for property rights, and other institutions necessary for growth. For example, it may adopt a social policy that lessens income inequality with a view toward facilitating continued and sustained growth. The public goods provided by a government can be regarded as negative costs. In accordance with the level of government repression and the amount of public goods provided by the state, the investor formulates his strategy to maximize his utility between consuming today and investing for tomorrow. In general, the lack of government intervention in the marketplace strengthens economic incentives. It should also be mentioned that a government does improve investment conditions by providing goods and services such as transportation, communications, defense, education, and the rule of law. All this indicates that democracy most likely promotes growth through indirect channels rather than directly.

In the cross-country setting of chapter 1, the economic growth patterns in Latin America and North America have been significantly different. North, Summerhill, and Weingast (2000) contrast Latin America with North America and theorize on the difference between the two regions in economic growth. Both regions started as colonies, were endowed with bountiful resources, and became independent about the same time. Then one region became the engine of economic growth in the world, while the other's economies stagnated and vacillated.

They offer a theory of political order to explain the difference (North, Summerhill, and Weingast 2000). While political order can emerge in two ways—an authoritarian society based on coercion and a consensual society based upon social cooperation—it is the latter that provides the political foundation for economic development. Consensual order requires that states provide credible commitment to political institutions and citizen rights. In this society, citizens agree that their political system is desirable and are willing to live under and defend it. Certain of their rights, citizens ensure that the state cannot violate their substantial social, economic, and political life. The government must be credibly committed to establishing, maintaining, and protecting those rights (North, Summerhill, and Weingast 2000).

While North, Summerhill, and Weingast (2000) refrain from identifying the "consensual society" with a democratic society, clearly a democracy is far more likely to possess the qualities mentioned above than an autocracy. Compared to North America, Latin America is lacking in political freedom, political stability, and policy certainty. These political conditions have important implications consistent with the political-order theory by North, Summerhill, and Weingast (2000). A democracy is more likely to provide credible commitment than an autocracy, because the former rules by social consensus and through political stability. In other words, democracy promotes growth and development, among other things, by reducing political instability and increasing policy certainty. Chapter 5 and chapter 9 will test these two propositions separately.

The recent work by Bueno de Mesquita et al. (2003) shows that governments can redistribute two types of goods: public goods that are enjoyed by all members of the society and private goods that are exclusively distributed to members of the pivotal group that sustains governments in power. Different types of political regimes have different structures in terms of the size and composition of a winning coalition necessary to sustain a government. For instance, authoritarian regimes require a small winning coalition to remain in power compared to the democratic regimes, and thus face smaller pressure for economic performance than the latter. Their argument is consistent with the model here in the sense that authoritarian governments impose greater (opportunity) costs on the economy than democratic governments, as the former have far less incentive than the latter to improve economic performance.

## 2.3   Some Casual Observations

To further analyze the effects of political freedom, political stability, and policy certainty on economic growth, I select a few countries on which to do a pair-wise comparison. An interesting comparison of Zaire and Botswana made by Smith (1994) is relevant to our discussion. Zaire is among the best economically endowed countries in terms of natural resources. It has enough arable land to feed the entire continent of Africa and enough hydro power to provide all of Africa's electricity, yet Zaire is among the poorest nations in the world. A striking contrast is nearby Botswana. Botswana's growth rate is among the highest for countries of at least one million in population; its economy grew at 5.2% per year from 1961 to 1998, comparable to high growth economies such as Taiwan and South Korea. Zaire's economy, by contrast, "grew" at a negative 2.9% rate throughout the corresponding period (figure 2.1).[11]

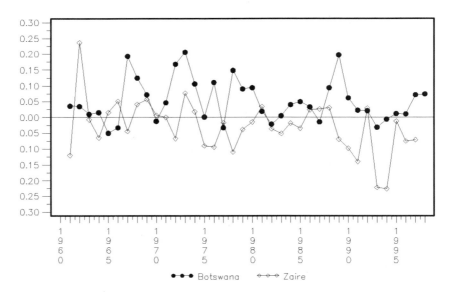

**Figure 2.1**
Growth rate of real GDP per capita, Botswana and Zaire

The main reason for the difference is political environment. Botswana has a decentralized multiparty political system, as characterized by Gastil (1983–1989). Elections have been held every five years since 1965. Amnesty International has consistently rated Botswana highest for human rights in Africa (even higher than Britain). Botswana enjoys a free press, universal primary education, and an absence of political prisoners (Smith 1994).

In contrast, Zaire has been politically characterized by a one-party system (noted by Gastil as "nationalist one party: military dominated"), political repression, human rights violations, and government corruption. The four decades of Mobutu's dictatorial rule ruined the economy in Zaire; meanwhile the dictator usurped huge wealth for himself. Large productive enterprises were owned and managed by the government, which substantially interfered in the economy. The political climate in Zaire was turbulent, while it was serene in Botswana. Compared to only one government crisis and an utter absence of coups d'état, revolutions, riots, or assassinations in Botswana from the 1960s through the 1980s, Zaire had eight government crises, eleven riots, one coup d'état, twelve revolutions, and at least three assassinations of major politicians in the same period of time (Banks 1999).[12] One argument that can be made from the comparison of Zaire and Botswana is that political freedom may contribute both directly and indirectly to economic growth and development. To begin with, freedom provides a fair and competitive economic, social, and political context for investment and growth through the framework of rule and law. Moreover, it may further improve the likelihood of sustained economic growth by reducing political instability, as freedom encourages the resolution of conflict in a peaceful manner. Therefore, the reduction in political instability, as shown in the following cases, may increase economic growth, since stability increases the value of investment for the future.

In addition to political freedom, political stability is critical to economic growth. Cape Verde and Zambia are another pair of sub-Saharan nations with very different growth trajectories. From 1960 to 1998, Cape Verde's economy grew annually at an average of 3.3%, which was the fourth highest growth rate in sub-Sahara, following those of Botswana, Seychelles, and Mauritius. Meanwhile, the average growth rate of the real GDP per capita for the same period in

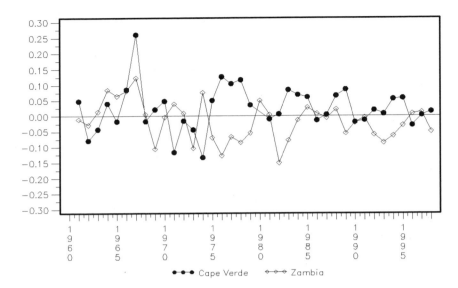

**Figure 2.2**
Growth rate of real GDP per capita, Cape Verde and Zambia

Zambia was −1.7%, the third lowest in the region, only better than the Central African Republic and Zaire (figure 2.2).[13]

The levels of political freedom in both nations during this period were similar, with both under "unfree" or "partly free" governments until 1992 (Freedom House, various years). The average score of civil liberties in the Freedom House data for the period of 1975 to 1999 was 4.56 for Cape Verde and 4.72 for Zambia. However, Zambia had more political instability than Cape Verde. For the same period, the former had one political assassination of a leading politician, four major riots, two antigovernment demonstrations, and one revolution, while the latter had only one antigovernment demonstration and one revolution (Banks 1999).

Cape Verde has experienced fewer riots, assassinations, and antigovernment demonstrations than Zambia. Sometimes, however, societies with greater freedom can be associated with more antigovernment demonstrations and riots as the result of little or no government repression. As the freedom levels between the two countries here are similar, the lack of demonstrations and riots can be accounted for by the lack of political instability rather than government repression. All this suggests that the lower growth rate in

Zambia could be driven by political instability, if not the lack of political freedom.

Finally, policy certainty plays an important role in economic growth. There may be a high level of political instability, as represented by the frequency of government change, but as long as the existing policy is preserved in the future, the negative effect of political instability on economic growth can be significantly offset. While investors may still be wary of government change, such caution may be mitigated if the two parties involved in a power transfer hold similar views about running the economy and managing the government.

The two nations selected for examination in this relationship are Bolivia and Thailand. Both nations have had a few unconstitutional government changes. From 1970 to 1995, each country had exactly the same number of coups d'état (five), and their levels of political freedom and civil liberties rights were similar, but their growth rates tell a different story. For the period of 1960 through 1995, while real GDP per capita grew on average 5.4% in Thailand, the comparable number for Bolivia was only 0.4%. Even if we include the GDP data for 1997–1998, when Thailand suffered from a major financial crisis, it still grew at an average rate of 4.5%, while Bolivia's average growth rate improved to 0.5%. Figure 2.3 shows that the year-to-year growth rates in Bolivia were significantly lower than those in Thailand for the two decades between 1976 and 1996.

What separated these two nations in economic growth is policy certainty. The level of policy certainty has been very high in Thailand, despite the appearance of significant political instability resulting from coups d'état. From 1932 to 1998, the country experienced 10 coups and 16 failed coup attempts (Morell and Samudavanija 1981, Schlossstein 1991). In terms of changing the course of the nation, military coups d'état in Thailand have never produced the same effects as those in Latin America. There are several major underlying reasons why an unusual constancy balances the seemingly endless political vicissitudes in Thailand. First, the Thai military shares with the civilian elite similar views regarding economic policy, and investors are confident that whoever gains power will not significantly deviate from previous policy. Second, the King provides a unifying presence that countervails the numerous government transfers. Furthermore, the preeminence of Buddhism in Thailand has eliminated the possibility of divisions in society along

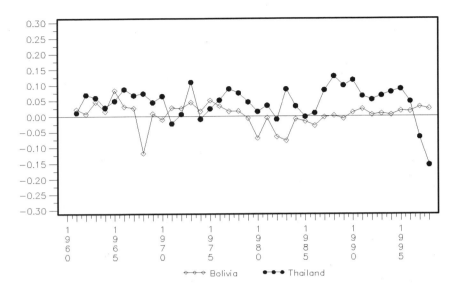

**Figure 2.3**
Growth rate of real GDP per capita, Bolivia and Thailand

religious lines. A further study of Thailand will be presented in chapter 4.

Compared with the essentially innocuous coups in Thailand, which had little effect on the economy, the Bolivian coups d'état have been malignant.[14] Political regime change in Bolivia represented very different social groups. For instance, the three regimes in Bolivia—Barrientos, Ovando, and Torres (1967 to 1971) represented polarized military regimes that met strong opposition not only from civilian segments but also within the military. While there was little policy difference between the ousted government and the new government in Thailand, the coups in Bolivia evinced a great deal of policy differences between the old and new regimes. While some regimes (e.g., Barrientos) were perceived to be an advocate of the agricultural and business sectors, others (e.g., Torres) were perceived as friendly to the labor sector (Klein 1992).

Policy consensus and certainty are also a result of the agenda of "shared growth." According to Campos and Root (1996), Thailand, like most other East Asian countries, has adopted a shared-growth strategy, resulting in a better life for every social class and the creation of a wealthy middle class. Since broad cross-sections in these societies have benefited from economic growth, social pressure groups advocating the continuation of a consistent economic policy and continued development have emerged. "In East Asia, the need to establish broad coalitional foundations was the motivation for leadership to create mechanisms for the technocratic formulation of policy. The institutions to ensure technocratic neutrality worked when top political leadership derived key coalitional support from economic policies that provided broad-based economic growth" (Root 1996, 149). The discussion in this chapter fits in well with this East Asian development scenario. The governments solicit social support by advocating shared growth benefiting every segment of society (Campos and Root 1996). The interests of various social groups coalesce, owing to the growth-oriented strategy. Meanwhile, the governments also adopt tactics to share, collect, and formulate information through various channels to direct and further develop the national consciousness and consensus regarding growth and development. For example, the Malaysian Business Council, the Economic Trend Review in South Korea, the state-sponsored industrial associations in Taiwan, and Singapore's National Wages Council have all facilitated a broad-based consensus among the government, business, and labor regarding growth policy (Root 1996).

When political change becomes inevitable, damage control can take place by preserving familiarities. The return of Hong Kong to China provides an example of avoiding or reducing uncertainty under political change. British rule was to end according to the 1898 treaty between Britain and the Qing Dynasty, which leased the New Territories to Britain for 99 years.[15] Pressured by British business interests in Hong Kong, the British government approached Beijing in the late 1970s to clarify the future of Hong Kong. An agreement between China and Britain, signed in Beijing in December 1984, stipulated that Hong Kong would revert to Chinese sovereignty in 1997. The territory, which would then be known as the Hong Kong Special Administrative Region of China, would be allowed to main- tain its own legal, social, and economic systems for at least another 50 years, with civil liberties guaranteed. However, China would assume responsibility for foreign affairs and defense. The subsequent Basic Law, promulgated by Beijing in 1990 to serve as Hong Kong's postcolonial constitution, took effect at midnight, July 1, 1997.

The British and Chinese governments' negotiations focused on how to reduce the political uncertainty surrounding power transfer in Hong Kong, as any adverse effect of the political change on the Hong Kong economy would mean bad business for both nations. Given the inevitability of Hong Kong's reversion to Chinese sovereignty, the best strategy for both parties was to maintain the status quo in Hong Kong. In other words, the negative effect of regime change was minimized by mitigating the differences between the contending parties.

The Basic Law helped promote policy certainty by allowing Hong Kong a high degree of autonomy and by preserving the existing capitalist system and political freedom. It could continue to enjoy its existing executive, legislative, and independent judicial power. The document assuaged the people of Hong Kong, satisfied British interests, and laid a foundation to support China's long-term political strategy for its reunification with Taiwan. The agreement between Britain and China thus minimized political and social uncertainty brought about by the political regime change in Hong Kong. Conflict concerning political reforms in Hong Kong did erupt between the Chinese government and the Governor of Hong Kong, Christopher Patten, during the last few years of British dependency. However, the agreement, signed by the two governments more than ten years before the actual power transfer took place, and the Basic Law, promulgated seven years before the reversion, provided important foundations on which to prepare for a transition with the least possible policy uncertainty. They were directly conducive to the continued prosperity of a Hong Kong governed by a different regime.

These examples demonstrate that none of the three political variables—political freedom, political stability, and policy certainty —is a sufficient, or even necessary, condition for economic growth. The effect of coups d'état on growth may be negligible if policy certainty is high. When the new government is perceived to be the same as the previous government regarding policy content and execution, the investor will normally discount regime change. Investors may not make a full commitment to long-term investment, but neither would they completely withdraw their capital from the market. Similarly, if policy certainty is low but the probability of the current government's remaining in power is high, the investor may still want to invest, despite the sharp difference between the government and its (unlikely successful) opposition. The worst scenario for economic growth is a nation where political stability and policy certainty are very low, with no political freedom.

It should also be mentioned that political freedom, political stability, and policy certainty may not all occur in the same country. While political freedom may increase the level of stability, a statement to be tested in chapter 5, it is unlikely that freedom and stability are perfectly correlated. Indeed, sometimes a country with full freedom may be a country with high political instability (e.g., the post-Marcos Philippines). Similarly, high freedom may not square well with policy certainty. If an antimarket socialist party replaces a probusiness party through a democratic election, investors may request a regime change to restore the former probusiness policy (e.g., Chile in 1973). The model does not reflect a scenario in which the investor has full knowledge and information about the new party's policy effects and adopts actions to promote the cause of the party, even through terrorism and violence. Despite these limitations, I will empirically test in the following chapters whether political instability reduces economic growth and investment. In general, I believe that radical government change generates uncertainty that dampens economic activities, including investment.

Figure 2.4 simulates a three-dimensional scenario, using growth as the dependent variable, political freedom and political stability as the independent variables, with the level of policy certainty kept fixed. For the purpose of simulation, both freedom and stability are standardized to the range of zero to one, with one indicating the highest level of stability or certainty. The simulation demonstrates that to maintain a high level of economic growth, a nation needs both political stability and political freedom. In a country where political freedom is high but political stability is low, investors will be concerned about the continuity of the current policy and policy environment. In a country where political stability is high but freedom is low, a repressive government policy will not allow investors to maximize the growth-enhancing level of investment, although there can still be some growth because of high political stability.

In the case of no stability and no freedom, the growth rate is the lowest (the corner closest to the reader). The combination of high political stability but low political freedom is still able to generate some growth (the left corner). Similarly, the combination of low political stability but high political freedom (the right corner)

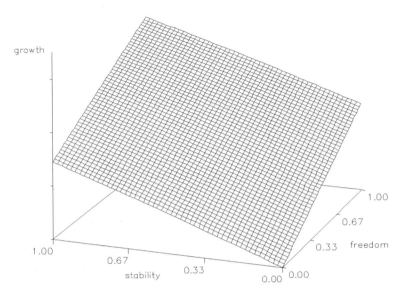

**Figure 2.4**
Growth, freedom, and stability

achieves some growth. However, the scenario of high stability and high freedom produces the best growth outcome (the farthest corner). The same result can be obtained for freedom and policy certainty, or stability and certainty, while keeping stability or freedom constant. The combined effects of freedom, stability, and certainty are extremely important political factors weighing heavily on the mind of an investor. Together they define the political foundation of a nation's economic management and market activities.

## 2.4  Summary and Policy Implications

The model in section 2.1, the discussion in section 2.2, and empirical evidence in section 2.3 point to some fundamental political elements that are conducive to economic growth: political stability, political freedom, and policy certainty, which all lead to a relatively high growth rate. However, it is important to note that none of the three variables (freedom, stability, certainty) is by itself a *sufficient* or *necessary* condition for economic development. An undemocratic country may still enjoy economic growth if the country is politically stable or economically efficient (for instance, Taiwan in the 1970s and the 1980s). On the other hand, a democracy may experience an economic slowdown if it suffers from the lack of political stability and policy certainty (for instance, Russia and Poland during the early 1990s).

Furthermore, political stability and policy certainty may offset each other. When contending parties share very similar political and economic views, government change should have little effect on capital accumulation and growth, even though the probability of a government transfer may be high. For example, despite coups d'état in Thailand in the 1970s and in South Korea in the 1980s, in both cases economic policies were consistent between the overthrown governments and the new ones, causing little disruption in either country's economy. Similarly, a wide difference between the opposing parties may not matter to an individual if he thinks that the current government is very stable and the probability of its being replaced is close to nil (for instance, Malaysia).[16]

Political instability can be discounted when policy polarization is minimized and vice versa. In Venezuela, opposition parties used to reach policy consensus before engaging in competition for the national office. In this case, regardless whichever party won, the policy course had already been set. In Colombia in the 1950s, the presidency carried an 18-year period. Policy polarization was discounted, as it could take years for any government change to happen again.[17] However, for any level of political freedom, investors prefer a politically stable and certain society to a politically stable but uncertain, or politically certain but unstable, society.

This study suggests that a nation can achieve "economic miracles" by reducing political instability, building policy certainty, and increasing political freedom—all of which this chapter has identified as important for improving a country's economy. These variables constitute the political foundation of nations' development strategies and the best set of common denominators in national-development success stories.

# 3        Measuring Political Freedom, Stability, and Certainty

*Technological man can't believe in anything that can't be measured, taped, or put into a computer.*

Clare Boothe Luce

Much debate has raged over the quantification of political variables, particularly that of political freedom or democracy, which is largely based on subjective assessment. The major limitation of using a subjective variable is that we may not exactly measure the concept we have in mind, and thus may suffer from the so-called validity problem in operationalization. The advantage of using subjective variables lies in the fact that the implications of theoretical arguments can still be evaluated on a consistent basis. If the empirical results are consistent with the theory of certain testable hypotheses, then confidence will increase regarding our advancing understanding of the relationships under scrutiny. Meanwhile, the use of these variables exposes their limitations and imperfections, emphasizing the need to improve our measurement of political systems and structures. This in turn will lead to progress in the social sciences.

Three general issues concerning the measurement of democracy or other political institutional variables exist, and they should not be conflated. The first issue is whether measures from various works *independently* conducted, but using *correlated* concepts, can produce similar degrees of measurement. If they do, our confidence in the validity and reliability of the data will increase on the grounds that similar concepts lead to similar measurement results, and that these results are repeated in independent studies. Second, even though these variables are highly correlated, reflecting some substantial common elements among them, they do not necessarily capture within-country political dynamism in the same way. Some political events may be given more emphasis in one measure than in others. Finally, some measures of democracy are discrete (e.g., the regime-change indicator in Gasiorowski 1996 or the measure of democracy in Przeworski et al. 2000), while others are "continuous" (e.g., the Polity index of institutionalized democracy, the Gastil index of political rights and civil liberties, and the Bollen index of liberal democracy). The degree of democracy, as proxied by political freedom, should not be misunderstood as a state of democracy. In this book, the degree of democracy, through the employment of continuous measures, is typically used to avoid categorical denomination of a country as a democracy or nondemocracy. Methodologically, it can be controversial to lump countries of different levels of political freedom in one category; conceptually, varying degrees of political freedom may lead to incremental changes in economic performance.

Major advances have been made in measuring political freedom since the 1980s, due to numerous important empirical works that have utilized those variables. This chapter examines the concepts and definitions of democracy. It also critiques various indicators of democracy. Furthermore, it operationalizes political stability/ instability and policy certainty/uncertainty. These variables will be utilized in the empirical testing in the rest of the book.

## 3.1   Political Freedom and Liberal Democracy

In this book, the terms *democracy* and *political freedom* will be used interchangeably. Democracy or political freedom is meant to be the degree of liberal democracy, which is consistent with the idea of an incremental state of democracy, rather than the idea of a dichotomous state of either democracy or nondemocracy. This definition is operationally necessary for hypothesis testing of alternative arguments found in the literature regarding the incremental effects of democracy on economic development.

What Westerners consider democracy, non-Western cultures often think of as a specialized "Western democracy." This was the cry, for instance, in the 1997 election victory of the People's Action Party of Singapore, in which the PAP won 81 of the 83 Parliament seats. The PAP leader (and Singapore's prime minister) declared his party's triumph as a "victory over Western democracy," which was advocated by his opponents (*Guoji ribao* 1997).

What, then, is Western democracy? Schumpeter emphasizes the procedural aspects of democracy, defining *democracy* as "that institutional arrangement for arriving at political decisions in which individuals acquire the power to decide by means of a comprehensive struggle for the people's votes" (Schumpeter 1976, 269). In Schumpeter's procedural version, democracy is nearly devoid of normative values such as the intrinsic utility of personal freedom and equality; an institutional arrangement for elections would be sufficient to qualify a society as democratic. Thus, Japan—with its relatively high degree of civil, political, and economic freedom—would be equivalent with Singapore or Malaysia, where personal and individual freedom is routinely sacrificed for the developmental goal of the state. Nonetheless, there are scholars who use and apply this definition of *democracy*. One World Bank publication, for instance, deemed Malaysia a "politically stable democracy" (World Bank 1993, 13).

Despite his rather simplistic definition of *democracy*, Schumpeter posits that the success of his "value-free" democratic system depends on some not so value-free conditions, including (1) a sufficient group of politicians who possess both good moral character and political ability; (2) constraints on the scope of government decision making; (3) a professional bureaucracy that not only administrates effectively but can also give advice (and even instruction) to politicians; (4) democratic self-control, meaning that politicians respect the results of elections; and (5) a large degree of tolerance for differences of opinion (Schumpeter 1976, 289–296). These conditions demonstrate Schumpeter's recognition that democracy is meant to protect individual freedom by fostering tolerance and self-restraint on the use of power, thus limiting the state's penetration of society (Kim 1993).

Other scholars who emphasize the procedural aspects of democracy include Lipset, who defines democracy as a "political system which supplies regular constitutional opportunities for changing government officials" (Lipset 1959, 71). Huntington defines democracy as a political system "to the extent that its most powerful collective decision-makers are selected through periodic elections in which candidates freely compete for votes and in which virtually all the adult population is eligible to vote" (Huntington 1984, 195). Finally, Przeworski defines democracy as "a system in which parties lose elections," because the outcomes of democratic processes are uncertain and determined by the people (Przeworski 1991, 10).

In contrast to the relatively value-free conceptions of procedural democracy, some scholars emphasize the notion that democracy is value-laden, and thus based on normative ideals. For instance, Sartori argues, "Democracy is uniquely open to, and hinged on, a *fact-value* tension. It can be said that only democracy owes its very existence to its ideals.... The term *democracy* then has not only a descriptive or denotative function but also a normative and persuasive function" (Sartori 1987, 8). Aware of the distinction between procedural democracy and liberal democracy in terms of their respective implications, Diamond writes,

There are two conceptions of democracy that are current in academic and public policy discussions, and we need to distinguish between them. A minimalist "electoral" form of democracy considers the presence of regular, competitive, and multiparty elections that are largely free and fair as the essence of democracy. A more expansive—and, to my view, meaningful and necessary—conception recognizes that elections occur only intermittently, that officials who are elected may not hold effective power in the country, and that true political choice and accountability require much broader pluralism and freedom. (1997, 3)

In line with this argument, the concept of liberal democracy intends to capture the intrinsic value of political freedom under democracy. For instance, Margolis defines liberal democracy as a political system that "emphasizes facilitation of individual self-development and self-expression as the primary goals of government. The object of the government is to keep open for the individual a wide range of options and values" (Margolis 1979, 26). Bollen, in turn, defines democracy as a function of two essential elements: political liberties and democratic rule. *Political liberties* refers to the freedom of citizens to express political opinions and to form or participate in any political group. Democratic rule concerns the government's accountability to the population and the entitlement of individuals to participate in the government directly or through representation (Bollen 1993). Vanhanen uses similar terminology for democracy, defining *democracy* as "a political system in which ideologically and socially different groups are legally entitled to compete for political power and in which institutional power holders are elected by the people and are responsible to the people" (1990, 11).[1]

It is this concept of liberal democracy that is utilized in this chapter and the rest of the book, rather than that of procedural democracy (which, without "the requisites for liberalism," allows for one-party dominance and control over the state machinery to influence and determine electoral results). The following section discusses three major indices of democracy that, to a substantial extent, tend to measure the liberal, rather than the procedural, aspects of democracy.[2]

### Measures of Democracy

Three indices for degrees of democracy have been used in the literature on democracy: Bollen's liberal democracy index, Gurr's institutionalized democracy index, and Gastil's political rights and civil liberties score.[3] None of these take dichotomous values to indicate either the presence or absence of democracy; instead they treat democracy as a *continuous* variable. This practice has two advantages: First, it avoids arbitrary decisions in categorizing borderline cases of democracy (Bollen and Jackman 1989). Second, it shares the conceptual position put forward by Dalton, who holds that the "process of democratization is open-ended" and argues that "democratization and the expansion of citizen influence is a continuing process" (1996, 2). Though these variables do possess terminal values indicating the extremes of most free or most unfree, their use in studying the incremental effects of democracy on economics and the influence of economics on the consolidation or weakening of democracy is superior to a dichotomous democracy variable.[4]

### The Bollen Index
Bollen defines *liberal democracy* as a function of political liberties and democratic rule. Political liberty is a function of citizens' ability to freely express a variety of political opinions in any medium and to form or participate in any political group. Democratic rule is a function of a national government's accountability to the general population, and of the citizens' entitlement to participate directly or via representatives in the government. Therefore, Bollen's concept of liberal democracy can be reduced to two dimensions: political freedom and popular sovereignty. The measure of the first dimension is based on freedom of group opposition, freedom of the press, and government sanctions. The latter dimension, popular sovereignty, is constructed from executive selection, legislative selection, and election fairness.

Banks' political-opposition variable, Gastil's political-rights measure and Banks' legislative-effectiveness measure are a few of the
basic political variables from which the total score of liberal democracy is derived. The value of the liberal-democracy index ranges
from 0 to 100, with 100 representing the freest. Data are available for
102 countries for the years 1960, 1965, and 1980.

### Polity Data and Institutionalized Democracy
The data set developed by Gurr and associates offers a wide range of
annualized variables, including centralization of political authority
and identification of major shifts in polity or political regime. It covers a long span of historical periods from the early nineteenth century to the present. Gurr offers a composite index of institutionalized
democracy, conceived of as the following elements: the presence of
competitive political participation, the guarantee of openness and
competitiveness of executive recruitment, and the existence of institutionalized constraints on the exercise of executive power. In Gurr's
index, the value of democracy ranges from 0 to 10, with 10 representing the most democratic. The data series starts from 1800 (for 22
countries) to the present for more than 150 nations. The operational
indicator of institutionalized democracy is derived from coding the
competitiveness of political participation, the openness of executive
recruitment, and the constraints on the chief executive. The democracy indicator is an additive (0 to 10) 11-point scale, constructed
using these weights to capture those traits conceptually associated
with democracy (Harmel 1980; Gurr, Jaggers, and Moore 1990).

### The Gastil/Freedom House Survey
Political freedom is also measured by using the data sets developed by Gastil (1983–1989) and the Freedom House (1990–present)
researchers, who score nations on two separate seven-point scales
measuring their levels of political rights and civil liberties. In terms
of political rights, those countries rated at one come closest to political democracy, while seven indicates those most unfree. Under
Gastil's and Freedom House's criteria of democracy, elections are held
freely, fairly, and competitively in democratic countries, and opposition parties play an important role in checks and balances. If a
country holds national elections to determine the formation of a
government but opposition parties play no vital roles or are pre-
vented from being substantial political competition, the country is

not considered a free country in Gastil's data set. Accordingly, it will not be ranked high in political rights (that is, it will not receive a lower-number score). A prime example is Singapore—it has elections, but the role played by opposition parties is minimal. In every election held since the inception of the city-state in 1965, the People's Action Party (PAP) has overwhelmingly won national office. The score on political rights for Singapore has been typically four or five on the seven-point scale (seven indicating the most unfree), and despite its functioning electoral system, it currently ranks second from the bottom on political rights among the Pacific Asian countries examined in the first section of this chapter.

States that receive a score of two are still regarded free, though political violence, discrimination against minorities, military intervention, and political corruption occasionally impair political rights. India, for instance, was placed in this category from 1972 through 1991 for reasons of political violence and discrimination against minorities. Political rights in India have deteriorated since 1990, engendering a score of three for 1991–1992 and 1992–1993, four for 1993–1994 through 1995–1996. In contrast, Taiwan was assigned a rating of two in the Freedom House categories of political rights and civil liberties in 1997, thus entering the ranks of free nations after "successfully completing its democratic transition to a competitive multiparty system with free and fair presidential elections" (Freedom House 1996, 3).

Countries receiving a score between three and five are considered partly free. They have the same negative factors that hold for countries scoring two, plus other forms of political abuse, such as civil war, extensive military intervention in politics, the existence of a strong royal influence, unfair elections, or the domination of a single party. Singapore falls into the category of partly free countries because of the dominance of the PAP.

Countries that receive a score of six or seven are considered unfree. These states are likely to be ruled by a single party, military dictatorships, autocrats, or theocracies. The difference between partly free and unfree nations lies in the minimal freedoms that citizens in the former category possess, such as the right to organize national political parties and to compete in national elections. The difference between countries designated six and seven also lies in whether local governments are elected competitively and whether minorities have some political autonomy. For those countries that fall in the seven category, even these limited freedoms are nonexistent, or extreme political violence prevails. Indonesia was classified as unfree from 1991 to 1997, when the political-rights score changed from five to six in 1991, and then from six to seven in 1994.

The civil-liberties score also ranges from one to seven, with seven representing the most unfree. A country with a score of one enjoys freedom of association, assembly, demonstration, speech, and religion, as well as free and independent media and court systems. Residents of these nations also possess freedom to do business on an equitable basis without excessive government corruption, and freedom to organize unions and other private groups. By 1996 the Philippines had made sufficient improvements in civil liberties to move itself from partly free to free. Countries that receive a score of two on the civil-liberties score are relatively weak in some of the above areas, although they generally espouse these principles (e.g., South Korea from 1993 to 1996). Countries rated at three, four, or five have progressively fewer of those freedoms listed above. Government repression asserts itself in the form of government censorship, political terror, and prevention of free association. For example, the civil-liberties score for India has been three or four since 1980–1981. Countries that receive a score of six have partial freedom in religious beliefs and business activities (e.g., Indonesia since 1993–1994). In nations receiving a score of seven, however, even these partial freedoms are nonexistent (e.g., China since 1989–1990, when the students' prodemocracy demonstration in Beijing ended in bloodshed).

Like all ordinal data derived on the basis of some subjective criteria, the Freedom House survey data are not free from limitations in measurement. Bollen (1993) shows that the political-rights and civil-liberties scores may suffer from regional bias. He compares the political-participation variables from Gastil's data set and Banks' data set, and concludes that while Banks' data favor Eastern European countries, Gastil's tend to give Latin American countries relatively low scores, as described above.

As a way to verify Bollen's remarks (1993), I seek evidence in the correlation among Bollen's liberal-democracy index, Gastil/Freedom House's political rights and civil liberties, and Polity's institutionalized-democracy index. I first transformed all these variables so that they take a range between zero and one, with one representing the most free. The formulas for the transformation of political rights and civil liberties are as follows:

$$\text{Political rights } (\text{PR})_i = \frac{7 - \text{political rights}_i}{6}$$

$$\text{Civil liberties } (\text{CL})_i = \frac{7 - \text{civil liberties}_i}{6}$$

The formulas for the transformation of the liberal-democracy index and the institutionalized-democracy index are these:

$$\text{Liberal democracy } (\text{LD})_i = \frac{\text{Liberal democracy}_i}{100}$$

$$\text{Institutionalized democracy } (\text{DEMOC})_i = \frac{\text{Institutionalized democracy}_i}{10}$$

In these formulas the left-hand-side variable is the transformed variable, and the right-hand-side variable is the original variable in the data.

Table 3.1 shows simple statistics for the four democracy indices. The means for them are similar, except in the case of institutionalized democracy, while the standard deviation for the latter is the highest of the four indices. DEMOC also has the most observations, as its data has been collected since the early nineteenth century. The beginning year for PR and CL is 1972/1973, and the three years data for LD are 1960, 1965, and 1980. If we use the years common to DEMOC, PR, and CL (between 1972 and 1998), then the number of observations for DEMOC is 3,693, and the number of observations for PR and CL is 4,416. In other words, DEMOC reflects more years worth of data, while PR and CL cover more nations.

Table 3.2 presents the correlations among political rights, civil liberties, institutionalized democracy, and liberal democracy. These

**Table 3.1**
Simple statistics for political rights, civil liberties, institutionalized democracy, and liberal democracy

| Variable | N | Mean | SD |
|---|---|---|---|
| Political rights | 4,752 | 0.495 | 0.375 |
| Civil liberties | 4,752 | 0.496 | 0.327 |
| Institutionalized democracy | 13,800 | 0.318 | 0.381 |
| Liberal democracy | 269 | 0.552 | 0.326 |

**Table 3.2**
Correlations among democracy indicators

|  | DEMOC | LD | PR | CL |
|---|---|---|---|---|
| DEMOC | 1.000 | 0.872 | 0.920 | 0.864 |
| LD |  | 1.000 | 0.941 | 0.885 |
| PR |  |  | 1.000 | 0.922 |
| CL |  |  |  | 1.000 |

indices are highly correlated, which shows the internal consistency of their relationships. The correlation between political rights and civil liberties is very high, even though some countries score lower on political rights than on civil liberties—indicating a democratically oriented electoral system with some isolated civil-liberties violations (e.g., Germany and India)—while others score lower on civil liberties than political rights—indicating a relatively closed authoritarian system that boasts some civil liberties (e.g., Tonga and Indonesia).

Institutionalized democracy and liberal democracy are more strongly correlated with political rights than with civil liberties, which makes sense. Political rights occur in the domain of political participation and democratic procedures, whereas civil liberties emphasize freedoms of association, assembly, demonstration, expression, religion, independent media, and independent courts, as well as the freedom to do business on an equitable basis without excessive government interference or corruption, and the freedom to organize unions and other private groups. The correlation of 0.92 between PR and DEMOC and the correlation of 0.94 between LD and PR show that using these variables interchangeably could well be justified.

The use of each of the four indicators has its advantages and disadvantages. The strength of Bollen's liberal-democracy index lies in its theoretical coherence, but its usefulness is tremendously handicapped by its lack of observations in terms of years as well as countries. Gurr's institutionalized-democracy indicator has a long time-series span and wide coverage of countries. Its main drawback is that when a political transition occurs, the variable is recorded as missing, thus providing no information on the country's level of political freedom for that year. For instance, when Romania experienced a revolution that deposed its communist regime in 1989, its institutionalized-democracy variable received no value. For the same year, Gastil assigned a score of seven to Romania to indicate the general political climate in that country.

The civil-rights variable may not be a good choice, however, as the correlation of civil liberties with liberal-democracy and institutionalized-democracy indicators is low compared to those of the political-rights index, which indicates that some elements in the domain of liberal democracy are absent from the civil-liberties measure. For its part, the major limitation with political rights is that its beginning year is 1972, which means that using it would exclude a significant number of observations in the study of long-run economic and political performance.

The lack of time series in the political-rights data, however, is compensated by the extent of their coverage. For instance, in 1989 the Gastil/Freedom House data covered 201 countries or areas, while the Polity data included only 138 polities. As political rights and institutionalized democracy are very highly correlated, this book will use the latter if the period under study goes back before 1972, but will use the former if the period starts after 1972. This criterion is determined by efficiency. We want to include as many countries as possible (and so use the Freedom House data), but when the period of study is many years prior to 1972 in the case of long-run economic performance, I will resort to the Polity data.

Figure 3.1 shows the annual trend of the average levels of freedom in the world as determined by the two data sources discussed above. The start year of 1973 was chosen because that was the first year for which the Gastil/Freedom House data were available. DEMOC is the degree of institutionalized democracy. PR is political rights. The formulas for DEMOC and PR are the same as the ones used for table 3.1. It is clear that the world in which we live has become much freer since 1989. From 1973 to 1977 the level of freedom in the world declined. Overall, from 1977 to 1989 world freedom trended slightly upward. For the standardized values, PR is consistently higher than DEMOC until 1989. After 1989 the two series closely match. This difference between these two variables could have been caused by some systematic change regarding the communist countries. After 1989 the Soviet bloc collapsed, and some of the countries transformed into liberal democracies. It is not coincidental that the two series started to converge in the post-Soviet world.

The difference between DEMOC and PR also results from the difference in the two variables' subjects. It has been argued that while PR

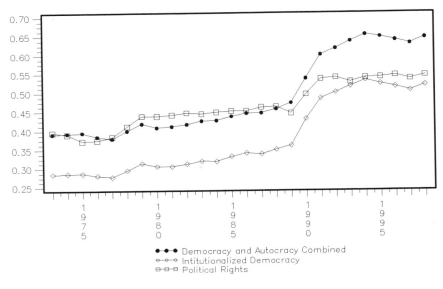

**Figure 3.1**
Political freedom in the world, 1973–1998

focuses on liberal democracy's espousing freedoms, DEMOC may also emphasize procedural democracy with checks and balances (Burkhart 1998). A new variable DEMOCRACY AND AUTOCRACY COMBINED was created to examine this hypothesis. It is a combination of the institutionalized-democracy (DEMOC) and autocracy (AUTOC) indices from the Polity project. The variable AUTOC in the Polity data reflects the degree of civil liberties and rights. The formula for the combined variable is $((1 - \text{AUTOC}/10) + \text{DEMOC}/10)/2$, as AUTOC ranges from 0 to 10, with 10 as the most autocratic. Thus, the new variable captures both the political constraints of DEMOC and the freedoms of AUTOC. From 1973 to 1989, the combined series seems to match PR well; after 1989, it exceeds PR by an increasing margin. The correlation between this combined variable and PR for the same 3,765 observations in table 3.2 is 0.917, which is lower than DEMOC and PR, indicating that DEMOC and PR are probably interchangeable under most circumstances. Therefore, among all possible variables of political freedom or the degree of liberal democracy, I choose to use DEMOC and PR in the analysis of economic performance in this book.

## 3.2   Political Stability/Instability

Political instability as conceived of in this book's theoretical model is related to change of government. Of all variables, the one most appropriate for the concept of government change in the model is the coup d'état, which is defined as "extraconstitutional or forced changes in the top government elite and/or the effective control of the nation's power structure," including but not exhausted by successful revolutions (Banks 1979, 17).

However, the probability of government change is not directly observable, and political "stability and instability," as indicated by government change, are "relative tendencies, not discrete states" (Sanders 1981, 57). What we observe in reality is the discrete phenomenon of government change. There can be a significant chance of government change, but we may not describe such a scenario as a half change, since government change either occurs or does not occur.

To account for the relationship between the all-or-nothing nature of the transfer of the executive power and the relativity of political instability, I use the limited-dependent-variable estimation method. This method defines the probability function of extraconstitutional government change as a continuous variable, characterized as a response to economic and political conditions.[5] The choice of the dependent variable is critical to capturing the idea of political instability in the model.

As discussed in the last chapter, although both irregular government change and major regular government change are categorized as major government change, they can be entirely different, hence the definitional shortcoming. The former is a regime change occurring outside the constitutional framework, whereas the latter is a government change from one party to another within the constitutional framework. While it may be argued that major regular government change and minor regular government change have different impacts on—or result differently from—growth and freedom, this difference pales in comparison to the difference between regular and irregular government change.[6]

Given any kind of polity,[7] irregular power transfers represent radical changes that replace the current regime with a new one, while regular government change conforms to the constitution and represents social, political, and economic adjustments rather than qualitative changes. It is certainly difficult to consider the power transfer from Prime Minister James Callaghan to Prime Minister Margaret Thatcher as having the same policy implications as that from President Salvador Allende to General Augusto Pinochet, or from the Shah Pahlavi to Ayatollah Khomeini. Yet all three of these events would be classified as major government change (Alesina et al. 1996). While irregular government change and major regular government change both involve a substantial turnover of leadership, they are qualitatively distinct. In the following analysis, therefore, government change refers specifically to irregular government change.

Similar to the treatments in Cukierman, Edwards, and Tabellini (1992) and Feng (1997a), the probability function of government change is here defined by four categories of variables: economic variables measuring the government's recent economic performance (e.g., previous levels of inflation, consumption, and income), political events accounting for significant political incidents that may signal an imminent government change (e.g., riots, assassinations, general strikes, and revolutions), political structures indicating systemic stability (e.g., the selection of the effective executive of the state, parliamentary responsibility, and the effectiveness and selection of the legislature), and finally dummy variables grouping countries according to their continents so as to control for systemic effects not explained by the model. The probability of a political-regime change for each country in any given year during the period 1951 to 1995 is then estimated from the fitted values of the logit model using pooled time-series cross-national data.

The following discusses the definitions and operationalizations of those variables used in the logit model to estimate the probability of an irregular government change. All economic variables are from Summers and Heston 2000, and all definitions of political variables are directly taken from Banks 1999.

### Dependent variable

IRREGULAR GOVERNMENT CHANGE This variable is defined as an extraconstitutional change in top-level government in a given year, be it by forced removal of top officeholders or by taking effective control of the nation's power. Unsuccessful coups are not counted.

## Independent variables

INFLATION This variable is the percentage of price changes in the gross domestic product (GDP).

REAL GDP PER CAPITA This variable is an index of real income per capita based on purchasing-power parity.

ASSASSINATIONS This variable is defined as any politically motivated murder or attempted murder of a high government official or politician.

STRIKES This variable counts any strike of 1,000 or more industrial or service workers that involves more than one employer and is aimed at national government policies or authority.

GUERILLA WARFARE This variable measures any armed activity, sabotage, or bombings carried on by independent bands of citizens or irregular forces aimed at overthrowing the present regime.

GOVERNMENT CRISES This variable refers to any rapidly developing situation that threatens to bring down the present regime, excluding popular revolts.

PURGES This variable refers to any systematic elimination of political opposition within the ranks of the regime or the opposition by jailing or execution.

RIOTS This variable measures any violent demonstration or clash of more than 100 citizens that involves physical force.

REVOLUTIONS This variable counts any illegal or forced change in the top government elite, any attempt at such a change, or any successful or attempted armed rebellion whose aim is independence from the central government.

ANTIGOVERNMENT DEMONSTRATIONS This variable refers to any peaceful public gathering of at least 100 people with the primary purpose of displaying or voicing opposition to government policies or authority. It excludes demonstrations of a distinctly antiforeign nature.

TYPE OF REGIME This variable classifies regimes into the following types: (1) civilian, (2) military-civilian, (3) military, (4) other. All regimes that do not fall into one of the foregoing categories lack an effective national government.

NUMBER OF MAJOR CONSTITUTIONAL CHANGES This variable accounts for the number of basic alterations in a state's constitutional structure, the extreme case being the adoption of a new constitution that significantly alters the prerogatives of the various branches of government. Examples of the latter might be the substitution of a presidential government for a parliamentary government, or the replacement of monarchical rule by republican rule. Constitutional amendments that do not have significant impact on the political system are not counted.

MONARCH A dummy variable that takes the value one if the chief executive of the country is a monarch and zero otherwise.

PRESIDENT A dummy variable that takes the value one if the chief executive of the country is a president and zero otherwise.

MILITARY A dummy variable that takes the value one if the chief executive of the country is the military and zero otherwise.

PREMIER A dummy variable that takes the value one if the chief executive of the country is a premier and zero otherwise.

EFFECTIVE EXECUTIVE SELECTION This variable differentiates the ways in which the executive of the country is selected: (1) election of the effective executive by popular vote or the election of committed delegates for the purpose of executive selection, (2) selection by an elected assembly or by an elected but uncommitted electoral college, (3) any means of selection not involving a direct or indirect mandate from an electorate.

DEGREE OF PARLIAMENTARY RESPONSIBILITY This variable measures the degree to which a premier must depend on the support of a majority in the legislature's lower house in order to remain in office. (0) Irrelevant. Office of premier does not exist. (1) Absent. Office exists, but there is no parliamentary responsibility. (2) Incomplete. The premier is, at least to some extent, constitutionally responsible to the legislature. Effective responsibility is, however, limited. (3) Complete. The premier is constitutionally and effectively dependent upon a legislative majority for continuance in office.

SIZE OF CABINET This variable is the number of ministers of cabinet rank, excluding undersecretaries, parliamentary secretaries, ministerial alternates, etc. It includes the president and vice president under a presidential system, but not under a parliamentary system. Chiefs of state are excluded, except under a presidential system.

NUMBER OF CABINET CHANGES This variable measures the number of times in a year that a new premier is named and/or 50% of the cabinet posts are occupied by new ministers.

LEGISLATIVE EFFECTIVENESS This variable measures the checks and balances between the legislature and the country's chief executive. (0) None. No legislature exists. (1) Ineffective. (2) Partially Effective. The effective executive's power substantially outweighs, but does not completely dominate, that of the legislature. (3) Effective. The legislature possesses significant governmental autonomy, typically including substantial authority in regard to taxation and disbursement and the power to override executive vetoes of legislation.

LEGISLATIVE SELECTION This variable measures the competitiveness of the elective process of the legislature. (0) None. No legislature exists. (1) Nonelective. Examples would be the selection of legislators by the effective executive or by means of heredity or ascription. (2) Elective. Legislators (or members of the lower house in a bicameral system) are selected by either a direct or indirect popular election.

ASIA A dummy variable that takes the value one for Pacific Asian countries and zero otherwise.

AFRICA A dummy variable that takes the value one for sub-Saharan countries and zero otherwise.

LATIN AMERICA A dummy variable that takes the value one for Latin American countries and zero otherwise.

OIL A dummy variable that takes the value one for OPEC countries and zero otherwise.

All independent variables take a one-year lag to reduce the possibility of endogeneity. Most variables in the logit model have the expected sign, even though not all are statistically significant, as there may be serious multicollinearity among political variables that are highly correlated. In addition, serial correlation in the panel data may be a problem, as it biases the parameter estimates. I chose a logit model because I am interested in the final outcome—namely, the probability estimation—rather than the significance level of an individual parameter estimate, even though the latter may yield interesting information about its individual effect on government change. Similarly, I ran a logit model on the probability of major regular government change. The probability estimation of minor regular government change can be calculated by subtracting the estimation of irregular government change and major regular government change from one. Table 3.3 reports estimates of the probability of irregular government change, which is the operation-

**Table 3.3**
Estimates of the probability of irregular government change, 1950–1995

| Variable | Estimate | Wald $\chi^2$ | Prob |
|---|---|---|---|
| Intercept | −2.181 | 4.369 | 0.037 |
| Inflation | 0.285 | 0.993 | 0.319 |
| GDP per capita | −0.0003 | 20.641 | 0.000 |
| Assassinations | −0.0033 | 0.002 | 0.965 |
| General strikes | 0.224 | 3.737 | 0.053 |
| Guerrilla warfare | 0.069 | 0.646 | 0.422 |
| Government crises | 0.467 | 15.403 | 0.0001 |
| Purges | −0.067 | 0.446 | 0.504 |
| Riots | 0.058 | 1.046 | 0.306 |
| Revolutions | −0.073 | 0.212 | 0.645 |
| Demonstrations | −0.137 | 2.236 | 0.135 |
| Constitutional change | −0.105 | 0.298 | 0.585 |
| Regime type | −0.049 | 0.047 | 0.829 |
| Monarch | 0.522 | 0.431 | 0.512 |
| President | 0.563 | 0.527 | 0.468 |
| Military | 0.465 | 0.324 | 0.570 |
| Premier | 0.809 | 5.330 | 0.021 |
| Executive selection | 0.038 | 0.073 | 0.787 |
| Parliament responsibility | −0.481 | 3.781 | 0.052 |
| Cabinet size | −0.025 | 3.024 | 0.082 |
| Cabinet change | 0.301 | 5.170 | 0.023 |
| Legislative effectiveness | −0.457 | 5.277 | 0.027 |
| Legislative selection | −0.017 | 0.009 | 0.926 |
| Asia | −0.292 | 0.395 | 0.530 |
| Africa | −0.362 | 0.601 | 0.438 |
| Latin America | 0.421 | 0.806 | 0.369 |
| Oil | 0.685 | 3.487 | 0.062 |

| Criterion | Intercept only | Intercept and covariates | $\chi^2$ |
|---|---|---|---|
| AIC | 1358.662 | 1213.057 | |
| SC | 1365.078 | 1386.278 | |
| −2 log L | 1356.662 | 1159.057 | 197.605 |
| Score | | | 178.104 |

AIC: Akaike information criterion. SC: Schwarz criterion. L: likelihood statistic. Score: score statistic.
$N = 4{,}517$

alization of the theoretical variable $(1 - \pi)$, indicating the probability of the current government losing office in the model of chapter 2.

In the logit regression of table 3.3, an increase in real GDP per capita decreases the likelihood of irregular government change, whereas general strikes and government crises increase the probability of such change. The variable "antigovernment demonstrations" has a negative effect on irregular government change, and is statistically significant at the 10% error level in a one-tailed test. This may reflect the fact that antigovernment demonstrations are a legal means by which citizens in a democracy, where irregular government change is generally infrequent, can express their dissatisfaction and discontent with the government. One interesting finding regarding political structures and political instability is the role played by the legislature. Irregular government change is significantly lower where the legislature has a higher degree of responsibility and effectiveness, which suggests that a strong and democratically elected legislature inhibits irregular government change. The size of the cabinet also reduces the likelihood of an irregular government change. The number of officials at the ministerial level in an executive branch may indicate a mature bureaucratic system with well-defined divisions of labor, which should reduce those irregularities that breed political instability. Finally, countries with a premier as the executive and oil-producing countries tend to have a higher level of irregular government change than otherwise.

Figure 3.2 shows the annual trend of aggregate political instability in the world. Since the probability value for irregular government change is small, the value in the figure is amplified by a factor of 10. The graph shows that political instability, as measured by the probability of irregular government change, peaked in 1971. As mentioned in the previous chapter, many Latin American countries experienced military coups d'état in the 1960s and 1970s. Since the mid-1980s, the probability of irregular government change has declined in the world. We are living in a world with comparatively greater political freedom and less political instability.

## 3.3 Policy Certainty/Uncertainty

Policy uncertainty focuses on uncertainties generated by changes in policies, rather than political systems, and can be measured through

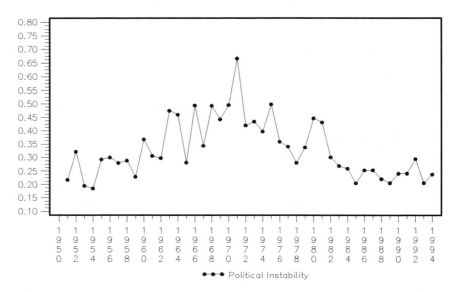

**Figure 3.2**
Political instability in the world, 1950–1994

the "volatility of the institutional framework or through the volatility of outcomes" (Brunetti and Weder 1998, 516). Rodrik (1991) and
Dixit (1989) discuss the theoretical impact of policy uncertainty upon
private investment and assert that policy uncertainty generates a
negative effect on investment by creating a reward for waiting;
therefore, an increase in uncertainty will reduce investment.

Policy-uncertainty variables have been constructed from the standard deviation of inflation (Grier and Tullock 1989) and from the
variances of GDP, government consumption expenditure in GDP,
money growth, domestic credit expansion, and government-budget
deficits (Aizenman and Marion 1993) and from the standard deviation of black-market premiums on foreign exchange, the standard
deviation of real-exchange-rate distortion, changes in the constitution, and changes in the institutional framework (Brunetti and
Weder 1998).

In contrast to these measures of economic policy uncertainty, this
chapter focuses on politically motivated policy uncertainty. In the
theoretical model presented in chapter 2, policy uncertainty or
certainty is associated with policy polarization between opposing
political parties. In previous works I have used such variables as

assassinations, revolutions, riots, and strikes to measure polarization or policy uncertainty,[8] all of which reflect the scale and intensity of the disagreement over a country's political management. Two limitations are worth mentioning. First, in reality, the lack of such violence in a country does not necessarily mean that the country enjoys political harmony, as would be the case for a highly repressive government that could effectively suppress opposition acts. Second, these political behaviors are the consequences or causes of policy uncertainty rather than policy uncertainty itself. Policy uncertainty originates in differences over specific policies. In this large-sample quantitative analysis, it is impossible to look into these specific policies, so here I choose to use income distribution as an indicator of policy certainty. Social, political, and economic conflict in a country often results from income distribution, which is perhaps the single most important politicoeconomic variable (Chen and Feng 1999). A high degree of wealth disparity polarizes people into extremely rich and extremely poor classes, leaving little or no room for a middle class strong enough to compromise the demands of the two extremes. The lack of compromise between the extremes ushers in political and social conflict, which is reflected in the struggle of political parties that efficiently utilize the opportunity created for them by how wealth is distributed in the nation. Of all income-distribution variables to be discussed in full detail in chapter 9, I construct the policy-certainty variable by subtracting the Gini coefficient from one. The larger this variable, the more broadly wealth is possessed and the stronger the degree of policy certainty. Policy uncertainty in this book is proxied by the Gini coefficient itself.

The close relationship between wealth distribution and polarization can be depicted by Chinese political history in the early twentieth century (Chen and Feng 1996b). In the 1920s the Communist Party of China (CPC) strategized to seize national office by winning support from the country's economic losers under a highly unequal wealth-distribution system. Following the strategy laid out in an article written by Mao in 1926, the CPC strove to win over semitenant peasants, poor peasants, middle peasants, master handicraftsmen, petty intellectuals, students, primary and secondary school teachers, office clerks, junior lawyers, petty traders, and national capitalists (Mao 1966). After Mao assumed the party leadership in 1936, the CPC succeeded in canvassing support from the poor peasantry, who represented more than 90% of the Chinese population. The CPC proceeded to consolidate its power base in the countryside by redistributing wealth from the rich to the poor, grew steadily in the war against Japan, and eventually drove the Nationalists to Taiwan. The moral is that if wealth distribution had been relatively equal, the CPC would not have had a raison d'être, let alone a means to wage battles and wars against the Nationalists.

The use of income distribution as an index of policy certainty can also be supported by the theory of politics expounded by Bueno de Mesquita and Root (2000) and Bueno de Mesquita et al. (2003).[9] In such a theory, the government provides a public good that benefits everyone and a private good that benefits only the members of the winning coalition. The government competes with the opposition by forming a winning coalition in the selectorate. The size of the government coalition reflects how different the government policy is from the preference of the citizens at large. The relevancy of this model to the measurement of policy certainty through equality is that if income/wealth distribution is relatively equal, then the coalition sought by the government and its opposition must be large. Consequently, both parties will converge toward the interests of this large group of population, producing an outcome that reinforces policy cloning between the two opposing parties.

### 3.4   Joint Examination of Freedom, Stability, and Certainty

Figure 3.3 jointly examines political freedom, stability, and certainty. Political freedom is measured by DEMOC, stability by one minus two times the probability of irregular government change, and policy certainty by subtracting the Gini coefficient from one. The aggregate data over the period of 1960 to 1995 are used for the three variables for more than 134 countries. The countries in the sample are classified into Asia and the Middle East (balloons), Africa (cylinders), Central and South America (flags), North America and Europe (squares), and Oceania (clubs).

Interestingly, the pattern that emerges is that the five groups of countries can be largely characterized by the three fundamental political variables. North American, European, and Oceanic countries tend to be high on all three political variables, followed by Asian countries. The Central and South American countries are relatively low on policy certainty and political stability, and the African countries are low on political freedom and policy certainty. In the

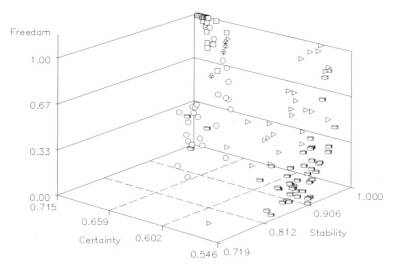

**Figure 3.3**
Freedom, stability, and certainty of nations by region, 1960–1995

three-dimensional graph of political freedom, stability, and certainty, countries tend to form regional clusters. From right to left, we find African countries (cylinders), Latin American countries (flags), Asian countries (balloons), Oceanic countries (clubs), and North American and European countries (squares). The grouping of the countries in the graph is not accidental at all. On the contrary, it is underscored by the political theory of economic growth presented in chapter 2, which explains why some Pacific Asian countries and the G-7 countries share the same pattern of economic growth, while some Latin American and sub-Saharan nations experience similar trajectories in their economic development.

Figure 3.4 selects the 32 nations that constitute the motivating puzzle examined in chapter 1. The operationalization of the theoretical variables makes it possible to investigate the existence of a pattern indicative of the political determinants of economic growth. Political differentiation is even stronger in the four groups of selected nations than in the larger sample of figure 3.3. The G-7 nations (squares) are homogeneously high on political freedom; the only outlier country is France. They are also high on policy certainty and political stability. No unconstitutional government change occurred in this period of time for those nations, and equality characterized

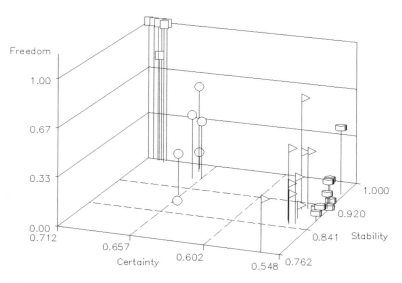

**Figure 3.4**
Freedom, stability, and certainty of 32 nations by regions, 1960–1995

their income distribution, which provided a great deal of policy certainty. The six Asian countries (balloons) should also fare well in the
light of the theory. Among the six Asian countries, Indonesia had the
lowest level of political freedom and was low on political stability.
Thailand, the country next to Indonesia, also was low on stability
because of its military coups d'état, even though those political
power transfers perhaps did not mean much in terms of instability,
as discussed in chapter 2. In general, these Pacific Asian countries
had relatively high policy certainty; their governments have been
able to pursue long-term, consistent growth-enhancing economic
policies thanks to broadly based support.

The nine Latin American countries (flags) were low on policy certainty and political stability. Their record of policy certainty was
better only than the sub-Saharan African countries in the sample,
and their record of political stability was the worst among the four
groups. The country that stood at the corner of low political stability
and low policy certainty was Bolivia, which had the slowest growing
economy in the Latin American group.

The sub-Saharan countries (cylinders) registered the second worst
political stability, pulling ahead of the Latin American countries, and
had the worst policy certainty in the study. Also, the African nations

had very low political freedom, though their repressive governments tended to retain power. The autocratic governments in sub-Sahara seemed to outlive their autocratic counterparts in Latin America. Zimbabwe was an outlier in this group, with its relatively high political freedom and political stability.[10] It should be mentioned in passing that Zimbabwe also enjoyed the highest level of real GDP per capita among the selected sub-Saharan countries. Its real GDP per capita was 3,022 international dollars in 1998. From 1960 to 1998, its average annualized real-GDP-per-capita growth rate was 1.22%, close to double that of second placed Cameroon (0.67%) in the group.

The measurement of political variables identified in the model of chapter 2 is instrumental in isolating differential growth patterns of the four groups of countries introduced in chapter 1. While the African countries' low political freedom and high policy uncertainty may have caused economic underperformance, the Latin American countries' high political instability and policy uncertainty may have been the reason for their unsustainable economic growth. The next chapter further tests the effects of these political variables on long-run growth, using the full sample and controlling relevant economic variables.

# 4         Testing the Political Determinants of Long-Run Economic Growth

*Hypothesis testing is my religion.*
Bruce Bueno de Mesquita

The preceding chapters have theoretically yielded the political conditions of long-run economic growth and have operationalized those political variables. The puzzle raised in chapter 1 has been answered in part by casually examining the data in light of the political theory of economic growth expounded in chapter 2. The objective of this chapter is to test the effects of the political determinants on economic growth in a multivariate setting. In particular, three main features of political institutions will be tested for their impacts on economic growth and socioeconomic development. On the basis of the theoretical discussion in chapter 2, I argue that long-run growth will increase as political freedom increases, political instability decreases, and policy uncertainty declines.

Empirically, in this chapter we will find that policy uncertainty is a major defining characteristic of economic growth. Policy uncertainty impedes growth and investment by increasing the value of withholding assets and decreasing the value of present investment. Wealth disparity is a weak foundation for policy consensus, making it difficult for a government to adopt consistent policy for long-run growth. Additionally, the economy slows down when the probability of irregular government change is high. Political freedom, however, does not show an effect on growth as strong as policy uncertainty or political instability. Rather than bearing directly on growth, the impact of political freedom tends to be indirect through variables that affect economic growth. Finally, the economic control variables included in the regression yield evidence that strongly supports both the exogenous and endogenous growth theories.

## 4.1  Methodology

The focus of this work is the secular trend of economic growth over a fairly long period of time, rather than dynamic change, transitional crises, or external shocks, all of which tend to be short-run phenomena. In keeping with this research interest, I analyze cross-section data instead of time-series data in order to obtain evidence that is tolerably insensitive to short-run factors. The advantage of this method is that it allows me to examine *long-run* trends of economic performance and political institutions. This research method has been popularized by a growing list of scholars, including Scully (1988); Kormendi and Meguire (1985); Barro (1997); Levine and Renelt (1992); Persson and Tabellini (1994); Mankiw, Romer, and Weil (1992); Helliwell (1994); and Alesina et al. (1996). The major characteristic of the methodological common ground shared by these studies is the employment of cross-country analysis, which requires averaging the values of the relevant variables for a fairly long period of time. The empirical models in this chapter are rooted in this methodological foundation.

Barro (1997) points out some problems related to using the short-run dynamic approach, including the fact that the "precise timing between growth and its determinants is not well specified at the high frequencies characteristic of 'business cycles.' For example, relationships at the annual frequency would likely be dominated by mistiming and, hence, effectively by measurement error" (Barro 1997, 15). Also, in connection with the potential benefits of using a time-series approach (which focuses on within-country variation of the variables), there is the notion of the fixed effect of the country—that is, the phenomenon under study is determined by country-specific political, economic, social, and cultural particulars. Fixed effects are often removed by first-differentiating all variables of the time-series data. This practice suffers from several disadvantages, such as the loss of cross-country information and the inaccuracy of timing as measured by lags.[1]

One additional problem is that political data such as political rights or institutionalized democracy may suffer from measurement errors related to time series. For instance, comparing some sub-

Saharan African countries, McHenry (2000) finds that political events used to measure democracy or political rights are not precisely reflected on an annual basis. The use of aggregate data mitigates the within-country time-series inaccuracies while attaching importance to cross-country variation.

Finally, the lack of within-country variation in certain countries' political freedom renders differencing methods highly ineffective: since the change in political freedom in these countries tends to be zero, and since the cross-country variance has been removed, these methods treat a considerably democratic country (e.g., New Zealand) the same as a consistently totalitarian country (e.g., North Korea).

Despite the potential pitfalls mentioned above, if handled appropriately time-series analyses have an advantage when it comes to studying the *dynamic change* of the relationship between political and economic development. Some works adopting various time-series models—such as those by Gasiorowski (1995), Burkhart and Lewis-Beck (1994), and Przeworski et al. (2000)—have unearthed important dynamic mechanisms involving political and economic change using annual data. The time-series method used in these works is consistent with the objective of their research, which is a relatively short-term changing relationship. However, the aim of this chapter is to uncover the aggregate, long-term relationships between political and economic development, but the analysis here complements the findings concerning short-run relationships.

Another important issue involved in this kind of analysis is endogeneity. Political institutions and economic performance have long been thought of as being mutually related, as being both consequences and determinants. There has been a host of works on the causal effects of democracy on growth, but ever since Lipset (1959), numerous scholars have also examined the requisites for democracy, including economic development. It is generally agreed that the relationships between the political and economic dimensions are complex. For instance, while political institutions have been determined to exert a tremendous influence on economic performance, it has been argued that the ability of both authoritarian and democratic leaders to maintain power is partly a function of economic performance, which in turn depends on the conduct of economic policy. Furthermore, the coherence and continuity of policy are determined both in the initiation phase and during the consolidation phase, when success rests on building bases for social support.[2]

Thus, the possibility of reverse causation is one possible objection to the use of political variables as independent variables (Knack and Keefer 1995). It is plausible that under certain circumstances, political turbulence (e.g., coups, revolutions, riots, strikes, etc.) is caused by economic difficulties (Londregan and Poole 1990). Barro (1991) treats economic growth as endogenous, while raising the possibility of reverse causation of political uncertainty (e.g., revolutions and coups). In their study of inflation, Cukierman, Edwards, and Tabellini (1992) explicitly assume that political instability is the exogenous variable, arguing, "Political stability also reflects other, permanent, or slowly changing features of a political system. Political institutions, culture, tradition, underlying conflicts, cleavage of population into organized groups, and the extent of political participation and the involvement of the citizens are all semipermanent features of a country that affect its stability" (Cukierman, Edwards, and Tabellini 1992, 550). In the same light, Fukuyama observes the permanency of political systems in the case of democratization:

Democratization is an autonomous political process ... that is dependent on a variety of political factors including: the apparent success of democracy relative to its authoritarian competitors in other countries; the fortunes of war (and peace) in the international system; the skill and competence of the individual leaders who seek to create and consolidate democratic systems; and sheer accident. There are also cultural obstacles to stable democracies, such as religion, ethnicity, preexisting social structure, and the like, that are independent of the level of economic development and affect the possibility of democracy. (1993, 102)

In their empirical study, Alesina, Özler, Roubini, and Swagel (1996) unequivocally find that causality runs from political instability to economic performance. The empirical results of Newman and Thompson (1989) lead to the conclusion that social development is more likely than economic development to be the "exogenous" variable. In this chapter I assume that political institutions are exogenous, but I will loosen this assumption in the next chapter, explicitly allowing both political systems and political stability to be endogenous.

Fully realizing the importance and inevitability of the interaction of these two sets of factors, I use in this study either a simultaneous-equation system, to account for the reverse-causation problem, or previous values of political variables as instruments to account for current economic performance and social change.

Another problem particularly limiting the work of political scientists is that they fail to consider relevant economic variables in their investigations of economic growth and political institutions. Parsimony is often given as the reason for the exclusion of economic variables; the unavailability of data is also responsible for their omission. In this study, I try to keep every model as simple as possible, yet I also try to include all of the relevant control variables, according to findings in the literature.

Finally, in the social sciences, few propositions are free from anomalies. The enterprise of scientific research is to find regularities and laws while taking into consideration exceptions to these rules. In this book, not only do I examine general theories and derive statistical evidence to test the hypotheses related to the theories, but I also conduct various case studies. Case studies, as Bates writes, are useful "to find the mechanisms that generate the variation we capture statistically and to account for cases that deviate from these trends" (Bates 1996, 2). Some of these cases are consistent with the theories and statistics in the book, lending additional support to them. Others apparently run counter to the theoretical implications and statistical results, casting doubt upon them. I make an extra effort in this chapter to analyze why these anomalies occur, so that the circumstances under which the general rules work well can be better understood.

## 4.2  The Statistical Model

The basic multivariate statistical model to test the three implications is $g_i = \alpha + \beta x_i + \gamma y_i + \varepsilon_i$, where the subscript refers to country $i$, $g$ denotes the average growth rate in real GDP per capita, $x$ is a set of political variables designed to capture political freedom, political instability, and policy uncertainty, $y$ is a set of control variables mostly measuring economic conditions, and $\varepsilon$ is the error term.

Since the theoretical model in the previous section reflects a long-term relationship between the political environment and economic development, I examine the average cross-country data for a sufficiently long period of time. In this study, the period covers 35 years, stretching from 1961 through 1995.[3] The selection of years is based on two factors. First, the effective testing of the model in chapter 2 requires a period long enough to study the secular trends of economic growth. Second, the exclusion of the few years beyond 1995 avoids some nonsecular trends such as the economic bubble inflated by "dot coms" and the subsequent economic recession. Empirically, the included period is important, as it spans the 1960s and 1970s, which saw a few authoritarian regimes doing seemingly well, and the late 1980s and early 1990s, which witnessed the dismantling of authoritarian regimes and their controlled economies.

As discussed in chapter 3, political instability is measured by the probability function of irregular or unconstitutional government change, political freedom or democracy is operationalized by the institutionalized democracy index in the Polity data, and policy uncertainty is proxied by the Gini coefficient.[4] In light of the theory presented in chapter 2, the following hypotheses are made:

- Economic growth increases as political freedom increases.
- Economic growth decreases as political instability increases.
- Economic growth decreases as policy uncertainty increases.

It is very important to control the testing of the above hypotheses with relevant economic variables; otherwise the results obtained for political variables could be substantially biased. Many economic variables have been considered determinants of economic growth, including investment, human capital, international trade, and inflation. In Levine and Renelt's (1992) systematic study of a wide range of economic factors that may account for long-run aggregate economic growth, trade and investment are identified as major inputs for growth, though the effect of trade on growth weakens when controlled by investment. Levine and Renelt (1992) also find that the initial level of development has a negative effect on growth, conditional upon the level of human capital, which has invariably been found to exert a positive impact on growth. In two separate studies, Barro (1991, 1997) has found that among a multitude of variables, the initial level of GDP, the initial level of human capital, the fertility rate, government consumption, an index of the rule of law, and trade all have some effect on growth. Mankiw, Romer, and Weil (1992) have obtained similar results regarding the effects on growth of initial levels of economic development, savings, and human-capital accumulation.

Among economic control variables, this chapter focuses on the initial level of development, the initial level of education, investment, inflation, birth rates, and property rights (economic freedom).

In the neoclassical model of growth, which numerous empirical findings have supported, a nation's growth rate tends to be negatively related to its level of development (Solow 1956; Barro 1991, 1997). The implication of these theoretical and empirical results is that for countries with similar preferences and technologies, poor countries tend to grow faster than rich countries, thus converging toward the same level of income (hence, the "convergence hypothesis"). The main reason for this phenomenon in neoclassical growth models is diminishing returns to reproducible capital. Poor countries typically have low ratios of capital to labor and, consequently, high marginal products of capital. They therefore tend to grow at higher rates. In this study I use real GDP per capita in 1960, the data for which comes from Barro and Wolf (1989), as an indicator of the initial level of economic development. It is expected that the initial GDP per capita will have a negative effect on growth.

In contrast, human capital plays a critical role in endogenous growth models, which hold that knowledge-driven growth can lead to a constant—or even increasing—rate of return. In Romer's work, for instance, human capital is the major input to research and development, since people innovate technologies necessary for continued growth (Romer 1990). Therefore, countries with larger initial human capital stocks are more likely to create new products, and therefore will grow faster than other countries. Empirical evidence has revealed a positive relationship between education and growth.[5] In this study, the elementary school enrollment rate in 1960 is employed as a proxy for the initial stock of human capital (Barro and Wolf 1989). I hypothesize that the initial level of human capital has a positive effect on growth.

Investment has long been considered an engine of growth. According to Kormendi and Meguire (1985) and Levine and Renelt (1992), investment share of GDP has a significant and positive effect on growth. Some studies of the relationship between growth and capital investment in developing countries have borne out the positive influence of capital formation on growth (Robinson 1971, Tyler 1981, Levy 1988). Following Kormendi and Meguire (1985), Barro (1991), and Levine and Renelt (1992), I include the ratio of domestic investment to GDP as a control variable in this study. This variable is averaged for the period 1960–1995, and the data are from Summers and Heston (2000). It is expected that domestic investment has a positive impact on growth.

The theoretical arguments regarding the effects of inflation on growth appear to be in conflict. As Grier and Tullock (1989) explain, the Tobin-Mundell hypothesis states that anticipated inflation causes portfolio adjustments, which lower the real rate of interest while raising investment and growth. Yet Stockman (1981) finds that higher anticipated inflation reduces economic activities, thus lowering investment and growth. However, Gregorio (1993) suggests that the effect of the inflation level on investment is negligible, provided that the elasticity of intertemporal substitution is sufficiently small. Several empirical cross-country studies tend to find a negative effect of inflation on growth.[6] The data for inflation are from Summers and Heston (2000), and the variable is constructed from the GDP deflator for the countries in this study.[7]

The standard deviation of inflation is a measurement of the variability of inflation. Some scholars maintain that variance in inflation causes uncertainty in the market information of prices, thus reducing economic activity (Hayek 1944, Friedman 1977). Others suggest that variance in inflation may be considered a proxy for macroeconomic uncertainty (Gregorio 1993), which in turn can spark capital flight, pessimistic perceptions, and delays in investment decisions. Empirically, some works document that the standard deviation of inflation is negatively related to growth (Grier and Tullock 1989), whereas others find that neither inflation nor the standard deviation of inflation is robustly correlated with growth or investment share of GDP (Levine and Renelt 1992). The data on variability of inflation is constructed from the GDP deflator in the data compiled by Summers and Heston (2000).

Birth rates negatively affect economic growth. Feng, Kugler, and Zak, in several recent works (2001, 2002), derive and test a set of conditions linking politics to growth through fertility rates. A rapid increase in population decreases human capital and transfers resources away from production, resulting in a decrease in long-run economic growth. Barro (1997) empirically finds that high fertility rates tend to have a negative effect on economic growth, while Przeworski et al. (2000) find that population growth pronouncedly reduces economic growth. In this chapter I adopt crude birth rates (CBR), defined as the number of births per 1,000 population, as a measure of population increase. The data are from the *World Development Indicators* (World Bank 2000). I expect that birth rates will have a negative effect on growth in a regression.

The protection of property rights, or economic freedom in general, has been found to have a positive effect on long-run economic growth. Empirical studies of political economy and growth have unequivocally determined that economic freedom enhances economic growth. Chen and Feng (1996) find that economic freedom, measured by Scully's economic liberty index,[8] has a significant effect on growth. Similarly, Knack and Keefer (1995) and Chen and Feng (1996) find that a state's institutional strength, proxied by the Business Environment Risk Intelligence (BERI) indicator and the International Country Risk Guide (ICRG) indicator, has a significant and positive effect on growth. Moreover, the effect of political instability on growth, as measured by Barro (1991) through revolutions and coups, becomes much weaker when controlled by these indicators.[9] Finally, Clague, Keefer, Knack, and Olson (1995) use a measure known as "contract-intensive money" (CIM) to estimate the effect of financial institutions on growth; the higher a nation's CIM ratio is, the stronger its institutional framework is presumed to be.[10] Their statistical results support the hypothesis that nations with a higher CIM measure will have higher levels of real GDP per capita, growth of real GDP per capita, and private investment. In this study I utilize a measure of economic freedom presented in Gwartney, Lawson, and Block (1996) and predict that economic freedom will have a positive effect on economic growth. These results are summarized in table 4.1.

## 4.3   Empirical Results

Before running the multivariate regression on economic growth, it is useful to examine correlations among the variables above (table 4.2). Because of the complex interrelations characteristic of a dynamic development process, there could exist a high correlation between certain variables, thus causing a multicollinearity problem for the multivariate testing of the variables identified in the last section. Because of space limitations, the following notations are used: GROWTH (growth rates of real GDP per capita), $\text{GDP}_{60}$ (real GDP per capita in 1960), $\text{PRIM}_{60}$ (the elementary school enrollment rates in 1960), INV (investment share in GDP), INF (inflation), INFV (the standard deviation of inflation), BIRTH (crude birth rates), ECONF (economic freedom), FREE (political freedom), INST (political instability), and UNCER (policy uncertainty).

**Table 4.1**
Summary of the variables

| Variable | Sign | Data source |
|---|---|---|
| *Policy variables* | | |
| Political freedom | + | Polity 1998 |
| Political instability | − | Constructed 2000 |
| Policy uncertainty | − | Deininger and Squire 1996 |
| *Control variables* | | |
| Initial level of development | − | Barro and Wolf 1989 |
| Initial level of education | + | Barro and Wolf 1989 |
| Investment | + | Summers and Heston 2000 |
| Inflation | ? | Summers and Heston 2000 |
| Inflation variability | − | Summers and Heston 2000 |
| Birth rates | − | World Bank 2000 |
| Economic freedom | + | Gwartney et al. 1997 |

Dependent variable: growth rates of real GDP per capita.
Source: Summers and Heston 1995, 2000.

The relationship between democracy and growth is weak. This binary finding is consistent with the ambiguous relationships found for political democracy and economic growth in the literature (see appendix 4.A for a brief discussion of the literature on democracy and growth). The weak correlation between freedom and growth displayed in the table, however, is likely to be inconclusive, as we also find a strong positive correlation between democracy and development, yet it is known that developed countries tend to grow more slowly due to the convergence effect. Leaving everything else out of the equation, we are likely to find that a democracy has a low growth rate, which may or may not be true in multivariate testing. Thus, we should exercise caution about a simple comparison of growth under autocracy and democracy.

Table 4.2 also shows that both democracy and growth are positively correlated with investment, education, and economic freedom, and negatively correlated with birth rates, political instability, and policy uncertainty. Therefore, democracy may contribute to growth through these variables, which points to the importance of studying the indirect effects of democracy on growth through its influence on such variables as education and investment.

By contrast, political instability and policy uncertainty are both negatively correlated with growth at a fairly high level. Moreover, they are also strongly and positively correlated with births and

**Table 4.2**
Correlation matrix of variables in the growth equation

| | GROWTH | GDP$_{60}$ | PRIM$_{60}$ | INV | INF | INFV | BIRTH | ECONF | FREE | INST | UNCER |
|---|---|---|---|---|---|---|---|---|---|---|---|
| GROWTH | 1.000 | 0.193 | 0.463 | 0.237 | 0.240 | 0.105 | -0.317 | 0.410 | 0.170 | -0.425 | -0.334 |
| GDP$_{60}$ | | 1.000 | 0.564 | 0.423 | 0.023 | -0.135 | -0.757 | 0.411 | 0.717 | -0.601 | -0.335 |
| PRIM$_{60}$ | | | 1.000 | 0.591 | -0.003 | -0.114 | -0.798 | 0.463 | 0.609 | -0.554 | -0.488 |
| INV | | | | 1.000 | -0.157 | -0.187 | -0.495 | 0.292 | 0.392 | -0.531 | -0.443 |
| INF | | | | | 1.000 | 0.847 | 0.078 | -0.165 | -0.025 | 0.137 | 0.089 |
| INFV | | | | | | 1.000 | 0.216 | -0.295 | -0.169 | 0.226 | 0.148 |
| BIRTH | | | | | | | 1.000 | -0.396 | -0.655 | 0.666 | 0.649 |
| ECONF | | | | | | | | 1.000 | 0.378 | -0.234 | -0.298 |
| FREE | | | | | | | | | 1.000 | -0.595 | -0.381 |
| INST | | | | | | | | | | 1.000 | 0.641 |
| UNCER | | | | | | | | | | | 1.000 |

negatively correlated with investment and education. Therefore, political instability and policy uncertainty may actually have compounding effects on economic growth through direct and indirect channels. It should also be noted that the relationship between political instability and policy uncertainty is positive, as expected. Thus, the interaction between them could have a spillover impact on economic growth.

Economic growth is positively correlated with education and economic freedom, but negatively correlated with births. Similarly, the level of development ($GDP_{60}$) is positively correlated with education, investment, and economic freedom, but negatively correlated with birth rates. Education is highly negatively correlated with birth rates as well. All of this indicates that demography is a critical piece in the development puzzle. The variance of inflation and the level of inflation are strongly positively correlated, showing that there may be a vicious cycle caused by spirals of price increases. The convergence effect cannot be found in table 4.2, and the sign is wrong. This result is consistent with the literature, which finds that the convergence effect will take place only after being controlled by other variables, such as education (Barro 1991).

Table 4.3 presents results of multivariate statistical analysis. Because heteroskedasticity could be important across countries, the standard errors for the coefficients are corrected on the basis of White's heteroskedasticity-consistent covariance matrix (White 1980).

Column (1) is an economic model of growth. Column (2) presents a political model of growth. Columns (3) through (6) are political-economic models that respecify column (1) and column (2) by varying the set of included political variables controlled by economic variables. The results indicate that political freedom, or democracy, as I shall often say, tends to have a positive effect on growth, though the level of statistical significance varies when controlled by different sets of economic and other political variables. All three theoretical variables take their expected signs in all regressions where they are entered. Thus, democracy appears to be positively related to growth, while political instability and policy uncertainty have negative effects on growth. However, only political instability and policy uncertainty are statistically significant. The lack of significance of the parameter estimate for democracy warrants some careful analysis. It is premature to declare that democracy has no impact on economic growth.

**Table 4.3**
Regression results on growth

| | (1) | (2) | (3) | (4) | (5) | (6) |
|---|---|---|---|---|---|---|
| INTERCEPT | -0.0314* | 0.0678* | 0.0321* | 0.0341* | 0.0499* | 0.04870* |
| | (0.0135) | (0.0118) | (0.0133) | (0.0133) | (0.0141) | (0.0147) |
| $GDP_{60}$ | -0.0062* | — | -0.0068* | -0.0068* | -0.0064* | -0.0070* |
| | (0.0011) | | (0.0012) | (0.0011) | (0.0010) | (0.0011) |
| $PRIM_{60}$ | 0.0019 | — | 0.0008 | 0.0011 | 0.0086 | 0.0073 |
| | (0.0074) | | (0.0074) | (0.0073) | (0.0074) | (0.0074) |
| INV | 0.0008* | — | 0.0008* | 0.0007* | 0.0007* | 0.0006* |
| | (0.0002) | | (0.0002) | (0.0002) | (0.0002) | (0.0002) |
| INF | -0.032 | — | -0.0552 | 0.0698 | -0.0672 | 0.0968 |
| | (0.1044) | | (0.1047) | (0.1041) | (0.0998) | (0.1022) |
| INFV | -0.0009 | — | -0.0040 | -0.0063 | -0.0069 | -0.0113 |
| | (0.0196) | | (0.0200) | (0.0194) | (0.0187) | (0.0090) |
| BIRTH | -0.0009* | — | -0.0009* | -0.0008* | -0.0005** | -0.0006* |
| | (0.0002) | | (0.0002) | (0.0002) | (0.0003) | (0.0002) |
| ECONF | 0.0030* | — | 0.0029* | 0.0035* | 0.0032* | 0.0036* |
| | (0.0013) | | (0.0013) | (0.0013) | (0.0012) | (0.0012) |
| FREE | — | 0.00003 | 0.0003 | — | — | 0.0002 |
| | | (0.00065) | (0.0009) | | | (0.0006) |
| INST | — | -0.1105** | — | -0.1178** | — | -0.0803** |
| | | (0.0658) | | (0.0534) | | (0.0474) |
| UNCER | — | -0.0012* | — | — | -0.0009* | -0.0008* |
| | | (0.0003) | | | (0.0003) | (0.0003) |
| $\bar{R}^2$ | 0.595 | 0.302 | 0.591 | 0.609 | 0.634 | 0.635 |
| $\sigma$ | 0.011 | 0.015 | 0.012 | 0.011 | 0.011 | 0.011 |

Dependent variable: growth rates of real GDP per capita.
*Statistically significant at the 0.01 error level in a one-tailed test.
**Statistically significant at the 0.05 error level in a one-tailed test.
Standard errors are in the parentheses and are constructed from White's (1980) heteroskedasticity-consistent covariance matrix.

Whether democracy has a positive or negative effect on economic growth in all empirical analyses is a problem of specification. There are three statistical possibilities that affect whether democracy has a positive or negative, significant or insignificant, effect on growth. First, most advanced economies also boast a high degree of democracy. Second, most advanced economies also tend to grow slowly, when we control for relevant variables such as education. Third, the effects of democracy on growth may be a result of the other variables included in the regression. If we put the first two possibilities together, the implication is that democracies tend to have a low growth rate. Nothing can be farther from the truth if we argue, from the above premises, that democracy slows economic growth. If we focus on the third possibility, then democracy tends to show statistical insignificance.

Statistically, we can test the null hypothesis that democracy retards economic growth, or that democracy has no effect on growth, with the following model:

$$\text{GROWTH} = \beta_0 + \beta_1 \text{ GDP}_{60} + \beta_2 \text{ EDUCATION}_{60} + \beta_3 \text{ DEMOCRACY} + \varepsilon$$

In this very parsimonious model, the inclusion of the education variable will help identify the convergence effect. The inclusion of the output-per-capita variable corrects the spurious result that highly democratic nations (which tend to be rich economies) have low growth rates. The parameter estimates from the above model are as follows, with the parameters' standard errors in parentheses ($\bar{R}^2$ is adjusted $R^2$):

$$\text{GROWTH} = -0.003 - 0.003 \text{ GDP}_{60} + 0.027 \text{ EDUCATION}_{60}$$
$$\qquad\quad (0.004) \quad (0.001)^* \qquad\quad (0.007)^*$$

$$\qquad + 0.019 \text{ DEMOCRACY} + \varepsilon$$
$$\qquad\quad (0.007)^*$$

$$\bar{R}^2 = 0.30, \quad \sigma = 0.016, \quad N = 113$$

*Statistically significant at the 0.01 error level in a two-tailed test.

We have some fairly clear evidence that democracy leads to growth when we control for the size of the economy and level of education.[11] The danger of a hasty conclusion based on a misspecified model is clear. The correction of this potential specification error is to include relevant control variables, which may lead to different problems: the efficiency of the estimate of the policy variable decreases, since the standard error of the estimate may increase with the inclusion of control variables. The trade-off is between bias and efficiency.

The effect of democracy on growth is likely to attenuate when a certain set of control variables is included. Two phenomena characterize these variables. First, they have an impact on economic growth. Second, democracy determines them. The usual candidates for this set of variables are education, investment, inflation, economic freedom, population growth, political instability, and policy uncertainty as indexed by income distribution.

Take the relationship between growth, democracy, and income distribution, for example. In table 4.3, policy uncertainty as measured by income inequality has a strong negative effect on growth. Furthermore, income distribution can be affected by other variables, particularly political freedom. It is hypothesized that democracy leads to more evenly distributed wealth than other political systems. While chapter 9 will exclusively study the relationship between political institutions and income distribution, it can be argued here that political freedom contributes to economic growth through the channel of income distribution. Political freedom will be found less significant when controlled for income distribution, if it mainly affects growth via that route. This occurs when income distribution is one of the major drivers of economic growth and political freedom directly contributes to income equality rather than economic growth. This relationship can be represented by figure 4.1, which shows the relationship between growth, inequality, and political freedom or democracy, after all other variables such as human capital, investment, inflation, political stability, and level of development are fully taken into consideration.

It is clear that without income equality, political freedom will be greatly associated with economic growth, as their common area is relatively large. With income equality (or inequality) included, the exclusive overlap between political freedom and growth becomes marginalized. Given the hypothesis that political freedom increases income equality, thus leading to growth, it can be deduced from figure 4.1 that political freedom may have little direct effect on growth once its potential indirect effects (such as physical capital formation, human capital accumulation, inflation, political instability, and policy uncertainty) and the effect of income distribution on

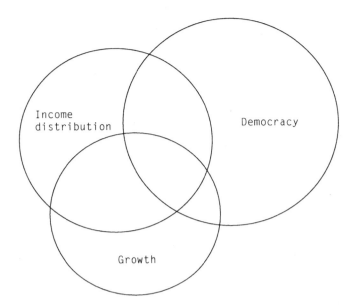

**Figure 4.1**
A hypothesized relationship among growth, inequality, and freedom

growth are taken into account. Indeed, the direct effect of political
freedom on growth is weak and ambiguous. Herein lies the key to
the literature's controversy and debate regarding the relationship
between democracy and growth (see appendix 4.A). The relevance
of democracy to growth is a complex issue. Conclusions based on
overly simple statistics prove to be nothing but confusion. When we
study democracy and growth, we have to take a much broader view
of how democracy suffuses the facilitating environment for economic
growth.

Most control variables hold their expected signs and are statistically significant. We have strong evidence of the convergence
hypothesis. The initial level of the economy has a negative and
highly significant effect on growth. With other factors fixed, a relatively small poor country tends to grow faster than its large, rich
counterpart. As noted in the last section, neoclassical growth
models (e.g., Solow 1956) imply that the growth rate of real GDP
per capita tends to be negatively related to the starting level of income per capita, with the main reason being diminishing returns to
capital. The convergence hypothesis is identified after other con-

**Table 4.4**
Standardized parameter estimates

| Variable | Standardized estimate |
| --- | --- |
| INTERCEPT | 0.000 |
| GDP PER CAPITA, 1960 | −0.703 |
| ENROLLMENT, 1960 | 0.116 |
| INVESTMENT SHARE | 0.350 |
| INFLATION | 0.285 |
| INFLATION VARIANCE | −0.183 |
| BIRTH RATES | −0.310 |
| ECONOMIC FREEDOM | 0.229 |
| POLITICAL FREEDOM | 0.040 |
| POLITICAL INSTABILITY | −0.137 |
| POLICY UNCERTAINTY | −0.300 |

ditions, such as economic and political constraints, are taken into consideration.

Among other findings, investment has a positive effect on growth, an increase in birth rates decreases growth, and economic freedom promotes growth. Neither inflation nor variability of inflation is statistically significant. Finally, the primary-school-enrollment rate has the expected positive sign but remains statistically insignificant in all regressions shown in table 4.3. The lack of significance for education is caused by the inclusion of the birth variable: The correlation between the enrollment rate and the birth rate is 0.80. If birth rates were excluded from column (1), the parameter estimate for enrollment rates would be 0.0182. With a standard error of 0.0069, the enrollment variable would be statistically significant at the 0.01 error level.

Finally, table 4.4 presents the relative magnitudes of the variables by comparing standardized estimates of their regression coefficients, which denote the change in the dependent variable in terms of its standard deviation, given a one unit change in the standard deviation of the independent variable.

Table 4.4 shows the standardized estimates of regression (6) of table 4.3. Here the most powerful variable for predicting growth is the initial level of real GDP per capita, which demonstrates that the conditional convergence model is a good way of forecasting future growth after controlling for political and economic variables.

Investment share, economic freedom, education, and birth rates are also useful indicators of growth. Regarding the political variables, however, democracy does not appear to be an important variable explaining growth. Political instability and policy uncertainty are better indicators than democracy. Despite the apparently relatively weak effects of democracy, democracy, as argued earlier, should have considerable impact on economic growth through its influence on the other variables that contribute to growth. Thus the political environment can have considerable impact upon economic growth.

## 4.4 Continental Effects

Several studies have empirically established the continental effects of economic growth. It has been found that Latin America and sub-Saharan Africa tend to have a negative effect on growth, while East Asia is likely to produce a positive effect on growth, with other variables kept constant. While some interpretations have been offered to identify the latent variables underlining the continent variables, none of the interpretations has been hinged on political factors (Barro 1997, 30–32). In this book, chapter 1 started with the puzzle of economic growth based on regional patterns, chapter 2 deduced a political theory of economic growth, and chapter 3 mapped economic growth to measurements of the three major political variables identified in the model. Here, to ascertain the relationship between our three policy variables and these continents, I replicate table 4.3, controlling three continent dummy variables: Africa, Pacific Asia, and Latin America. The results are reported in table 4.5.

A few interesting results emerge from the inclusion of the continent variables. First, the policy variables—political freedom, political instability, and policy uncertainty—are robust in the sense that the magnitudes of the parameter estimates do not weaken, and in some cases (e.g., regression (12)) even increase, after controlling the continent variables. This indicates that these variables extend beyond these particular regions and may hold universally.

Regression (7) controls the continent variables in the economic model and thereby replicates the literature's results, namely, showing that Africa and Latin America have a negative effect on growth whereas Pacific Asia has a positive effect. All three continent variables are statistically significant at the 10% error level. The political model in regression (8), however, shows that only Pacific Asia is significant. Latin America and sub-Saharan Africa not only become statistically insignificant, but the former even changes its sign from negative to positive. This result indicates that the political model is a key to solving the "mysterious" continent effects. In other words, the negative effect of Latin America or sub-Saharan Africa on growth may be largely due to the political institutions characterized by those three variables (political freedom, instability, and uncertainty).

Regressions (9) to (11) introduce one political variable at a time in the economic model, controlling the continent variables. It was found in (9) that while Pacific Asia and Latin America maintain significant effects on growth, Africa loses significance when the democracy variable is included. Therefore, democracy is likely to be a major factor in African economic development. In a multivariate cross-section statistical analysis of long-run growth and democracy of the 40 sub-Saharan African countries, Feng (1996) finds that a country ruled by a democratic government is likely to grow faster than an autocracy.

In regression (10), the parameter estimate for Latin America becomes statistically insignificant after political instability is included, indicating that political instability underscores the negative effect of the Latin American dummy variable found in the literature. The inclusion of the political-instability variable, however, does not directly make sub-Saharan Africa or Pacific Asia insignificant. Political instability may run different courses in those two continents compared to Latin America. Indeed, the next section portrays Thailand as a case in which apparent instability does not significantly affect growth in the presence of the nation's particular political setting.

When the policy-uncertainty variable enters together with the continent dummy variables in regression (11), not only do the parameter estimates for Latin America and sub-Saharan Africa become statistically insignificant, their signs are reversed. This finding provides a further solution to the mysterious continent effects. Both continents, particularly Latin America, lack political consensus, largely due to a huge disparity in wealth distribution. Most likely this lack of policy consensus, rather than the continent itself, is what causes the economy to falter in many of the two regions' countries. By contrast, the parameter for Pacific Asia remains significant. Pacific Asia, unlike Latin America, does not have rampant, persistent, regionwide problems of income inequality. The fast-growth

**Table 4.5**
Regression results on growth

|  | (7) | (8) | (9) | (10) | (11) | (12) |
|---|---|---|---|---|---|---|
| INTERCEPT | 0.0289* (0.0142) | 0.0621* (0.0211) | 0.0258** (0.0148) | 0.0357* (0.0146) | 0.0690* (0.0223) | 0.0759* (0.0225) |
| GDP$_{60}$ | -0.0053* (0.0012) | — | -0.0055* (0.0012) | -0.0060* (0.0011) | -0.0060* (0.0011) | -0.0068* (0.0012) |
| PRIM$_{60}$ | 0.0062 (0.0089) | — | 0.0054 (0.0080) | 0.0022 (0.0082) | 0.0068 (0.0078) | 0.0026 (0.0080) |
| INV | 0.0007* (0.0002) | — | 0.0007* (0.0002) | 0.0006* (0.0002) | 0.0007* (0.0002) | 0.0006* (0.0002) |
| INF | 0.0747 (0.1028) | — | -0.0933 (0.1054) | 0.0992 (0.1026) | -0.0757 (0.1003) | 0.1156 (0.1016) |
| INFV | -0.0010 (0.0193) | — | -0.0129 (0.0198) | -0.0126 (0.0191) | -0.0089 (0.0188) | -0.0149 (0.0190) |
| BIRTH | -0.0007** (0.0003) | — | -0.0006** (0.0003) | -0.0006** (0.0002) | -0.0006** (0.0002) | -0.0005** (0.0002) |
| ECONF | 0.0019† (0.0014) | — | 0.0019† (0.0014) | 0.0021† (0.0014) | 0.0023** (0.0014) | 0.0025** (0.0014) |
| FREE | — | 0.0003 (0.0006) | 0.0005 (0.0006) | — | — | 0.0005 (0.0006) |
| INST | — | -0.1355** (0.0756) | — | -0.1135** (0.0661) | — | -0.1012† (0.0644) |
| UNCER | — | 0.0011** (0.00065) | — | — | -0.0013** (0.0006) | -0.0015** (0.0006) |
| AFRICA | -0.0055† (0.0043) | 0.0016 (0.0065) | -0.0050 (0.0043) | -0.0058† (0.0042) | 0.0077 (0.0071) | 0.0091 (0.0072) |

| | | | | | | |
|---|---|---|---|---|---|---|
| PA | 0.0097† | 0.0287* | 0.0108** | 0.0101† | 0.0104** | 0.0109** |
| | (0.0063) | (0.0065) | (0.0064) | (0.0062) | (0.0061) | (0.0062) |
| LA | −0.0060† | 0.0081 | −0.0057† | −0.0030 | 0.0077 | 0.0121† |
| | (0.0041) | (0.0084) | (0.0041) | (0.0043) | (0.0072) | (0.0074) |
| $\bar{R}^2$ | 0.616 | 0.441 | 0.615 | 0.625 | 0.635 | 0.660 |
| $\sigma$ | 0.011 | 0.013 | 0.011 | 0.011 | 0.011 | 0.011 |

Dependent variable: growth rates of real GDP per capita.

*Statistically significant at the 0.01 error level in a one-tailed test.

**Statistically significant at the 0.05 error level in a one-tailed test.

†Statistically significant at the 0.10 error level in a one-tailed test.

Standard errors are in the parentheses and are constructed from White's (1980) heteroskedasticity-consistent covariance matrix.

economies in Asia—Singapore, Taiwan, and South Korea—all have
low levels of income inequality, although the relatively slowly
growing economies—the Philippines, Indonesia, Thailand, and Malaysia—all have relatively high levels of income inequality. Therefore, the negative effect of policy uncertainty on growth should be
strengthened when controlling for Pacific Asia—an inference supported by the comparison between regression (5) and regression (11).

Regression (12) combines the full political model with the economic model, controlling the continent dummy variables. Again,
some continent effects identified in the literature—i.e., negative
effects of Latin America and sub-Sahara Africa on growth—
completely disappear. Pacific Asia still has a significantly positive
value, indicating that certain factor(s) excluded in the regression
may cause this region to have good economic growth.[12] The most
important finding of all regressions in table 4.5 is that politics lies
behind the veil of the mysterious continental effects. *While the dearth
of political democracy and the existence of policy uncertainty are a drag on
the economic growth of sub-Saharan Africa, political instability and policy
uncertainty underscore the lack of economic performance in Latin America.*

## 4.5   A Case Study: Thailand

When it comes to anomalies, reality may appear to contradict theory.
Thailand is an interesting case that can be used to refute or support
the proposition that political instability decreases economic growth.
Despite apparently high levels of political instability, Thailand's per
capita income increased from $537 in 1963 to $887 in 1988, exceeding
the growth rate of many other lower-middle-income countries by a
large margin (Balassa 1991, 188–189), even though its 1997 financial
crisis has raised questions about the foundation of its economic
growth. Alternatively, Thailand's growth lags behind other Pacific
Asian economies (e.g., Taiwan, Singapore, and Hong Kong) where
political instability is low. In general, frequent military coups d'état
in Thailand have not generated the same pernicious effect on growth
as those in some Latin American countries, although such political
turbulence may have been disadvantageous for Thailand's growth,
compared to its politically calm counterparts in the region.

There are two important lessons to be drawn from political instability in Thailand. First, government change as the result of a coup

d'état does not have to instill political uncertainty into the economy if both the overthrown government and the coup leaders share the same commitment to a market economy. "Thai politics revolve around personalities, not ideology" (Fletcher and Gearing 1996, 22). Second, given the prevalence of the monarchy in the tradition and culture of Thailand, a change of government as the result of a coup d'état does not have the same consequence as in nations of other cultures, where such a permanently unifying national political figure does not exist. Therefore, a country with regular coups d'état is still able to manage growth if its fundamental principles remain unchanged, polarization is alleviated, and economic freedom prevails.

Thailand had 25 governments from 1932 to 2001, many of which emerged as a result of major political crises. During this period, the country experienced 10 coups and 16 failed coup attempts (Morell and Samudavanija 1981, Schlossstein 1991). From March 1975 to November 1997, the average life span of a Thai government was 24 months, the shortest being two months under Suchinda and the longest 100 months under Prem. Table 4.6 illustrates some details of these government changes. The statistics ostensibly depict a highly unstable political system. The high frequency of power transfer in Thailand appears mind-boggling, especially in light of the long-term Asian model of government change seen in Japan, Singapore, Malaysia, China, and Indonesia. But despite the kaleidoscope of power transfer by legal as well as illegal means, the actual fundamentals of the Thai political system are secure. "Shifts in Thai political power that have resulted in wholesale changes in government tend to reflect differences among the ruling elite rather than any underlying systemic weakness of instability" (Schlossstein 1991, 17).

In spite of government change, political and economic foundations remain intact in Thailand. Ordinarily, the coups are outcomes of a power struggle among the military elite, amounting to nothing more than a battle for who stands at the helm of a ship without altering the course of navigation. The coups in Thailand "rarely have obstructed government processes or undermined the principal underpinnings of the state, nation, king, and religion" (Neher 1992, 650).

For centuries, the Thai political system revolved around the monarchy as the basis of governance and legitimacy. The military

**Table 4.6**
Government changes in Thailand

| Prime minister | In office | Duration (months) | Means of selection |
|---|---|---|---|
| Manopakon | 1/1932–6/1933 | 12 | Coup |
| Phahon | 6/1933–9/1938 | 63 | Parliament[a] |
| Phibun | 12/1938–8/1944 | 68 | Parliament |
| Khung[b] | 8/1944–8/1945 | 12 + 2 + 4 | Parliament |
| Thawi | 8/1945–8/1945 | 0.5 | Interim |
| Seni | 9/1945–1/1946 | 4 | Interim |
| Pridi | 3/1946–8/1946 | 4 | Parliament |
| Thawan | 8/1946–11/1947 | 15 | Parliament |
| Phibun (2) | 4/1948–9/1957 | 114 | Coup |
| Phot | 9/1957–12/1957 | 3 | Interim |
| Sarit[c] | 2/1959–12/1963 | 58 | Coup |
| Thanom | 12/1963–10/1973 | 10 + 118 | Succession |
| Sanya | 10/1973–2/1975 | 16 | Interim |
| Khukrit[d] | 3/1975–1/1976 | 10 | Parliament |
| Seni (2) | 4/1976–10/1976 | 7 | Parliament |
| Thanin | 10/1976–10/1977 | 12 | Coup |
| Kriangsak | 11/1977–2/1980 | 28 | Coup |
| Prem | 3/1980–8/1988 | 100 | Parliament |
| Chatichai | 8/1988–2/1991 | 30 | Parliament |
| Anand[e] | 2/1991–2/1992 | 12 + 3 | Interim |
| Suchinda | 3/1992–5/1992 | 2 | Coup[f] |
| Chuan | 9/1992–6/1995 | 33 | Parliament |
| Banharn | 7/1995–11/1996 | 16 | Parliament |
| Chavalit | 11/1996–11/1997 | 12 | Parliament |
| Chuan (2) | 11/1997–2/2001 | 39 | Parliament |

a. Parliament was restored through a coup.
b. Khung was again prime minister from January to March 1946 and from November 1947 to April 1948.
c. Thanom was prime minister for 10 months while Sarit was treated for cirrhosis in the United States.
d. Seni was prime minister for about 20 days before Khukrit.
e. Anand was again prime minister from June to September 1992.
f. Suchinda was chosen by Parliament but his selection was the result of a coup.
Source: Ockey 1996, 345–360, 347, and my observation since the Banharn government.

revolution in 1932 brought an end to absolute monarchy. "However, a fusion of military power and royal legitimacy was reestablished. The living symbols of 'nation, religion, king' were displayed by the military leadership as the rationale for their continuing dominance of the political process" (Morell and Samudavanija 1981, 4).

When the King intervenes in the political process to restore equilibrium, he serves as a focal point for restraining excesses. He legitimizes the political leadership of the elite so long as they exercise power within tolerable though vaguely defined limits, and he is also considered the system's last resort, accessible by individual petitioner and public opinion alike. (Schlossstein 1991, 177)

Officially, the King has very limited political power, tasked in part with approving the prime minister, maintaining regular visits to rural Thai villages, and sponsoring environmental projects (Schloss-stein 1991, 177). His influence is, however, keenly felt everywhere in the nation. "The overwhelming sense in Thailand today is that regardless of the form of government, as long as the substance of the monarchy prevails, the people will be happy" (Schlossstein 1991, 142).

The case of Thailand demonstrates the complexity of particular realities. It can be argued that the lack of policy polarization and uncertainty related to the coups in Thailand made its economy a success story, compared to some Latin American countries, where coups were the results of deep political cleavages and devastated the economies. Alternatively, it can also be argued, on the basis of a comparison between Thailand and other Pacific Asian nations (e.g., Singapore, Taiwan, and Korea), that political instability in Thailand did have some negative impact on its economy, though its damaging effect was far from that in Latin America. The bottom line is that for economic growth, political stability is preferred to political instability, and among political instabilities, less is preferred to more.

## 4.6   Summary and Policy Implications

This chapter tests the hypotheses derived from chapter 2, utilizing the operationalization of the variables developed in chapter 3. It finds that political instability and policy uncertainty affect economic growth negatively, while the effect of democracy on growth is statistically insignificant. I have argued that democracy may actually promote growth by facilitating some factors that themselves increase economic growth. Such factors include investment, education, birth rates, economic freedom, income distribution, and political stability. The case study in section 4.5 reinforces the theoretical implications and statistical results in the preceding sections, suggesting new possibilities when the assumptions of the model are relaxed.

It is important to note, as discussed in chapter 2, that the parameter estimate for any policy variable is a partial equilibrium and is obtained while keeping other variables constant. None of the three variables (political freedom, political stability, and policy certainty) is by itself a *sufficient* or *necessary* condition for economic development, but a combination of the three variables will have pronounced effects on economic growth. A politically unfree, unstable, and uncertain nation is destined to have its economy wrecked.

In the name of growth, a nation should reduce and eradicate the hotbed of policy polarization, namely wealth inequality. A nation should also maintain a stable political system that safeguards the stable infrastructure of investment and growth. However, a nation may sometimes face the dilemma of a choice between political stability and political freedom. China and Russia have adopted different sequences of political and economic reforms and have achieved different outcomes in their efforts to revitalize their economies. The statistical results and empirical evidence in this chapter indicate that evolutionary transformation toward political freedom under a stable political system can achieve greater economic success than radical political change amid upheavals and turbulences.

This chapter has found strong evidence of the convergence hypothesis. While a country cannot do much about its initial level of development, it can work on human-capital accumulation, physical-capital formation, income distribution, economic environment, and political infrastructure to loosen the constraints of the economy and have higher growth rates. While this chapter shows how these constraints work for or against growth, the remaining chapters in this book indicate how these constraints may be changed for the specific purpose of improving growth.

Though political freedom does not show particularly strong effects on growth in the multivariate regressions, it crucially affects growth through the other variables included in the statistical testing, I argue. The rest of the book will investigate these indirect effects of democracy on growth. Chapter 5 deals with the joint effects of democracy, stability, and growth. Chapter 6 analyzes three political models of inflation. Chapter 7 investigates the effects of democracy and stability on private investment. Chapter 8 delves into the political interpretation of human-capital formation. Chapter 9 centers on the effect of democracy on income distribution. Chapter 10 focuses on political freedom and economic freedom. Finally, chapter 11 looks into the political determinants of population growth.

Democracy, Stability, and
Growth: A Simultaneous
Approach

*We have no intention, however, of making a fetish of democracy. It may well be true that our generation talks and thinks too much of democracy and too little of the values which it serves.... Democracy is essentially a means, a utilitarian device for safeguarding internal peace and individual freedom.*

Friedrick von Hayek

In chapter 4, democracy was found statistically not to affect economic growth. However, examination of the data also shows that democracy may lower political instability, thus indirectly increasing economic growth. In light of this finding, this chapter studies the joint evolution of political stability, liberal democracy, and economic growth. Such an approach will not only help place into a proper perspective the contradictory hypotheses and evidence presented in appendix 4.A regarding the effects of democracy and stability on economic growth, but also explain worldwide political transformation under the name of the third wave of democratization:

Political freedom was relatively low in the world prior to 1975. The years between 1960 and 1975 witnessed a reversal of the democratic trend of the 1950s, reducing the number of democracies from 36 in 1962 to 30 in 1975. Subsequently, at least 30 countries made democratic transitions between 1974 and 1990, in what is now known as the third wave of democratization. (Huntington 1991, 12)

The study of democratization has been dominated by the political-agent approach, which focuses on the short-run strategic interactions among political actors, in contrast with the structural approach, which examines long-term relationships between democracy and structural variables such as economic development.[1] "The protagonists in the struggles for democracy could not and did not believe that the fate of their countries would be determined either by current levels of development or by the distant past. They maintain that, albeit within constraints, democratization was an outcome of actions, not just of conditions" (Przeworski and Limongi 1997, 176). Under the political-agent approach, scholars such as Przeworski (1991), Casper and Taylor (1996), Kaufman (1986), Karl (1986), Gillespie (1991), Marks (1992), and Zhang (1994) treat democratic transitions as a sequential process characterized by erosion and fall of authoritarian rule and by subsequent democratic consolidation, emphasizing the strategic relationship between the dictatorship and its opposition and focusing on how the authoritarian regime relinquishes power following concessions from the opposition through a pact. The separate roles played by major parties including the military, church, or international actors are also examined in the political agent approach (e.g., O'Donnell and Schmitter 1986, Remmer 1989, Youngblood 1990, and Berryman 1984). In this area of research, political stability is often a more important topic than democracy itself.

The structural approach in the study of democratization is almost synonymous with the modernization thesis postulated by Lipset (1959), who argues that economic development results in improved education and enlarges the middle class, fostering "receptivity to democratic political tolerance" (Lipset 1959, 83–84). Dahl (1989) refines this theme by examining how economic development promotes the decentralization of the central government and the dissemination of democratic ideas. Huntington (1991) takes an extreme position by making economic development almost a necessary condition for democracy. Political scientists and economists have tested the modernization thesis in various forms, resulting in a rich array of both confirming and challenging statistical evidence (e.g., Barro 1997, Feng and Zak 1999, Przeworski et al. 2000, Bueno de Mesquita et al. 2003). The structural approach is not limited to economic development, as other structural determinants of development are frequently added to this mix. Huntington (1993), for example, proposes that cultural values, traditions, institutionalization, and ideologies contribute to democratization. Huber, Rueschemeyer, and Stephens (1993) focus on the relative strengths of interest groups as determined by wealth distribution as an important factor for democratization.

This chapter takes a third approach. It studies democracy, political stability, and economic growth as jointly evolving phenomena. The two aforementioned approaches do not consider the reversed effects of growth and development on democratization, which in turn affect the next stage of democratization, nor do they consider the interactions between political freedom and political stability as conditioned by economic growth. The latter omission is critical, as many arguments made under the rubric of the political-agent approach concern political stability or instability, characterized in this book as regular government change and irregular government change. A structural understanding of the relationship between political stability and democratic values can inform and empower the political-agent approach.

This chapter attempts to answer three specific questions: What are the effects of democracy on economic growth both in itself and through political stability? What are the relationships between political stability and democratization? And how does growth contribute to democratization both by itself and by affecting political stability? The empirical testing in this chapter will focus on the period of the third wave of democratization (1975–1989), the most exciting one and half decades in the last century in terms of worldwide political change and economic transformation (this and the following chapters can be read as independent essays by themselves. Their coverage in terms of countries and years is determined by historical or regional interest, data availability, or a need to compare with other works).

Chapter 5 is organized as follows: Section 5.1 develops the central theoretical argument of this study and outlines its methodology. Section 5.2 specifies the component equations in the system and describes the data. And section 5.3 presents the results and analysis of the simultaneous-equations system, which help reveal the interactions among democracy, political stability, and growth.

## 5.1 A Simultaneous-Equations Model

In chapter 4 the political forces that drive economic decisions are assumed to be exogenous, and this in a theoretical model helps to derive conclusions by keeping the directions of the variables tractable. But in reality, very few variables are exogenous. As an extension of my earlier work on democracy, political stability, and economic growth (Feng 1997a), this chapter will delineate a multiequation model that takes the endogeneity of both political variables and economic growth into consideration.

Helliwell, who finds the estimated partial effect of democracy on subsequent economic growth to be negative but insignificant, identifies an important clue in the puzzle of democracy's effect on growth (Helliwell 1994, 235–236). This insignificant negative effect, according to Helliwell, is counterbalanced by the positive indirect effect that democracy exerts on growth through education and investment. Parallel to Helliwell's argument, the positive indirect effect of democracy on growth through the channel of political stability is also an area worthy of study. Such a study can be theoretically framed and empirically implemented through a simultaneous-equations model that includes growth, government change, and democracy as endogenous variables.

In the simultaneous-equations system defined below, the endogenous variables are economic growth, democracy, and government change. Government change here is classified into a set of mutually exclusive groups: irregular government change, major regular government change, and minor regular government change. As in chapter 3, irregular government change is defined as power transfer that occurs outside of constitutional arrangements. Major regular government change is defined as government change that takes place within the constitutional framework and involves a change of the ruling party. Finally, minor regular government change refers to the kind of government change that takes place under the constitution, with the same party remaining in power.

Two objectives are achieved with this model setup. First, types of government change are differentiated, and second, political change thus defined is endogenized together with political democracy and economic growth. The following sections discuss the theoretical relationships between government change and growth, between government change and democracy, and between democracy and growth.

## Instability and Growth

Regular and irregular government changes should have different impacts on economic growth. Specifically, severe and radical political change, such as a coup d'état, instills a great amount of uncertainty into the marketplace, slowing, and even reversing, economic growth. The drastic changeability of government control serves to indicate alteration of the parameters circumscribing economic activities. As economic agents have to pay entry or exit costs when they invest, actual or anticipated fundamental changes in the government compel them to decrease their investment to minimize these costs (Feng and Chen 1997). Economic growth is thus retarded because of the political uncertainty resulting from potential fundamental change in the political control of the nation.

By contrast, regular government transfers take place within the framework of a nation's constitution. Major regular government change often implies that the ousted government's economic performance was not satisfactory, and voters chose a new government for its potential to improve the economy. In a simultaneous-equations model where irregular government change is also entered as an endogenous variable, regular government change may represent political adjustment to market conditions so that the economy will reposition itself for growth. In contrast to uncertainty caused by regime interruption resulting from irregular government change, major regular government change offers policy adjustment without a fundamental change in the political order. In the short run, major regular government change may create uncertainty in some economic areas, and its effect on growth may be ambiguous. In the long run, however, major regular government change reflects a pattern of system adjustability and government accountability in favor of economic performance. It is thus likely to produce higher growth.[2]

Similarly, a minor regular government transfer represents a political adjustment rather than a radical change, reflecting continuity of government policy and possibly providing the political stability necessary for economic growth and development. Minor regular government change has two advantages: the government is allowed sufficient time to formulate long-term economic plans without giving in to pressures or temptations for short-term political gains, and investors benefit from the low-risk costs of policy changes since they do not have to concern themselves with the possibility of significant political shifts. In the context of a popularly elected government, minor regular government change offers "democracy without turnover" (Huntington 1991). In this study, the likelihood of minor government change—which requires that the same party to remain in office—is combined with the likelihood of no government change. The conceptual reason for the combination of minor government change with no change is that the two are almost synonymous. The technical reason (elucidated in the next section), is that Banks' (1999) data contains no information on government change from which minor regular government change alone can be constructed. Therefore, "minor government change" hereafter refers to both government transfers that keep the same party, and often the same person, in power, as well as to no government change. Both are hypothesized to increase the rate of economic growth, with other factors kept constant.

Finally, growth is likely to have a positive impact on the legitimacy of the government, while its effect on substantial government change should be negative. Rapid economic growth increases the popularity of the current government, thus diminishing the likelihood for its ouster either within a constitutional context or through unconstitutional means. The government party is either punished or rewarded for its economic performance, and the probability of its reselection for office increases if its economic record is good. Two implications arising from this analysis are that improvement in the economy should decrease the chance of regime or irregular government change, and that a good economy likely increases the probability of minor regular government change. However, the effects of growth on major regular government change can be ambiguous. Growth may be induced by the expectations of citizens that a new government will not only advocate growth-promoting policies but will also have the ability to successfully carry them out. Furthermore, growth may inspire new ideals or create new challenges that require major policy adjustments best initiated under the circumstances of political competition in a democratic system. In contrast to the study of elections and economies in democracies, which typically involves time-series analysis of short-run dynamics in democratic elections,[3] this chapter uses aggregate cross-sectional data to investigate the effect of long-run economic growth on the average probability of government change for both democracies and autocracies. Therefore, the empirical results to be obtained in this chapter may be significantly different from the literature that focuses on industrialized democracies.

## Instability and Democracy

Defined as a degree of liberal democracy, rather than as a dichotomy, democracy is directly related to government turnover, affecting both regular government change and regime change. While the former political change takes place within the existing political system, the latter type implies a fundamental alteration of the constitution or rules of the political game. Nondemocracies are characterized by either irregular government change, in which the country is trapped in a historical cycle of coups d'état (Londregan and Poole 1990, 162–163), or by an absence of substantial change in government, in which it is led by the same party for decades (Bienen 1993). By contrast, democracy encourages political competition within a constitutional context and tends to bring about government change through party politics, thereby increasing the chances of a substantial transfer of power between political parties. In the long run, this reduces the possibility both of one party holding on to power for a long time and of abrupt, profound unconstitutional government change.

The five theses on democratization and external conflict summarized by Solingen (1996) can be applied to an analysis of the relationship between democratization and regime stability. The conditions favoring democracy that scholars cite are those promoting interstate cooperation and reducing conflict. These conditions also have an impact on reducing irregular government change, which, like interstate conflict, invariably involves the use of force. The first proposition is that government must have domestic legitimacy and be accountable, the argument being that legitimacy granted to the leader through democratic means in a liberal democracy has a dampening effect on the use of force or violence because, on a Kantian conception, the citizen consents to and supports the democratic regime (Doyle 1983, 1986; Van Evera 1993). The second proposition argues that free speech, electoral cycles, and the public-policy process all function as restraints and limits on democratic leaders, preventing the adoption of extreme policies (Bueno de Mesquita and Lalman 1992, Ember, Ember, and Russett 1992, Weingast 1997). The third thesis maintains that political openness, strengthened by information technology, makes compromise and cooperation easier, thus reducing political uncertainty and distrust (Keohane 1984, Bueno de Mesquita and Lalman 1992, Starr 1992). The fourth proposition emphasizes the credibility of commitments made by democratic governments. Since such governments are assumed to have a greater respect for the rule of law and are more likely to develop self-enforcing rules to limit their behavior, greater interstate cooperation should result (Doyle 1983, Siverson and Emmons 1991, Gaubatz 1996, Weingast 1997). Finally, the people in democracies tend to have an aversion toward political violence embedded in their normative liberal-democratic values (as discussed above), which decreases the possibility that force will be used to overthrow a government or to repress the people (Schumpeter 1955, Doyle 1986). While each of these five theses links democracy with regional cooperation, they also synergistically account for the peaceful resolution of domestic political issues, including government change according to the constitution. Therefore, major regular government change characterized by peaceful power transfer between contending parties is likely to be a feature of democracy, while irregular government change underscored by political violence and polarization tends to be associated with nondemocracies.

Japan has been a quintessential example of democracy without turnover—of repeated minor regular government change within the context of a democratic system. Nonetheless, major regular government change eventually did occur in Japan in 1993, when the long-ruling Liberal Democratic Party was voted out after 38 consecutive years in power. By contrast, its two autocratic neighbors, China and North Korea, as well as some African countries studied by Bienen (1993), saw only minor regular government change during the same period without any major government change at all. Therefore, democracy, in the long run, has a negative effect on minor regular government change. Democracy, in general, increases the probability of major regular government change, lessens the chances of irregular government change, and in the long run decreases the propensity toward minor regular government change.

Furthermore, regular government change and irregular government change should have different effects on democracy. Londregan and Poole (1990) establish that past coups d'état increase the probability of future coups d'état. Likewise, irregular government transfers are likely to be followed by other irregular transfers. While major regular government change enhances constitutional adjustability and system flexibility, irregular government change disrupts the constitution and is thus more likely to herald successive undemocratic governments than to consolidate the democratic process. The general implication is that major regular government change promotes democracy, and irregular government change leads to a decrease in democracy. Finally, for lack of substantial party competition, minor regular government change may, in the long run, erode democracy.

### Democracy and Growth

The central argument in this chapter is that democracy is likely to have a significant indirect effect on growth through its impact on political stability. I expect to find that democracy has a positive effect on major regular government change and a negative effect on both irregular and minor regular government change. Meanwhile, both types of regular government change promote economic growth, whereas irregular government change retards economic growth. Therefore, the net effect of democracy on growth through the route of political instability is theoretically ambiguous.

Regular government change is likely to have a positive effect on growth, as it tends to represent political and economic adjustments responding to the demands of a society, including economic stimuli. In contrast, irregular government change exerts a negative impact on growth, as it incorporates a large degree of political uncertainty into the costs of doing business. Therefore, democracy enhances growth where it increases the probability of major regular government change and where it decreases the probability of irregular government change. One reason that the literature produces conflicting empirical findings on the relationship between democracy and growth is that the indirect effect of democracy on growth through the channel of political change has not been taken into consideration. One should note that neither the "compatibility school" nor the "conflict school" has theoretically explored the effect of democracy on growth as conditioned by political stability.

Democracy's indirect effect on growth through its effect on minor regular government change remains theoretically ambiguous. For the reason given above in the discussion of the instability-democracy nexus, while democracy tends to increase the probability of major regular government change (postulated to be positively related to growth), it may reduce the probability of minor regular government change (also postulated to be positively related to growth). Thus, whether or not democracy promotes growth through its impacts on major and minor regular government changes depends upon the trade-off between the loss of growth resulting from the reduction in the probability of minor regular government change and the increase of growth resulting from the augmentation of the probability of major regular government change. It will be important to empirically discover not only to what degree of significance democracy may decrease the likelihood of minor regular government change, but also how significantly minor regular government change may promote growth.

The effects of growth on democracy may be ambiguous in terms of the time horizon. In the long run, continuous growth will eventually lead to a high level of development, which has a positive effect on democracy (Chen and Feng 1999; Feng and Zak 1999, 2002). But in the short run, growth may strengthen the hand of a dictator and provide his government the excuse for sacrificing democracy and freedom to maintain the existing rate of development. Therefore, while the long-term effect of growth on democracy is positive, the short-run effect may be negative. Since this study involves a fairly long period of time, the aggregate effect of growth on democracy is expected to be positive.[4]

*The Statistical Model*

In order to estimate the interactions between democracy, stability and growth as stipulated above, I define the following simultaneous-equations system:

$$P_1 = \lambda_{p_1} P_{2,3} + \gamma_{p_1} G + \zeta_{p_1} D + \alpha_{p_1} X_{p_1} + \varepsilon_1$$

$$P_2 = \lambda_{p_2} P_{1,3} + \gamma_{p_2} G + \zeta_{p_2} D + \alpha_{p_2} X_{p_2} + \varepsilon_2$$

$$P_3 = \lambda_{p_3} P_{1,2} + \gamma_{p_3} G + \zeta_{p_3} D + \alpha_{p_3} X_{p_3} + \varepsilon_3$$

$$G = \gamma_g P + \zeta_g D + \alpha_g X_g + \mu$$

$$D = \gamma_d P + \zeta_d G + \alpha_d X_d + \varphi$$

Variables here have the following meanings:

$P_{ij}$ = a set of government change variables

$P_1$ = probability of irregular government change

$P_2$ = probability of major regular government change

$P_3$ = probability of minor regular government change

$G$ = annual rate of economic growth per capita

$D$ = degree of democracy

$X$ = a set of predetermined variables

$\varepsilon, \mu, \varphi$ = error terms

The coefficients $\lambda$, $\gamma$, and $\zeta$ take into consideration the contemporaneous feedbacks from change of government, growth, and democracy, while the $\alpha$ coefficients measure the effects of the predetermined variables. Note that $P_1$, $P_2$, and $P_3$ involve three kinds of mutually exclusive government transfers.

The method used in this chapter is three-stage least-squares (3SLS) estimation, which generalizes the two-stage least-squares method to take account of the error-term correlations between equations. It requires three steps: first, calculating the 2SLS estimates of the identified equations; second, using the 2SLS estimates to estimate the structural equations' errors, and then using these errors to estimate the contemporaneous variance-covariance matrix of the structural equations' errors; and third, applying generalized least squares to the large equation representing all of the identified equations of the system. The 3SLS estimator is consistent and generally asymptotically more efficient than the 2SLS estimator. If the disturbances in the different equations are uncorrelated, so that the contemporaneous variance-covariance matrix of the disturbances of the structural equations is diagonal, 3SLS reduces to 2SLS (Greene 1993).[5]

## 5.2  Data and Specification

This section delineates the details of the execution of the research design set up in the last section. The period of time under study is 1975–1989. This historical context was selected because it was the period of democratization. By focusing on this historical period, we can gain a substantial understanding of politicoeconomic causes and effects associated with the third wave of democratization, a series of changes that has vastly transformed the world.[6]

## The Growth Equation

One of the endogenous variables, economic growth, is defined as the average growth rate of real gross domestic product (GDP) per capita in Summers and Heston's data set. As in chapter 4, the growth equation includes a group of economic control variables identified by previous studies as important stimulants of economic growth.[7] These variables consist of economic development, educational attainment, investment share in GDP, economic freedom, and income distribution—all at initial, rather than current, levels.[8] There are the previous theoretical arguments regarding the effects of initial economic conditions on growth. In addition, the lagged variables also help alleviate the potential endogeneity problem caused by the indirect effect of democracy on growth via development, education, investment, economic freedom, and income distribution. To better understand the indirect effects of political institutions on growth through these channels, the following chapters will examine each of these factors and how political institutions influence them.

## The Government-Change Equations

Government-change equations estimate a set of probabilities of government change. The probability of irregular government change is constructed as in chapter 3: the major-regular-government-change variable is derived by differentiating irregular government change (e.g., coups d'état) from major government transfers, which include both extraconstitutional government changes and government transfers from one party to another through constitutional means. An indirect estimation of minor regular government change is derived by taking the difference between one and the sum of the estimated probabilities of irregular government change and major regular government change, thus representing the likelihood of minor government change and no government change at all, even though the variable is termed "minor government change."

In the three government-change equations, the estimate of the past probability of government change is used as the predetermined variable. The hypothesis is that the past causes the future. Indisputably, discontinuity of regime occurs from time to time, as when an old regime is overthrown and a new one emerges with a set of significantly different fundamentals. However, path dependence often plays a strong role in regime transitions. History, tradition, culture, and ideology all are actively involved in nation building. A country that has a history of military coups d'état may continue to experience irregular government change, even after the country has made a transition to democracy.

Specifically, the annual probabilities of government change over the period of 1951 to 1975 are averaged to serve as instrumental variables in the simultaneous-equations system. Note that this will not introduce a bias against African countries that gained independence in the 1960s, as the data for them start only upon the inception of their nationhood.

The initial irregular government change, the initial major regular government change, and the initial minor regular government change are each entered into their own corresponding equation.[9] These predetermined variables provide a historical context in which the current government change takes place. Because of historical continuity, it is expected that the past probability will have a positive impact on the current probability.

The initial level of the Gini coefficient is included as a control variable in the government-change equations. Ideally, income distribution should be endogenized. Owing to the relatively large number of equations in the system, I treat income distribution as a control variable here and use its initial level to alleviate the endogeneity problem. It will be studied as an endogenous variable in chapter 9. While the effect on growth of the Gini coefficient has been identified as negative, its effect on the probability of government change is ambiguous because income concentration can be related to either power deterioration or power consolidation. Income inequality may breed political chaos and violence, thus increasing the likelihood of irregular government change (Feng and Gizelis 2002), or it may contribute to the centralization of power, thereby reducing the likelihood of government change (Feng and Zak 1999). Therefore, after controlling for economic growth and democracy, the effects of income distribution on government change are theoretically ambiguous. The other exogenous variables in the equation are the initial level of real GDP per capita and the elementary school enrollment rate in 1960, both of which control for initial social and economic conditions.

## The Democracy Equation

To measure liberal democracy, I turn to the political-rights data provided by Gastil and Freedom House. There is no necessary condition for characterizing a political system as democratic; rather, democracy is treated as a variable. As operationalized in the previous chapter, the value of liberal democracy ranges from zero to one, with one representing the most democratic, averaged for the period of 1975 to 1989. The political-rights data begin in 1972–1973, which, when combined with the economic-freedom data starting in 1975 and the political instability data ending in 1989, constrain the aggregate analysis to the period of 1975 to 1989.

Real GDP per capita and the primary-school-enrollment rate for 1960 are also included in the democracy equation. Helliwell confirms a robust positive relation between the level of per capita income and education, on the one hand, and the adoption of democracy, on the other. This suggests that there "appear to be no clearly defined thresholds or prerequisites—just a strong tendency for democracy to become the chosen and maintained form of government as countries get richer and as education levels increase" (Helliwell 1994, 246). These results suggest that democracy has an intrinsic value that is increasingly sought after as populations become better off financially and better educated. The level of GDP per capita is also established by Bilson (1982, 107–108) as the only statistically and substantively significant independent variable for democracy.

Income inequality is entered in the democracy equation through the use of Gini-coefficient data. As in the case of the probability of regime change and income inequality, the effect of the Gini coefficient on democracy may be ambiguous. A positive effect of income inequality on democracy may be related to a combination of two phenomena. First, a rise in the level of economic development may increase income disparity (Kuznets 1955). Second, an increase in national income promotes democracy (Lipset 1959, Feng and Zak 1999, Chen and Feng 1999). A positive effect of income inequality on democracy may also be an indicator of partisan politics. As income disparity enlarges, different interest groups will emerge, thus presenting opportunities for the formation of politically competing groups. Under certain circumstances, the clash between interest groups will increase the likelihood of major regular government change, as is consistent with democratic politics. Therefore, from a political point of view, income inequality may increase the likelihood of the creation of democratic politics and procedures. This argument is that democracy should emerge when income inequality is on the rise. Yet from a different point of view, the enrichment of the middle classes as the result of economic development will narrow the gap in wealth, leading to a still higher level of development and thus promoting regime transition toward democracy. Theoretically, therefore, the effects of income inequality on democracy can be positive or negative.

Given the possibility that the increase in income will bring about income disparity and that income inequality is likely to lead to either a peaceful or violent democratic transition (depending on its effects on irregular government change), it would be in the interest of authoritarian leaders to keep income inequality low while endeavoring to increase their growth-led legitimacy. Indeed, this may be quite applicable to contemporary Pacific Asia, where governments attempt to improve income equality while increasing economic growth.

Authoritarian developmental societies, such as Singapore, Indonesia, Malaysia, and South Korea before its democratic transition, have been undergoing what Campos and Root call "shared growth." They argue that policies that promote this concept are the reason behind the fast growth of East Asian economies (Campos and Root 1996).

The authoritarian leaders in these nations have the political incentive to keep income inequality low, especially when growth is high. Land reforms and rural development, investment in education, promotion of small business, and the enrichment of low-income groups are all means to reduce income disparities and to increase broad-based support for development strategies (Campos and Root 1996, 50–75). Therefore, income equality might be positively associated with a development-oriented authoritarian government whose legitimacy depends on economic growth, which, as we have found, requires that income inequality not be severe.

Finally, two dummy variables are added to the democratic equation to account for possible cultural effects.[10] Huntington suggests that Islam and Confucianism have been inhospitable to democracy while conducive to authoritarian rule (Huntington 1984, 1991, 1993).

"Islam ... rejects any distinction between the religious community and political community.... To the extent that governmental legitimacy and policy flow from religious doctrine and religious expertise, Islamic concepts of politics differ from and contradict the premises of democratic politics" (Huntington 1991, 28). The variable ISLAMIC takes one for the countries where Islam is the largest religious group and zero otherwise. These countries in the data set are Algeria, Chad, Comoros, Egypt, Gambia, Guinea, Ivory Coast, Mali, Mauritania, Morocco, Niger, Nigeria, Senegal, Somalia, Sudan, Tanzania, Tunisia, Afghanistan, Bahrain, Indonesia, Iran, Iraq, Jordan, Kuwait, Malaysia, Oman, Pakistan, Saudi Arabia, Syria, United Arab Emirates, Yemen, and Turkey (*Encyclopedia Britannica* 1994, 783–785).[11]

The Confucian culture is similarly regarded as bereft of certain democratic elements. "Confucian societies lacked a tradition of rights against the state; to the extent that individual rights did exist, they were created by the state. Harmony and cooperation were preferred over disagreement and competition. The maintenance of order and respect for hierarchy were central values. The conflict of ideas, groups, and parties was viewed as dangerous and illegitimate. Most important, Confucianism merged society and the state and provided no legitimacy for autonomous social institutions at the national level" (Huntington 1991, 24). In the same context, Fukuyama holds that Confucian societies produce political and social hierarchies that provide the basis for an "overt form of paternalistic authoritarianism in countries like Singapore" (1993, 103). In contrast, some Asian scholars strongly disagree with the position taken by Huntington and Fukuyama. For instance, Kim (1991) holds that in South Korea the strong moralistic orientation of the political elite and political behavior, the tradition of dissent and protest often practiced by Confucian officials and intellectuals, and an egalitarian tendency all originated in Confucianism, which in turn has fostered democratization in South Korea. The variable CONFUCIAN takes one for South Korea, Taiwan, Singapore, and Japan, nations in which Confucianism has been regarded as the major cultural influence. If Huntington's cultural hypothesis of democracy holds, the parameter estimates of the two variables will be negatively signed and their statistical strength will be significantly different from zero.

**Table 5.1**
Definitions of variables in table 5.2

| Variable | Definition |
|---|---|
| GROWTH | Average annual percentage increase of per capita real GDP for 1975–1989 (Summers and Heston 2000). |
| DEMOCRACY | The mean value of political rights, 1975–1989 (Gastil 1975–1989). |
| IRREG CHANGE | The average probability of an irregular government change, 1975–1989 (constructed from Banks 1999). |
| MAJ REG CHANGE | The average probability of a major regular government change, 1975–1989 (constructed from Banks 1999). |
| MIN REG CHANGE | The average probability of a minor regular government change, 1975–1989 (constructed from Banks 1999). |
| GDP PER CAP$_{75}$ | Real GDP per capita in 1975 (Barro and Wolf 1989). |
| PRIM$_{60}$ | Enrollment rate in primary school in 1960 (Barro and Wolf 1989). |
| INVESTMENT$_{75}$ | Average real gross domestic investment (private and public) as a percentage of GDP for 1950–1975 (Summers and Heston 2000). |
| ECONF$_{75}$ | The 1975 value of the experts-based indictor of economic freedom (Gwartney et al. 1995). |
| GINI$_{75}$ | The 1950–1975 averages of the Gini coefficient value (Deininger and Squire, 1996). |
| ISLAMIC | A dummy variable for a country where Muslims make up the largest religious group (*Encyclopedia Britannica* 1994). |
| CONFUCIAN | A dummy variable for Japan, South Korea, Singapore, and Taiwan. |

## 5.3   Empirical Analysis: Three Sets of Nested Relationships

The results in table 5.2 are telling in that they support the hypotheses about the differential effects of regular and irregular government change on growth, while producing many other interesting results. Such results include the effects of democracy on growth, the relationship between democratic values and political stability, and the consequences of growth on democracy. The following subsections focus on each of these topics.

### *The Indirect Effects of Democracy on Growth through Political Stability*

Democracy is found to have a salient impact on economic growth by reducing political regime change and regularizing government change under a constitution. The growth equation clearly demonstrates that

**Table 5.2**
Joint estimation of growth, democracy, and government change (3SLS)

|  | GROWTH equation | IRREGULAR equation | MAJOR REG equation | MINOR REG equation | DEMOCRACY equation |
|---|---|---|---|---|---|
| GROWTH | — | −63.371* (11.159) | 17.585* (5.770) | 10.974** (4.983) | −3.194 (5.343) |
| IRREG CHANGE | −0.016* (0.003) | — | 0.294* (0.104) | 0.094 (0.078) | −0.136** (0.064) |
| MAJ REG CHANGE | 0.061* (0.011) | 3.168* (0.739) | — | −0.792* (0.187) | 0.441* (0.161) |
| MIN REG CHANGE | 0.057* (0.013) | 3.123* (0.823) | −0.898* (0.192) | — | −0.290† (0.196) |
| DEMOCRACY | −0.066* (0.022) | −2.444** (0.991) | 1.360* (0.411) | 0.321 (0.342) | — |
| INTERCEPT | −0.066* (0.023) | 3.109* (1.381) | −1.145* (0.406) | −0.719** (0.344) | 0.564** (0.247) |
| GDP PER CAP$_{75}$ | −0.012* (0.002) | −0.788* (0.101) | 0.214* (0.083) | 0.108† (0.060) | −0.065 (0.059) |
| PRIM$_{60}$ | 0.016 (0.012) | 1.051† (0.799) | −0.344 (0.330) | −0.135 (0.179) | 0.037 (0.238) |
| INVESTMENT$_{75}$ | 0.0002 (0.0118) | — | — | — | — |
| INFLATION | −0.003 (0.006) | — | — | — | — |
| ECONF$_{75}$ | −0.016 (0.063) | — | — | — | — |
| GINI$_{75}$ | −0.075* (0.030) | −5.155* (2.123) | 0.028† (0.077) | 1.219* (0.433) | 0.025 (0.564) |
| IRREG CHANGE$_{75}$ | — | 0.121 (0.129) | — | — | — |
| MAJ REG CHANGE$_{75}$ | — | — | −0.027 (0.077) | — | — |
| MIN REG CHANGE$_{75}$ | — | — | — | 0.088 (0.111) | — |
| CONFUCIAN |  |  |  |  | −0.211** (0.120) |
| ISLAMIC |  |  |  |  | −0.032 (0.054) |

Degrees of freedom: 322.
System weighted $R^2$: 0.842.
System weighted $\sigma$: 4.777.
*Statistically significant at the 0.01 error level in a one-tailed test.
**Statistically significant at the 0.05 error level in a one-tailed test.
†Statistically significant at the 0.10 error level in a one test.
Standard errors in parentheses.

instability involving drastic political change is harmful to economic growth, as irregular government change has a significant negative effect on growth. At the same time, both types of regular government change have a significant positive effect on economic growth. Table 5.2 also shows that democracy reduces the probability of irregular government change and contributes to major regular government change. Its effect on minor regular government change is statistically insignificant. Therefore by differentiating among the types of government change, we have a new understanding of democracy's indirect effect on growth via irregular and major regular government changes. The results in table 5.2 significantly reduce the ambiguity of democracy's effects on growth by showing that democracy promotes major regular government change but inhibits irregular government change, thus positively impacting growth in two ways. Rapid economic growth requires a stable political regime that is capable of adjusting to circumstances by changing—through constitutional means—the party in power or the ruling coalition of parties. Democracy is likely to provide these conditions, thus indirectly boosting economic growth by inhibiting regime interruption while enhancing policy adjustability. Although democracy takes a negative sign in the growth equation, it would be premature to conclude that democracy leads to slower growth.

Empirically, the net total effect of democracy on growth is found to be positive. According to the results in table 5.2, the direct negative effect was overshadowed by the positive indirect impacts of democracy on growth, with a net effect of 0.056.[12] Overall, an increase in democracy by one unit will increase the growth rate by about 0.056. Democracy is measured here as a variable ranging from zero to one, with one being full democracy and zero full autocracy. The 5.6% can be thought of as, with all other factors kept constant, the average difference in effect between a full democracy and a full autocracy on economic growth. This is a large gap in wealth accumulation. If an economy expands at 5.6% every year, it will double approximately every 12.72 years. This finding has enormous implications for our understanding of the nexus between democracy, political stability, and economic growth.

It should be noted that by the design of the instrumental variables, the feedbacks between democracy and investment and education have been excluded. Helliwell has found a positive effect of democracy on investment and education, both of which in turn exert a positive impact on growth (Helliwell 1994). The net total effect of democracy on growth, which has been found to be positive, is very likely to be much larger when such contemporaneous interactions are taken into consideration. The following chapters will study the effects of political institutions on these factors, which themselves promote or decrease growth.

The sustainability of government favors the conflict-school argument that a mainstream regime is needed to carry out consistent economic policy, and the adjustability of the political system favors the compatibility-school argument that growth presupposes a free, democratic political system. The empirical significance of this trade-off is identified by examining the effects of minor regular government change and major regular government change on growth, as well as the effects of democracy on the two kinds of regular government change. On the one hand, the results in table 5.2 show that the effect of minor regular government change on growth and the effect of major regular government change on growth are both positive and significant. Regime stability, underscored by regular elections, and government stability, represented by the same party remaining in office, both create a positive environment for long-run growth. On the other hand, I found that democracy has a significant positive effect on major regular government change and a statistically insignificant effect on minor government change. All of this implies that if there is political freedom, the sustainability of the government and the adjustability of the political system can power long-run economic growth.

### Democratic Values and Political Stability

The above statistical finding also helps to understand the relationship between democratic values and democratic stability, which has been studied by various scholars. While Almond and Verba (1963), Lipset (1960), Dahl (1971), Huntington (1968), and Lijphart (1980) all emphasize the positive effect of democratic values on democratic stability, Berry (1970) focuses on the premise that democratic stability is the cause of democratic values. Both views can be correct.

Democratic stability requires acceptance of democratic ideas. Without democratic stability, however, democratic ideas will be stifled. This dynamic relationship is important for fledgling democracies, such as Taiwan and the Philippines. If voters lack an education in democratic ideals and practices, they will not seek to defend a democratic constitution when usurpers come along. However, if a new democratic society is seized in political chaos, democratic principles will be doubted and challenged.

The evidence in table 5.2 demonstrates that democracy has a positive effect on major regular government change, and vice versa. At the same time, democracy has a negative effect on irregular government change, and vice versa. Under the norms of a democratic constitution, democracy means "a system in which parties lose elections" (Przeworski 1991, 10), or in the terminology adopted here, a system in which major regular government change takes place and irregular government change should not occur. If we equate the regularization of constitutional government change and the absence of irregular government change with democratic stability and the degree of democracy with democratic values shared by the government and the people, then table 5.2 indicates democratic ideas promote democratic stability, and vice versa.

This finding—that democratic ideas promote democratic stability, and vice versa—is consistent with Weingast's (1997) proposition that democratic values and democratic stability are associated. The pivotal question is: How can we promote a common set of values toward the appropriate role of government? On the basis of the statistical findings in this chapter, it is plausible that democratic values enforce the mechanism for solving the coordination dilemma, and political stability provides, under certain circumstances, vital room for negotiation and compromise so that citizens may achieve consensus.

In addition, both democratic values and democratic stability may be caused by other factors. For instance, economic growth inhibits the likelihood of irregular government change by making it easier for various political groups to reach a consensus for protecting their rights from infringements by the state. Economic growth may also increase shared democratic values by inducing major regular government change, which in turn further raises the level of democracy. Indeed, the statistical results in this chapter reconcile the argument that democratic values cause stable democracy (Almond and Verba 1963, Lipset 1960, Dahl 1971, Huntington 1968, Lijphart 1980) with the argument that democratic stability causes democratic values (Berry 1970).

*Economic Growth and Democratic Evolution*

The critical link between economic development and democratic transition lies in the relationship between growth and government change. Growth has a strong negative impact on irregular government change; its effects on regular government transfers, including both major and minor government change, are positive. Growth promotes democracy predominantly by augmenting major regular government change and reducing irregular government change. In the democracy equation, irregular government transfer weakens democracy, yet major regular government change strengthens democracy. This might indicate that the consolidation of democracy is likely to result from a political system that promotes competition and political change, whereas decay or loss of democracy to authoritarian rule is the likely outcome of extraconstitutional political change.

The life of a regime is positively associated with the growth of its economy. In line with the findings of Sanders (1981) and Londregan and Poole (1996), this work finds that the probability of a government being overthrown by a coup d'état appears to be substantially reduced by a relatively high rate of economic growth. By comparison, growth leads to an increase in the probability of minor regular government change, confirming the finding that good economic performance increases a ruling party's popularity and improves its chance to be reselected for office. The regression results in table 5.2 also indicate that growth and major regular government change have a positive relationship, suggesting that growth has certain "destabilizing" effects on the political status quo as well.[13]

That growth promotes major regular government change seems to run counter to the finding in industrialized democracies that the incumbent is more likely to win office when the economy is strong than otherwise (Lewis-Beck 1988, Sanders 1995). There is a distinction in research design between this work and the works that have found the above relationship. The latter usually use a dynamic model based on the data of annual, or even greater, frequency. The countries studied under this approach have almost invariably been developed societies that are also mature democracies. This work adopts an aggregate analysis using a longer trend and studies a wide range of countries, democratic and autocratic alike. Growth being a determinant of major regular government change is consistent with the evidence that growth promotes democracy, since having major regular government change is considered the most important aspect of being a democracy (Przeworski et al. 2000).

Furthermore, the long-term effect of growth on democracy contrasts with a possible negative short-run effect. As discussed above, autocratic regimes may utilize their good economic performance to consolidate their power. Therefore, the direct effect of growth on democracy may be ambiguous, but it can also be argued that although dictators may be able to use the short-run effects of growth to keep themselves in power, each increment in the development of an economy raises the odds in favor of democracy.

This interaction of the long-term and short-term effects of growth on democracy may have rendered the growth variable in the democracy equation insignificant. Combined with the findings from the three political-instability equations, this result indicates that although the direct effect of growth on democracy is negative, the indirect effects of growth on democracy are positive (by promoting major regular government change and by inhibiting irregular government change). This is one of the important implications that emerge from the study of democracy and growth by adding political stability to the simultaneous-equations model. This finding—that growth tends to increase the likelihood of democracy through its indirect effects of increasing major regular government change and decreasing irregular government change—is a link between growth and democracy that has been missed in the literature.

It is through those political mechanisms that the prospects for democratization and consolidation of democratic values increase or decrease. Improvement in the livelihood of a nation enhances the desire of a people for a higher order of freedom (that is, political freedom) and decreases irregular government change. Using an explicit mathematical model, Feng and Zak (1999) and Zak and Feng (2003) show that development induces some individuals to act in their own self-interest rather than follow the development plan of the government. Wealthy agents, for instance, have preferences for a growing bundle of goods. As agents move further from subsistence consumption, they become accustomed to making choices for maximizing their utility over a large set of goods. Their political awareness concurrently grows, and they tend to make political decisions along the same lines as their economic decisions—that is, their menu for political choice increases as well. Ultimately, the newly wealthy lose their identification with the political goals of the party in office and begin to act according to the dictates of their own self-interests. Political parties will form in response to newly emerging interest groups, and political realignment will take place in order to amass and marshal new social demands. All of this activity is conducive toward substantial change in government.

Calvert (1994) indicates that the cooperative equilibrium of a social order fails when the underlying conditions induce agents to act in accordance with their own self-interest. Denzau and North (1994) term this loss of identification with mainstream politics the loss of a "shared mental model," which occurs when wealth increases. In a previous work, North (1988) names this process the "loss of the social contract," and Trebilock (1995) argues that democracy as a "psychological imperative" for self-recognition follows the empowerment of the middle class.

The argument that is being made here—that growth leads to political change—is similar to, yet distinct from, the above propositions. It is similar in the sense that political interest groups, driven by development, are the catalysts for major political change. However, it diverges in the sense that growth-led change is likely to take place as regular government change rather than as regime interruption. A clear implication here is that economic growth is more likely to lead to a peaceful evolution from procedural democracy to substantive or liberal democracy, instead of to revolution. The finding in this section implies that democratic transition will take place as the result of political evolution nurtured by economic development. Lack of economic development, in contrast, will weaken the social and economic foundations for compromise and cooperation among various interest groups, making the coordination problem discussed by North, Summerhill, and Weingast (2000) even more difficult to resolve.

Furthermore, irregular government change decreases growth, and the reduction in growth leads to more political upheavals, which further reduce democracy. Londregan and Poole (1990) have found "coup traps," but what actually makes more sense are mutually reinforcing "twin traps": the "coup trap" and the "poverty trap." The other side of the coin posits growth as the key. Economic development increases the chances for peaceful evolution toward democracy through substantial government change within constitutional procedures or through the revision of the constitution to meet new social and political demands. The political development of South Korea and Taiwan attests to the nexus between economic development and democratic transitions.

In both South Korea and Taiwan, the demise of authoritarianism was closely associated with the relative decline of the autonomy, coherence, and capacity of the state. First, after a quarter century of rapid economic accumulation, the material and organizational resources and analytical capacity of the state economic bureaucracy could no longer keep up with the complexity of the economic structures and the organizational expansion of big business. The business elite became more responsive to market changes and less susceptible to government directives.... Second, with the accumulation of material resources in the private sector and through social struggles and accommodations in various arenas, the state's control over the people and their behavior steadily declined over time.... In Taiwan, the penetration of the party-state into the organized sectors of the civil society has steadily receded since the early 1980s. The upsurge of social movements, in the form of citizen petitions, demonstrations, wildcat strikes, civic disobedience, and riots, upset the imposed social tranquility and loosened the grip of the authoritarian state on civil society at the grass-roots level.... Finally, in the political arena, the political opposition played the most critical role in bringing about the decline of authoritarian rule. The strengthening of the opposition provided various social groups and isolated individuals with a collective alternative. (Chu 1996, 26–38)

The parallel between economic development and political development in South Korea and Taiwan has left us with an optimistic message: Democratic transition can occur peacefully and naturally as the result of economic development. The statistical finding and the historical discussion here both indicate that "elections have turned out to be the principal mechanism through which changes in the social structure, brought about by rapid capitalist development, were translated into a political force for weakening the entrenched authoritarian order and for pushing the democratization process forward" (Chu 1996, 30).

### Findings on Control Variables

The conditional convergence hypothesis has withstood a strict test using simultaneous-equations-system estimation. Given the political institutional variables, the rate of growth is negatively related to the level of development. With the same level of democracy and political stability, less developed countries grow faster than developed countries. Education, investment, and economic freedom are not statistically significant. It should be noted that the use of the initial values of these variables precludes their contemporaneous effects on growth. For instance, economic freedom in 1975 may be enhanced over the period of 1980 through 1985, which then exerts a strong impact on growth. As chapter 10 demonstrates, political freedom has a tremendous impact on economic freedom. Political freedom, however, was relatively low in the world prior to 1975. Furthermore, significant improvement in economic freedom did not happen until in the 1980s and 1990s, when globalization was gaining momentum. The effect of the initial level of economic freedom in 1975 on subsequent growth tends to be weak, as economic freedom lacked a significant boost from political freedom and globalization during the period of 1960 through 1975.

Similarly, investment for the period of 1951 through 1975 may not be fully responsible for the growth during the period of 1975 through 1989, as continued growth requires timely investment or a change in investment patterns determined by technological innovation. There was relatively little effective use of computers throughout the 1960s and 1970s, while continued growth in the 1990s required significant investment in information technology. The use of these initial values helps militate against reverse causation. Nonetheless, it removes their contemporaneous effects on growth.

The effect of income inequality on growth is again found to be negative and statistically significant, even in the presence of political-institution variables. Its effect on political stability seems to be consistent with the power-consolidation scenario. We cannot find evidence from this sample that income disparity leads to an increase of irregular government change, with other factors kept constant. On the contrary, income inequality is negatively correlated with the probability of irregular government change. The evidence is consistent with the notion that a concentration of wealth may be combined with a concentration of power, preventing irregular government change from occurring. Similarly, income inequality increases the likelihood of the same party remaining in power. This finding is consistent with the scenario described by Bueno de Mesquita et al. (2003). Under an autocracy, the size of the winning coalition is small, and the government allocates social resources to its members so that the political elite may retain power. The reward to the winning coalition through the reallocation of social resources increases income inequality, which, however, improves the chance of the government remaining in office.

The statistical results also indicate that an increase in the initial level of development reduces the probability of irregular government change and increases the probability of both major regular and minor regular government change. Again, we have evidence that economic development is one of the best weapons against political instability and violence.

The average estimates of the probabilities of irregular, major regular, and minor regular government change for the period of 1950 to 1975 are not statistically significant in the government-change equations after current interactions between political stability and freedom are introduced. It is possible that a proper lag structure is needed to robustly test path dependence.

After controlling for the endogeneity of political stability, the parameter estimates for education and initial development are not statistically significant in the democracy equation. Initial development and education would have been positive and significant in the democracy equation if it had been estimated without the political-instability variables.[14] The positive impacts of development and education on democracy attenuate in the presence of political stability.

Finally, the signs of the two cultural dummy variables are as expected, but only the Asian one is significant. Given the same levels of income, education, and political stability, it takes East Asian and some Southeast Asian countries longer to evolve into democracies. When South Korea and Taiwan turned democratic in the 1990s, they already enjoyed massive social wealth as Third World countries; their per capita income levels were much higher than most other new democracies. Their late entry into the democracy world can be ascribed to their culture, which places a strong emphasis on social order and hierarchy. However, in this chapter, I reiterate, democracy is measured in degrees. Religious and cultural factors may register much stronger impacts on democratic transition, which is best measured by a dichotomous variable.

## 5.4   Summary and Policy Implications

This chapter contributed to the study of the political economy of growth in several major respects. The simultaneous-equations approach to the study of the relationships between growth and political stability and between growth and democracy allowed us to identify the indirect effect of democracy on growth through its impact on political stability. This work isolates three forms of political stability, thus clarifying earlier misconceptions about regime stability and government stability. The findings reported here support those of Alesina, Özler, Roubini, and Swagel (1996) in the sense that regime change adversely affects growth. At the same time, they replicate Londregan and Poole's (1990) evidence that growth has a negative effect on coups d'état. Additionally, they show support for the argument that growth increases the probability of the same party remaining in power. Thus, the inclusion of democracy as an endogenous variable strengthens the feedbacks between growth and political instability.

The following are the three major findings of this chapter: First, an ambiguous total effect of democracy on growth was exposed. While democracy may have a negative direct effect on growth, it can have a positive indirect effect on growth through its impact on the probability of regular and irregular government change. On the one hand, major regular government change has a positive effect on growth, and irregular government change has a negative effect on growth. On the other, democracy has a positive impact on major regular government change and a negative impact on irregular government change. Therefore, overall, democracy indirectly promotes growth by allowing major regular government change and reducing irregular government change.

Second, this study reconciles the contradictory arguments and evidence presented by Almond and Verba (1963), Dahl (1971), Lipset (1960), Huntington (1968), and Lijphart (1980) in one corner and Berry (1970) in the other. While the former set of scholars emphasize the effect of democratic values on democratic stability, the last focuses on the impact of democratic stability as the cause of democratic values. The results derived from the simultaneous-equations model in this chapter indicate that democratic values and regime stability reinforce each other. The evidence shows that while democracy increases major regular government change, major regular government change favors democratic values. Additionally, democracy was found to inhibit irregular government change, which is the antithesis of democratic stability. This result is consistent with Weingast's (1997) proposition that democratic values and democratic stability are correlated. The difference between this work and that of Weingast is whether or not the resolution of the coordination problem should be considered to be embedded in democratic values shared by representative citizens, therefore requiring at least some degree of political stability. This is an important new avenue of empirical research. It would be of great interest to discover how the resolution of the coordination dilemma is related to democratic values and political stability, be it as a cause or an effect.

Third, this study contributes to the understanding of the growth-generated dynamics promoting democratic transitions. The results in this chapter provide support for the theoretical argument by Feng and Zak (1997), Zak and Feng (2003), Calvert (1994), Denzau and North (1994), and North (1988) that development induces behavioral changes in members of a society, thus creating a motive for independence from government by dictatorship. But the results in this chapter also show that a democratic transition is more likely to take a peaceful and evolutionary approach, rather than a revolutionary one. Economic growth contributes to peaceful evolution from procedural democracy to liberal democracy through the activation of party politics, particularly through promoting major regular government change (which is conductive to democracy), and through reducing irregular government change (which has a pernicious effect on democracy).

A major policy implication is that democracy provides a stable political environment that reduces unconstitutional government change at the macro level. Yet along with regime stability, democracy offers flexibility and the opportunity for substantial political change within the political system. Taken with the potential positive indirect effects of democracy on growth through the channels of price stability, investment, education, income distribution, property rights, and population growth—the order of topics for the rest of the book—this juxtaposition of macropolitical certainty and micropolitical adjustability should be regarded as the ultimate basis for sustainable economic growth and expansion.

# 6

## Political Institutions and Inflation: An Evaluation of Three Models

*The power of taxation by currency depreciation is one which has been inherent in the State since Rome discovered it.*

J. M. Keynes

This chapter studies the effects of the political environment on inflation. As the results in chapter 4 and chapter 5 indicate, the effect of inflation on growth is not statistically significant. But while the impact of inflation on growth may not be as consequential as that of investment in reproducible capital on growth, price stability greatly affects economic behavior and imposes political consequences (e.g., the ouster of incumbents because of such economic factors as high inflation, low employment, and/or slow economic growth). Together with economic growth, external balances, and full employment, inflation control is a major economic-policy objective of a nation. Furthermore, because its source resides—at least in part—with the political office holder, inflation is one of the political mechanisms government can manipulate to transfer social wealth to reward particular constituencies.[1] As aptly put by Don Paarlberg,

Inflation, defined as a general increase in prices, is the world's greatest robber. A covert thief, inflation steals from widows, orphans, bondholders, retirees, annuitants, beneficiaries of life insurance, and those on fixed salaries, decreasing the value of their incomes. Inflation extorts more wealth from the public than do all other thieves, embezzlers and plunderers combined.

Inflation, a Jekyll and Hyde character, is not only a great robber but also a great benefactor. Inflation is the world's greatest giver, doling out benefits to debtors, hoarders of goods, owners of property, government (for which it reduces the burden of the public debt), and, over time, owners of common

stocks. The largesse thus bestowed on the debtor class and owners of property exceeds the combined total of all charities, contributions, and donations.
(Paarlberg 1993, xi)

Inflation is generally regarded as an operational malfunction of the
economy, potentially able to decrease economic growth. Not being a
Pareto optimal solution, it robs some social groups to enrich others,
and even those who earlier benefited from inflation may eventually
turn against it as their economic gains require deflationary measures.
It is normatively something to be openly shirked by all governments,
yet some governments generate higher inflation than others.[2] Two
elements link a government to inflation: *motives* and *capacity*. Certain
regimes, as described below, use inflation to finance governmental
activities, including rewards to their constituencies, while others
simply lack the capacity to restrain inflation, even if they so desire.

The preceding chapter identified the indirect effect of democracy
on growth through the inhibition of irregular government change
and reduction of macropolitical uncertainty. Political institutions
characterized by political freedom and regime stability may have
some influence on macroeconomic phenomena (such as inflation)
that, along with political institutions, ultimately affect saving,
investment, and economic growth. The task of this chapter is to
identify the impact of political institutions on inflation. If we find
that certain features of politics have a restraining effect on inflation,
then the usefulness of the political infrastructure in promoting
growth will be better understood and, in a practical sense, be further
strengthened.

Inflation is both an economic and political phenomenon. Fred
Hirsch correctly notes that it is "the end-product of the existing
monetary instrumentalities and the use made of them. The instrumentalities represent the technique; their management or manipula-
tion ultimately rests on political determination and on the social and
economic forces that in turn underlie political decisions or confine
them within a certain range. Economic factors, and they alone, can
explain how inflation happens, but economic factors alone cannot
explain why" (Hirsch 1978, 263).

The proximate economic sources of inflation have been identified
as excess money and spending (as a result of government spending),
scarcities (e.g., shortage of oil and other natural resources), increases
in wages (e.g., the influence of powerful labor unions), and expecta-
tional momentum from all of these areas (Lovett 1982, 94–106). In

terms of economic structures, factors said to have a positive impact on inflation include urbanization concomitant to a tremendous rise in urban infrastructure, rapid expansion of production facilities incidental to industrialization, government protection of so-called "infant industries," and finally, increased demand for imports, which tends to result in the devaluation of the home-country currency and to subsequent inflationary pressures (Baer 1991).

As noted by Goldthorpe (1978), these economic explanations of inflation often have been treated as exogenous in the study of inflation, although many important works have shown that the state— through its power to determine the money supply—has ultimate responsibility for inflation when it results from a rapid growth in money supply (Friedman 1956, 1960; Hayek 1959, 1960; Johnson 1972). The role played by the government and political institutions is particularly important for long-run inflation (in contrast to short-run inflation, which, more or less, is caused by the economic conditions mentioned above). Willett (1988); Roubini and Sachs (1989); Edwards and Tabellini (1991a); Roubini (1991); Grilli, Masciandaro, and Tabellini (1991); and Cukierman, Edwards, and Tabellini (1992) all empirically demonstrate that political institutions and incentives do indeed matter in the government's use of seigniorage and its implementation of monetary policies to deal with subsequent inflationary pressures.

Among political economists who have focused on government behavior as a clue for inflation, Obstfeld (1991) suggests that the lack of government credibility may generate a bias toward debts and inflation, especially when the government is short-lived. Edwards and Tabellini (1991a) obtain the result that societies with high political polarization and heterogeneity have more difficulty in reducing inflation through institutional means, implying that their political institutions are not credible. Tabellini and Alesina (1990) find that public debt can be used strategically by a current government to influence the policies of a future government with a different political agenda. Similarly, Cukierman, Edwards, and Tabellini (1992) illustrate that the more unstable and polarized a country, the more likely the government will depend on seigniorage to finance its spending. Additionally, there is a substantial body of literature on central-bank independence, much of which finds that the more independent the central bank, the lower the level of inflation (Banaian et al. 1988).

All of these works have made important contributions to our understanding of inflation. My point of departure for this chapter lies in examining the effects of broader political institutions than have been studied by economists. The particular focus will be on a joint examination of three political models of inflation: political freedom, political stability, and political capacity. A study of inflation is important given the argument that inflation has a negative impact on private investment and growth. Thus, if democracy reduces inflation—with everything else kept constant—the effect of democracy on private investment and growth is likely to be positive; if inflation is higher in democracies than autocracies, then the effect of democracy on private investment and growth may be negative.

This chapter is organized as follows. Section 6.1 introduces the theoretical arguments and reviews empirical findings concerning political institutions and inflation. Section 6.2 presents a preliminary examination of the data on inflation in light of three political-institutional models. Section 6.3 specifies a multivariate model while discussing the variables in the model. Section 6.4 discusses the findings and implications of statistical testing.

## 6.1    Political Freedom, Stability, and Capacity: Three Models

In terms of the structural effects of political institutions on inflation, three characteristics have been viewed as responsible for inflation: the degree of democracy, political-regime stability, and government political capacity. Democracy is linked to inflation because the democratic political system can be seen as a political infrastructure built on the rise of organized labor, which in turn is empowered and strengthened by the system. Organized labor groups in democracies are thus able to translate demands into wage-push inflation, narrowing the range of political options available to governments and making deflationary policy politically infeasible (Goldthorpe 1987).

Inflation is also viewed as a consequence of macropolitical uncertainty. Alesina and Tabellini (1990); Tabellini and Alesina (1990); Persson and Svensson (1989); and Cukierman, Edwards, and Tabellini (1992) all use an intertemporal model based on rationality assumptions to discover the equilibrium conditions for the use of seigniorage. Their theoretical models boil down to the conclusion that under circumstances of political instability, a government will rely on seigniorage to finance its operations, rather than improve an inefficient tax system to increase tax receipts, since the current government may not remain in power long enough to benefit from an improved tax system.

Finally, it is argued that inflation is caused by a political elite's inability to subdue and control interest groups pressing for inflationary policies from which they benefit. A strong government is capable of mobilizing the population and efficient in extracting resources from the nation's material pool. Therefore, some argue that a government with high political capacity is in a better position to curb inflationary demands (and even adopt a deflationary policy) than a government with weak political capacity (Arbetman and Kugler 1995, Al-Marhubi 1997, Alcazar 1997). According to these authors, political capacity is independent of regime type, as there exist weak and strong authoritarian regimes as well as weak and strong democratic ones, which implies that the degree of democracy may not be a strong factor influencing price stability.

The three political models of inflation are examined on their assumptions and implications in the following subsections.

## Democracy and Inflation

According to Goldthorpe (1987), postwar inflation was produced by distributional conflict. The argument assumes that inflation was caused by large demands from workers, and an increase in their power allowed them to translate such demands into wage-push inflation. A democratic political system enhances the power of organized labor; therefore, inflation rises as a consequence of labor demands on a democratically elected government. Various writers have noted a fundamental dilemma for democracy regarding inflation. Discontented workers at first exert pressures for a democratic system; then, after the apparatus of political democracy is established, workers are able to extract "both a social safety net and the legal basis for a free trade union movement." This in turn leads to "more equitable distribution rewards" (Smith 1992, 3).[3] On this line of reasoning, the growth of the working class's organized political power under a democratic government detracts from the efficiency of the capitalistic market and may produce inflation as a result of demands for increases in their welfare (Smith 1992, 3).

A government has three ways to finance itself: through taxation, debt, and monetization.[4] Under a democratically elected government, political parties campaigning under a platform calling for a tax increase will not be popular. Similarly, issuance of large amounts of government debt will lead to an increase in interest rates for borrowers (e.g., mortgage and automobile loan rates), also making the government unpopular. That leaves monetization a means of financing government while delaying the impact on the economy, thus creating an opportunity for the state to spend without undertaking unpopular measures.

There are two other incentives for a democratic government to use inflation to finance itself. A government can reduce its real burden of debt through inflation, making payment to creditors less expensive in real terms. Second, deficit spending makes government-provided goods and services look "cheaper" than they really are, which may lead people to demand more of these goods and services (Buchanan and Wagner 1977, 99). These assumptions are part of the foundations for several theories of the political economy of elections in democracies. By comparison, a dictatorship is not constrained by short-term election concerns and is thus in a better position to withstand the demands of labor. Authoritarian governments have a two-fold advantage in that they do not have to yield to the wages and social-security benefits demanded by the working class, and they can increase taxes without being ousted from office. However, it should be noted that according to this perspective, these incentives to increase the money supply are not unique to democracies; on the contrary, they may be shared by autocracies. What makes the latter different is the lack of political constraints, which allows it to make effective use of other political means besides inflation to finance government or reward constituencies. Hence, scholars who maintain that inflation is inherent in democratic societies base their arguments on the lags in the inflationary consequences of an election,[5] the lack of information for voters and voter ignorance of long-term consequences, and the self-interest of politicians—all of which are supposed to lead to a larger than preferable size of government and to accelerate the inflation rate.

Democracies are beset by the political sources of inflation discussed above, but autocracies certainly are not immune to similar problems. Many autocracies have a deeply embedded potential for social and political instability. Without democratic means of resolving conflict and because of deficiencies in political trust and compromise, an autocratic government may have to use redistribution mechanisms to win support from median citizen interest groups.[6] These governments can adopt inflationary policies that favor one group or groups over others. Until the mid-1970s, inflation served the governments of many Latin American countries as a mechanism for resource allocation and income redistribution. As Baer notes, "It is clear that in many Latin American countries the shifting of resources from one sector or social group to another has been politically easier to achieve through inflation than through more explicit government decisions" (1991, 49). Though Baer does not specify which Latin American countries adopted an inflationary policy to redistribute income, all Latin American countries—except Colombia, Costa Rica and Venezuela—were classified as autocracies in the mid-1970s (Gasiorowski 1996). Thus, one can conclude that inflation is very likely to occur in autocracies to redistribute income.

Another source of reasoning connecting democracy to inflation lies in identifying the level of political uncertainty caused by the political regime. As mentioned by Peacock and Ricketts, "A political system that presents an individual voter with highly uncertain outcomes, and which gives him no assurance that he will not become the victim of the strategic behavior of others, will be ill-equipped to provide a solution to the problem of inflation" (1978, 127). Roemer (1995) argues that a dictatorship produces political stability and its citizens can predict the economic policies of the state. A democracy, by contrast, involves political turnover of the government, thus leaving citizens uncertain about future policy. His argument implies that if the objective function is to maximize investment and growth, citizens would simply choose a development-oriented dictatorship, with South Korea and Taiwan as paradigms; if they choose democracy, they do so because of the intrinsic value of freedom. In other words, there exists a trade-off between material consumption and civil liberty. The foregone opportunity of economic growth is political freedom. Since the relationship between growth and democracy has been dealt with in chapter 5 and the relationship between political freedom and economic freedom will be tackled in chapter 10, I will not discuss the trade-off between growth and freedom here. Rather, the focus will be on the condition in Roemer's argument that leads to growth. This condition is premised upon the relatively low level of political uncertainty generated by a stable, growth-oriented dictatorship and the relatively high level of political uncertainty caused by government turnover in a democracy. The variant political-business-cycle and partisan theories seem to indicate that inflation is inherent to democracy.

However, the implication that inflation is higher under a democracy than an autocracy requires some additional assumptions. There are two important assumptions implicit in the thesis that dictatorships are stable. The first (as discussed in the preceding chapter) is that there is no irregular government change. The second is that policy change under democratic government involves radical policy discontinuities rather than minor adjustment. As the results of the preceding chapter show, when these two assumptions are loosened, dictatorship has a higher level of uncertainty than a democracy, since the latter reduces the probability of irregular government change, which causes political and economic uncertainty.

A key assumption made by Roemer and others is that dictatorships are oriented toward maximizing the welfare of their nations, or at least oriented toward growth by operating market economies. In other words, while there is little or no political freedom, the autocracy allows a high degree of economic freedom. This is a strong and significant assumption. As Barro mentions, "History suggests that dictators come in two types, one whose personal objectives often conflict with growth promotion and another whose interests dictate a preoccupation with economic development" (Barro 1996). The factors determining the two types of dictator have not been well studied in the literature and remain a lacuna in our knowledge. To assume one type of dictatorship is a convenient strategy toward initial progress with a model, but interpretation of the subsequent theoretical results must be qualified with the caveat that they were obtained under an overly restrictive assumption.

As we found in chapter 5, nations with low political freedom and poor democratic institutions tend to engender political instability, which may lead to inflation. Two examples suffice here. Political instability has been the leading element in the political economy of Argentine inflation. From 1940 to 1982, after which Argentina could finally be characterized as a democracy, the country was led by at least 18 chief executives. Of these, only 2 died in office and 1 resigned—the other 15 gained and lost power through military coups (Snow 1979, 54). The 1955 coup against Perón was followed by a military government, which lasted two and half years, and a civilian government under Frondizi, which lasted three years. After

Frondizi came another period of military rule, followed by another three years of civilian rule under Illia, and then seven more years of military control under three different regimes. Finally, a second Perónist era lasted for three years, only to be replaced by another military junta, which remained in power from 1976 to 1982.

During this period, prices increased by a factor of one million, and inflation averaged around 35% per year (Pothier 1982, 187). Neither authoritarian nor short-lived semidemocratic regimes could control inflation in Argentina. To be sure, some of the blame may be placed on three interest groups—the agricultural industry, unions, and bureaucrats—and their push for economic welfare. Diaz-Alejandro claims that the inflation of 1948–1955 can be "viewed as resulting from the struggle among urban workers, urban entrepreneurs, the public sector, and the rural sector to maintain the gains or recover the losses in real income sustained during the 1946–1955 boom" (Diaz-Alejandro 1970, 122). The general political environment did not provide a hospitable vehicle for reducing inflation. Military coups intensified the political uncertainty, and the populace's demands for improvement in their welfare may have just been in response to the deterioration in livelihoods caused by economic and political mishaps.

The other example I briefly explore is Spain. Compared to Argentina, Spain's postwar authoritarian rule seemed stable. However, the uncertainty of political change is an issue of probability rather than a discrete phenomenon of change versus no change. Many elements of political instability lie in an authoritarian society, all of which may lead eventually to fundamental change in the political system. Between 1963 and 1972, during which the Spanish economy grew at a cumulative rate of 7.6%, its consumer price index rose from 100 to 181, compared to a rise from 100 to 150 in the European democracies (Coverdale 1982, 225–226). During the final years of the Franco regime, Spain's inflation rate went even higher. The assassination of Franco's heir-apparent, Carrero Blanco, seriously weakened the government, and the new cabinet led by Carlos Arias Navarro had no intention to adopt politically unpopular anti-inflation measures (Coverdale 1982, 226). Neither the last Franco government nor the first two governments under the restored monarchy undertook serious measures to curb inflation. By the summer of 1977, the Spanish economy experienced severe problems involving "slow growth, falling investment, rising unemployment, spiraling inflation, and a deficit of the current external account" (Coverdale 1982, 229). Meanwhile, democratic Europe continued to control inflation better than authoritarian Spain.

Wittman (1989, 1995) argues that democratic institutions are efficient and therefore can reduce political uncertainty. He demonstrates that democracy is organized to promote wealth-maximizing performance, since its processes are competitive and its political agents are rewarded for efficient behavior. In particular, he maintains that all of the notions about the efficiency of the market can be applied to democratic mechanisms and institutions. Democratic institutions are efficient because the actions of candidates and voters mitigate the problem of rational voter ignorance, and rivalry between political parties reduces politicians' rents via competition. In addition, strong political institutions, as found in democracies, decrease transaction costs.

Finally, a skeptical perspective, exemplified by Kurth's (1982) historical analysis, considers inflation an outcome of economic development, differentiated by the timing of entry into the international market. The nations that industrialized earliest, such as the United Kingdom and the United States, were the first to have a competitive advantage in consumer goods and were able to develop relatively strong commercial banks. The domination of their products, such as textiles, in the international market made it desirable for them to adopt deflationary policies. The nations that industrialized later— such as Germany, Italy, Russia, and the Latin American countries— had to depend on industrial investment banks to develop their capital-intensive products. In these countries, coalitions were formed around the policy of deflation or inflation.[7] In this context, inflation is fundamentally determined by the level of development rather than by the type of polity.

## Political Instability and Inflation

Severe political upheavals, especially those that involve a change of regime due to war and revolution, often cause hyperinflation.[8] In some extreme cases, inflation can be staggeringly high. For example, Germany's price index went from 96 in January 1914 to 115,900,000,000,000 in June 1924 (Sargent 1982). Similar cases occurred in Austria, Hungary, and Poland in the midst of high public deficits and their governments' use of the central bank to finance operations following the costly First World War. During the late 1940s, the prospect of the government changing from the Nationalists to the Communists sent inflation sky-rocketing in China, as consumers and investors were deeply concerned about the value of their assets; they feared that the new postrevolution government might not honor the currency used in the old regime.

Hyperinflation does not erupt regularly in the day-to-day world, but high inflation does occur from time to time. High inflation, according to Leijonhufvud (1992), involves an increase in prices of 8 to 10 percent per month. The annual percentage rate is considered meaningless in this context, except in retrospect. It is important to determine whether political institutions have anything to do with the rise of inflation in the absence of great social and political upheavals (such as warfare), leading to hyperinflation.

There are several reasons for the positive relationship between political instability and inflation. First, political instability adds to the risk premium, leading to increased demand for money. Second, incentives to use currency increase with the prospect of approaching political instability, as there is no point in storing currency lest it completely loses value. Third, political instability will drive the citizens of a country to exchange home currency for foreign currency, leading to currency depreciation and additional inflation. Fourth, an unstable political regime may use fiscal means to buy off opposition or reward supporters. If a government has to spend more towards political stability in a polarized society, higher inflation follows. In some industrializing countries, growth and inflation are concurrent because of industrialization, urbanization, and increased demand for imports. Without political uncertainty and instability, inflation can be well estimated; consequently, its harm is reduced to the margins. With political instability and crisis, uncertainty causes large variances in inflation. This variance leads to misallocation of resources and worsening welfare, resulting in spirals of social and political resentment and continued increases in the inflation rate.

Cukierman, Edwards, and Tabellini (1992) base their argument for a positive relationship between political instability and inflation upon a different set of premises. They maintain that countries with more unstable and polarized political systems will have less efficient tax structures, and thus will have to rely more heavily on seigniorage, increasing the upward pressure on inflation. They propose that political incumbents will choose to inflate the economy as a way of financing the operation of government, since the alternative of improving the tax-collecting apparatus will not likely be to their benefit, as they may not remain in power for the next period.

### Government Political Capacity and Inflation

Scholars argue that unstable governments and weak governments are the two types of government most likely to generate seigniorage or an inflation tax. The two terms sound similar semantically. Yet there remains a fundamental distinction between the two in a government's rationale for choosing to raise taxes or to use inflation to finance government operations. An unstable government relies on seigniorage when it is aware that it may not remain in power in the future period, thus choosing not to improve the efficiency of the tax system (Cukierman, Edwards, and Tabellini 1992). Weak governments, on the other hand, depend on seigniorage because they are not sufficiently strong or able to improve the efficiency of the tax system (Alesina and Drazen 1989, Aizenman 1992). In short, an unstable government is not *willing* to improve the tax system, while a weak government is not *capable* of making it function efficiently. In either case, an increase in the use of seigniorage ensues. In a test of these two hypotheses, Edwards and Tabellini (1991a) find support only for the government instability thesis.

However, Alcazar (1997) argues that party coalitions (used by Edwards and Tabellini) are inappropriate as a measure of government capacity on the grounds that they better indicate the political autonomy of a government than the relationship between the government and its selectorate. Adopting the concept of relative political capacity (RPC) and the operationalization of relative political extraction (RPE), to be introduced later in this chapter, Alcazar finds that a government's relative political capacity has a dampening effect on seigniorage, particularly in developing countries (thus confirming the views of Alesina and Drazen [1989] and Aizenman [1992]). One serious limitation in Alcazar's work is that her result is not controlled by the effect of political instability on seigniorage. It can be argued that relative political capacity is affected by the political instability inherent in the political system. Specifically, the higher the level of political instability, the less capable the government is. One may argue about reverse causation from political capacity to political instability, but by excluding the political-instability variable, the RPC variable may reflect some effect of political instability on seigniorage. Hence, Alcazar's finding that higher political capacity leads to lower levels of seigniorage remains inconclusive and must be accepted with some caution.

Similarly, Al-Marhubi (1996), as well as Marina Arbetman and Jacek Kugler (1995), find that relative political capacity has a negative impact on inflation rates. The former work studied inflation in 14 Latin American countries from 1972 to 1985, while the latter examined inflation in 9 Eastern European countries for the period of 1984 to 1990. Again, the conclusion that government political capacity decreases inflation is obtained without controlling for political instability in the system.

The central argument in this chapter is that political systems, political instability, and government capacity all affect inflation, but in different ways. The scholars who argue that inflation is inherent in democratic systems ignore the fundamental issue of the indirect effect of democracy on regime stability. Their studies typically focus only on democratic countries, emphasizing the contradictions between labor and capital under a democratically elected government. These studies lack a comparative evaluation of democracies and nondemocracies battling with inflation. Further, the democratic nature of a particular political system may in itself have little direct influence on inflation, as different forms of governments may adopt the same inflation-inhibiting policy. For instance, New Zealand and Thailand have had very similar inflation levels despite the fact that the former has been a democracy and the latter has been an autocracy for most of its independence.

Similarly, governments of the same type may have very different attitudes toward inflation. Both Germany and Italy are democracies, but 5% inflation in the former country will raise a specter of fear, while the citizens of the latter may sleep quite peacefully with a 20% inflation rate. The pattern of saving and consumption, together with national culture and ethos, may determine people's reaction to inflation. In spite of the lack of a persuasive argument for the direct influence of a democratic regime on inflation, democracy may create a congenial environment for price stability. I have argued elsewhere in this book that democracy leads to political stability by reducing the likelihood of military coups d'état and other radical changes of the political regime, thus providing some degree of macropolitical stability upon which a strong financial market can be built. Major

**Table 6.1**
Regime type and inflation, 1961–1991

| Regime | Indicator | N | Mean | SD |
|--------|-----------|-----|-------|-------|
| Autocracy | GDP | 2,025 | 0.246 | 3.149 |
|  | CPI | 1,703 | 0.231 | 3.947 |
| Democracy | GDP | 1,024 | 0.509 | 4.500 |
|  | CPI | 988 | 0.527 | 4.857 |
| Semidemocracy | GDP | 183 | 0.106 | 0.174 |
|  | CPI | 178 | 0.104 | 0.168 |
| Transitional | GDP | 127 | 0.900 | 6.981 |
|  | CPI | 107 | 0.326 | 0.689 |

government change under a democratic system *does* generate political uncertainty, but compared to that caused by irregular government change, the effect of regular democratic government change on inflation is marginal.

## 6.2   Preliminary Empirical Evidence

In this section I examine some preliminary statistical evidence of the relationship between political institutions and inflation, first exploring the distribution of regime types and inflation. In accordance with the taxonomy of political regimes provided by Gasiorowski (1996), political regimes are classified into four groups: autocracy, democracy, semidemocracy, and transitional polity.

The data for inflation are constructed from the price deflator for gross domestic product (GDP), and the consumer price index (CPI) published by the World Bank (1993). The GDP price level presents a comprehensive measure for a nation's rate of inflation, while the consumer price index reflects price changes that affect consumers. These two indices are highly correlated.

The information in tables 6.1 and 6.2 seems to support the argument that an autocracy is more capable of controlling inflation than a democracy. A *t*-test reveals that the difference between autocracy and democracy in their levels of inflation is statistically significant at the 10% error level, using the assumptions of both equal and unequal variances.

By contrast, semidemocracies have significantly lower levels of inflation and lower variability of inflation than both autocracies and democracies. This result led me to examine the composition of

**Table 6.2**
*t*-tests of inflation under democracy and autocracy

| Regime | N | Mean | SD | Std error | t | Prob > \|t\| |
|---|---|---|---|---|---|---|
| *Using the GDP deflator* | | | | | | |
| Autocracy | 2025 | 0.246 | 3.149 | 0.070 | −1.679[a] | 0.093 |
| Democracy | 1024 | 0.509 | 4.500 | 0.141 | −1.880[b] | 0.062 |
| *Using the CPI* | | | | | | |
| Autocracy | 1703 | 0.231 | 3.947 | 0.099 | −1.632[a] | 0.102 |
| Democracy | 988 | 0.527 | 4.857 | 0.155 | −1.724[b] | 0.085 |

a. Assumes equal variance.
b. Assumes unequal variance.

this group of regimes. Indeed, quite a few growth-oriented non-democracies are classified as semidemocratic, such as Malaysia and Singapore. The governments in these two countries have adopted a policy to compel their populations to save and invest.[9] A complete list of the semidemocratic countries used in the analysis is as follows: Algeria (1991), Burkina Faso (1972–1973), Gabon (1965–1967), Lesotho (1967–1969), Nigeria (1969–1982), Senegal (1961, 1979–1991), Sierra Leone (1969–1972), Sudan (1966–1968, 1987–1988), Tanzania (1963–1964), Uganda (1963–1965), Zambia (1965–1970), Zimbabwe (1981–1989), Guatemala (1987–1991), Honduras (1961–1962, 1983–1991), Panama (1990–1991), Argentina (1961–1965, 1974–1975), Bolivia (1961–1963), Ecuador (1961–1962, 1969, 1980–1983), Paraguay (1990–1991), Peru (1961, 1964–1967), Bangladesh (1980–1981), Malaysia (1972–1991), Pakistan (1973–1976), Singapore (1966–1991), Sri Lanka (1984–1992), Thailand (1987–1990), Switzerland (1961–1970), and Turkey (1984–1986).

Since these countries are defined as neither full autocracies nor full democracies, they may offer empirical evidence in support of opposite arguments on political systems and inflation. Scholars who argue that autocracy assures financial stability may find examples in this group of countries. Similarly, scholars who maintain that democratic processes result in low inflation can also find examples in this set of nations.

Table 6.3 examines the correlation between inflation and political instability, using annual data. The three indicators of political instability developed in chapter 3 and chapter 5—irregular government change, major regular government change, and minor regular government change—are used here to clarify the relationship between

**Table 6.3**
Correlations between political instability and inflation

|                    | Irregular change | Major regular change | Minor regular change |
| ------------------ | ---------------- | -------------------- | -------------------- |
| Inflation (GDP)    | 0.095            | 0.115                | 0.027                |
|                    | (0.001)          | (0.001)              | (0.023)              |
| Inflation (CPI)    | 0.112            | 0.099                | 0.044                |
|                    | (0.001)          | (0.001)              | (0.065)              |

**Table 6.4**
Correlations between political instability and inflation

|                    | Irregular change | Major regular change | Minor regular change |
| ------------------ | ---------------- | -------------------- | -------------------- |
| Inflation (GDP)    | 0.348            | 0.041                | −0.110               |
|                    | (0.001)          | (0.400)              | (0.022)              |
| Inflation (CPI)    | 0.436            | 0.042                | −0.015               |
|                    | (0.001)          | (0.388)              | (0.018)              |

political instability and inflation. In particular, I expect a positive correlation between inflation and irregular government change, but a negative relationship between inflation and minor regular government change. Inflation and political instability appear to be positively related, consistent with our expectation, though the strength of the association is low enough to say that there is virtually no relationship between inflation and any form of political instability. The lack of association is likely due to the possibility that political instability has a lagging effect on inflation.[10]

To correct this problem, table 6.4 uses aggregate levels of inflation over the period of 1961–1991 and aggregate levels of political instability over the period of 1950–1980. The pattern of the relationship between the annual data and the aggregate data is very distinct: a salient association between inflation and political instability has emerged in the aggregate data, and the correlation between inflation and propensity for irregular government change is fairly strong. By comparison, the relationship between inflation and major regular government change is weak, as less political uncertainty should be engendered by constitutional government change than by unconstitutional or extraconstitutional regime change. Finally, the correlation between inflation and minor regular government change has now turned negative, although the association is not very strong.

Of the three kinds of government change, minor regular change is associated with the lowest levels of instability. In this case, political instability is perhaps a misnomer, as certainty—rather than uncertainty—is the outcome of this type of government change.

Next I check for the relationship between government political capacity and inflation, since the strength and efficiency of the government are an important variable that bridges economics and politics. Organski and Kugler develop a concept of political capacity. This concept "attempts to capture whether elites have the tools to tap into human and material resources in their societies ... and use them for national purposes" (Organski and Kugler 1980, 69). The concept focuses on "the capacity of the political system to carry out the tasks chosen by the nation's government in the face of domestic and international groups with competing priorities" (Arbetman and Kugler 1997, 1), and it pivots on a government's capacity to extract revenue. As governmental operation depends upon resources extracted from the population, governments cannot survive—let alone govern—without such resources.

Taxes are exact indicators of governmental presence. Few operations of governments depend so heavily on popular support—or on fear of punishment. Revenues affect so directly the lives of most individuals in society, and few are avoided so vigorously. Without some form of tax revenue, there is no national unity, and no control. Failure to impose and extract taxes is one of the essential indicators of governmental incapacity to obtain and maintain support. (Organski and Kugler 1980, 74)

Guided by this theoretical principle, Arbetman and Kugler create a measure of political capacity called relative political extraction (RPE), as it estimates the government's political capacity to extract resources against a benchmark model in which the extraction of resources is determined by economic factors. This measure is obtained in three steps (Arbetman and Kugler 1995). First, an ordinary least-squares regression is run on the following model:

$$\frac{\text{tax}}{\text{GDP}} = \beta_0 + \beta_1(\text{time}) + \beta_2\left(\frac{\text{mining}}{\text{GDP}}\right) + \beta_3\left(\frac{\text{agriculture}}{\text{GDP}}\right)$$
$$+ \beta_4\left(\frac{\text{exports}}{\text{GDP}}\right) + \varepsilon.$$

In the second step, the predicted value for the tax ratio is obtained using the parameter estimates derived from the first step. In the third step, the following ratio is calculated:

$$\text{RPE} = \frac{\text{actual government revenue}}{\text{predicted government revenue}}$$

If the above ratio is larger than 1, then the government is defined as "strong," since it collects more taxes than otherwise predicted by economic factors. Such a government is also regarded as politically capable and efficient. If the ratio is less than 1, then the government fails to collect the taxes it is expected to obtain and is regarded as politically less capable.

The use of the concept and measure of relative political extraction has produced an established literature on government capacity and conflict (e.g., Organski and Kugler 1980, Tammen et al. 2000) and has motivated various works that study political institutions and economic development (e.g., Snider 1996; Alcazar 1997; Feng, Kugler, and Zak 2000, 2001). RPE is orthogonal to political freedom and independent of the nature of a polity. Therefore, "a major virtue of this concept is that it is not institution specific ... [and] can be applied equally to systems with varying degrees of democracy and authoritarian control" (Willett 1997, 297).[11]

The aggregate data are checked to see if any cyclical or lagging problems have weakened the relationship between inflation and government capacity. The correlation between the mean of inflation and the mean of relative political extraction for each country during the period of 1961–1991 is not only low, but is signed opposite to the expectation of the argument that a weak government tends to have a higher level of inflation. The Pearson correlation coefficient is $-0.064$ for inflation, constructed from the GDP deflator, and RPE and $-0.045$ for inflation, constructed from the CPI, and RPE.

The relationship between political institutions and inflation implied by the above should be accepted with two caveats. First, we still do not know the causal relationship between political systems and inflation. We have a global pattern presenting a general tendency, but the pattern itself may be spurious after intervening variables are considered. Second, the means in the table were generated from annual data; a few outlier countries with a long span of years in the data can significantly alter the aggregate statistics. The next section tests the three institutional models—the political-instability model (Edwards and Tabellini 1991a, 1991b; Cukierman, Edwards, and Tabellini 1992), the political-capacity model (Arbetman and

Kugler 1995, Al-Marhubi 1997, Alcazar 1997), and the democracy model—on inflation through multivariate statistical estimation.

## 6.3  Model Specification and Data

Following the aggregate analysis design in Edwards and Tabellini (1991a, 1991b), I use the average inflation rate (derived from the consumer price index for the period of 1970 to 1992) as the dependent variable. This period was chosen to compare with similar works (Arbetman and Kugler 1995, Al-Marhubi 1997, and Alcazar 1997). One historical event causing worldwide inflation was the oil-price crises in the 1970s. The effect of external oil-price shocks in the 1970s may cause countries with various types of political institutions to react in ways different from the 1980s. In the analysis, in addition to the period of 1970 through 1992, I also run two separate regressions, one for the 1970–1980 period and the other for the 1980–1992 period. The data on inflation are constructed from the *Social and Economic Indicators* compiled by the World Bank (1993b). It should be noted that the multivariate model estimated here is a reduced form of inflation, as money supply is omitted. It is assumed that all the policy variables in the three political-institution models affect inflation through change in the money supply.

In the instability model, the most important variable affecting inflation (as discussed in the preceding sections) is political change. Edwards and Tabellini (1991a, 1991b) and Cukierman, Edwards, and Tabellini (1992) find that a higher level of political instability leads to a higher level of seigniorage, and thus a higher level of inflation. Among various forms of political instability, the most serious one is extraconstitutional, or regime, change (as argued in chapters 3 and 4). The studies by the above authors, however, have not separated unconstitutional government change from major, yet constitutional, government change. Another weakness of their studies, as pointed out by Alcazar (1997), lies in their use of party coalitions as a measure of government capacity. This measure regards "political weakness as a political struggle *within* the government," while "a struggle between the government and its selectorate is what forces the government to avoid increasing taxes to satisfy public demands" (Alcazar 1997, 84). I include two variables to measure the level of government control of the population, as explained later in my discussion of the political-capacity model.

For political instability, I include the probabilities of irregular and regular government change in the empirical model as indices of the uncertainty engendered by political turnover. I expect that the probabilities of irregular government change, as well as of major regular government change, will have a positive impact on inflation. While it is straightforward that the higher the probability for irregular government change, the higher the level of inflation, major regular government change (in which the ruling party or the ruling coalition of parties changes) also contributes to a certain degree of uncertainty that may increase inflation. For indices of political instability, I resort to measures of the three kinds of political change explained in chapters 3 and 5. As there may be a reverse relationship between inflation and political instability, lagged values of political instability are used to estimate future inflation.

The democratic nature of the political system and the capacity of the government are also important variables to be considered here. Unlike the political-instability variables, they are less directly responsible for inflation. In addition, the effect of democracy on inflation should depend on the circumstances under which inflation occurs. During the oil-price crisis of the mid-1970s, a democratic government in response to social pressures may have taken active measures to address the inflationary problems caused by price shocks. In contrast, an autocracy may not be under as much pressure under the same circumstances. Alternatively, in the case of chronic inflation caused by domestic problems, it may be difficult to predict whether democracy or autocracy does better in controlling inflation. Since this is an aggregate analysis, I use the index on political rights and civil liberties compiled by Raymond Gastil and Freedom House. The index is operationalized to have a range from zero to one, with one representing the most democratic.

In the political-capacity model, the key variable has been the level of government capacity. An important lesson from the East Asian countries is that a strong, efficient government is able to strengthen institutional credibility, organize the society for shared and collective activities, and implement a consistent growth-oriented strategy (Root 1996). Arbetman and Kugler (1995), Al-Marhubi (1997), and Alcazar (1997) all find that a higher level of government political capacity leads to a lower level of inflation. However, their work leaves two issues unresolved. First, the effect of political capacity on inflation is not controlled by political instability. To find whether the instability model or the capacity model better explains inflation, variables of both indices must be used. Unfortunately, this is not the case, so the comparative explanatory power of the two models remains unsettled. Second, the design in this chapter utilizes aggregate rather than time-series data. The disadvantage of the former design is that some information is lost in aggregation, but its strength is that it looks at a relatively longer period of time and examines the average effect, which is less idiosyncratic and less susceptible to surprises.

Though the level of political capacity has been used in the literature on inflation, I believe that government political capacity significantly affects inflation through the macropolitical uncertainty caused by the *changeability* of the government's capability to control society. Feng and Chen (1997), using the changeability of government political capacity as a proxy for macropolitical uncertainty, suggest that macropolitical uncertainty causes macroeconomic uncertainty. It can be argued that the more variable the government's capacity, the less clear its signals and directions in its control of the nation. Thus uncertainty in the marketplace increases, and inflation is likely to ensue. The operational difference between the probability of irregular government change and the changeability of government political capacity lies in the fact that the former points to the likelihood of one political system replacing the other, while the latter mainly applies to the strength of government within the existing system. As in Feng and Chen 1997, this index for macropolitical uncertainty is measured by the standard deviation of relative political extraction (RPE). I expect that this variable will have a positive sign with considerable statistical strength.

While the positive relationship of the level and variance of political capacity has vast implications for statecraft and government survival, its implication in the context of this chapter is that unlike the RPE-variance variable, political capacity tends to have an ambiguous effect on inflation. While a strong and efficient government may have the power to reduce inflation, it also has other political and economic goals that may require a change of its relative political capacity (RPC). Therefore, higher RPC may lower inflation if reducing inflation is the major policy objective. However, higher RPC may increase inflation, since it will contribute to higher variability of political capacity. Thus, though I expect higher variances of RPC to lead to higher inflation, higher RPC may or may not lead to higher inflation.

In other words, I expect that RPE will be insignificantly different from zero in hypothesis testing. Likewise, democracy may reduce the likelihood of irregular government change—thus fending off the rise of inflation—but it also increases the likelihood of major regular change, which may increase inflation. The net result of the impact of democracy on inflation, like the effect of RPC on inflation, is ambiguous.

Among the economic structural variables, I include the following: real GDP per capita, the agricultural share of GDP, the trade share of GDP, urbanization, and the fiscal deficit.[12] In addition, I also use two other variables not included in previous studies: the industry share of GDP and a dummy variable for Latin American countries. Hence, this study into the effects of political institutions on inflation includes all the various structural variables used in Edwards and Tabellini 1991a, 1991b and Alcazar 1997 as control variables. I now turn to explaining the use of these variables in the model.

It has been speculated that the size of a nation's economy may have something to do with inflation. Edwards and Tabellini (1991a) maintain that as an economy develops, the government's taxation system will become efficient and as a result seigniorage will be used less as more taxes are collected. Thus, with everything else kept constant, the more developed a nation, the lower its level of inflation. A second argument holds that a higher level of development leads to a higher level of inflation. The premise for this assertion is based upon the assumption that urbanization and industrialization—the two major economic sources of inflation (as discussed in section 4.1)—are positively correlated with the level of development. An alternative explanation for the positive relationship between the levels of development and inflation is based on Hirsch's (1976) argument of "positional goods." According to Hirsch, as societies become richer, consumers' tastes shift to a class of goods he terms "positional," which are finite in quantity (e.g., a house on the ocean), quality (e.g., a Mercedes-Benz), or both (e.g., a painting by Rembrandt). This change in preferences gives rise to a market reaction, which leads to a rise in the price of these goods much greater than the price of goods in general. Therefore, "economic success on the conventional reckoning contributes in this way to frustration, tension, and inflation" (Hirsch 1976, 273). The data used to measure the level of development are real GDP per capita from Summers and Heston 2000.

I also include urbanization among the economic structural variables. As argued by Baer (1991), urbanization drastically increases the need for housing, schools, health clinics, and other kinds of infrastructure that (for various reasons) are best provided by the public sector. The increase in the need for public spending, coupled by a lack of sufficient tax receipts due to inefficient tax systems, creates inflationary pressures. Therefore, urbanization is expected to have a positive effect on inflation. Nonetheless, since from the perspective of seigniorage, tax-collection costs are lower in cities than rural areas, higher levels of urbanization should be negatively associated with the use of seigniorage and inflation (Edwards and Tabellini 1991a). The degree of urbanization is indexed by the portion of the population living in cities of at least 100,000. Industrialization requires that the government provide the necessary infrastructure, such as freeways and communications systems. As with urbanization, lack of adequate tax revenues means that the government may have to rely on seigniorage. Therefore, industrialization puts inflationary pressures on the government and the economy. There is, however, a counterargument regarding this relationship from the point of view of seigniorage. As in the above argument regarding the level of development and inflation, industrialized societies are likely to develop relatively efficient tax-collection systems that decrease the need to use seigniorage to finance the government and reduce the potential of inflation. The level of industrialization is proxied by the GDP share of manufacturing and mining, and data are constructed from the *Social and Economic Indicators* from the World Bank (1993b).

Likewise, there are opposing arguments on the relationship between trade and inflation. In terms of the cost of tax collection, trade provides a tax base that is cheap and politically easy to tax, hence the effect of trade on seigniorage and inflation should be negative (Edwards and Tabellini 1991a, Alcazar 1997). A conflicting argument is that currency overvaluation is often concomitant with a large import share of GDP. Devaluation is difficult when the government wants to appeal to import-substituting industries, which benefit from imports of cheap capital goods, or the urban working class, which favors cheap, imported foodstuffs (Baer 1991, 47). Here the GDP share of exports and imports of goods and services, also termed as "openness" of the economy, is used. Again, the data are constructed from the World Bank's *Social and Economic Indicators* (1993b).

It has been argued that the share of agriculture in GDP should have a positive effect on seigniorage, since the agricultural sector is the most difficult to tax (Edwards and Tabellini 1991a, Alcazar 1997). Therefore, from the perspective of monetization, it can be expected that a large proportion of agriculture in GDP will lead to a relatively high level of inflation. Additionally, as argued by Kurth (1982), the agricultural sector benefits from an inflationary economy and is thus likely to join a coalition with workers to pressure the government for inflationary policies. In this study, value added in agriculture as a percentage of GDP is used; the data are constructed from the World Bank's *Social and Economic Indicators* (1993b).

Government spending in general has a strong potential for spurring inflation.[13] A government may not spend its money as "rationally" as individuals do, because of various coordination problems—prisoners' dilemma, collective action, principal-agent coordination, standard operating procedures, and bureaucratic politics —all of which may lead to overspending and overconsumption, causing more money to chase fewer goods. Additionally, government consumption often involves borrowing and deficit spending. The possibility that a government may have to monetize its debts hangs over the economy, driving consumers to spend their financial assets today rather than waiting for tomorrow. Such an increase in consumer spending is analogous to a run on a bank: the prophecy is self-fulfilling simply because people believe it. Another rationale for connecting government spending with increased inflation is that an increase in government debt increases interest rates (with the money supply held constant). The demand for money is sensitive to interest rates because an increase in rates increases the velocity of money, thereby leading to a boost in the price level (Protoparadakis and Siegal 1987, 36).

In this chapter I include the ratio of the difference between government revenue and spending to GDP, and I expect that the higher the government deficit, the higher the level of inflation. This hypothesis has not always been supported in previous studies. For example, Peacock and Ricketts (1978) find no relationship between the growth of the public sector and inflation. Their finding is perhaps in part attributable to the fact that the size of the government is proxied by the ratio of tax receipts to GDP. As stated earlier in this chapter, tax share may not indicate the real size of the public sector, as government has other means (i.e., monetization and borrowing) of financing itself. Second, as Peacock and Ricketts admit, they have not controlled their result for political systems: "It is perhaps understandable that our rather crude cross-section comparisons, including countries with vastly different political systems ranging from confederate Switzerland to Franco's Spain, should prove so inconclusive" (1978, 136). Since this study controls for these aspects, I hypothesize that government deficit spending has a positive effect on inflation. The data on government fiscal deficits are constructed from the World Bank's *Social and Economic Indicators* (1993b).

Finally, a dummy variable is created for the Latin American countries, many of which experienced high inflation in the late 1970s and the early 1980s. These countries suffered from overvaluation of their currencies, yet had strong political coalitions that resisted devaluation (Crystal 1994). More important, perhaps, Latin America faced inflationary pressures because rapid urbanization and industrialization required the government to invest in socioeconomic structures, but the relatively weak governments could not raise enough revenue through taxation, since high-income groups successfully resisted being taxed. This situation inevitably led to budget deficits and a general rise in prices, both of which were worsened by the debt crisis of the 1970s (Baer 1991, 51, 54). The Latin American experience, not replicated elsewhere, was unique in the countries' level of modernization, the state-society relationship, and their integration in world financial markets. It is expected that this dummy variable will be positively related to inflation. These variables are summarized in table 6.5.

## 6.4  Empirical Evidence

Table 6.6 presents regression results from the model discussed in the last section. Columns (1), (2), and (3) test the three political-institution models for the period of 1970 to 1992. Of these, the instability model seems to work the best, followed by the capacity model. The results indicate that the higher the probability of irregular government change, the higher the level of inflation. Additionally, changes in government political capacity affect inflation: the larger the variance of this capacity, the greater the inflation rate. Both results indicate that political institutions matter in price stability. The two variables—political instability and government capacity—can be thought of as respective indices of regime stability and government

**Table 6.5**
Summary of model specification

| Variable | Sign | Data source |
|---|---|---|
| *Policy variables* | | |
| Political freedom (FREE) | ? | Freedom House 1999 |
| Irregular gov. change (PROBIRCH) | + | This book |
| Regular major gov. change (PROBMJCH) | + | This book |
| Regular minor gov. change (PROBMNCH) | − | This book |
| Relative political extraction (RPE) | ? | Arbetman and Kugler 1997 |
| Standard deviation of RPE (RPESD) | + | Arbetman and Kugler 1997 |
| *Control variables* | | |
| Industrial share of GDP (INDUSTRY) | ? | World Bank 1993 |
| Agricultural share of GDP (AGRICLTR) | + | World Bank 1993 |
| Urban population (% living in cities of >100,000 people) (URBAN) | + | World Bank 1993 |
| Percentage of imports and exports in GDP (TRADE) | ? | World Bank 1993 |
| Government deficit as a percentage of GDP (DEFICIT) | + | World Bank 1993 |
| Real GDP per capita (REALGDP) | ? | Summers and Heston 2000 |
| Latin America (LATAMER) | + | Barro and Wolf 1989 |

Dependent variable: change of consumer price index.

stability. While the former indicates the likelihood of a fundamental change in the current political system, the latter measures the struggle for control between government and selectorate. Change in both kinds of political institutions appears to affect inflation.

Column (4) presents a "full" model that incorporates the three institutional models. Again, irregular government change and changes in government political capacity have a positive impact on inflation. The other political variables are not statistically significant. Columns (5) and (6) present the results of a retest of the full model for the periods of 1970–1980 and 1980–1992, respectively. The first period witnessed the worldwide inflation caused by the oil-price hikes of the OPEC nations. The domestic economic adjustments made necessary by this external shock and the subsequent level of inflation probably differed from other periods, when inflation was more or less caused by domestic problems. Lagged values of political instability are used in both equations to mitigate potential reverse-causality problems. In (5), political instability for the period of 1960–1970 is used, while political instability for the period of 1970–1980 is used in (6).

The results of (5) and (6) vary significantly. For the period of 1970–1980, the probability of major regular government change (rather than that of regime change) appears to increase inflation, democracy is found to decrease inflation, and the level of government capacity (instead of its variance) seems to cause inflation. The combination of these results presents an interesting pattern. When inflation is caused by external shocks and economic adjustments are necessary, a free country is more capable of reducing inflation than an unfree country, but only under the circumstances that major regular government change occurs infrequently and that the government is not too "strong." This implication is consistent with the notion that a democratically elected government is more constrained than an autocracy in making policies. When the whole nation is affected by inflation caused by external shocks, a democracy has to consider the overall social concerns related to price increases, and thus adopts a deflationary policy. The paradox is that democracy increases the likelihood of major constitutional government change, which adds to political uncertainty. Thus a democracy reduces inflation because of its commitment to, and constraints from, society, while it may also increase the level of inflation, since it induces major regular change through elections. Furthermore, the dampening effect of democracy on inflation in this case is also conditioned by the political capacity of the government. If the ruling elite is strong and capable, it can distance itself from social concerns and may not have strong incentives to control price increases.

From 1980 to 1992, after the world inflation caused by the oil-price increases passed, a different combination of political variables emerged. Above all, the probability of regime change and the variance of government strength appear to cause inflation. As seen in the full model for the whole period (column (4)), a relatively high probability of irregular government change is found to lead to relatively high inflation, and a relatively high variability of government political capacity over time is found to be conducive to relatively high inflation. Both variables are statistically significant under any conventional criteria.

Among the economic-structure variables, the GDP shares of agriculture and industry are consistently positive in sign and statistically significant in all regressions except in column (1). While it has been

**Table 6.6**
Three political-institution models on inflation

| Variables | Instability model (1) 1970–92 | Democracy model (2) 1970–92 | Capacity model (3) 1970–92 | Full model (4) 1970–92 | Full model (5) 1970–80 | Full model (6) 1980–92 |
|---|---|---|---|---|---|---|
| INTERCEPT | -2.976** (1.141) | -2.824** | -3.943* (1.454) | -4.910* (1.462) | -0.736 (0.300) | -8.922* (2.497) |
| PROBIRCH | 12.412* (3.661) | — | — | 14.074* (3.848) | -0.594 (0.646) | 24.567* (6.477) |
| PROBMJCH | -1.125 (2.353) | — | — | -0.073 (2.793) | 0.904† (0.482) | 1.650 (4.628) |
| PROBMNCH | 0.039 (2.213) | — | — | -0.424 (2.182) | -0.440 (0.490) | -0.738 (3.907) |
| FREE | | -0.446 (0.627) | | 0.215 (0.745) | -0.362* (0.136) | 0.447 (1.269) |
| RPE | | — | 0.219 (0.417) | 0.627 (0.458) | 0.272* (0.087) | 1.083 (0.737) |
| RPESD | | — | 1.738** (0.892) | 1.957** (0.888) | 0.381 (0.262) | 4.332* (1.414) |
| INDUSTRY | 2.971 (1.936) | 4.388** (1.922) | 4.355** (1.967) | 3.221† (1.920) | 0.944** (0.429) | 7.451** (3.205) |
| AGRICLTR | 2.439 (1.905) | 3.905** (1.962) | 4.842** (2.025) | 3.901** (1.997) | 0.883** (0.413) | 7.392† (3.873) |
| URBAN | 0.015 (0.011) | 0.019† (0.011) | 0.020† (0.011) | 0.0142 (0.011) | 0.008* (0.002) | 0.020 (0.018) |
| TRADE | 0.150 (0.331) | -0.120 (0.329) | -0.072 (0.322) | 0.287 (0.324) | -0.145** (0.070) | 0.232 (0.523) |

| | | | | | | |
|---|---|---|---|---|---|---|
| DEFICIT | 11.456* | 11.746* | 12.180* | 11.748* | 0.827 | 14.576* |
| | (3.479) | (3.542) | (3.486) | (3.396) | (0.628) | 4.810 |
| REALGDP | 0.050 | 0.007 | 0.004 | 0.074 | −0.027 | 0.119 |
| | (0.066) | (0.071) | (0.061) | (0.073) | (0.017) | (0.112) |
| LATAMER | 0.918** | 1.440* | 1.465* | 0.631** | 0.141† | 2.099* |
| | (0.391) | (0.397) | (0.392) | (0.319) | (0.077) | (0.763) |
| $\bar{R}^2$ | 0.372 | 0.300 | 0.326 | 0.414 | 0.439 | 0.461 |
| $\sigma$ | 1.022 | 1.022 | 1.022 | 1.022 | 0.190 | 1.874 |
| $N$ | 90 | 90 | 90 | 90 | 76 | 88 |

*Statistically significant at the 0.01 level in a two-tailed test.
**Statistically significant at the 0.05 level in a two-tailed test.
†Statistically significant at the 0.10 level in a two-tailed test.
Standard errors in parentheses.

argued that a larger agricultural sector is likely to be associated with higher inflation, the impact of industrialization on inflation has been controversial (as summarized in the last section). The statistical finding is a positive effect of industrialization on inflation, thus confirming that social aspects act as causes for inflation (Baer 1991) and contradicting the monetization argument centered on the cost of tax collection (Edwards and Tabellini 1991a, Alcazar 1997).

Government fiscal deficits are found to have a positive impact on inflation in columns (1) to (6), consistent with Al-Marhubi's (1997) results. Because of the potential inverse relationship between inflation and deficits (which stipulates that high rates of inflation may reduce the real proceeds of taxes and thereby lead to budget deficits), the variable of fiscal deficits in table 6.6 was replaced with its lagged value to estimate current inflation. The result was highly consistent with table 6.6. Government fiscal deficits are a dominant structural determinant of inflation.

Urbanization is consistently positive in sign and statistically significant in columns (2), (3), and (5). Again, this result is consistent with the argument based on the social aspects of inflation (Baer 1991), but not with the argument derived from the hypothesis that urban areas are easier places for tax collection, thus both creating a lesser need for seigniorage and generating a lower potential of inflation. Real GDP per capita is positively signed in most of the results, but it is not significant, possibly because GDP is highly correlated with urbanization and industrialization.

Trade is ambiguously signed and is significant only for the period of 1970–1980. It appears that during the 1970s, the countries that had a larger combined share of imports and exports in GDP were more capable of curbing inflation than other countries, with all other factors kept constant. This finding seems to run against the argument that in economies dependent upon international trade, price levels were more susceptible to massive changes in the prices of the world market (e.g., oil price hikes) than were relatively closed economies.

Finally, the dummy variable for Latin American countries is statistically significant in columns (1) through (6). This result indicates that Latin American countries have some factor or factors (exclusive of the economic-structure variables included as controls in the model) that create systemic effects on inflation. Such factors could lie in the social or cultural realms. As implied in the last section, the relationships between government and interest groups in Latin American countries may be systematically different from those in other nations.

The preliminary bivariate statistics find that semidemocracies seem more capable of having low levels of inflation than other types of political regimes. In the context of multivariate testing, this means that inflation and political freedom have a nonlinear relationship in which the countries with the middle level of political freedom have the lowest inflation rates. In order to test this hypothesis, I transformed the ordinal variable on political rights and civil liberties into two binary variables. MID-FREE takes the value of one for countries that have a composite score for political rights and civil liberties between 0.33 and 0.66; otherwise MID-FREE takes a value of zero. Similarly, HIGH-FREE takes a value of one for countries whose composite freedom scores are greater than 0.66 and less than or equal to 1; it takes the value of zero otherwise. The low-freedom countries are those whose scores are below 0.33. These are the benchmark countries in the regressions including the two dummy variables MID-FREE and HIGH-FREE. Another dummy variable, SOC, is included, as countries in the sample may also have a socialist type of economy, where inflation is low or even zero as the result of central planning.

Table 6.7 shows the estimation results for three periods of time using the dummy variables indicative of the three levels of political freedom. After controlling for other political-institution and economic-structure variables, I could not find a strong nonlinear relationship between inflation and democracy. Indeed, the freest countries had the lowest level of inflation for the period of 1970 to 1980. For the other periods, the statistical significance of the freedom dummy variables is not very salient. For the whole period, the middle-freedom group has a higher level of inflation than the other two groups, though the statistical relationship is significant at only the 10% error level. The other information in table 6.7 is highly consistent with that in table 6.6.

## 6.5   Summary and Policy Implications

In discussing the three political-institution models of inflation and examining their empirical evidence, I found no statistical evidence that a democracy is more likely to generate inflation than an

**Table 6.7**
Inflation and revised democracy index

|            | (7) 1970–92      | (8) 1970–80      | (9) 1980–92      |
|------------|------------------|------------------|------------------|
| INTERCEPT  | −4.738*          | −0.981*          | −9.043*          |
|            | (1.385)          | (0.323)          | (2.448)          |
| PROBIRCH   | 13.604*          | −0.399           | 23.515*          |
|            | (3.719)          | (0.652)          | (6.042)          |
| PROBMJCH   | −0.065           | 0.875*           | 1.363            |
|            | (2.699)          | (0.484)          | (4.553)          |
| PROBMNCH   | −2.761           | −0.394           | −3.653           |
|            | (2.338)          | (0.497)          | (4.493)          |
| MID-FREE   | 0.687†           | −0.009           | 0.850            |
|            | (0.365)          | (0.065)          | (0.739)          |
| HIGH-FREE  | 0.021            | −0.200**         | 0.297            |
|            | (0.468)          | (0.080)          | (0.918)          |
| RPE        | 0.717            | 0.295*           | 1.255            |
|            | (0.454)          | (0.090)          | (0.755)          |
| RPESD      | 2.000**          | 0.486†           | 4.540*           |
|            | (0.863)          | (0.257)          | (1.443)          |
| INDUSTRY   | 2.851            | 0.959**          | 7.4678**         |
|            | (1.892)          | (0.437)          | (3.815)          |
| AGRICLTR   | 3.747†           | 1.080**          | 7.855**          |
|            | (1.940)          | (0.442)          | (3.815)          |
| URBAN      | 0.012            | 0.009*           | 0.018            |
|            | (0.010)          | (0.002)          | (0.018)          |
| TRADE      | 0.271            | −0.133**         | 0.177            |
|            | (0.316)          | (0.072)          | (0.526)          |
| DEFICIT    | 13.208*          | 1.024            | 17.213*          |
|            | (3.404)          | (0.665)          | (4.853)          |
| REALGDP    | 0.114            | −0.028†          | 0.155            |
|            | 0.070            | (0.016)          | (0.111)          |
| LATAMER    | 0.749†           | 0.130†           | 1.713†           |
|            | (0.415)          | (0.078)          | (0.836)          |
| SOC        | −0.267           | 0.004            | −0.924           |
|            | (0.414)          | (0.079)          | (0.826)          |
| $\bar{R}^2$ | 0.443           | 0.426            | 0.465            |
| $\sigma$   | 0.996            | 0.181            | 1.865            |
| N          | 90               | 76               | 88               |

*Statistically significant at the 0.01 level in a two-tailed test.
**Statistically significant at the 0.05 level in a two-tailed test.
†Statistically significant at the 0.10 level in a two-tailed test.
Standard errors in parentheses.

autocracy. Indeed, during the period of 1970 through 1980, demo-cratic governments had a better record in keeping inflation low than autocratic governments. The bivariate statistical evidence that a semidemocratic country is best equipped to fight inflation does not hold in a multivariate model. While there are inflation-generating elements in a democratic society, we need more evidence to support the claim that an autocracy is better than a democracy when it comes to reducing inflation.

Second, I found that political instability has a great impact on inflation. For the period of 1980–1992, regime instability in particular had devastating consequences for price stability. For the period of 1970 through 1980, it was major regular government change that affected inflation. Additionally, government stability as indexed by the changeability of government political capacity is more likely to increase inflation than the level of government political capacity.

Third, contrary to the findings of Arbetman and Kugler (1995), Al-Marhubi (1997), and Alcazar (1997), we found no evidence that a country with high relative-political-extraction rates has low inflation. If there is evidence that any relationship exists between inflation and political capacity, the relationship shows the opposite direction. For instance, higher relative political extraction resulted in higher infla-tion for the period of 1970–1980. Intuitively, this makes sense: The government will spend the resources it extracts. The higher the level of extraction, the higher the potential level of government spending, thus the higher the potential level of inflation. It is the level of vari-ance of government political capacity, however, that is the key vari-able explaining inflation in the government-capacity model. The major implication is that a government should maintain a stable policy course and avoid vacillation in policy execution.

The theoretical arguments, empirical evidence, and statistical analysis presented in this chapter show that no single political-institution model offers a complete political explanation for inflation. Aspects of all three models only partly affect price stability, given economic and other structural constraints.

# 7            Political Institutions and Private Investment

*One can make money under any policy situation as long as it does not change every fifteen minutes.*

Anonymous businessperson

As chapters 2 and 4 illustrate, economic growth and development depend upon a nation's capability to have its people invest in their economy. Investment has been found to be one of the most robust determinants for growth among all potential factors that may be conducive to economic development, with the fast-growing economies of the world almost invariably experiencing a high level of investment share of GDP.[1] The success story of economic growth in many countries is often attributed to one kind of investment in particular: a high level of domestic private fixed-capital formation in the form of equipment acquisition (De Long and Summers 1993). This relationship between political institutions and private fixed capital is the focus of this chapter, which extends the results in Feng 2001a by incorporating irregular government change, corruption, and international conflict into a model of private investment and foreign direct investment.

The intended contributions of this chapter are threefold. First, this chapter examines the three dimensions of political systems—political freedom, political stability, and political capacity—for their potential consequences on private investment. This chapter then compares these effects on both domestic private investment and foreign direct investment in order to facilitate our evaluation of a general framework for private investment. Finally, this chapter incorporates interstate conflict and cooperation, as well as economic openness and sanctions, into a domestic model, with a view toward investigating international connections with domestic and foreign direct investment.

Investment, particularly private investment, may be endogenous to a wide range of political and economic conditions, such as political- and financial-regime stability. In light of this book's central interest, I examine whether democracy and other major facets of political institutions have any significant effects on private investment. In this study, I focus on three political determinants that may affect property rights: political freedom, political stability, and government capacity. The major findings in this chapter may be summarized as follows: political freedom promotes private investment, particularly through the channel of improving human-capital formation. Political instability has a pernicious impact on private investment. Finally, government capacity adversely affects private investment through the *change* of its levels over time rather as a result of its level.

This chapter is organized into four sections. Section 7.1 reviews alternative analyses and implications of the relationships between democracy and investment, political stability and investment, and government capacity and investment. Section 7.2 specifies a multivariate statistical model to test various hypotheses. Section 7.3 presents multivariate findings on the relationships between political institutions and private investment. Section 7.4 investigates the effects of political institutions on foreign direct investment. The chapter ends with policy-relevant implications derived from the research presented in this chapter.

## 7.1 The Political Environment of Private Investment

Similar to the framework of the previous chapter, which explored the link between political institutions and inflation, this chapter examines the link between political institutions and private investment. The findings from this study will enhance our understanding of the role played by political institutions in economic development through private investment.

### Democracy and Investment

In light of the summary of the literature on democracy and growth in chapter 4, it is not surprising to find three similar general views on the relationship between democracy and investment. Corresponding to the three schools of thought on growth are three schools of thought on investment: the compatibility school, the conflict school, and the skeptics. Some scholars argue that an authoritarian system of strong political capacity is more likely to attract private investment than a democracy among developing countries (Gerschenkron 1962, O'Donnell 1978, O'Donnell and Schmitter 1986, Root 1996), yet others conclude that political freedom promotes private investment while autocracy forfeits it (Kormendi and Meguire 1985, Pastor and Hilt 1993, Pastor and Sung 1995, Helliwell 1994). Given the example of capital flight in Latin America in the late 1970s and the early 1980s, the former group would argue that an authoritarian government has the ability to establish effective controls on capital and the ability to retain it domestically. A democracy, without autocratic power, lacks the capacity to prevent capital from exiting the country. In contrast, the latter group maintains that government repression and lack of freedom are initial causes of capital flight.

Two major premises are typically utilized in the argument that democracy reduces incentives for private investment. First, democracy is thought to release needs for immediate consumption, reducing the pool of resources from which investments are made (Huntington and Dominguez 1975). Second, democracy gives the median voter opportunity to redistribute income toward the poor, reducing incentives to save and invest. After studying the flaws of populism, some economists have voiced the concern that there might be incentives in a democracy to expropriate capital, particularly if the median voter is poorer or has less capital than the average person, and/or the poor have extensive political rights (Dornbusch and Edwards 1991, Persson and Tabellini 1990, Alesina and Rodrik 1994).[2]

My objection to this view is based on the political nature of democracy. A democratic political system requires broad-based support and consensus to make the political process efficient and systematically secure. As argued in the preceding chapter, an autocracy may have the appearance of government stability but generally lacks the fundamental social basis for regime stability. While policy adjustment under a democratic government may help reduce long-term radical political change, an autocratic government has a potential for regime change. Between the two, investors prefer the democratic process, which often institutionalizes the redistribution system, to the political uncertainty, characterized by irregular government change, inherent in an autocratic system. Furthermore, findings in chapter 9 show that democracy is conducive to a reduction in income inequality. A strong middle class, combined with the institutionalization of the redistribution system, is likely in a democracy to reduce the circumstances by which the poor can expropriate wealth.

Numerous studies have shown a link between democracy, investment, and economic growth. Helliwell (1994), following an empirical test, maintains that democracy may have a positive effect on growth through the channel of investment. That is, democracy increases investment, which in turn spurs economic growth. Pastor and Hilt (1993) and Pastor and Sung (1995) test the relationship between democracy and private investment using pooled time-series data on Latin American and other developing countries and find that democracy does have a positive impact on private investment (Pastor and Hilt 1993, Pastor and Sung 1995). These empirical results seem to enhance Kormendi and Meguire's (1985) early finding that civil liberty has a positive impact on the share of investment in GDP in an aggregate sample of 47 countries during the postwar period of 1950–1977.

Three findings in this last study are interrelated and reveal an interesting pattern. First, the impact of civil liberty on growth is positive but relatively modest. Second, investment has a strong positive effect on growth. Third, the effect of civil liberty on the share of investment in GDP is positive and very pronounced. In fact, civil liberty is so overwhelming that it alone explains 45% of the variance in investment ratios, and its inclusion virtually eliminates the effects of all other variables (namely, initial income per capita, mean population growth, standard deviation of money supplies, standard deviation of real output growth, and mean growth rate of inflation), even though they are mostly statistically significant in the growth equation. It can be inferred from these results that civil liberty promotes growth mainly through the investment channel (Kormendi and Meguire 1985, 155–156). These findings suggest that democracy makes investment work, thus promoting growth, although the direct effect of democracy on growth may be minimal. A democratic system induces and enhances investment primarily through the protection of property rights, thus demonstrating the fundamental link between political institutions and private investment. Potential investors are not able to calculate the expected returns from their investments if they are uncertain of the extent of their capital ownership and are insecure in their capital gains. By securing rights for venture capitalists and technological innovators, democracy arguably makes one of the most important contributions to fostering economic growth.

A third view holds that investment is not related to political institutions but is affected by domestic coalitions among such interest groups as bankers, government bureaucracies, and labor. A notable phenomenon of decreased domestic investment is capital flight, as demonstrated by Latin American countries. The major economic reasons for capital flight include inflation and the failure to adjust a nation's exchange rate. Without such adjustment, a holder of an overvalued currency will have the incentive to exchange for a foreign currency and invest in a foreign country. Taxation is suggested as another factor, with higher taxes leading to lower appropriation of returns (as the model in chapter 2 implies), resulting in a decreased incentive to save and invest.

Maxfield (1990) argues that the institutional and organizational strength of banks results in particular economic-policy patterns and affects the integration of the financial market. When the links of private bankers to industry are close and independent monetary authorities govern the relationship between bankers and the state, bankers often form strong alliances, likely leading to free capital mobility and a probable shortage of domestic industrial capital (Maxfield 1990, 27). On the basis of a comparison of Argentina, Brazil, and Mexico, Maxfield rejects the view that political-regime type has a fundamental impact on capital flight. Both Argentina and Brazil were intermittently ruled by autocratic regimes during a period when capital flight from Latin America was phenomenal. However, the two countries adopted different economic policies: Argentina followed orthodox policies and had a high level of capital outflow, while Brazil used heterodox policies and enjoyed a low level of capital flight. In terms of the crises caused by the exit of capital, Argentina bears a closer resemblance to Mexico, which was less authoritarian. Although this case comparison led Maxfield to discount the effect of political regimes on investment, she cautions that we should not dismiss the political-regime explanation without further research (Maxfield 1990, 187–188). The connection between democracy and capital flight should be examined in the presence of political instability and polarization. Without controlling for these and other factors (including economic endowments), conclusions based upon isolated observations involving democracy and capital flight are merely conditional and preliminary.

Crystal (1994) expands Maxfield's coalition thesis by emphasizing the strength of labor and the government's ideological commitment to fighting inflation. He argues that the type of regime most capable of increasing and keeping investment in the home country is one that is "ideologically and politically capable of accepting the inflationary consequences of devaluation (including the erosion of real wages) and a trade policy that stressed export promotion" (Crystal 1994, 146). The issue then becomes a question of what kind of political system is most efficient in fighting inflation and promoting exports. The preceding chapter has found that under inflation caused by external shocks, a democratic government is more capable of curbing inflation.

Another way of looking at the relationship between regime and investment is from the perspective of income distribution. As summarized in the last chapter, Kurth's (1982) main theoretical thrust is that a strong middle class will tend to ally itself with industry and agriculture to support price stabilization and reduced inflation, in turn lessening the uncertainty encompassing the market and thus promoting private investment. The middle class can best achieve a deflationary policy in a democratic system, where "extreme" groups are excluded from the ultimate decision-making process by the rule of law.

As the model in chapter 2 implies, a strong middle class in a democratic society reduces policy polarization, making it easier to build policy consensus on the basis of powerful middle-income groups. This reduction of polarization renders government change relatively less important. Political momentum, when characterized by a strong middle class functioning in a democratic society, is able to reduce income inequality. According to a study by Alesina and Perotti (1996), this reduction mitigates social-political instability and consequently is conducive to investment. Democracy can thus reduce overall macropolitical uncertainty. This argument is consistent with the finding in chapter 5 that democracy is instrumental to reducing political instability while increasing the capacity of the political system for policy adjustment. A strong democracy tends to be built on the bedrock of a strong middle class whose values are consistent with private capital accumulation.

## Political Instability and Investment

Political stability is another important factor for private investment. It is generally accepted that a stable investment environment fosters private investment, but that a democratic political system is likely to provide sufficient stability and that its ability to induce greater private investment in a developing country have yet to be demonstrated empirically. According to Gastil, Malaysia and Zambia are listed as partly free. They are both ruled by a dominant party; both have had almost the same degree of political rights and civil liberties. The lack of democracy in Malaysia, however, could be cited as a benefit to its economic growth. The nation's political stability has been assured by the United Malays National Organization (UMNO), led with indisputable and uncontested authority by Prime Minister Mahathir, who is able to exploit the UMNO's absolute political majority to implement his economic policy. In contrast, the one-party dominance in Zambia has not been able to provide a healthy environment for private investment and economic growth. The Zambian economy continued to deteriorate during the time of this study. The average level of private investment as a percentage of GDP during the 1978–1988 period was only 2.4% in Zambia, compared with 15.7% in Malaysia (Pfeffermann and Madarassy 1991). In this example, the same degree of political freedom and government capacity is associated with two different outcomes in economic growth and private investment. This paradox leads us to another major policy variable in our framework of analysis: political instability. From the 1960s through the early 1980s, the probability of irregular government change in Zambia was twice as high as that in Malaysia, and the probability of minor regular government change in Malaysia was three times as high as that in Zambia. A study of the relationship between democracy and investment or between governing capacity and investment should be controlled for political instability.

Economic growth is sustained through saving and investment. When a political regime is unstable, consumers decrease savings and increase consumption, as savings may become worthless. Additionally, political upheavals often displace people or deprive them of jobs, making saving money unrealistic. Similarly, investors will decrease investment in fixed-capital stocks, such as factories or land, preferring to keep their properties and portfolios in forms that stand a better chance of retaining value, such as foreign currencies or gold. In times of political uncertainty, both the supply of investment capital by savers and the demand of capital by business will decrease. In addition, political instability makes job opportunities less attractive and less available, thus diminishing the potential pool of savings. Furthermore, it wreaks havoc with the efficient allocation of resources and the formation of fixed capital necessary for economic development. An impending political crisis will cause investors to put decisions to send their money into the market on hold and will compel consumers to spend.

Governmental change often meant a reversal of property rights. Under conditions of political instability, short-term investments with quick returns that could easily be exported were preferred to long-term commitments that could be held hostage when governments changed. If the underlying cause of instability—the absence of broad coalitional support for government—is not addressed, structural adjustment does little to alter the calculations of investors. (Root 1996, 152)

In this citation, the phrase "governmental change" apparently refers to irregular government change, extraconstitutional government change, or political-regime change, rather than regular government change under the constitution. Though regular government change, particularly major regular government change, may produce political uncertainty, it more or less represents policy adjustment. Any strong negative effect on economic activities by such political change (as was found in the last two chapters) is very unlikely, as regular government change seldom leads to a change in the ownership status of property. Root's (1996) argument provides a general sense of how political stability and investment are premised on security and protection of property rights. Nonetheless, his argument does not distinguish between irregular and regular government change, thus making its theoretical application to his cases (Singapore, Malaysia, and other East Asian countries) questionable. Irregular government change will cost investors dearly, while the negative consequence of regular government change should not be very serious. Hypothetically, regular government change in Singapore or Malaysia need not produce the degree of reduction in investment implied in the quotation. The impact of government change on investment in these countries should be very different from a case of irregular government change, as exemplified by the capital flight from China before and during the 1950s, when private enterprises in China were nationalized following the communist takeover with little compensation for their owners. In the face of impending political change, a rational investor will do his or her best to turn a threatened investment into an asset that has a better chance of retaining its value.

Political violence—such as riots, strikes, revolutions, and assassinations—also has an effect upon investment. Venieris and Sperling (1994) find that social-political instability (SPI) negatively affects savings in less-developed countries but has a positive effect in developed countries. This phenomenon is explained by the difference in the level of economic development. In the early phase of development, consumption-risk aversion is said to be low, with political instability increasing the propensity to consume. In later phases of development, consumption-risk aversion is considered high; an increase in political instability will decrease consumption but increase savings (Venieris and Sperling 1994, 235). This empirical result may reflect the fact that developed countries are all democracies, where irregular government change, as defined in chapter 3, occurs infrequently. Instead, these nations have regular government change, which serves to readjust and reorient government policy toward making the economy work.

By comparison, minor regular government change, where the ruling party remains in power, signals policy continuity and political consistency to investors and consumers. In a country where the same party rules, the tendency to save and invest will be high, keeping the political system and government capacity constant. Singapore and colonial Hong Kong are perhaps classical cases of this type of government. In the former, the leadership of People's Action Party carried out a consistent government campaign for national savings and investment since the nation's 1965 inception. In the latter, despite frequent change in the head of government and regardless of individual leadership, official policy regarding market operations in Hong Kong remained the same—making Hong Kong the true home of Adam Smith's ideals. The economy in this former British colony benefited from the policy consensus among British political parties on the issue of Hong Kong. Indeed, this benefit derived as much from the consistency of the policy as its content. In countries where regimes often change, investment tends toward the liquid and speculative, leaving these countries stuck with low-investment and low-productivity industries, rather than capital-intensive and knowledge-intensive enterprises requiring investment in real assets and technology that provide the foundation of advanced economies (Zak 2000).

An increase in the prospect of political regime change will directly and adversely affect private investment. Because of entry and exit costs—and because investment decisions are largely irreversible (Dixit 1989, Rodrik 1991, Pindyck 1993)—an uncertain environment leads investors to opt to wait for new information. The value of this option is very sensitive to the degree of uncertainty regarding returns on investment. Therefore, the level of prevailing uncertainty affects aggregate investment. Servén and Solimano (1993) have discussed the impact of different forms of uncertainty upon private investment, which include uncertainties in the demand schedule, future real exchange rates, and interest rates. However, of all the types of uncertainty influencing investment decisions, political-regime instability is the ultimate consideration. The other economic uncertainties pale beside the prospect of an ousted political regime. In addition, political uncertainty emanating from variation of government political capacity has an effect on government credibility, as mentioned by Servén and Solimano:

From a policy perspective the credibility of policy reform is an important source of uncertainty. Unless investors view the adjustment program as internally consistent and are convinced the government will carry it out despite the implied social costs, the possibilities of reversal will become a key determinant of the investment response. *Governments can reverse adjustment policies, but investors cannot undo decisions about fixed capital.* (Servén and Solimano 1993, 23)

In order to assure investors, the government must keep its political capacity consistent with the desired policy and maintain stability. As one businessman notes, "One can make money under any policy situation as long as it does not change every fifteen minutes" (Rodrik 1991). This is why bankers may prefer inflation to political instability. Under an inflationary government policy, investors can still make rational decisions about their investments, but they may not want to make any investments at all under conditions of political instability. While the above quotation may be an avid entrepreneur's overstatement, it is generally true that investors will be deterred from making long-term investments if the political capacity of the government, the level of political freedom, and the level of civil liberties in the country frequently change. As previously stated, investors are typically faced with certain start-up costs to initiate an investment, and these costs make investors especially sensitive to policy changes.

Empirically, Alesina and Perotti (1996) found that sociopolitical instability reduced investment in a sample of 71 countries. Their result is consistent with the findings not only of Barro (1991), but also of Alesina, Özler, Roubini, and Swagel (1996), and of Chen and Feng (1996), who find that political and social instability leads to a decrease in the investment share of GDP.

## Government Capacity and Investment

As implied by the preceding chapter on political institutions and inflation, scholars who argue that a strong government is more capable of reducing inflation than a weak government should in this context also argue that the same strong government is able to raise national savings and investment. One important assumption of this argument is that the strong government in question should be *growth-oriented*. Some literature has identified East Asian governments as such strong, growth-enhancing governments (Wade 1990, Root 1996, Campos and Root 1996).

A central interest in this chapter is the variability of government strength or capacity. As a measure of the uncertainty of the policy environment, government capacity is consistent with the measures of policy volatility,[3] which include the standard deviation of inflation (Grier and Tullock 1989); variances involving GDP, government consumption, money growth, domestic credit growth, and government deficits (Aizanman and Marion 1993); and the standard deviations of black-market premiums on foreign exchange and real exchange-rate distortion (Brunetti and Weder 1998). Unlike those studies that focus on the volatility of monetary or fiscal policy, this chapter investigates the changeability of government capacity as an index of the uncertainty of the policy environment. The fluctuation of government's strength over time instills uncertainty into the policy environment, as the populace is uncertain whether the government can or will realize its policy goal as originally formulated.

To assure investors, the government must keep its political capacity consistent with the desired policy, thus maintaining its policy stability. An interesting but seldom studied issue is the effect of variability of government capacity on private investment. The fluctuation of such capacity indicates that the government lacks consistency in its power to get a job done. Uncertainty about government effectiveness can be more adverse than the policy itself in deterring investors from committing their assets. Given a bad policy that is certain to be executed, the investor can still find ways to make money. But if the government lacks consistency in its policy execution, investors will delay investment until it becomes clear that the government is consistent in executing its policy.

### International Constraints: Economic Integration and Interstate Conflict

Just as domestic political institutions can affect investment, so can international factors. To a large extent, the domestic environment for investment is often constrained by international security and economic relationships between countries. The degree of openness to, or integration in, the world market may increase private investment. As a country specializes and exports, developmental gains from trade can contribute to high levels of growth. Export expansion, because of foreign competition, raises factor productivity and leads to growth through the efficient use of resources and the adoption of technological innovations. The economy expands as the result of integration into large international markets, giving rise to greater capacity utilization and gains of economy-of-scale effects. All this may lead an investor to increase his stake, as expected returns are higher in an open economy than in an autarky.

In contrast, international economic sanctions tend to reduce the openness of an economy, thus decreasing private investment in the target country for at least two reasons. First, economic sanctions are often politically motivated (as in the case of economic sanctions against Cuba and Iraq), increasing the political risks of doing business with the target country and reducing foreign direct investment. Second, the gains from an open economy are reduced because of economic isolation resulting from sanctions. As economic returns are reduced, domestic and foreign investors will refrain from making large investments in the sanctioned economy.

Interstate conflicts, such as militarized disputes and war, may also affect investment and economic growth. Over the years, scholarly studies have found that international conflict has a negative effect on international trade and foreign investment.[4] While it is likely that interstate conflict will curtail international economic transactions, such as foreign investment, its effects on domestic economic activities, such as domestic private investment, can be ambiguous. Though it can be argued that international conflict has a negative impact on domestic economies—as it often entails physical destruction and always engenders uncertainty, both of which lead to a decrease in investment—it can also be argued that international conflict (particularly militarized disputes) generates an intense need to utilize domestic productive factors with great flexibility (Kugler and Arbetman 1997). Some suggest that wars destroy distributional interest groups, improving the efficiency of the economy (e.g., Olson 1982). Finally, public spending on research and development in times of interstate conflict have a spill-over effect on the economy; the creation and diffusion of new technologies promoted by the government to enhance national security may eventually lead to economic expansion, particularly in the long run.

This chapter will include international economic and security relationships in a model of domestic private investment and foreign direct investment in an effort to study the determinants of investment. International cooperation fosters a spirit of commerce, improving conditions for foreign direct investment and creating a healthy general environment for domestic economic activities centering on private investment. International conflict impedes economic transactions, and thus reduces interstate commerce, though its effects on domestic investment can be ambiguous.

## 7.2   Specification and Data

This and the next sections use a statistical model to test the influence of democracy and macropolitical uncertainty on investment. The statistical testing will start from the basic model presented in Feng and Chen 1997:

$$\text{PRIVATE} = \alpha + \beta X + \gamma Y + \varepsilon$$

Here PRIVATE is private investment, $X$ is a set of political variables, including measures for political freedom, political stability, and government capacity; $Y$ is a set of relevant economic variables, and $\varepsilon$ is the error term. All data are averages for the period of 1978–1988, unless otherwise noted. The choice of countries and years included in the sample was determined by the availability of data on private investment. This aggregate analytical design is similar to the one used by Alesina and Perotti (1996), who conducted a cross-country analysis of average investment shares in GDP in 71 countries over the period of 1960–1985. The regression equations in this chapter may be considered an extension of their investment equation, which includes four variables on the right-hand side of the equation: a sociopolitical instability indicator, primary-education enrollment rates, inflation, and the magnitude of deviation of inflation levels from the sample mean. A similar model was constructed by Aizenman and Marion (1993), who estimate average private investment during the period of 1970–1985 by the initial level of real GDP per capita, initial primary-school enrollment rates, growth rates of real GDP per capita for the period of 1965–1970, and one variable each from a set of macroeconomic uncertainty indicators, such as public-investment share and government consumption.

### The Dependent Variable

The private investment data compiled by Pfeffermann and Madarassy (1991) are available for 40 countries when used along with the political variables, for 42 countries when used with other economic variables, and for 40 countries when used with both the political and economic data. All of these countries are less developed countries (LDCs), except Turkey and Portugal, which are in the OECD.[5] The dependent variable is private investment as a percentage of GDP (PRIVATE). Utilization of the data compiled by Pfeffermann and Madarassy (1991) has two advantages. Initially, the measure of private investment in the data set excludes financial investment and changes in inventories, focusing instead on fixed capital formation, such as investment in factories or equipment, which is essential for economic growth. Additionally, like several empirical studies (e.g., Pastor and Hilt 1993, Pastor and Sung 1995, and Feng 2001a) that adopt Pfeffermann and Madarassy's measure of private investment and utilize their operationalization, the model in this chapter estimates the same phenomenon studied in these other works.

### The Policy Variables

As noted above, Kormendi and Meguire (1985), Pastor and Hilt (1993), and Pastor and Sung (1995) identify a positive effect of democracy on private investment. A separate study in this book found that political freedom is positively related to economic freedom, thus increasing private investment. While chapter 10 will tackle the relationship between political freedom and economic freedom, it suffices here to say that evidence exists suggesting that a higher degree of political freedom leads to a higher degree of economic freedom, so political freedom should have a positive impact on private investment.

Since the model in chapter 2 tries to capture broad political freedom as a gauge of the business environment, FREE, a combination of indices of civil liberties and political rights (Gastil and Freedom House 1978–1988), is used here as an index for the degree of freedom. The indicator in our study is standardized to range from zero to one (with one representing the highest level of political freedom and civil liberties),[6] averaged from 1978 to 1988 for each country in the data set. Generally, I expect to see a positive sign on this variable.

The political-instability variable is operationalized as the probability of irregular government change (PROBIRCH). Compared to regular government change, irregular government change implies fundamental alteration of the political environment for investment. Thus a higher probability of irregular government change should cause the levels of private investment to decline.

Policy-environment uncertainty is operationalized as the degree of change in relative political extraction (RPE) and political freedom and as the number of deaths related to political events, adjusted by the population in a country. I take the standard deviations of the level of relative political extraction, the operationalization of which was detailed in chapter 5, and of the level of political freedom for a country over the 11 years in the data. Larger standard deviations indicate a larger degree of policy-environment uncertainty. I expect the signs on the parameter estimates of these two standard-deviation variables (RPESD and FREESD) to be negative.

Deaths will ensue in intensely contested political events, and thus DEATH captures the degree of political polarization. It is a better indicator of the severity of political turbulence than revolutions, coups d'état, strikes or riots themselves, because it differentiates the degree of violence both across different types of political violence (revolutions versus riots) and within the same type of political violence (a riot that lasts three days versus one that lasts three months). I expect that political deaths (DEATH) have a negative effect on private investment.

*Economic Control Variables*

Expected growth, inflation, the variability of inflation, primary-school enrollments, public investment, and the type of the economy are among the economic variables used. Expected growth is measured by the average growth rate of real GDP per capita over 1968–78 (EXPGRO), the 10 years prior to the period 1978–88 under study. Its sign is expected to be positive. Investors have a penchant to invest when they anticipate sustained economic growth based upon their assessment of past economic performance. In other words, the better the record of growth in the past, the more likely investors will invest in the future.

As stated in chapter 4, inflation may have ambiguous effects on investment, according to assumptions. The standard deviation of inflation is a measurement of the variability of inflation and is generally regarded as having a negative effect on investment. In this chapter, I expect the sign on both inflation (INF) and the standard deviation of inflation (INFSD) to be negative.

The primary-school enrollment rate in 1960 ($PRIM_{60}$) is used to measure the initial quality of the labor force, that is, the initial condition of human capital investment. In the context of investment, private investment will increase if investors anticipate a relatively high rate of return, and well-educated labor force is one of the conditions that can increase capital returns. High-quality labor can put capital to better use, thus earning better returns on the investment. I expect the sign on $PRIM_{60}$ to be positive.

Next, real GDP per capita in 1960 ($GDP_{60}$) is used to control for the initial level of the economy. On the one hand, the initial condition of the economy is found to be negatively associated with the rate of economic growth, possibly because of diminishing marginal returns; on the other hand, a higher initial level of GDP indicates a higher level of economic development and, concomitantly, a more sophisticated market system, which is conducive to investment. Therefore, the sign on $GDP_{60}$ tends to be ambiguous.

Public investment (PUBINV) is viewed either as crowding out private investment or as enhancing the expectations of private investors by providing infrastructure and a more buoyant aggregate market.[7] Governments may provide public goods (such as highway systems or communications networks) that increase the marginal product of private investment or may waste funds and divert resources to projects that do not encourage private investment. Therefore, public spending may increase or decrease private investment. Finally, a dummy variable (soc) is included to control for socialist economies; this variable takes a value of one for a socialist economy, zero otherwise.

Government corruption is included to measure the extent of economic freedom. Widespread corruption results in inefficient controls on the economy and encourages the operation of a black market. Foreign lenders and investors in particular may find it difficult to conduct business in countries where there is rampant financial corruption in the form of "demands for special payments and bribes connected with import and export licenses, exchange controls, tax assessments, police protection or loans" (International Reports, 1990, 10). Numerous studies have found that corruption reduces economic growth rates (Mauro 1995, Knack and Keefer 1995), which is consistent with the finding that corruption has a negative impact on foreign direct investment (Wei 1997a, 1997b). In this research I adopt the measure of corruption in the International Country Risk Guide (ICRG) data and expect that corruption (CORRUPT) has a negative effect on private investment.

### International Environment

For variables that reflect a country's general relations with the rest of the world, I utilize the World Events Interaction Survey (WEIS) data set, which has 22 categories subdivided into 61 event types covering 1966 to the present.[8] As in Gasiorowski (1986), an aggregate measure is taken of a country's conflictual or cooperative behavior. Four indicators are developed: the number of conflictual acts initiated by the country toward the rest of the world (v1con), the number of conflictual acts suffered by the country and initiated by the rest of the world (v2con), the number of cooperative acts initiated by the country toward the rest of the world (v1coop), and finally, the number of cooperative acts enjoyed by the country and initiated by the rest of the world (v2coop). It is expected that while international conflict may have an ambiguous effect on domestic private investment, interstate cooperation increases private investment, as a peaceful, cooperative international environment is consistent with, if not conducive to, domestic economic pursuit.

I also utilize the data set of economic sanctions by Hufbauer et al. (1990). The average number of years of economic sanctions against a country in the sample are adopted as an indicator of one kind of international adversity: economic isolation. Finally, the degree of economic openness is utilized as a measure of a country's integration with the world market (the percentage of exports and imports in the gross domestic product has been frequently employed as an indicator of economic openness). As indicators of globalization, international trade and investment often go together (Feng 2000d).[9] For the reasons discussed above, I expect to find a negative effect of economic sanctions (SANCTION) on private investment and a positive effect of economic openness (TRADE) on private investment. All of these variables are summarized in table 7.1.

### 7.3 Empirical Evidence: Domestic Private Investment

This section contains a multiple-step test of the link between political institutions and domestic private investment. Table 7.2 shows the regression results focusing on economic variables. Because heteroskedasticity could be important across countries, the standard errors for the coefficients are based on White's (1980) heteroskedasticity-consistent covariance matrix.

The expected growth rate and education are found to have positive and statistically very significant effects on domestic private investment. A higher expected rate of growth for the economy will induce investors to increase their investment. The initial level of education is consistent with human-capital accumulation, which improves the marginal product of physical capital and therefore leads to an increase in fixed-capital formation. Meanwhile, the size of the economy does not seem to affect the level of investment.

The standard deviation of inflation is found to have a negative influence on private investment, and its parameter estimate is statistically significant at the 5% level. Inflation appears to have a positive effect on private investment, consistent with the Tobin-Mundell hypothesis, though it is statistically insignificant. Theoretically, public investment may substitute for or complement private investment; empirically, it has a negative effect on private investment in our sample of 40 developing countries during the period of 1978 to 1988, though statistically such an effect is only marginal. The dummy variable for socialist economies is not statistically significant.

Table 7.3 presents parameter estimates for both political and economic variables. The combination of the two sets of variables considerably improves the estimates shown in table 7.2 and noticeably

**Table 7.1**
Definitions of variables in tables 7.2–7.5

| Variable | Definition | Source |
|---|---|---|
| PRIVATE | Average private domestic investment as % of GDP | Pfeffermann and Madarassy 1991 |
| FDI | Foreign direct investment stock | World Game Institute 1997 |
| EXPGRO | Expected growth rate of real GDP per capita | Summers and Heston 2000 |
| PRIM$_{60}$ | Primary school enrollment rates, 1960 | Barro and Wolf 1989 |
| INF | Inflation rates | Summers and Heston 2000 |
| INFSD | Standard deviation of inflation rates | Summers and Heston 2000 |
| PUBINV | Public investment as a percentage of GDP | Pfeffermann and Madarassy 1991 |
| SOC | Socialist economy, dummy variable | Barro and Wolf 1989 |
| CORRUPT | Government corruption | International reports |
| RPE | Relative political extraction of the government | Arbetman and Kugler 1995 |
| RPESD | Standard deviation of relative political extraction | Arbetman and Kugler 1995 |
| FREE | Political freedom | Gastil, various years |
| FREESD | Standard deviation political freedom | Gastil, various years |
| PROBIRCH | Probability of irregular government change | Banks 1995 |
| DEATH | Deaths in politically related events | Taylor 1985 |
| v1CON | Conflicts initiated by the country | Goldstein 1992 |
| v1COOP | Cooperation initiated by the country | Goldstein 1992 |
| v2CON | Conflicts is subject to the country | Goldstein 1992 |
| v2COOP | Cooperation received by the country | Goldstein 1992 |
| TRADE | Exports and imports as % of GDP | World Bank 1992 |
| SANCTION | Number/year of economic sanctions received | Hufbauer et al. 1990 |
| GDP | Real GDP per capita | Summers and Heston 2000 |
| POP | Population | Summers and Heston 2000 |
| LATAMER | Latin America, a dummy variable | |

**Table 7.2**
Economic model of private domestic investment

|                | (1)      | (2)      | (3)      | (4)      |
| -------------- | -------- | -------- | -------- | -------- |
| INTERCEPT      | 0.066*   | 0.064*   | 0.052*   | 0.041*   |
|                | (0.023)  | (0.021)  | (0.016)  | (0.014)  |
| EXPGRO         | 1.175*   | 1.149*   | 1.192*   | 1.146*   |
|                | (0.026)  | (0.259)  | (0.259)  | (0.288)  |
| $GDP_{60}$     | −0.003   | —        | —        | —        |
|                | (0.004)  |          |          |          |
| $PRIM_{60}$    | 0.079*   | 0.070*   | 0.067*   | 0.075*   |
|                | (0.022)  | (0.021)  | (0.021)  | (0.023)  |
| INF            | 0.230†   | 0.211    | 0.269    | —        |
|                | (0.192)  | (0.206)  | (0.207)  |          |
| INFSD          | −0.203** | −0.203** | −0.201** | 0.188**  |
|                | (0.110)  | (0.104)  | (0.102)  | (0.101)  |
| PUBINV         | −0.225†  | −0.163   | —        | —        |
|                | (0.166)  | (0.155)  |          |          |
| SOC            | 0.012    | —        | —        | —        |
|                | (0.070)  |          |          |          |
| $\sigma$       | 0.029    | 0.028    | 0.028    | 0.029    |
| $\bar{R}^2$    | 0.659    | 0.672    | 0.668    | 0.661    |

*, **, and † indicate that the estimated value is significantly different from zero in a one-tailed test at the 2.5%, 5%, and 10% error levels, respectively.
Standard errors in parentheses.

betters the fit. As expected, the probability of irregular government change and the standard deviation of government capacity both have a significant negative effect on domestic private investment. The standard deviation of political freedom affects private investment adversely, but it becomes statistically significant at the 10% level only when the probability-of-irregular-government-change variable is excluded from the equation. Political and policy uncertainty does appear to reduce fixed-capital formation. In addition, the number of political deaths, an indicator of the intensity of political violence and the degree of political polarization in the country, has a negative relationship with private investment, and its statistical significance is high across all equations in table 7.3.

When FREE and $PRIM_{60}$ are both used as regressors, the effect of FREE on investment is canceled. When the education variable is excluded, political freedom has a very significant positive effect on domestic private investment (see columns (8) and (9)). This result implies that in this particular sample, political freedom probably

**Table 7.3**
Politicoeconomic model of private domestic investment

|              | (5)       | (6)       | (7)       | (8)       | (9)       |
|--------------|-----------|-----------|-----------|-----------|-----------|
| INTERCEPT    | 0.090*    | 0.082*    | 0.075*    | 0.094*    | 0.105**   |
|              | (0.018)   | (0.017)   | (0.011)   | (0.025)   | (0.011)   |
| EXPGRO       | 1.296*    | 1.370*    | 1.275*    | 1.613*    | 1.534*    |
|              | (0.137)   | (0.151)   | (0.167)   | (0.183)   | (0.194)   |
| PRIM60       | 0.068*    | 0.059*    | 0.070*    | —         | —         |
|              | (0.013)   | (0.010)   | (0.012)   |           | —         |
| INFSD        | 0.084†    | —         | —         | —         | —         |
|              | (0.059)   |           |           |           |           |
| RPE          | −0.018    | −0.015    | —         | −0.007    | —         |
|              | (0.017)   | (0.014)   | —         | (0.018)   | —         |
| RPESD        | −0.206*   | −0.138*   | −0.167*   | −0.138*   | −0.179*   |
|              | (0.032)   | (0.043)   | (0.031)   | (0.033)   | (0.046)   |
| FREE         | −0.0004   | —         | —         | 0.043*    | 0.038*    |
|              | (0.014)   |           |           | (0.014)   | (0.014)   |
| FREESD       | −0.037    | −0.074†   | —         | 0.009     | —         |
|              | (0.055)   | (0.053)   |           | (0.066)   |           |
| PROBIRCH     | −0.203*   | —         | −0.167*   | −0.211*   | −0.188*   |
|              | (0.068)   |           | (0.062)   | (0.086)   | (0.081)   |
| DEATH        | −0.0007*  | −0.0008*  | −0.0007*  | −0.008*   | −0.007*   |
|              | (0.0001)  | (0.0001)  | (0.0001)  | 0.0002    | (0.0001)  |
| CORRUPT      | −0.002    | —         | −0.003    | —         | −0.014    |
|              | (0.013)   |           | (0.016)   |           | (0.019)   |
| $\sigma$     | 0.020     | 0.022     | 0.020     | 0.024     | 0.025     |
| $\bar{R}^2$  | 0.827     | 0.807     | 0.824     | 0.768     | 0.730     |

*, **, and † indicate that the estimated value is significantly different from zero in a
one-tailed test at the 2.5%, 5% and 10% error levels, respectively.
Standard errors in parentheses.

induces private investment through the channel of education.[10] Helliwell (1994) speculates that democracy may promote growth by bettering educational outcomes, and here we have some consistent evidence that democracy may contribute to private investment by enhancing education.

Government capacity has a negative sign, though it is not statistically significant. Whether a strong government is able to promote private investment is inconclusive from the data. On the one hand, a capable centralized government may be better positioned to implement its desired policy. On the other, a decentralized government may favor a market economy; the level of private investment depends on market incentives rather than government directives.

Among the economic control variables, expected growth of the economy and the initial level of education remain robust. Their positive effects on private investment hold even in the presence of political variables, which tend to have profound influence on private investment. In contrast, the effect of the standard deviation of inflation becomes weakened when included with the political variables. This effect is canceled when the impacts of political uncertainty are controlled with the probability of political regime change, the standard deviation of government capacity, political freedom, and politically related deaths, which indicates that political stability, political freedom, and variability of government capacity may be better indicators for the level of private investment than some of the variables accounting for macroeconomic uncertainty. The level of change in government capacity may have dominated the effect of change in inflation on investment, as the latter is very often the result of macropolitical uncertainty. Compared with macroeconomic uncertainty, macropolitical uncertainty—as indicated, for instance, by the standard deviation of relative political extraction—exerts a fundamental effect on private investment.

The regressions in table 7.4 incorporate international determinants of private domestic investment into the previous model. As conflict initiated and received and cooperation initiated and received are both highly correlated (with correlation coefficients above 0.90), they are entered separately into regression equations to avoid the multicollinearity problem. International cooperation is found to have a positive relationship with domestic investment. The more cooperative the home country is toward other countries (v1coop) and the more cooperative other countries are toward the home country (v2coop), the larger the private domestic fixed-capital formation as a percentage of GDP. A peaceful and harmonious international environment fosters and facilitates domestic market operation. In contrast, interstate conflict is also positively related with domestic private investment, though it is only marginally significant. It should be noted that it is the conflictive behavior of the home country toward the rest of the world, rather than the conflictive behavior toward the home country, that has this positive effect. For the reason discussed in the theoretical argument, belligerent states have to stimulate their economies to improve their position in conflict. In addition, foreign investment in the home country should decrease when there is interstate bellicosity, which further raises the need

**Table 7.4**
Politicoeconomic model of private domestic investment controlled by international environment

|  | (10) | (11) | (12) | (13) |
|---|---|---|---|---|
| INTERCEPT | 0.062* | 0.065* | 0.039* | 0.054* |
|  | (0.016) | (0.014) | (0.056) | (0.017) |
| EXPGRO | 1.133* | 1.301* | 1.129* | 1.310* |
|  | (0.474) | (0.161) | (0.134) | (0.152) |
| PRIM60 | 0.073* | 0.060* | 0.074* | 0.062* |
|  | (0.014) | (0.014) | (0.012) | (0.014) |
| RPESD | −0.190* | −0.161* | −0.151* | −0.142* |
|  | (0.034) | (0.032) | (0.034) | (0.035) |
| PROBIRCH | −0.117† | −0.141** | −0.084 | −0.122** |
|  | (0.074) | (0.074) | (0.076) | (0.075) |
| DEATH | −0.001* | −0.001* | −0.0008* | −0.0009* |
|  | (0.0001) | (0.0001) | (0.0001) | (0.00009) |
| v1CON | 0.00009† | — | — | — |
|  | (0.00006) |  |  |  |
| v2CON | — | 0.00003 | — | — |
|  |  | (0.00007) |  |  |
| v1COOP | — | — | 0.0004* | — |
|  |  |  | (0.00015) |  |
| v2COOP | — | — | — | 0.0002** |
|  |  |  |  | (0.0001) |
| TRADE | 0.016* | 0.011† | 0.019* | 0.013** |
|  | (0.007) | (0.008) | (0.006) | (0.007) |
| SANCTION | −0.006 | −0.001 | −0.023† | −0.011 |
|  | (0.016) | (0.017) | (0.016) | (0.017) |
| CORRUPT | −0.005 | — | −0.0002 | — |
|  | (0.016) |  | (0.014) |  |
| $\sigma$ | 0.020 | 0.020 | 0.018 | 0.019 |
| $\bar{R}^2$ | 0.826 | 0.834 | 0.856 | 0.846 |

*, **, and † indicate that the estimated value is significantly different from zero in a one-tailed test at the 2.5%, 5% and 10% error levels, respectively.
Standard errors in parentheses.

to increase domestic private investment. In addition, international trade was found to have a positive effect on private investment. As expected from the theoretical argument discussed earlier, the degree of economic openness is found to exert wholesome influence on domestic private investment.

Even after controlling for international factors, the variables representing domestic political institutions still hold their expected signs and remain statistically significant. While government-capacity stability and political-regime stability have a positive effect on domestic private investment, political violence reduces this effect. Expected growth and human-capital formation continue to have a positive sign, as expected. Economic sanctions and domestic corruption have a negative effect on domestic private investment, though only the sanction variable is statistically significant.

## 7.4   Empirical Evidence: Foreign Direct Investment

This section studies foreign direct investment and compares it to domestic private investment. As in the case of private domestic investment in equipment and plants, foreign direct investment involves fixed-capital formation. Developing and former communist countries attach great importance to foreign direct investment as the first step toward stimulating their economies (Pomfret 1994, McMillan 1995, Radice 1995). Recent research has suggested that foreign direct investment in low-income countries is important to their economic development.[11] Among national characteristics, it has been found that protests, demonstrations, strikes, riots, and government corruption have negative impacts on foreign direct investment.[12] By contrast, some cross-country analyses have established that security relationships may improve or impede interstate economic transactions, including trade and foreign direct investment (Nigh 1984; Gowa 1994; Feng 1994, 2000c).

By definition, foreign direct and private domestic investments both involve fixed-capital formation. However, as their sources are different, the effects on foreign direct and private domestic investments of the political and economic factors examined in the preceding section should also be different, as domestic and international constraints have variegated consequences on them. Few works, however, have studied the effects on foreign direct investment of both international and domestic institutions. Utilizing and expanding the model for private domestic investment, I test the effects of both domestic and international variables on foreign direct investment and then subject the statistical result to a comparison with that of domestic private investment.

On the basis of the model in the preceding section, features in the model used by Wei (1997a, 1997b) are added. As in Wei 1997a, 1997b, the dependent variable is the stock of foreign direct investment for 1990.[13] GDP and population are among my independent variables. A dummy variable for Latin America is a third included variable, which controls for distance and linguistic ties in Wei's model. Located in the Western Hemisphere, Latin America has a long tradition of economic interaction with more advanced nations. Because of its geographic proximity to the United States, Latin America receives a large share of foreign direct investment compared to other less developed countries (particularly, in sub-Saharan Africa).

Among all potential determinants of foreign direct investment, Wei (1997a, 1997b) focuses on corruption. He finds that corruption has a negative effect on foreign direct investment even after controlling for political stability. By comparison, others document that political instability and risks drop in significance once a proxy for economic openness is included in the regression.[14] Still others find that both political stability and government capacity have a significant effect on foreign direct investment when economic considerations, such as trade, are taken into account.[15]

The results in table 7.5 help in evaluating these different findings as well as the cross-country evidence on private domestic investment in the preceding section. Corruption has the expected negative sign, though it is statistically significant in only two out of five regressions in table 7.5. The findings of Wei (1997a, 1997b) regarding the effects of corruption on foreign direct investment are, to some extent, replicated here, while the politicoeconomic model presented in this chapter uncovers additional information. International variables have pronounced impacts on foreign direct investment. Interstate conflict and economic sanctions both decrease foreign direct investment, while economic openness has a very strong positive effect on foreign direct investment. In contrast, the effect of interstate cooperation on foreign direct investment is not statistically significant. Foreign direct investment appears to be more susceptible than domestic private investment to the international environment.

**Table 7.5**
Politicoeconomic model of direct foreign investment controlled by international environment

|  | (14) | (15) | (16) | (17) | (18) | (19) |
|---|---|---|---|---|---|---|
| INTERCEPT | −27.741* | −22.451* | −23.173* | −21.132* | −27.097* | −27.034* |
|  | (6.768) | (5.615) | (6.091) | (0.056) | (0.017) | (0.016) |
| GDP | 0.0002 | 0.0006 | 0.0007 | 0.0007 | 0.0003 | 0.0003 |
|  | (0.0006) | (0.0006) | (0.0007) | (0.0007) | (0.006) | (0.0006) |
| POP | 0.0002* | 0.0002* | 0.0002* | 0.0002 | 0.0002* | 0.0002* |
|  | (0.0000) | (0.0000) | (0.0000) | (0.0000) | (0.0000) | (0.0000) |
| EXPGRO | 52.390† | 82.284* | 50.898† | 76.570* | 50.302† | 46.790 |
|  | (39.100) | (32.175) | (33.267) | (29.983) | (38.022) | (38.161) |
| $PRIM_{60}$ | −0.880 | −4.065 | −1.395 | −2.294 | −0.802 | −0.556 |
|  | (5.506) | (4.106) | (4.563) | (3.918) | (5.449) | (5.514) |
| RPE | 13.942* | 12.931* | 13.232* | 11.922* | 13.843* | 13.830* |
|  | (3.869) | (3.303) | (3.605) | (3.732) | (3.920) | (3.900) |
| RPEV | 6.252 | 14.818† | 6.223 | 10.458 | 5.382 | 5.198 |
|  | (13.051) | (10.479) | (11.466) | (10.113) | (13.451) | (12.994) |
| PROBIRCH | 9.989 | 4.462 | −0.141 | 28.114 | 15.542 | 19.856 |
|  | (36.138) | (32.718) | (36.892) | (31.370) | (20.219) | (38.757) |
| DEATH | −1.830 | −1.654† | −0.867 | −1.822† | −1.402 | −1.124 |
|  | (1.447) | (1.206) | (1.108) | (1.220) | (1.555) | (1.557) |
| CORRUPT | −0.170 | −0.283 | −0.591† | −0.612** | −0.245 | −0.285 |
|  | (0.375) | (0.322) | (0.364) | (0.321) | (0.342) | (0.354) |
| v1CON | — | — | −0.081* | — | — | — |
|  |  |  | (0.038) |  |  |  |
| v2CON | — | — | — | −0.106* | — | — |
|  |  |  |  | (0.038) |  |  |
| v1COOP | — | — | — | — | −0.034 | — |
|  |  |  |  |  | (0.0616) |  |
| v2COOP | — | — | — | — | — | −0.030 |
|  |  |  |  |  |  | (0.034) |
| TRADE | 12.203* | 10.364* | 10.594* | 10.042* | 11.851* | 11.799* |
|  | (1.897) | (1.717) | (2.060) | (1.930) | (2.141) | (2.031) |
| SANCTION | — | −7.313* | −6.340* | −5.076* | −7.510* | −7.382* |
|  |  | (2.473) | (2.368) | (2.311) | (2.695) | 2.760 |
| LATAMER | 11.414* | 9.670* | 7.886* | 7.767* | 10.769* | 10.440* |
|  | (2.720) | (2.073) | (2.828) | (2.554) | (3.217) | (3.195) |
| $\sigma$ | 4.318 | 3.984 | 4.216 | 4.073 | 4.436 | 4.424 |
| $\bar{R}^2$ | 0.807 | 0.836 | 0.816 | 0.828 | 0.796 | 0.797 |

The figures in parentheses are the standard errors of the parameter estimates.
*, **, and † indicate that the estimated value is significantly different from zero in a one-tailed test at the 2.5%, 5% and 10% error levels, respectively.
Standard errors in parentheses.

The major political variables that affect domestic investment are no longer significant in the case of foreign direct investment. The probability of irregular government change and the standard deviation of government capacity mostly take the wrong sign and remain statistically insignificant. While the variable of deaths in politically related events maintains a negative relationship with foreign direct investment, it is marginally significant in only two out of five regressions in table 7.5. The one domestic variable that stands out is government capacity, which has a positive effect on foreign direct investment and is statistically significant at a high level. A strong and capable government seems to be popular with foreign investors. In contrast, political freedom (not reported) has a negative effect on foreign direct investment in this group of developing countries, though its significance drops sharply when international factors are included. As observed by Wei (1995), foreign direct investment largely occurs among OECD countries, all political democracies for the period under examination.[16] When foreign direct investment is made in less developed countries, the degree of political freedom in the host country does not seem to help attract foreign capital.[17]

Among the control variables, the size of the population and expected growth of the economy tend to be positively related to foreign direct investment. While population provides both labor and consumers to foreign investors, a stable growth trajectory in the past bodes well for future profitability, all of which may increase the level of foreign direct investment. Real GDP and initial education are not statistically significant in the regressions. The former is not significant because the economic effect is absorbed by the dummy variable Latin America, since the level of economic development is relatively high in this group of less developed countries. The lack of significance for the latter is robust; even the exclusion of GDP, which is highly correlated with education, cannot resuscitate its statistical significance.

I tentatively offer a comparative analysis of the different effects of domestic and international factors on private domestic investment and foreign direct investment. First, while political freedom fosters private domestic investment, its effect on foreign direct investment tends to be negative, and attenuates when international conflict is included. Second, while the effect of the probability of political-regime change on domestic private investment is negative and significant, this is not the case with foreign direct investment. Third, while the stability of government capacity is more relevant in domestic private investment than in foreign direct investment, government capacity is more relevant in foreign direct investment than in domestic private investment. Fourth, a strong government has an advantage in attracting foreign direct investment, though it tends to have a dampening effect on domestic private investment. Fifth, a nation's tendency toward cooperation with other countries is positively related to domestic private investment, and its tendency toward conflict decreases foreign direct investment, although it does not reduce domestic private investment. Sixth, economic openness has a positive effect on both private domestic investment and foreign direct investment, tending to be stronger with the latter than with the former. Likewise, economic sanctions decrease both domestic private investment and foreign direct investment, having a more pronounced negative impact on foreign direct investment than on private domestic investment.

## 7.5   Summary and Policy Implications

This chapter studies the effects of political institutions on private investment. Some suggest that political freedom, political uncertainty, and political instability all affect individuals' decisions to invest in the asset market. A high probability of irregular government change as well as a high level of variation in political capacity and freedom may result in macropolitical uncertainty, decreasing private domestic investment in the same way as macroeconomic uncertainty. An increase in the prospect of political regime change will directly and adversely affect private domestic investment, while the lack of consistency in government capacity to rule the nation and organize its society will also create political uncertainty in the marketplace. Because of entry and exit costs in an uncertain environment, investment decisions often involve exercising the option of waiting for new information. The value of this option is very sensitive to the degree of uncertainty regarding returns on investment. Therefore, the level of prevailing uncertainty consequentially affects aggregate investment.

To assure investors, the government must keep its political capacity consistent with its desired policy and maintain stability of political freedom and civil liberties. A government that vacillates in strength and on its policy positions does not help an economy. If it becomes essential that some policy change be made so that the economy can be repositioned for growth, a policy in favor of gradual adjustment seems preferable to a radical change. Situations that require the government to take action to change its political capacity or economic agenda are exemplified by changes in exchange rates, trade deficits, oil-price increases, and global economic recessions. Under these circumstances, the government must meet the challenge presented by the change.

Gradual adjustments involve moderate changes and can be realized with little uncertainty. Radical change, such as depreciating the national currency by a large margin to increase exports, will lead to drastic consequences because of a reallocation of resources. In the literature, it is not clear which kind of adjustment is better than the other, because the choice largely depends upon the social distribution of the costs of adjustment.[18] However, in this chapter we can reach the conclusion that drastic measures involving radical changes should not be followed. Inconstancy and variation of the government's control of the national economy—if continued and embedded—creates macropolitical uncertainty, which will reduce private domestic investment over time regardless of the distribution of adjustment costs. Gradual change of the status quo, if necessary, allows the government to build institutional credibility by degrees and, over time, helps reduce fear of uncertainty on the part of investors.

Political-regime instability is often out of a government's control. While a government can change its level of political capacity to suit a policy goal, it cannot easily do so to efficiently improve regime stability. Political-regime stability is embedded in the national culture and value systems and accentuated by particular political events that function as catalysts for political change. Some governments will use nonpolitical appeals in justification of their actions to subdue political dissent regarded as a threat to regime stability. For instance, the Chinese government resorted to force in ending the student demonstrations at Tiananmen Square for the sake of a stable environment for economic growth. In the long run, however, a democratic government remains preferable to an authoritarian one, even on grounds of regime stability, as democracy produces political stability through regular elections. The rules and procedures of the political selection process in democratic societies are based on social consensus, which is conducive to regularity and conventionality. Economically, reduction of political uncertainty reduces investment risk and narrows the variance of investors' expected returns. In addition to the advantages for investors of procedural and political consensus, political democracy indirectly enhances the positive prospects for private investment through promotion of economic freedom and improvement in the stock of human capital, both of which play a pivotal role in acquiring and utilizing private capital.

In the short-run, the political transition to democracy may negatively affect growth through economic uncertainty and adjustment determined by political change. Over the long haul, it facilitates the economic development of a nation, as a stable political system espousing economic freedom will boost economic growth in an environment with little political uncertainty. Yet transitions to democracy can occur with minimum uncertainty and as the economy continues to grow if an authoritarian government converges toward the policy position desired by the middle classes so that it will not be removed.[19] This scenario of political change results in peaceful political evolution rather than revolution.

Although this work does not investigate the causal relationship between domestic private investment and foreign direct investment, one can infer an association between the two. On the one hand, it has been found that interstate conflict decreases foreign direct investment; on the other, it has been found that the same interstate conflict may have a positive effect on domestic private investment. The evidence seems to indicate that a developing nation has to rely on its own private investment when it engages in international conflict, as interstate hostilities decrease foreign direct investment. The implication of this finding is that, ironically, interstate conflict may promote long-run growth of a nation through economic mobilization centered on private investment.

A nation can attract foreign direct investment by having a capable government. Strong and capable governance improves institutional credibility and is likely to assure foreign investors of the government's capacity to handle domestic politics. If a government adopts a policy to solicit foreign investors, a capable government can do better than a weak one. The evidence in this chapter indicates that international investors prefer a strong foreign government that provides an auspicious framework for their investment. If a nation's aim is to attract domestic private investment, it should have a stable government, as evidence in this chapter reveals that political stability, at both the system and government levels, increases private domestic investment. To secure the two kinds of investment, a nation also needs to adopt a cooperative policy toward other nations, as the evidence in this chapter indicates that interstate cooperation increases both domestic private investment and foreign direct investment.

The results in this research also have implications for the link between domestic political and economic development and international relations. The findings in this work demonstrate that a reduction in interstate conflict is generally associated with an increase in foreign direct investment, leading to a rise in economic growth. Additionally, economic development is a sufficient condition for transitions to democracy (Chen and Feng 1999) and necessary for democratic consolidation (Przeworski and Limongi 1997). Democracies are less likely to fight wars with each other.[20] A reduction in international tension is conducive to interstate commerce, which increases national welfare and improves the prospects for democratic transitions and consolidation. Such linkage enhances both world peace and economic prosperity.

# 8            The Political Economy of Human-Capital Accumulation

*All the difference which exists between classes and bodies of men is the effect of education.*

James Mill

Like the preceding chapter, this one deals with the effects of political institutions on the inputs of the production process. While physical-capital formation (e.g., plants and equipment) was the central issue of the last chapter, this chapter focuses on the impacts of political processes on human-capital formation. In his seminal work, Romer (1993) explains the different patterns of growth between developed and less developed countries by differentiating "idea gaps" from "object gaps." The former concept posits the view that nations are poor because their citizens do not have access to the ideas used by advanced industrialized nations to increase the value of economies; the latter holds that some nations are poor because they lack such capital goods as machinery and manufacturing equipment.[1] Romer believes that access to ideas is the key to economic growth in less developed countries. Instead of examining the accessibility of ideas from advanced nations, this chapter looks into the formation of human capital within the home country itself. A close link exists between the human-capital stock of a country and its use of imported ideas, because advanced ideas from other countries, even if accessible, cannot be absorbed efficiently and used effectively without a sufficient level of educational attainment. The effects of ideas are difficult to measure; thus a direct test is elusive. However, as ideas are connected to human capital, the generation of economic value depends on the interaction between the accessibility of ideas and the existence of human capital.

Human capital is accumulated through education, which also plays an important role in the formation of a state, as will be discussed below. In some concrete form, the normative aims of education, as made clear in reports submitted by member states to the International Bureau of Education (IBE) in Geneva, are that "education should develop the all-round intellectual, moral, physical and aesthetic capabilities of individual children and that education should contribute to the improvement of society" (Holmes 1985, 7–9).

The objective of this chapter is to identify patterns of political institutions, economic circumstances, and educational outcomes. As noted by Easterlin (1981), establishing and expanding formal schooling in large part depend on political conditions and ideological differences. As in other chapters, my primary interest lies in the effects of political systems and regime instability on national educational development.

## 8.1   Political Systems, Political Stability, and Human Capital

The concept of human capital has been defined as the process by which people—by means of education, training, or other activities—invest in themselves in hope of raising their future income (Woodhall 1987). The importance of human-capital accumulation was implied in chapter 4, where I said that advances of human and social development have their sources in technological innovation, as determined by human capital. Numerous articles, as well as various chapters of this volume, point to the empirical connection between human capital and economic growth (Romer 1990; Barro 1991; Mankiw, Romer, and Weil 1992; Benhabib and Spiegel 1994). In addition to its positive impact on economic growth through increased productivity, improvement in the stock of human capital betters a society by reducing crime, making markets efficient, speeding technological breakthroughs, and advancing the arts and sciences.

### Political Systems and Human Capital

While various studies have examined the effect of human capital on growth, the question remains as to what causes the differentiation in levels of human-capital formation across nations. Helliwell (1994) suggests that democracy may enhance economic growth through the channel of improving education. Though he does not produce any theoretical foundation for his suggestion, the data analysis in his work partially supports his claim. The impact of democracy on school enrollments is positive and statistically significant. But when the initial level of development is included in the equation, the estimated effect of democracy becomes smaller and less significant. So we have yet to see any conclusive evidence that democracy is conducive to education.

That democracy contributes to human-capital formation remains an important hypothesis for testing. If democracy does enhance the level and quality of educational attainment, the evidence for the superiority of democracy to other forms of political systems will be strengthened. In the preceding chapters, initial levels of education are used as measures of human-capital stocks to estimate the subsequent growth rates of countries. This has the advantage of avoiding the endogeneity problem: economic growth may positively affect education. The limitation, however, is that no explanation is given as to what may increase or decrease human-capital accumulation.

Romer (1993) has offered some indirect evidence regarding democracy's enhancement of human-capital formation. In a limited statistical test on the importance of ideas, the effects of initial levels of the economy on growth turn from negative to positive once some proxies for ideas are controlled. The more advanced countries, Romer argues, are better positioned than less developed countries to increase growth, because of their ability to generate and use new ideas.[2] This view runs directly counter to the argument that, with everything else constant, growth rates in developed countries should be slower than in developing countries, due to the principle of diminishing returns. What is of interest to this study is the premise that democracy is positively connected to human-capital accumulation, a confirmation of which would be consistent with Romer's finding, since advanced countries tend to be democratic in his sample. Therefore, what causes constant or increasing returns to capital may include contributions from political institutions, possibly by fostering a spirit of learning while facilitating education for a broad segment of the nation's population. In addition, the preceding chapter shows that the effect of democracy on private investment is positive, but this effect becomes less significant if education is included in the equation. One can speculate that this occurs because democracy increases private investment through the channel of education.

If true, an endogenous growth process that seeks development of human capital must be embedded in the political environment. The difference in the quality and quantity of education associated with human-capital formation can be accounted for by the differences between political systems, some of which provide more encouraging conditions than others when it comes to promoting education. This hypothesis will be scrutinized in this chapter.

Using a model initially developed by Becker and Tomes (1979) and extended by Aghion and Bolton (1990), Saint-Paul and Verdier (1993) conclude that redistribution under democracy does not necessarily have adverse effects on growth if public education is the main channel of redistribution. If the median voter is poorer than the mean and differences in endowments of human capital are the only source of income inequality, political equilibrium under a democracy with majority rule will lead to a higher level of spending for education, and therefore will generate higher growth. In other words, democratization and the extension of political rights in a society will lead to more redistribution, larger spending on public education, and a boost in growth and equalization of income. Saint-Paul and Verdier's model is empirically consistent with the history of the Western democracies, which have enjoyed sustained growth, a decrease in income inequalities, and an increase in political rights.

One example used by Saint-Paul and Verdier (1993) is the Third Republic of France, which liberalized political rights and civil liberties after the Second Empire of Napoleon III, giving public education a strong boost in the process. For French politicians of the day, the main objective in promoting education was not "only to diminish the religious influence and power of the Church in France but also to satisfy a political demand for more social mobility and less inequality in the French society" (Saint-Paul and Verdier 1993, 406–407).

That democracy enhances education can be seen also from the perspectives of both liberal and Marxist approaches. In the liberal paradigm, education is concerned with the acquisition of knowledge and aims at the full development of both the individual and society,[3] as the pursuit of knowledge is embedded in the struggle for freedom and democracy. "Knowledge and freedom are inevitably linked to education. Beginning with Plato, through the Stoics, to the contemporary with a particular place reserved for the Enlightenment, Reason was considered as the basis of freedom, and education was conceived as a way of liberation" (Szkudlarek 1993,

41). The advancement of education is consistent with the promotion of human freedom, including political freedom. As summarized by Green,

Mass education developed first and fastest in the Protestant countries of northern Europe, and in the Puritan states of northeastern United States. The primary impetus for this development came from the early recognition of Protestants, from the Reformation onwards, of the powers of education as a vehicle of proselytization. The enormous educational advances of the nineteenth century were a product of this early impulse, coupled with the intellectual thrust of the Enlightenment, and of the gradual secular movement towards political democracy, under the banner of liberal capitalism, during the nineteenth century. (1990, 28)

Learning includes some of the fundamental values cherished by society. Knowledge not only leads to self-enlightenment, but also moves society forward and betters the quality of human life. Knowledge can be dangerous to authoritarian political control, of course. Although the French Revolution brought about positive thinking regarding education and the advancement of knowledge in some circles, conservative town-council leaders in France successfully opposed expansion of secular primary education for much of the nineteenth century. The elites feared that mass education would increase the social expectations of the working class and rural peasants. Hence, the public school was seen as a political threat (Fuller and Rubinson 1992, 9). In this context, conservatives were led to use institutional and economic leverage to slow the growth of school enrollments (Gildea 1983). In much the same vein, Qin Shi Huang, the first emperor to unify China, burned books and executed intellectuals to minimize the danger to his rule. During the Cultural Revolution, when totalitarianism reached its zenith in China, the schools were closed and graduates sent to the countryside. Though schools were subsequently reopened, the total number of years required for a student's primary- and secondary-school education was reduced from 12 to 9, and the subjects of study were revamped to suit the political orientation of the nation.

Politics and education are clearly intertwined, as the state molds a country's educational system to realize its political agenda. A democratic society has to enhance its educational system because political competition assumes information and knowledge. Various studies have found that political participation is crucially determined by educational attainment: the educated are more actively involved in politics and more likely to vote than those who are less educated. At a system level, democracy functions on the basis of popular participation, which itself requires a sufficient level of education for the populace. "The connection between education and liberty was one that was fundamental to enlightenment philosophy. Freedom could only be vouchsafed by the vigilance and educated judgment of the people; democracy could only work if those who elected representatives to govern made enlightened choices" (Green 1996, 179).

Even some Marxist scholars argue that democracy and capitalism promote education. The Marxist view of education as a tool of politics is based on (or at least consistent with) the power thesis of Foucault:

We should admit rather that power produces knowledge (and not simply by encouraging it because it serves power or by applying it because it is useful); that power and knowledge directly imply one another; that there is no power relation without the constitution of a field of knowledge, nor any knowledge that does not presuppose and constitute at the same time power relations. (Foucault 1977, 27)

For Foucault, knowledge is a product of the political power structure, and vice versa. Along this line of thinking, Bowles and Gintis hold that schooling consists of disciplinary mechanisms to make individuals not only obedient but also useful to the state. According to Bowles and Gintis (1976), a capitalist society is a formally totalitarian economic system driven by profits and domination, in contrast to a formally democratic political system. In this structure, the educational system plays an important role in preparing individuals for the production process by providing technical and cognitive skills for adequate job performance. From this point of view, democracy does indeed promote education, though with the purpose of reproducing the social relationships necessary for the existence of capitalism.

On a somewhat different note, Madan Sarup claims that although education in a capitalist society apparently focuses on the quantity and quality of the labor force required by the economic system, "most workers in capitalist society are today unproductive" (Sarup 1982, 57). In the face of economic crises, according to Sarup, the state has increasingly cut expenditures on health, education, and other welfare services to redistribute "surplus value from unproductive expenditure to capital" (Sarup 1982, 57). Empirically, the experiences of advanced industrialized democracies do not support such a claim, as education has been continuously emphasized as a major policy issue by the left and right alike. Cuts in education and welfare may undeniably occur in times of economic difficulty, but they do not happen because the state is trying to transfer the wealth from the poor to the rich. Instead, they are necessary economic adjustments. Marxists often ignore the fact that voters matter in a democracy; unpopular cuts in social welfare can cost politicians their chance to get reelected. While the flaw of the Marxist argument lies in its oversimplification of class relationships, it does give some credit to a democratic political system for enhancing education, even though (from the Marxist point of view) the purpose of education is to serve the political system in favor of the owners of capital.

## Political Stability and Human Capital

One would expect that political instability has a negative impact on schooling. Such a negative effect can be seen from the perspective of both the investment decisions of individuals and the direct effect of instability on the provision of education. In the former case, students (and their parents) decide to reduce their demand for education because of either rational expectations or an adaptive process; in the latter, war and revolution directly make it impossible to learn, regardless of the investment decisions of students and parents.

As the accumulation of human capital involves investment under political uncertainty, the process of garnering knowledge per se is influenced by politics. In the second chapter, we observed how political institutions might affect economic growth through their impacts on investment. In particular, the government repression, the polarization of partisan politics, and the instability of the political regime all make investors withhold their assets. All of these political factors decrease the value of investment, including private investment in human capital. As with the relationship between political institutions and private investment, the present value of human capital will be greatly depreciated by an unfavorable political environment characterized by regime instability.

Expected earnings and other returns from education over a lifetime are crucial factors in the decisions about the types and amounts of education students seek (McMahon 1987). Once governments have made primary and secondary school compulsory, this rational decision-making process is especially true for higher education. In his classical treatise *Investment in Learning* (1977), Bowen argues that the total expenditure on higher education would not have been made unless students and their families, the citizenry, and philanthropic donors collectively believe that the returns justify the outlays. Political instability makes such rational calculation difficult. If actors are risk-averse, waiting is a valuable option for students and parents who take time to evaluate all their possibilities before deciding to commit their time and capital to learning. In addition, financial uncertainty generated by the prospect of political instability reduces the amount of schooling. When political instability is taken into consideration, it is no longer clear to students whether another five or six years of graduate study can lead to the employment opportunities for which they have worked, as political upheavals may vaporize such opportunities.

In the adaptive model, rational expectations are a lesser component of the decision-making process. Rather, students base their decisions on their knowledge of some immediate past incidents. In 1977 the Chinese government restored the college entrance exams, which had been discontinued during the Cultural Revolution (1966–1976). For 10 years, entrance to higher education had been determined on the basis of political loyalty; now the process was again presumably based on merit. Yet after the scores were announced, a student who found himself qualified to get into medical school was persuaded by his mother to pursue a liberal-arts major instead. A pediatrician herself, the mother had been sent to the countryside for eight years of "reeducation" during the Cultural Revolution. On the basis of her own experience, she did not want her son to become a medical doctor. Knowledge of what his mother (and her peers) had experienced crucially determined the son's decision regarding his education and career.

This story is consistent with Friedman's income hypothesis that expected future income can be estimated by applying a distributed lag to immediate-past incomes using geometrically declining weights. This practice allows the most recent experience to have the largest impact on decisions regarding future education. As most students do not yet have much in the way of "life experience," their expectations are based on those of their parents, relatives, friends, neighbors, or elders. Along this line of thinking, Katona concludes

that the formation of expectations is really guided by frequently repeated past experiences. He suggests that expectations based upon past events produce a "feeling that spreads over many people and influence action ..., whereas the cognitive (rational expectations) content of expectations may be vague and may differ from person to person" (Katona 1980, 33).

This argument stands in contrast to the rational-expectation thesis, which holds that the rational decisions of individuals are based on the assessment of the situation via the probability that some favorable or unfavorable event happens. Thus, rational expectations are subject only to random errors rather than immediate past experience. In the case of investing in learning, the rational-expectation approach, as shown in the preceding chapter, does imply that risk-averse students would postpone their decision to invest in human capital in the face of financial uncertainty brought about by political instability.

In addition, political instability reduces schooling by directly disrupting educational institutions. In some extreme cases, such as wars and revolutions, schools are forced to remain closed for reasons of safety or lack of financial resources. In countries where political instability is typically high and protracted, the adaptive model and the rational-expectation model both predict that political instability negatively affects education. From either perspective, if a country has a high level of political instability—characterized by both political violence and regime turnovers—it can be expected that human-capital formation is not healthy.

Some interesting side issues concern the different effects of political instability on students at various levels of education or by gender. For instance, the adverse effect of political instability on female education may be larger than that on male education. This speculation is based on two assumptions: First, females and males may differ in risk-taking tendencies. Second, the opportunity costs of male and female students receiving education under the circumstances of political instability may be perceived differently. Additionally, political instability may affect primary education more than higher education, as children are more susceptible and sensitive to political violence than adolescents or adults. At higher levels of education whether political instability has an effect is a more or less self-selective process. In essence, education is an investment process. Because of the different entry costs at different levels of education, the reactions of individuals to political instability will likely be quite varied.

## 8.2   Measurement of Human Capital

This section discusses the various approaches to measuring human capital. Generally speaking, human capital can be measured either quantitatively or qualitatively through certain aspects of educational attainment and performance. The following subsections discuss some of the major indicators of human capital in terms of their strengths and limitations.

### Enrollment Rates

The most frequently used measures of human-capital stocks are the primary-education enrollment rate or the secondary-school enrollment rate, used by (among others) Barro (1991); Levine and Renelt (1992); Levine and Zervos (1993); Romer (1993); Mankiw, Romer, and Weil (1992); Helliwell (1994); and Alesina, Özler, Roubini, and Swagel (1996). The definition of the enrollment rate is the ratio of the number of students actually enrolled at a certain grade level to the number of people in the age group for that level. Such a definition allows the enrollment ratio to be larger than one. For instance, the sum of the number of students enrolled from the designated age group for primary-school education (i.e., ages 6 to 11) plus the primary-school enrollment from other age groups can be larger than the number of students from the designated age group for primary school because of adult education or grade retention. The enrollment rate can be redefined by modifying the numerator to include only those enrolled from the designated age group so that the ratio ranges between zero and one. The limitation, in practice, is that information for such a redefined numerator is not as accessible as the total number of students enrolled, in developing countries (Barro and Lee 1993, 366).

School-enrollment rates for a certain year (for instance, the primary-school enrollment rate in the year 1960) are typically used in aggregate cross-country analyses, as exemplified by the works cited above. There are two reasons for the use of the initial level of enrollment. One is that by using the enrollment rate in a certain year (usually the first year of the aggregate analysis; for instance, the enrollment rate in 1960 for an aggregate study of the period 1960 through 1980), the idea of initial human-capital formation is captured. Second, by using the beginning-year education data, reverse causality problems are mitigated, if not completely avoided.

There are at least five potential problems related to the use of enrollment rates, particularly initial enrollment rates. First, the use of initial enrollment rates may not reflect precise lag information for the formation of human capital. The cycle of the educational process is long, as is the lag between the initiation of education and the realization of human capital. In other words, enrollment rates reflect a flow, while human capital represents a stock. The use of the initial-year enrollment can only be a rough approximation for human-capital formation.

Second, according to Chapman and Boothroyd (1988), the enrollment rates in some developing countries tend to be inflated. "In several countries, headmasters have been observed to inflate reported enrollment based on their experience that higher enrollment figures lead to more resources (supplies, textbooks, budget) being allocated to the school" (Chapman and Boothroyd 1988, 418). In addition to intentional reporting of false data, sources of inaccuracy include failure to report data because of "lack of clarity about who is responsible for reporting data, lack of incentives to report data or lack of communication," and unintentional reporting of inaccurate data caused by teachers not having "adequate systems to maintain school records or not understanding what is meant by the types of data being requested" (Chapman and Boothroyd 1988, 417, 419).

Third, enrollment ratios do not take dropout rates into consideration. The enrollment data are usually collected at the beginning of the school year, but students may later drop out. Another related issue is class attendance. According to Fredriksen, actual school attendance was 30% below the registered number for the first grade in some rural areas of China (Fredriksen 1991); by comparison, attendance in five large public-school districts in New York state (i.e., Buffalo, New York City, Rochester, Syracuse, and Yonkers) was 90% for kindergarten through grade three (Feng 1992, 101). Low attendance causes an undereducation problem and implies a reduction in the effective hours actually spent at school. This is in contrast to the stark phenomenon of students dropping out and receiving no schooling at all.

Fourth, as Barro and Lee (1993) point out, lack of information on migration and mortality precludes a precise picture of the number of students eventually added to the human capital of the nation, while enrollment ratios do not differentiate abnormal enrollments, such as grade retention, from normal enrollments.

Finally, enrollment ratios do not necessarily reflect progress in learning. Easterlin (1981) cites Spain as an example of how educational attainment is not easily measured via enrollment ratios. His finding shows that Spain was above Italy and Russia in enrollment rates, but its economic growth was poor, in large part because Spanish education was strongly controlled by the Roman Catholic Church well into the twentieth century. "The children of the masses received only oral instruction in the Creed, the catechism, and a few simple manual skills.... Science, mathematics, political economy, and secular history were considered too controversial for anyone but trained theologians" (Thut and Adams 1964, 62). As with other quantity-types of data on education, enrollment ratios entail a lack of mechanisms to link the quantity of education to the quality of education.

It should be noted that despite these limitations, enrollment rates remain the most frequently used indices for human capital in the empirical literature on growth and development. Other measures, discussed below, attempt to correct the limitations of enrollment rates. However, these measures have created new problems more difficult to assess (as they complicate the original limitations in enrollment rates), and they make less data available in terms of the coverage of countries.

### Adult Literacy Rates

UNESCO defines adult literacy as enough education so that the person "can both read and write a short simple statement of his everyday life" (Carceles 1990). Conveniently, the rate of adult literacy is generally defined as the ratio of the literate adult population to the total adult population. In comparison with enrollment rates, adult literacy rates do not have the undesirable lag between the flow and the stock of education. In a sense, adult literacy is part of human capital, while school enrollment is a means of realizing human capital. Scholars such as Romer (1990) and Barro (1991) have used this index of human capital.

The most serious potential problem associated with measuring the literacy rate is its failure to capture an advanced level of human-capital accumulation. By the definition given above, the criterion of literacy is minimal and, as such, the variable cannot measure the sophistication and complexity of human-capital stocks. Another potential problem lies in the language used in reading and writing. For example, as the official language of many developing countries in Africa is that of the erstwhile colonial power, it is not clear whether those capable of reading and writing in their native languages, but not in English or French, are considered literate.

### Educational Attainment

Scholars have sought to address these problems associated with enrollment and adult-literary rates. The most ambitious approach is Barro and Lee's (1993) measure of human capital through two variables: the percentage of the population who receive a certain level of education and the average years of education in the population.[4] Focusing on the educational attainment of the total population aged 25 and over, their benchmark panel-estimation sample contains at least one observation and, in most cases, three or more, for each of the 129 countries between 1945 and 1985. Using the available census data as benchmarks, Barro and Lee then estimate the missing observations at four broad levels of classification: no schooling, first-level total (the sum of incomplete and complete first-level education), second-level total (the sum of first- and second-level education), and higher (which refers to post-secondary-school education). The percentage of the population receiving no schooling, first-level schooling, second-level schooling, or higher education is derived from the data on school-enrollment ratios and population by age. Finally, the average years of schooling are derived by summing up the average duration in years for various education cycles.

The educational-attainment data comprise two categories: the percentage of the national population who accomplish a certain level of education (e.g., primary or secondary education) and the average years of schooling. Though considered an improvement over the data on enrollment rates, similar problems are also inherent in attainment data because gross enrollment rates are used in estimating both types. In the estimation of attainment, problems such as inflated reports of enrollment rates, grade retention, dropouts and absenteeism remain unresolved.[5]

A more basic problem for attainment data lies in the lack of a way to adjust for the quality of education, which is at the core of human-capital formation. It is quite doubtful that a year of education at the first grade in the United States is equivalent to a year of education at the same level in Zaire. In addition, there is a great difference in the outcome of one academic year's education across different regions, states, counties, or school districts *within* nations, including the United States. In Orange County, California, "two years of math are enough for a high school diploma from Anaheim Union. Laguna Beach's high school demands three. Most high schools require four years of English; in Garden Grove, three is enough" (Menendez 1996). The quality and content of education are almost nonissues in the measurement of attainment data. Voicing misgivings about the quality of education, an education expert says, "I think people are worried that we allow graduation of students who don't have adequate levels of knowledge and skills for success in life. . . . Yet we let them out of high school and give them a diploma. And that diploma becomes less meaningful if it's not linked to expectations."[6] Thus, quantity of schooling is only a crude measure of academic excellence and human capital.

Aside from the quality issue, school years may vary a great deal from country to country. Children in China used to go to school six days a week for eleven months a year, while their counterparts in the United States attended school five days a week for ten months a year. Under two admittedly unreliable presuppositions—that the quality of instruction is the same and that students attending both systems have identical endowments—the school that has more in-class hours should turn out better students than the school with fewer hours.

The above discussion demonstrates that no measure of human capital is perfect; each is the result of compromises researchers have to make; so each has its particular strengths and weaknesses. With these limitations in mind, the next section will test the relationships between education and political institutions. Without better measures of human capital, the statistical analysis here uses some of the best available indices of human capital.

**Table 8.1**
Average years of schooling by regime type

| Regime | All | Male | Female |
|--------|-----|------|--------|
| Autocracy | 2.76 | 3.55 | 1.98 |
| Democracy | 7.48 | 7.81 | 7.13 |
| Hybrid | 4.39 | 4.90 | 3.80 |

## 8.3   Some Preliminary Data on Education and Democracy

Tables 8.1 through 8.4 tabulate democracy and education. It should be emphasized here that the relationship shown between education and polity may be spurious, as it is not controlled by income and other variables, and we know that mature democracies tend to have higher incomes than autocracies. The type of political regime is differentiated as "democracy," "autocracy," and "hybrid," using the criterion in the Freedom House data.[7] After the polity data is merged with the education data by Barro and Lee (2000), we have six years of data from the two data sets (1975, 1980, 1985, 1990, 1995, and 2000).

First, I look at the distribution of average schooling years, controlled by regime type. Recall that this variable is defined to be the average schooling years in the total population over age 25. In table 8.1, democracy is associated with a significantly higher level of average schooling years than autocracy. The average number of schooling years under democracies is 2.7 times that under autocracies and 1.7 times that under hybrids. When average schooling years are broken down by gender, we find that the difference in averages by gender is far smaller for democracy than autocracy. Women's average number of schooling years under democracy is 91% of their male counterparts; under autocracy, women's schooling years attain only 56% of their male counterparts. For hybrids, this percentage is 77%. Democracies seem far more capable of promoting women's education than autocracies. That the average number of schooling years is relatively close between men and women under democracies is consistent with the principle of gender equality, which is more likely to be advocated and practiced under democracies than autocracies.

Table 8.2 shows the percentage of population that completed primary-school education. Again, two major findings emerge.

**Table 8.2**
Percent of population that completed primary school

| Regime | All | Male | Female |
|--------|-----|------|--------|
| Autocracy | 8.21 | 9.89 | 6.61 |
| Democracy | 17.36 | 16.52 | 17.74 |
| Hybrid | 12.68 | 13.69 | 11.71 |

**Table 8.3**
Percent of population that completed secondary school

| Regime | All | Male | Female |
|--------|-----|------|--------|
| Autocracy | 4.69 | 6.09 | 3.28 |
| Democracy | 15.87 | 15.86 | 15.57 |
| Hybrid | 7.84 | 8.69 | 6.94 |

**Table 8.4**
Percent of population with higher education

| Regime | All | Male | Female |
|--------|-----|------|--------|
| Autocracy | 1.70 | 2.43 | 0.97 |
| Democracy | 7.19 | 9.08 | 5.42 |
| Hybrid | 3.37 | 4.28 | 2.46 |

Democracies have a higher percentage of population with primary education completed, and inequality between the male and female percentages of the population with primary education is the least in democratic states. Indeed, democracy has a higher percentage of women that completed primary-school education than men did (17.8% versus 16.5%).

In table 8.3 the percentage of the population completing secondary education is 15.87 under democracy but 4.69 under autocracy (3.38 times as many). For higher education (table 8.4), this percentage is 7.19 under democracy, but only 1.70 under autocracy (4.22 times). Note that the higher the level of education, the larger the difference between democracies and autocracies. The ratio of educated females to males is in favor of democracy at all levels of completed education.

Because the relationship between regime type and education may be found to be spurious after other relevant variables are controlled, we need to conduct a multivariate statistical analysis of education and politics. For instance, most democratic countries have high incomes, and high incomes are positively correlated with education. Therefore, the positive relationship found above between democracy and education may not hold once we control for incomes.

## 8.4 Model Specification

The following basic multivariate statistical model is proposed to test the impacts of political institutions on education and human capital:

$$\text{EDU}_i = \alpha + \beta X_i + \gamma Y_i + \varepsilon_i$$

Here EDU is human-capital formation as measured by the portion of the population that has completed post-secondary-school education and the average years of schooling,[8] $X$ is a vector of political institutional variables (specifically, political freedom and political instability), $Y$ is a vector of control variables including income levels, $i$ is the subscript for a country, and $\varepsilon$ is the error term.

The focus on higher education is based on several concerns. First, as discussed in the section on measuring educational attainment, most of the problems associated with attainment data tend to occur at lower levels of education. Second, a population of college-educated people indicates the formation of human capital, while it would be unrealistic to call a population that completed only primary or secondary school the critical agents of knowledge. Third, because schooling at the elementary or secondary level tends to be compulsory (even if primary or secondary school is not mandatory, it is a priority largely determined by national income), differences in the portion of the population who received education at these levels should be small across polities. The completion of college education, however, is a choice and should be the litmus test of the political system's impact on education. The other dependent variable—the average number of years of schooling—is chosen for two reasons. First, it has become one of the most frequently used proxies for human capital. Second, it indicates a period of time that potentially spans all levels of education. Barro and Lee's (2000) data set contains five-year-interval data for 138 countries (among which data are missing for some developing nations), starting from 1960 and ending in 2000.

Among political-institution variables, the degree of institutional-ized democracy from the polity data will be used as a measure of the degree of democracy. This variable is chosen over Gastil's freedom data because of its longer annual coverage. The educational data start in 1960, but Gastil's freedom data start in 1972, and the institu-tionalized-democracy data date back to the nineteenth century. The generated probability of irregular government change will be used as an index of political instability. Both variables take a 10-year lag to mitigate the endogeneity problem.[9] Another political variable to be included is the history of democracy. This variable indicates the number of years of democratic rule in a country and is based on the political-regime data compiled by Gasiorowski (1996). It assumes a lagged value of 20 years prior to the education data. As it indicates cumulative years of democratic history, plus a 20-year lag, this vari-able is expected to significantly reduce the endogeneity problem. On the basis of my discussion in the preceding section, I expect that democracy has a positive effect on human-capital formation and that political instability has an adverse effect on education, particularly educational quantity as measured by years of school.

Among the control variables, the level of economic development is included in the regression, since expansion of schooling is regarded as a function of economic development (Easterlin 1981). As with private investment in the preceding chapter, investment in human capital will increase where the economy has bright prospects. A growing economy needs educated personnel with expertise to spur future growth. I expect that the level of development has a positive impact on education. To mitigate reverse causality, real GDP per capita with a 10-year lag is used. These data are from *The Penn World Table* (Summers and Heston 2001).

In addition, continent dummy variables are used for Africa, Asia, and Latin America to control for systemic relationships not cap-tured by the political-institution and economic variables. Among the elusive effects is the cultural factor: as certain cultures centered on specific core religious or philosophical tenets (e.g., Confucianism or Protestantism) have been regarded as conducive to the pursuit of education. A brief examination of Chinese history reveals a positive connection between learning and promotion of good government, and according to Confucius himself, scholastic excellence makes good statesmen. However, as argued above, since culture itself is an ontologically complex and multidimensional process, it is difficult to isolate the cultural variable. In this study, the continent variables are employed with the hope that some effects of latent systemic variables, such as culture and tradition, can be captured.

## 8.5 Empirical Analysis

The regressions in table 8.5 show that institutionalized democracy and democratic history are both positively related to the percentage of the population who have completed postsecondary education when the level of income per capita is controlled. Real GDP per capita is the strongest predictor of education here. However, in its presence, institutionalized democracy and history of democracy in particular remain significant. Given a certain level of income, a longer history of democracy means a larger portion of the population having completed postsecondary education.

**Table 8.5**
Regressions on post-secondary-school education

| Variable | M/F | M | F | M/F | M | F |
|---|---|---|---|---|---|---|
| INTERCEPT | 1.054* | 1.912* | 0.204 | 0.528 | −0.334 | 1.404* |
| | (0.426) | (0.501) | (0.400) | (0.457) | (0.430) | (0.543) |
| FREEDOM | 0.016** | 0.019† | 0.014† | — | — | — |
| | (0.009) | (0.011) | (0.008) | | | |
| HISTORY | — | — | — | 0.095* | 0.090* | 0.099* |
| | | | | (0.011) | (0.010) | (0.013) |
| INSTABILITY | −0.639 | 0.576 | −1.745 | −1.447 | −2.406 | −0.426 |
| | (2.880) | (3.380) | (2.697) | (2.889) | (2.716) | (3.433) |
| GDP | 0.567* | 0.700* | 0.444* | 0.438* | 0.323* | 0.567* |
| | (0.034) | (0.040) | (0.032) | (0.039) | (0.036) | (0.046) |
| ASIA | 1.318* | 1.547* | 1.045* | 2.173* | 1.872* | 2.420* |
| | (0.418) | (0.492) | (0.392) | (0.443) | (0.417) | (0.527) |
| AFRICA | −0.658† | −1.20** | −0.111 | 0.048 | 0.538 | −0.435 |
| | (0.466) | (0.547) | (0.434) | (0.514) | (0.483) | (0.611) |
| LATAMER | 1.509* | 0.755† | 2.227* | 2.123* | 2.849* | 1.367* |
| | (0.418) | (0.490) | (0.391) | (0.438) | (0.412) | (0.521) |
| $\bar{R}^2$ | 0.485 | 0.525 | 0.387 | 0.538 | 0.453 | 0.561 |
| $\sigma$ | 3.156 | 3.704 | 2.956 | 3.073 | 2.900 | 3.652 |

*Statistically significant at the 1% level in a one-tailed test.
**Statistically significant at the 5% level in a one-tailed test.
†Statistically significant at the 10% level in a one-tailed test.
Standard errors in parentheses.

Between institutionalized democracy and history of democracy, the latter appears to have a more pronounced effect on post-secondary education. Political instability, however, is not statistically significant.

Asian and Latin American nations tend to have a larger portion of their population holding higher-education degrees than the benchmark group of nondummy nations. This percentage is about two points higher in Asia and Latin America.

The regression results for average schooling in table 8.6 are informative. First, controlled by income per capita, both institutionalized democracy and history of democracy seem to have a positive relationship with the average number of years of schooling for males and females separately as well as for males and females combined. The degree of democracy and the years of democracy are both associated with more years of schooling, and this result is statistically significant even after being controlled for by income levels.

**Table 8.6**
Regressions on average years of schooling

| Variable | M/F | M | F | M/F | M | F |
|---|---|---|---|---|---|---|
| INTERCEPT | 4.406* | 4.753* | 3.408* | 3.624* | 4.442* | −2.906* |
| | (0.214) | (0.210) | (0.229) | (0.224) | (0.225) | (0.238) |
| FREEDOM | 0.015* | 0.014* | 0.016* | — | — | — |
| | (0.004) | (0.004) | (0.005) | | | |
| HISTORY | — | — | — | 0.045* | 0.035* | 0.050* |
| | | | | (0.005) | (0.005) | (0.006) |
| INSTABILITY | −3.603* | −2.529* | −4.572* | −3.078* | −2.446† | −4.024* |
| | (21.446) | (1.419) | (1.547) | (1.414) | (1.417) | (1.505) |
| GDP | 0.360* | 0.339* | 0.380* | 0.311* | 0.301* | 0.327* |
| | (0.017) | (0.017) | (0.018) | (0.018) | (0.019) | (0.020) |
| ASIA | −0.255 | −0.141 | −0.543* | 0.204 | 0.216 | −0.012 |
| | (0.209) | (0.206) | (0.224) | (0.216) | (0.217) | (0.230) |
| AFRICA | −1.516* | −1.607* | −1.495* | −1.093* | −1.258* | −1.027* |
| | (0.233) | (0.229) | (0.250) | (0.251) | (0.256) | (0.267) |
| LATAMER | −0.196 | −0.683* | 0.247 | 0.099 | −0.458** | 0.596* |
| | (0.209) | (0.206) | (0.224) | (0.214) | (0.215) | (0.228) |
| $\bar{R}^2$ | 0.693 | 0.689 | 0.683 | 0.727 | 0.711 | 0.722 |
| $\sigma$ | 1.573 | 1.545 | 1.685 | 1.492 | 1.495 | 1.589 |

*Statistically significant at the 1% level in a one-tailed test.
**Statistically significant at the 5% level in a one-tailed test.
†Statistically significant at the 10% level in a one-tailed test.
Standard errors in parentheses.

Second, the effects of political instability on the average number of years of education differentiated by gender are telling: it affects women more pronouncedly than men, almost by twice as much. As suggested earlier, the explanation might be that female students are more risk-averse than male students under circumstances of political instability, which can be related to women's assumed vulnerability in the face of political violence. The other potential reason is that political instability increases the risk premium for education, as political chaos and displacement may tremendously diminish the future returns from education. Since the cost of education goes up with the risk premium and a culturally informed value system often favors men over women when it comes to careers, households decide to provide education for their sons over or ahead of their daughters.

While the effect of political instability on the percentage of the population that completed postsecondary education is not statistically significant, its impact on the average number of years of schooling is very strong, possibly due to the fact that postsecondary education involves self-selection. Those most likely to be affected by political instability in their pursuit of education are those at the lower levels of education. Students who enter universities and colleges have finished their primary and secondary education, and are thus better equipped to finish educational goals than those in the initial years of schooling. As a result, higher education is relatively robust in the face of political instability when compared to primary education.

The regional dummy variables indicate that the average number of years of schooling in African countries are shorter by about one year than the benchmark of nondummy countries, with other factors kept constant. For Latin American countries, the average number of years of education for their female populations are slightly longer than the rest of the nations. However, those of their male populations are slightly shorter, with other factors kept constant.

It should be pointed out that the parameter estimates in tables 8.5 and 8.6 are very robust for democracy during different periods. In addition to the ending year 2000, I also experimented with the years 1995, 1990, 1985, 1980, 1975, and 1970. The results for democracy remain highly consistent, though the effects of political instability on education attenuate.

### 8.6   Summary and Policy Implications

As in the preceding chapter, we have found evidence of effects of political institutions on human-capital formation. National education plays a crucial role in forming and accumulating human capital, which is an important source of economic growth and social development. This is especially true for developing countries, since education provides a way to narrow the gap of ideas between the developed and less-developed countries. With sufficient increases in educational attainment and improvements in educational quality, advanced ideas from other countries can be absorbed efficiently and used effectively. Education is thus important. This chapter identifies the nuanced effects of democracy and stability on national educational development.

I have thus strongly confirmed Helliwell's (1994) hypothesis that democracy may enhance economic growth through the channel of educational improvement, in contrast to the partial support he obtained in his empirical analysis. This confirmation was made possible by using the average number of years of schooling and the percentage of the population with higher education, which are more refined data than gross school enrollments. Democracy's impact on the length of schooling and the percentage of the population that completed higher education is found to be positive and statistically significant.

In addition to democracy's intrinsic value in terms of personal freedom, nations benefit from democracy because of its utility in fostering conditions for economic and social development and its indirect effects (e.g., through the channels of education and investment) on the course of development.

Political instability, as estimated by the probability of irregular government change, adversely affects human capital formation. It has more of a dampening effect on female education than on male education, more on the lower levels than on higher levels of education.[10] On the supply side, educational environments deteriorate under the circumstances of political upheavals, though schools might still remain open. A lack of financial resources, an orientation away from academic excellence, or both may cause deterioration in education. The morale of teachers and incentives for them to train students are also affected negatively. On the demand side, the expected returns from education decrease as political instability increases. When political uncertainty is high, students rationalize away or discount the benefits of learning, while the educational process itself is likely characterized by scholastic lethargy or a lack of interest in learning, thus resulting in low test performance.

A consolidated democratic political system is the key to successfully accumulating human capital. A democracy with little prospect of regime change fosters the spirit of learning among all children through the principle of equal opportunity and inspires scientific breakthroughs buttressed by academic freedom. In addition, political stability is also important for improving human capital. It has both direct and indirect effects on education. Its direct effects have been shown in this chapter. Indirectly, political stability promotes long-run growth, thus increasing national income and wealth, which in turn lead to an improvement in education.

One important component of a national development strategy is to improve human-capital formation and accumulation, which requires both high quality and large quantities of education. Democracy is conducive to creating a broad-based national education as well as academic excellence, contributing to physical-capital formation by improving human-capital stocks. The preceding chapter found that democracy has a positive impact on private investment; however, the effect is less significant when the role played by human capital is controlled. This chapter shows that democracy promotes human-capital formation, which (according to the preceding chapter) is positively related to private investment in equipment and machinery. Therefore, by producing human capital—itself compatible with increasing private investment—democracy actually expands the physical-capital formation necessary for economic growth.

# 9        Democracy and Income Inequality Reconsidered

*When wealth is centralized, the people are dispersed. When wealth is distributed, the people are united.*

Confucius

A major aspect of this chapter's investigation is the effect of democracy on income equality. In addition to income equality, a society's goals and aspirations may include equality before the law and equal opportunity (including financial opportunity). Some scholars have argued that if the goal is to study how far a society has progressed towards equality, one must study the laws of that society. Other scholars argue that studying the legal framework of a society is not sufficient to understand equality, as discrimination may fall outside of legality. Still different arguments tackle equality of opportunity. For instance, if human-capital investment is important for future income, then initial levels of start-up capital become essential for future well being. Even in the absence of discrimination, the opportunity to acquire education and its potential benefits would not be equal if the financial constraints imposed on the attainment of education vary among individuals (Hyland 1995, 14).

While agreeing that equality has many facets and implications, I focus in this chapter on just one aspect of equality—income equality. My focus on the reduced form of the relationships between income equality and political systems implies that politics may also affect other variables that have impacts on income distribution. Since income inequality has been found to exert a negative impact on growth in chapter 4, the existence of a relationship between income equality and democracy would be just another channel through which democracy indirectly determines growth. If democracy displays a negative effect on income inequality, it would imply that democracy is another tool with which to combat social poverty and improve national welfare. While my other research also looks into the effect of income distribution on political systems (e.g., Feng and Gizelis 2002), my aim in this chapter is to unearth the variation in income inequality across countries as determined by the degree of democracy.

## 9.1  Theories and Findings on Democracy and Income Distribution

Political scientists, political sociologists, and economists take different methodological and substantive stances regarding the relationship between democracy and income inequality. While the first two look at the direct causal relationships between democracy and income inequality, the last are likely to take income distribution as given and then build their political-economic models on the basis of the median-voter theorem. The advantage of the political science/sociology approach is that the effect of democracy on income distribution can be directly examined. In contrast, a benefit of the economic approach is that income distribution as a source of economic growth or related areas (such as property rights protection, education, and fertility) can be investigated. The design of this book dictates that we examine both approaches so as to obtain a general picture of political systems and income distribution.

### The Political Models

In their review of democracy and economic development, Sirowy and Inkeles (1990) examine the theoretical relationship between democracy and income distribution and review the empirical evidence. The literature that they review falls under three models: the Democratic Model, the Authoritarian Model, and the Skeptical Model. The first model argues that democracy leads to a reduction in income inequality if certain political mechanisms operate: "Democracies are conceived to tend to neither adopt economic growth polices that directly attempt to deprive specific social groups of their relative economic shares nor are they free to ignore the voices of mobilized sectors of the population due to their legitimate needs. Because of electoral mechanisms and rights to opposition and participation, democracies are relatively open to battles over the distribution of societal resources" (Sirowy and Inkeles 1990, 135).[1] In essence, the democratic processes shift political power away from the rich toward the middle-income groups, ultimately resulting in a relatively even distribution of wealth. The theoretical implication from this model is that democracies are more likely than autocracies to reduce income inequalities.

In contrast, an authoritarian regime can pursue policies benefiting the few at the cost of the majority without being ousted. The rich minority has the financial power, as well as effective incentives, to influence the political elite to adopt policies favorable to augment their income. Additionally, it is suggested, an authoritarian regime has fewer constraints in dealing with multinational corporations and is able to work out transactions benefiting a small sector of domestic constituents as well as foreign actors, at the expense of the poor domestic sector (Evans 1979, Kaufman 1979). Brazil in the 1960s, Chile after 1973, Iran under the shah, Nepal, Saudi Arabia, and Ethiopia appear to be just a few of the cases that support the connection between authoritarian regimes and income inequality (Bollen and Jackman 1985, 439).

Bollen and Jackman (1985, 440) challenge the Democratic Model by questioning its assumptions that democracies adhere to the median-voter model, that low-income groups demand redistribution, and that inequality is perceived as being unjust. Similarly, Nelson (1987) cautions that the pattern of political participation may be crucial in understanding income distribution. Political participation may vary across democratic countries. Differences could be caused, for instance, by social or demographic structure. A highly rural democracy may take a different position on income distribution than a highly industrial one, thus blurring a distinctive role in income distribution played by the type of political regime.

The Authoritarian Model views authoritarian governments as more capable of improving income inequality than their democratic counterparts. While this model assumes that democracies are receptive to social demands, it also asserts that the really disadvantaged social groups lack the power to make their voices heard in the first place. Income inequality is thus a consequence of political inequality in terms of deficient political representation. This dilemma is particularly true for developing countries, where democracies are not fully consolidated and political rents are up for grabs (Beitz 1982, Huntington and Nelson 1976). By contrast, autocracies may offer better protection for the politically disadvantaged groups in terms of political and economic interests. This view is consistent with Hayek's observation that "while an equality of rights under a limited government is possible and an essential condition of individual freedom, a claim for equality of material position can be met only by a government with totalitarian powers" (Hayek 1976, 83). The Authoritarian Model, however, has so far failed to systematically identify the circumstances under which autocracies have the incentive to protect their socially, politically, and economically disadvantaged groups.

Finally, the Skeptical Model has two variants. The functionalist view argues that the relationship between democracy and income equality is spurious; the intervening variable should be a nation's economic development. In other words, after the level of economic development is controlled, the effect of democracy on income distribution will disappear. Industrialization determines the employment structure of the nation, resulting in varying income levels. In addition to disregarding the political mechanisms unique to the democratic process, this argument assumes no connection between democracy and development, thus linking income distribution only to the level of development (Marsh 1979, Kerr et al. 1969). The functionalist view depoliticizes the development process and gives serious consideration to Kuznets's (1955) thesis on the relationship between income inequality and economic development.

By contrast, the Marxist view downplays the importance of political systems in income distribution and focuses on class conflict (Sirowy and Inkeles 1990, 136). One major variable in the Marxist theoretical structure is the relative strength of capitalist and labor classes. While capitalists may be relatively strong in some democracies, they are weak in others, leading to higher income inequalities in the former than the latter. After the relative strength of capital versus labor is controlled, any systematic relationship between political systems and income distribution should attenuate or disappear. This model assumes that democratic processes are not important, and that the majority of voters cannot have any substantial influence. Such an assumption has been revealed to be untenable, as income transfer and social-welfare policies do occur in a wide range of capitalist welfare states, such as Sweden and Canada. In addition, developed countries—where capitalism is strongest—tend to be associated with the lowest level of income inequality. A quick examination of the data on Gini coefficients shows that the five countries with the lowest average income inequality all have long-standing capitalist economies: the United Kingdom (26.25), Spain (26.25), Belgium (27.01), Luxembourg (27.13), and the Netherlands (28.59), while the five countries with the highest average income inequality are developing economies: South Africa (62.30), Gabon (61.23), Sierra Leone (60.79), Brazil (57.84), and Zimbabwe (56.83). (For a summary of the Gini coefficients in the sample, see appendix 9.A.)

### The Economic Models

Economists, assuming democratic processes in which the median voter determines the tax rate, choose to base their models on the political mechanisms of income distribution and economic growth. Intuitively, when the decisive voter is poor relative to the average voter, he faces a relatively low opportunity cost of redistribution through tax prices. Consequently, if the mean income is above the median income, a voter majority emerges proposing a redistribution of income from the rich to the poor. As shown by various economists, inequality tends to be positively associated with the level of taxation and redistribution (Romer 1975, Roberts 1977, Meltzer and Richard 1981).

Using this finding as their conceptual foundation, Alesina and Rodrik (1994), Persson and Tabellini (1994), and Perotti (1993) all analyze how income distribution affects growth through the channel of a public tax-collecting sector, which is perceived to affect growth in terms of either public investment or simply through redistribution.[2] The key assumption for all of these models is the median-voter theorem, which asserts that the median voter determines a tax rate and a balanced budget, and thus affects economic growth through the public sector's inputs in the marketplace. In this process, the political mechanism and the economic structure are integrated.

Alesina and Rodrik (1994) predict that the greater the inequality of wealth and income, the higher the tax rate and the lower the growth rate. The key feature of their model is that individuals differ in their endowments of capital and labor. Growth is driven by expansion of the capital stock and by productive government services financed by a tax on capital. If government services are productive, a small tax on capital leads to provision of the public good for the benefit of all. However, different individual endowments of capital and labor imply that individuals have different ideal rates of taxation. An individual whose income is completely derived from capital returns prefers a tax rate on capital that maximizes the economy's growth rate. Other agents prefer a higher tax, with a subsequent lower growth rate for the economy. The lower an agent's relative capital income, the higher his ideal tax rate and the lower his ideal growth rate. According to the median-voter theorem, the less the median voter is endowed with capital, the higher the tax rate and lower the growth rate. As the model specifies that the redistribution of income is monotonically and negatively related to growth, income inequality is predicted to have an adverse impact on the subsequent growth rate.

Persson and Tabellini (1994) also predict that higher inequality is associated with lower growth. The inverse relationship between income inequality and growth in their model is more immediate than in that of Alesina and Rodrik. An individual born poorer or richer than the average has, respectively, less or more capital than the average person. Thus, individual preferences for redistribution can be ranked by their idiosyncratic endowment. The equilibrium political variable here is the redistribution value preferred by the median voter born with the median endowment. A better-endowed median voter favors relatively less redistribution. Since redistribution monotonically depresses growth, income inequality—as represented by a poorly endowed median voter—would lead to relatively high income redistribution, which in turn causes a decrease in growth rates.

Perotti (1993) distinguishes between the roles played by median voters in a poor country and in a rich country. In a poor country, growth is engendered by the upper-income class's investment in its human capital. The two requisite conditions for growth in a poor country are that the upper-income class is initially rich enough, and that the middle-income class is close enough to the upper-income class not to have an incentive to tax the rich heavily. Such taxation would prevent the rich from investing in human capital. A rich country faces just the opposite problem, as continued growth there depends on the low-income class investing in its human capital.

Accordingly, the two conditions for growth in developed countries are that the low-income class is initially not too poor to invest in human capital, and that the middle-income class is close enough to the low-income class so that sufficient income redistribution would help the low-income class invest in its human capital. Indeed, the median voter in a rich country trades off more redistribution than presently desired for a higher per capita income in the future—possible only if the low-income class can invest today.

In addition to this connection between growth and income distribution through fiscal policies such as taxation, the linkage between the two has also been established through various *sociopolitical instability* (SPI) models. Some scholars argue that income inequality causes political instability when the poor expropriate the wealth of the rich through informal and illegal means. This results in further deterioration of property-rights protection and a rise in nonproductive activities to obtain income, e.g., illegal means such as burglary and armed robbery (Zak 2000, Alesina and Perotti 1996, Gupta 1990, Venieris and Gupta 1986). When development does not benefit the low-income classes, their frustration grows and their opportunity costs of engaging in nonproductive means to make a living become smaller. Therefore, as the distribution of wealth widens, sociopolitical instability increases. Sociopolitical instability caused by income inequality adversely affects growth for three reasons, as summed up by Zak (2000). First, SPI may reduce growth in terms of income redistribution policies implemented to alleviate sociopolitical instability; second, the government may use coercion on opposition, thus diverting resources from productive sectors; third, SPI may lead to the downfall of the current government, thereby adding to political uncertainty. The empirical results of Alesina and Perotti (1996) demonstrate that income inequality causes sociopolitical instability, leading to a reduction in investment.[3]

A third approach to income distribution and growth, as summarized by Perotti (1996), focuses on income distribution and investment, assuming that agents borrow to improve their future position. Galor and Zeira (1993) assume that investment in education will enhance future growth. If the constraints on borrowing are small, people can borrow in the present to invest in future gains through education. But if it is difficult to borrow for education, those without financial resources must forego education and remain trapped in poverty for generations. Therefore, given sufficiently large budget constraints on investment in education, income distribution will matter a great deal in promoting or inhibiting growth, since leaving a large portion of society uneducated causes a shortage of the human capital necessary for continued growth. Furthermore, Galor and Zhang (1993) extend the study of education and income distribution to that of fertility. Given the distribution of income, a higher fertility rate decreases the average resources for each child's education; with budget constraints, investment in human capital will be further reduced. Relatively unequal income distribution, combined with high fertility rates, thus leads to low investment in education.

A fourth approach endogenizes the fertility decision, which is subject to effects from both income and substitution. The income effect refers to the fact that when income increases, the demand for children increases as well, thus resulting in an increase in fertility; the substitution effect implies that when income increases, one's opportunity cost for having more children increases, thus leading to a dampening effect on fertility. For the extremely low-income classes, the income effect dominates the substitution effect, as the opportunity cost foregone as a consequence of having children is low. Thus a small increase in human capital leads to a general increase in children. For high-income classes, the substitution effect dominates the income effect, as the opportunity cost of having additional children is relatively large. In this context, children are "inferior" goods for high-income classes, implying that an increase in human capital will lead to fewer children. Redistribution from the rich to the poor will likely increase the low-income group's opportunity cost of having children when appropriately large redistributed wealth translates into investment in human capital. Therefore, income redistribution may induce those who cannot afford education to invest in human capital; the increase in human capital in the society will then lead to economic growth (Becker, Murphy, and Tamura 1990; Perotti 1996). It should be noted that even though the argument based on the income and fertility nexus appears to have the same implication as those based on the income and tax or income and SPI nexus (that is, that equal income distribution leads to growth), the latter two cases treat income distribution as the initial condition, while the former treats it as dynamic. In other words, income redistribution as a means of reducing income inequality is negatively associated with growth in the income-tax and income-SPI models, but it is positively associated with growth in the income-fertility model.

*Empirical Findings*

Although the empirical findings in each of these works is basically consistent with the theoretical implications of the particular model posited on growth and income equality, the relationship between political systems and income equality is not quite clear because of the direct link of growth to income distribution, with the latter treated as fixed. "The empirical verdict on these models is then still open: the reduced form seems to be capturing something, while the main elements of novelty of these models, the underlying political process, seems to be less well supported by the data" (Perotti 1991, 315).

Perotti (1996) addresses the political mechanisms of how income distribution affects growth by comparing the interaction term of income distribution and democracy. This interactive variable is included in the fiscal model, which specifies that the median voter affects income redistribution through taxation, which in turn affects growth. While the first effect is hypothesized to be positive, implying that a strong middle class will favor lower taxes, the latter effect is supposed to be negative, implying that redistribution reduces growth. In such a recursive model, the income share of the middle class is found to have a positive effect on growth, but the interactive term of the middle-class income share and democracy is far from significant. Furthermore, the marginal rate of taxation is found to have a significant and positive effect on growth, running counter to the fundamental argument of the fiscal model. By comparison, the SPI model works well statistically, as the empirical data show that income equality decreases sociopolitical instability, thus reducing SPI's negative impact on growth. Perotti's (1996) empirical results are also consistent with the endogenous-fertility model and the constrained-education-investment model: Income equality reduces fertility and thus increases growth; the indirect effect of income equality on growth is therefore positive. Similarly, the indirect effect of income equality on growth through investment in education is also positive.[4]

Perotti (1996) represents one of the most exhaustive statistical analyses of growth and income distribution yet published in the economics literature. It lacks, however, a focused analysis of the political system per se, though the author mentions the importance of political processes in income distribution. The interactive term of income distribution and democracy is not sufficient for examining the political mechanisms of income distribution. Like other economists who study income distribution and growth, Perotti treats income distribution as exogenous. The interactive term is intended to distinguish a democracy from a nondemocracy, yet it does not make income distribution endogenous to political systems. The specification that the interactive term should be positive when income distribution is more important in determining fiscal policy and growth in democracies than in nondemocracies does not directly address the question of whether or not democracy leads to a relatively even income distribution. In a study of the effects of political systems on income distribution, it is fundamentally important that income distribution be treated as completely endogenous.

As these economists' models assume that a country adopts a democratic procedure for voting in which the median voter is crucial, it remains an open question as to whether such theoretical models are sufficiently generic to include nondemocratic countries and whether the attendant empirical results are applicable to nondemocratic countries. Even in democracies, the political mechanism of the median voter is assumed rather than theoretically developed. Given the median-voter theorem and the proportional income tax, some nonpolitical factors (such as the age composition of the population or the productivity of the labor force) may present important considerations. More important, the initial level of income inequality is treated as fixed in these models. The issue of great interest in our study is whether different political systems will lead to different levels of income inequality. As Zak (1997, 2000) correctly notes, the market system does not completely determine the distribution of income. Rather, differences in income are also due to *exogenous* factors, such as education, intelligence, sociopolitical conditions, and government redistribution policies. Instead of assuming income inequality as a given, it is essential to endogenize income distribution as part of the economic and social phenomena conditioned by political institutions.

As the design of the book is to identify both the direct and indirect effects of political institutions on economic performance, it is essential that the effects of democracy and other major aspects of political institutions on income inequality are examined and tested. If it turns out that democracy does have a positive impact on income equality, as has been argued under the democratic model, then democracy's positive indirect effects on growth will be further illuminated.

In contrast to the quite robust findings on the relationship between income inequality and growth, empirical evidence on democracy and income inequality has been ambiguous. Sirowy and Inkeles (1990) survey twelve papers dealing with the effects of democracy on income inequality, of which seven find a negative impact of democracy on inequality and five discern no significant effect.[5] Two of the twelve articles, one by Bollen and Jackman (1985) and the other by Muller (1988), are considered "superior to the others" on the grounds of sample coverage, assessment of endogeneity, and controls for the source-of-income data (Sirowy and Inkeles 1990, 151). Nonetheless, each offers different findings on the relationship between democracy and inequality.

Having conducted a rigorous analysis, Bollen and Jackman (1985) find that political democracy does not affect inequality, nor does inequality affect democracy. Their work remedied several major methodological insufficiencies found in previous studies, including sample composition, income-data adjustment, the endogenous effects between democracy and inequality, and the nonlinear effects between development and inequality. While essentially following the same methodology, Muller (1988) takes a different topical approach from Bollen and Jackman (1985). For Muller, it is not the level of political democracy in a certain year that is important, but the years during which a democratic political system has been in existence. He argues that only when democracy is consolidated may political mechanisms for income equality become functional.

If the egalitarian influence of democracy is in reality a long-term incremental effect, then relatively new democracies should not be expected to be as egalitarian as old ones, even if they have the same level of democracy in a given year.... Given the existence of an egalitarian political structure, it is plausible to expect that, over time, as the more numerous poorer members of the population organize into unions and other interest groups, and as parties of the social democratic left develop a solid electoral base, win seats in legislatures, and participate in or control the machinery of government, democracy becomes associated, in a *facilitative* sense, with a gradual reduction of economic inequality. (Muller 1988, 50, 51, 65)[6]

Empirically, Muller finds that a country's years of democracy have a positive effect on income equality: the longer a country remains democratic, the higher the income equality in the country.

The findings of the two studies need not be inconsistent, as one deals with the level of democracy and income distribution at a point in time, while the other is concerned with the relationship over a period of time. This chapter will essentially test the same statistical models used by Bollen and Jackman (1985) and Muller (1988), utilizing recent data from the World Bank (which covers more countries over a longer period of time than these two studies). Moreover, I introduce a new explanatory variable to measure the density of democratic experience. Because it has a dynamic component, it is different from the static democracy variable used by Bollen and Jackman. It is also different from the one used by Muller, as this variable emphasizes short-term dynamism rather than long-term history.

## 9.2   Measurement Issues

This section deals with measurement issues concerning income distribution. The income-distribution data deserve lengthy treatment, as they are considered the murkiest among the social and economic data. In terms of model specification, this section will closely follow the papers by Bollen and Jackman (1985) and Muller (1988), who have laid down a solid methodological framework on the topic.

The empirical study of income distribution has been handicapped by the lack of reliable and comparable cross-country data. Weede (1997) presents one instance of potential data incompatibility. He compares two data sets of income inequality data, one compiled by Paukert (1973), the other by the World Bank (1985). Weede's work demonstrates that the correlation between the income-inequality variables in the two data sets is 0.53 for 12 industrialized countries and 0.69 for all 37 cases. Both correlations are below the usual standards in psychometrics.

The data problems facing the study of income distribution are multidimensional, and discrepancies may have been caused by a combination of factors. For instance, surveys on income distribution can be national or regional. Among regional surveys, some are conducted in rural areas, others in urban areas. It can be assumed that a national survey obtains a higher level of accuracy than a regional one. Additionally, surveys can be based on either a household or the economically active person in a household. The latter income distribution is regarded as more skewed than the former, thus representing a higher degree of inequality (Perotti 1996, 155; Bollen and Jackman 1985, 441, 445).[7] Furthermore, income can be either pretax or posttax. This difference can be systematically large, as common sense reveals that gross income will represent higher inequality than net income. Taxation can be a great equalizer. Normally, after-tax income leads to an income distribution that is less unequal than pretax income. Finally, the constrained-education-investment and endogenous-fertility models assume wealth rather than income distribution, and the former is more skewed than the latter.[8]

Some of these problems can be solved through estimation. Bollen and Jackman (1985) use a dummy variable to control for surveys of individual income. Perotti (1996) employs an average-ratio operator to adjust the difference between household and individual surveys. The construction of the adjustment factor involves three steps: First, the average is taken of the income-distribution variable; for instance, of the top quintile share, $\bar{q}_5^h$, for all observations based on household income and the top quintile share, $\bar{q}_5^i$, for all the observations based on individual income. Second, an average factor is constructed by dividing the former by the latter, i.e., $x = \bar{q}_5^h / \bar{q}_5^i$, which shows the extent to which the top quintile income share by households differs from the top quintile income share by individuals. Third, the average factor is applied to the value of the top quintile share for those countries that have data on income distribution by individuals only; in this case, the estimated top quintile share by households is $\hat{q}_5^h = x \cdot \bar{q}_5^i$. The same method can be extended to adjust the other discrepancies noted above.

This chapter focuses on four measures of income inequality: the middle income share, used by Perotti (1996), which is the summation of the shares by the third and fourth income quintiles; the ratio of income share of the fifth quintile to the first and second quintiles, used by Bollen and Jackman (1985); and the fifth income quintile and the Gini coefficient, both used by Muller (1988). There are two reasons for examining these indices. First, since they were used by previous studies, it is appropriate to use their variables to test their models so that empirical results are comparable. Second, political institutions affect the whole range of income distribution rather than a particular segment, so in order to examine the effects of political systems on income distribution, it is important to investigate

**Table 9.1**
Means of income distribution (household versus individual)

| Measure | Household | | | Individual | | | Avg factor |
|---|---|---|---|---|---|---|---|
| | Mean | Std error | N | Mean | Std error | N | |
| Gini (Muller) | 38.225 | 8.276 | 359 | 37.565 | 9.830 | 206 | 1.018 |
| Middle (Perotti) | 0.390 | 0.042 | 322 | 0.371 | 0.034 | 171 | 1.050 |
| Ratio (B&J) | 2.930 | 1.578 | 322 | 2.782 | 1.632 | 171 | 1.051 |
| Upper (Muller) | 0.441 | 0.074 | 322 | 0.445 | 0.076 | 171 | 0.992 |

**Table 9.2**
Means of income distribution (income versus expenditure)

| Measure | Expenditure | | | Income | | | Avg factor |
|---|---|---|---|---|---|---|---|
| | Mean | Std error | N | Mean | Std error | N | |
| Gini (Muller) | 36.968 | 6.922 | 130 | 38.288 | 9.361 | 435 | 0.966 |
| Middle (Perotti) | 0.373 | 0.025 | 104 | 0.386 | 0.043 | 389 | 0.967 |
| Ratio (B&J) | 2.522 | 1.072 | 104 | 2.974 | 1.698 | 389 | 0.848 |
| Upper (Muller) | 0.439 | 0.056 | 104 | 0.443 | 0.079 | 389 | 0.991 |

all relevant measures. Tables 9.1, 9.2, and 9.3 explore measurement problems related to income distribution.

Table 9.1 presents information on the means of the four income inequality measures in Deininger and Squire's (1996) data set by both household and individual distributions; the average factor for each of the four measures is also provided. The difference between the two distributions is negligible in the middle quintiles, the upper quintile, the Gini coefficient, and the ratio of the upper quintile to the bottom quintiles. Bollen and Jackman (1985) are justified in using a dummy variable to control for the individual distribution, as the dummy variable is statistically significant in their analysis. In the data for this chapter, the average discrepancy between household and individual income distributions appears minimal.

Table 9.2 shows the means of income distribution as measured by income and expenditure. Except for the ratio, the difference in the other measures is not very large. Of the four measures, the ratio of the upper quintile to the bottom two quintiles is particularly sensitive to systematic differences in how the surveys are conducted. The

**Table 9.3**
Means of income distribution (gross versus net income)

| Measure | Gross | | | Net | | | Avg factor |
|---|---|---|---|---|---|---|---|
| | Mean | Std error | N | Mean | Std error | N | |
| Gini (Muller) | 44.416 | 8.513 | 287 | 33.842 | 7.416 | 252 | 1.225 |
| Middle (Perotti) | 0.377 | 0.046 | 258 | 0.392 | 0.030 | 223 | 0.960 |
| Ratio (B&J) | 3.436 | 1.785 | 258 | 2.210 | 1.007 | 223 | 1.555 |
| Upper (Muller) | 0.468 | 0.078 | 258 | 0.410 | 0.056 | 223 | 1.144 |

upper-quintile share is systematically larger as measured by income rather than by expenditure, and the lower quintile share is smaller as measured by income than by expenditure. The ratio absorbs both tendencies, leading to a larger degree of systematic discrepancy. Indeed, close examination of data of the first and second quintiles shows that only the first quintile has a sizable discrepancy. While the mean of the first-quintile income share as measured by expenditure is 0.073, it is 0.060 as measured by income, resulting in an average factor of 1.22. For the second quintile, the two values are 0.115 and 0.111, and the average factor is 1.004. The first-quintile income share appears to be systematically lower when measured by income rather than by expenditure, resulting in a systematically higher ratio of the fifth quintile to the first two quintiles as measured by income rather than expenditure.

Table 9.3 presents information on the measures of the relevant income-distribution variables as measured by gross and net income. Compared to both the household versus individual method and the expenditure versus income method, the gross-income versus net-income method is prone to systematic discrepancy. It can be argued that the way taxes are collected in a large cross-section of countries tends to reduce income inequality rather than increase it. This hypothesis appears to be confirmed by the information in table 9.3.

The gross-income method makes a nation look more unequal than the net-income method by an average of 23% on the Gini scale. In a more detailed picture, the fifth-quintile income share is 14% larger as measured by gross income than as measured by net income. The first-quintile income as measured by gross income is, on average, only 67% of that as measured by net income (0.051 versus 0.076).

Finally, second-quintile income as measured by gross income is 84% of that as measured by net income (0.102 versus 0.122). Combined with the systematic upward trend for the upper quintile under the gross method, the ratio of the fifth quintile over the bottom quintiles is 56% larger under the gross-income method than under the net-income method. It is this kind of systematic discrepancy in the data against which one needs to be guarded.

Overall, the middle quintile shares (the third and fourth quintiles) used by Perotti (1996) are the most robust measure because they are relatively insensitive to measurement mechanisms generating systematic bias. The fifth quintile is also quite robust overall, though certain adjustments need to be made for the difference between the gross- and net-income methods. The use of the Gini coefficient and, in particular, the ratio of the upper to the bottom quintiles require some systematic adjustments to purge or alleviate the discrepancy factor. This can be achieved by the averaging method used by Perotti (1996), or by the use of dummy variables in a multivariate model, as used by Bollen and Jackman (1985).

Another problem related to the income-distribution data is the paucity of high-quality data available for large-sample cross-country analysis. The largest samples in the research on the relationship between democracy and income inequality are the 60 observations in Bollen and Jackman 1985 and the 55 observations in Muller 1988.[9] The present study relies on the recent data compiled by Deininger and Squire (1996), who cull 680 high-quality cases from 2,623 observations for the period of 1947 through 1995. The data cover 86 countries or regions, ranging from the United States in 1947 to Belarus and Estonia in 1995. In combination with the data on explanatory variables, as well as the adjustment between the net- and gross-income methods, there are a total of 82 countries available for the cross-country analysis in this chapter.[10]

## 9.3   Model Specification

The model used in this chapter to test the relationship between democracy and inequality is a combination of the models used by Bollen and Jackman (1985) and Muller (1988). Bollen and Jackman made three major advances over previous work. First, they considered a nonlinear association between development and inequality *à la* Kuznets (1955) by including both the level of development and the quadratic form of development to measure the rate of change of the development effect on inequality. Second, they made adjustments between survey data based on household-income distribution and on individual-income distribution by incorporating a dummy variable that measures the fixed effect of individual income in the model. Third, they tackled the endogeneity issue regarding democracy and inequality by using a simultaneous-equations system involving two-stage least-squares (2SLS) estimation. In addition, they considered the international position (i.e., core, periphery, or semiperiphery) of each nation, based on the world-system theory (Wallerstein 1974, 1979). In this connection, they included data on the population between ages 0 through 14 because they assumed that high population growth engenders income inequality by expanding the proportion of the national population in low-income groups (Ahluwalia 1976). Rapid increase in the population of the low-income groups will aggravate the inequality problems of periphery and semiperiphery countries.

In the presence of these control variables, the policy variable under examination in Bollen and Jackman (1985) is democracy's effect on income inequality, indexed by the ratio of the fifth-quintile income share to the first- and second-quintile income shares. The data on democracy are based upon Bollen's index of liberal democracy for 1965.[11] As discussed in chapter 3, this variable is highly correlated with the political-rights variable in the Freedom House world-survey data. The data on income distribution are from the World Bank. There are a total of 60 observations available for analysis, 40 of which were taken between 1960 and 1970. The juxtaposition of the 1965 democracy data with the income-inequality data, ranging from 1958 to 1975, is based upon the assumption that the inequality data are chronologically stable. Compared to some other political and economic variables, income distribution does evince a pattern of relative stability over time, though some countries (such as several in Latin America) do vary considerably in their income distribution across years. By contrast, the income-distribution data for developed countries (excluding France) are relatively stable over the years. The assumption of stable income distribution is necessary for the use of the democracy variable, fixed at one year, 1965. Two problems may arise from this assumption. First, though distribution data are stable compared to data for most other variables, some countries do have a considerable standard deviation over time (e.g.,

**Table 9.4**
Income distribution by standard deviation of the Gini coefficient

| Country | Frequency | Mean of Gini | SD |
|---|---|---|---|
| *Ten countries with the smallest standard deviation* | | | |
| Morocco | 2 | 39.20 | 0.01 |
| Zambia | 2 | 50.56 | 0.63 |
| Seychelles | 2 | 46.50 | 0.71 |
| Pakistan | 9 | 31.50 | 0.86 |
| Belgium | 4 | 27.01 | 0.88 |
| Netherlands | 12 | 28.59 | 0.95 |
| Greece | 3 | 34.53 | 1.07 |
| Denmark | 4 | 32.08 | 1.26 |
| United States | 45 | 35.28 | 1.29 |
| Japan | 23 | 34.82 | 1.35 |
| *Ten countries with the largest standard deviation* | | | |
| Egypt | 4 | 38.00 | 4.32 |
| Panama | 4 | 52.43 | 5.01 |
| Guatemala | 3 | 55.68 | 5.18 |
| Uganda | 2 | 36.89 | 5.50 |
| Chile | 5 | 51.84 | 5.76 |
| Peru | 4 | 46.34 | 5.86 |
| Turkey | 3 | 50.36 | 5.98 |
| France | 7 | 43.11 | 6.07 |
| Sri Lanka | 9 | 41.71 | 6.10 |
| Guyana | 2 | 51.49 | 6.60 |

France, Sri Lanka, and Guyana), compared to others (e.g., the Netherlands, the United States, and Japan).

Table 9.4 presents the 10 countries with the smallest standard deviation of the Gini coefficient and the 10 countries with the largest. The difference shown between the two groups is quite substantial, challenging the assumption that income distribution is generally stable over time and across nations.

Second, and more important, such an assumption discounts the dynamic change due to the interaction between democracy and inequality. Not only is income distribution assumed to be stable, so is, implicitly, the degree of democracy. As shown by Muller, however, the change in income inequality may have been caused by the history of a democracy in terms of years, so that the longer the country remains democratic, the more likely income inequality is reduced (Muller 1988). The assumption of stability precludes the study of the dynamic effect of the history of democracy on income inequality. Additionally, Bollen and Jackman's (1985) finding that the level of liberal democracy has no effect on income inequality may have resulted from the possibility that remote democratic values may have little to do with recent changes in income distribution. The income distribution in a country in 1975, for example, may not be responsive and sensitive to the degree of democracy it had in 1965. Though it can be assumed that political systems represent slowly evolving and semipermanent institutions, it would shed extra light on the relationship between democracy and inequality if this assumption can be relaxed and replaced with a model that allows for consequences of recent changes in the political system or political rights.

Otherwise using essentially the same model as Bollen and Jackman (1985), Muller (1988) pivots his study on the chronological effect of the history of democracy on income inequality. His alternative-policy variables are the years in which a country remains democratic and a qualitative variable that distinguishes among a "new democracy" (less than a generation, approximately 20 years old), "relatively new democracies" (more than one but less than two generations), "relatively old democracies" (more than two but less than three generations), and "very old democracies" (three or more generations). Muller's major thesis is that it is the years of democracy, rather than the level of democracy, that affects income inequality, because it takes years for democracy to work out the political mechanisms to redistribute wealth. These mechanisms include strengthening grass-roots interest groups and forming political procedures and structures for the transmission of citizens' demands. Even at the same level of democracy, it is difficult—if not impossible—for a new democracy to equal an old democracy's capacity to reduce income inequality, assuming that a relatively equal distribution of wealth is on the democratic agenda. Muller's findings essentially support his hypothesis. After controlling for development, world-system position, and population composition, the democratic-experience variable has a significant and negative effect on income inequality, while the level-of-democracy variable is far from statistically significant.

A disturbing problem is that the relationship between the years of democracy and income inequality may not be linear, or even monotonic. An overly long course of democracy may not give an old democracy an advantage over those newly emerged. Admittedly, young democracies need a certain amount of time to consolidate and develop their redistribution systems, but it need not take many generations to achieve this goal. For instance, Muller credits the United States with a history of 102 years as a democracy at its data point (1975), while Germany has only 25 years at its data point (1975).[12] Though democracy in the United States is four times as old as in Germany, Germany's income inequality was lower than that of the Untied States. As discussed earlier, it is appropriate that we examine the political system up to the point at which income distribution is observed; nonetheless, we should be careful about how far we want to look back. The events in the previous few decades, rather than the past century, may be more relevant as determinants for income distribution. In other words, there is a contrast between a long-term institutional effect that can be measured by years of democracy and a short-run dynamism that reflects political changes more recently affecting income distribution. It is the short-run effect that should carry more weight, as it is chronologically more closely related to the observation of income inequality and substantively more meaningful as an explanation than what happened a long time ago.

Even with all of these potential limitations, the papers by Bollen and Jackman (1985) and by Muller (1988) represent the most thorough investigation of democracy and income inequality.[13] The present work benefits from the solid groundwork laid by these two articles, such as considerations of nonlinearity, simultaneity, sample composition, and systematic measurement problems. This chapter attempts to expand the previous findings by using the data recently improved by Deininger and Squire (1996), covering 82 countries. When combined with the other available political and economic data, the data surpasses the number of nations covered by Bollen and Jackman by 22, and by Muller by 32 (see appendix 9.A). I will use the four measures of inequality discussed above and also alternative measures of democratic experience differentiated into both long-term and short-term dynamics.

The four major indices for income inequality cover most of the inequality measures utilized in various studies on income inequality; they are highly correlated with each other, as indicated in table 9.5. The Gini indicator measures the general level of inequality, based on the difference between the hypothetically perfect equality and the underlying Lorenz curve. The second measure used here, the income

**Table 9.5**
Correlation statistics for measures of inequality

|         | GINI    | MIDDLE  | RATIO   | TOP     |
|---------|---------|---------|---------|---------|
| GINI    | 1.000   | −0.794  | 0.918   | 0.970   |
|         | (680)   | (607)   | (607)   | (607)   |
| MIDDLE  |         | 1.000   | −0.782  | −0.893  |
|         |         | (607)   | (607)   | (607)   |
| RATIO   |         |         | 1.000   | 0.929   |
|         |         |         | (607)   | (607)   |
| TOP     |         |         |         | 1.000   |
|         |         |         |         | (607)   |

Number of observations in parentheses.

share for the fifth quintile (TOP), measures the concentration of income in the richest 20% of the population. These are the "two most commonly used measures" (Muller 1988, 53). As they are very highly correlated, the benefit of using both of them in the same study (as Muller does) may not be substantial. The combined income of the third and fourth quintiles (MIDDLE) is important because it captures the idea of the "middle class," whose income share is usually associated with the concept of equality. It is highly positively correlated with the third-quintile income group, where the median voter lies. The advantage of using the combined share of the third and fourth quintiles lies in the finding that it is less sensitive to measurement errors than simply using the third-quintile share (Perotti 1996, 154). The relative income share of the fifth quintile to the combined income shares of the first two quintiles (RATIO) measures polarized income inequality between the rich and poor. Some scholars maintain that the Gini coefficient is sensitive to the middle of a distribution (Allison 1978), and the ratio is used to adjust for the relative insensitivity of the Gini to the top or bottom share (Bollen and Jackman 1985, Perotti 1996). Table 9.5 shows that the Gini is better correlated with TOP than with MIDDLE.

It should also be noted that the RATIO measure adopted by Bollen and Jackman (1985) better reflects general inequality in a country than the MIDDLE measure used in Perotti (1996). While the correlation between GINI and RATIO is 0.92, it is −0.79 between GINI and MIDDLE. Therefore, the Gini coefficient and the ratio measure used by Bollen and Jackman seem to be the best measures for a broad picture of income inequality.

The selection rules for the observations are (1) that only the latest observations are used, and (2) that the income basis must be un-equivocally declared in terms of either gross or net income. The assumption behind the first rule is that the latest data tend to benefit from the use of a standardized methodology and are therefore of higher quality than previous data. Additionally, by choosing the latest year in which the income data are available, it is possible to extend the years of political data that precede income-distribution data in order to allow for the examination of short-term, as well as long-term, effects of political mechanisms on income distribution. The second rule omits those cases for which we are unsure whether they are based on gross or net income. Without such information, it is impossible to make the necessary adjustments. As the discrepancy between gross income and net income is large, the failure to make adjustments between the two sources of data would make subse-quent analysis ambiguous, if not misleading. Conformity with these requirements yields 82 countries for this study. It should be noted that the sample to which the two selection rules are applied consists of all the data up to 1995, a total of 680 cases.

For democracy variables, I use the political rights indicator in the Freedom House annual survey and the Liberal Democracy Index by Bollen (Gastil, various years; Freedom House 1990; Freedom House, *Freedom Review*, various years; Bollen 1980, 1990, 1993). While the former variable has been used in the preceding chapters of this book, which makes it a primary candidate for the democracy variable in the current chapter, the latter was used both by Bollen and Jackman (1985) and by Muller (1988).[14] As discussed in chapter 3, the corre-lation between the two variables is very high. Indeed, it is the high-est among four indicators for political rights and freedom ($r = 0.93$), even higher than that between political rights and civil liberties, the twin variable of political freedom in the Freedom House data set (see table 3.2). The political-rights scores seem to be the most desirable substitute index for liberal democracy.

The use of the political-rights variable allows us to conduct an analysis of the political dynamism up to the point in time when the income-inequality data are collected. In contrast, the benefit of using the liberal-democracy index allows this study to be compared to previous works on the same topic. Both variables are measured con-tinuously, which prevents an arbitrary decision categorizing a coun-try as a democracy or nondemocracy.[15] By comparison, Persson and

Tabellini (1994) and Perotti (1996) classify countries into the binary variable of democracy or nondemocracy in their studies of income equality and democracy. It is debatable whether some countries, particularly those rated as democracies by Persson and Tabellini (1994), should have ever been classified as democracies by the standards of political scientists. For example, Persson and Tabellini (1994) rate Bangladesh, Zimbabwe, and Senegal as democratic, while these countries have consistently been rated as "partly free" or "not free" since 1972 by both Gastil and the Freedom House surveys.[16] Person and Tabellini (1994) also rate Hong Kong as democratic, despite the fact that Hong Kong did not have an elected government in its entire history as a British colony or elected legislators until the 1990s.[17]

Along with the political rights data and the liberal democracy index, I also adopt the years-of-democracy measure, as defined by Muller. This measure captures the long-term effect of democratic institutions on income distribution. However, this variable is very skewed, with some old democracies having existed for more than a century, while others have just recently turned democratic. So I designed a variable named *weighted democratic experience*. This variable takes a lag of four years prior to the data year of income distribution, and is confined to the period in which the Gastil and Freedom House data are collected.

The advantage of constructing this latter variable is twofold. First, it measures the *density* of democratic experience, as the years of democracy are weighted by the years for which the country is in the data set. Weighted democratic experience equates the United States with Germany in terms of the density of democratic experience, in contrast to the large difference in terms of democratic years as measured by Muller's approach. Second, this variable contrasts long-term democratic experience with some short-term implications, as it is confined to the initial year 1972. For instance, if the income data were collected in 1994, then weighted democratic experience would take the average years of democracy for the period of 1972–1990. The use of a four-year lag places this variable prior to the GDP variable, which takes a three-year lag, thus mitigating the confusion of income effects. In addition, as this variable is bounded in 1972, it captures the relatively recent democratic experience of these countries. To be sure, the quality of democratic politics varies across countries and is path-dependent. The same score in the data given to a recent democracy in 1975 and an old democracy in the same year may confound certain path-dependent variations. What matters, however, is the difference in the explanatory power of the long-term indicator or the short-term indicator. I believe that income distribution is more sensitive to recent political experience than to remote political history. I also believe in path dependence, in the sense that the recent experience is related to, and rooted in, the past. But path dependence also implies that recent events have a larger impact on the current situation than more remote historical events. Both the long- and short-run measures of democratic experience are designed to capture the political dynamics responsible for the evolution of income distribution. But between the two, income distribution should be more sensitive to short-run experiences.

Next, as in Bollen and Jackman (1985) and Muller (1988), some indicators of economic development are included to control for both linear and nonlinear relationships between development and inequality. It has been proposed that inequality increases in the early stages of economic development and declines when the economy evolves to advanced stages of industrialization.[18] Bollen and Jackman use GNP per capita and its quadratic form for this measure. Muller adopts energy consumption per capita in 1965 for the same purpose, maintaining that GNP per capita is not comparable across nations because of difficulties in adjusting for exchange rates. This study escapes these problems by utilizing data on real GDP per capita based upon international dollars derived from purchasing-power-parity comparisons. These data are from *The Penn World Table* data set compiled by Summers and Heston (2000).

International dollars avoids the difficulty of calculating real exchange rates by taking account of different levels of purchasing power across various countries. Additionally, it is superior to an energy-consumption measure because it reflects a broader and more general approach to economic development. Figure 9.1 plots income distributions against income levels. The latter data are from *The Penn World Table* (Summers and Heston, various years), and the former data are from Deininger and Squire (1996), for both developing and developed countries. It reveals what seems to be a weakly U-shaped (instead of an inverted U-shaped) pattern between GDP per capita and the Gini coefficient. It should be noted that the variance of inequality is larger in the earlier, rather than later, stage of develop-

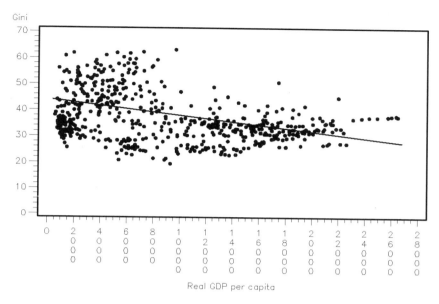

**Figure 9.1**
Development and inequality

ment. In a bivariate model, $\text{GINI} = 41.06 \ (0.589) - 0.0005 \times \text{RGDPCH}$ ($5.383\text{E} - 05$); the numbers in the parentheses are standard errors. When squared RGDPCH is added to the bivariate model, the improvement in the goodness of fit is negligible.[19] In general, there seems to be a negative linear (if not slightly U-shaped) relationship between income inequality and development. In the data, an increase in real GDP per capita by 1,000 international dollars will decrease the Gini coefficient by 5 points on the 100-point scale. GDP per capita squared is also included in the model to reflect the possibility of a nonlinear effect of income on income distribution, though I do not expect it to be significant.

The next variable to be discussed is the ratio of the population of age 14 or under to the total population. This variable is included to account for the hypothesis that income inequality is aggravated by an upsurge in the number of children, particularly in low-income families, which may have been caused by the income effect discussed earlier. The share of population aged 14 or under is a potentially important demographic variable. It should be negatively correlated with the share of population over age 65, a variable used by

Perotti.[20] Like the population share of 65 or over, $POP_{14}$ is likely proxying for the fertility rate, which decreases as income equality increases under the endogenous-fertility model.[21]

I also include variables for world-system position, as in Bollen and Jackman (1985) and Muller (1988). World-system theorists argue that the interaction between developed countries and developing countries aggravates income inequality in the latter group of countries, enriching a coterie while pauperizing the overwhelming majority (Wallerstein 1974, 1979; Chirot 1977). "The ongoing process of a world-economy tends to expand the economic and social gaps among its varying areas in the very process of its development" (Wallerstein 1974, 350). These varying areas refer to the core, periphery, and semiperiphery. According to the formal classification by Snyder and Kick (1979), the group of core-states consists of advanced industrialized countries. Similarly, the semiperiphery areas comprise states that were the core-areas of earlier versions of the world economic system, such as Turkey, Ireland, and Israel,[22] while the periphery is made up of most of the developing countries.

From the world-system perspective, the economic relations between core countries and periphery (including semiperiphery) countries are intertwined in such a way that benefits the core countries' development and harms the periphery countries' development. This kind of economic interface worsens the plight: the well-being of the majority of people in the periphery decreases as the result of unfavorable conditions imposed on them by the core nations. According to the Kuznets (1955) thesis, however, the periphery countries consist of those whose economic development has been accelerated, consequently engendering an increase in income inequality. Thus, under either theory, we are likely to find that being in the periphery has a more pronounced negative impact on income inequality than being in the core.[23]

It should be noted that neither the study by Bollen and Jackman (1985) nor the one by Muller (1988) has found a significant effect of periphery or semiperiphery status on income inequality. The lack of statistical significance of these structural positions may be due to the lack of variation caused by a limited sample size. While Bollen and Jackman examined 45 developing countries and Muller studied 34, this chapter collects data on 59 developing countries. The improvement in both the quality and quantity of data on income distribution and political institutions might improve our statistical analysis of the nuances that have escaped scholarly scrutiny before.

Finally, I add a dummy variable to indicate the seven countries in Pacific Asia: three newly industrializing countries (NICs) in Pacific Asia (South Korea, Singapore, and Taiwan) and the four new exporting countries (NECs) in the region (Indonesia, Malaysia, Thailand, and the Philippines). As mentioned early in chapter 2, these countries typically have a low level of income inequality. The Confucian or Islamic culture prevalent in these countries encourages social compassion and a traditional emphasis on wealth egalitarianism, both consistent with social equality. Nonetheless, in terms of the rationale of political-regime legitimacy, relatively equal wealth distribution in these societies may result from political elites wishing to maximize their political returns by increasing economic growth, which, as shown in chapter 4, depends upon a low level of income inequality. Following the strategy of "shared growth," the political elites in these countries consciously adopt policies designed to stimulate growth while militating against income inequality. "Sharing gave the less fortunate a stake in the economy, thereby discouraging disruptive activities and diminishing the risk of regime failure. It also enabled the regimes to concentrate on promoting rational economic policies by reducing the need to constantly contend with issues of redistribution" (Campos and Root 1996, 2). Growth combined with welfare balance is the hallmark of East Asian development. With everything else kept constant, being one of the Pacific Asian countries is negatively associated with income inequality. Table 9.6 presents the expected effects of the political and economic variables on income inequality.

To avoid or alleviate the endogeneity issue, all the continuous independent variables take values that occur prior to the year in which the income-distribution data were collected, as suggested by Muller (1988). The variable for political rights (PR) takes the average value of the political-rights score for the three years in the Gastil or Freedom House data prior to the year of the income-distribution data. For instance, if the income-distribution data are collected for 1993, then PR is the average of the political rights scores from 1990 through 1992. Similarly, the prior value of Liberal Democracy Index (LDI) is employed to estimate income distribution. Since the LDI data exist only for 1960, 1965, and 1980 and only 7 out of 82

**Table 9.6**
A summary of theoretical arguments in parametric format

| Sign | Symbol | Independent variable | Data source |
|---|---|---|---|
| − | PR | Political rights | Gastil and Freedom House (various years) |
| − | LD | Liberal democracy | Bollen 1980, 1990, 1993 |
| − | DE | Democratic experience | Gasiorowski 1996 |
| − | WDE | Weighted democratic experience | Gastil and Freedom House (various years) |
| − | GDP | GDP per capita | Summers and Heston 2000 |
| ? | $GDP^2$ | GDP per capita squared | Summers and Heston 2000 |
| + | $POP_{14}$ | Portion of population of age 0–14 | World Bank 1993 |
| + | SEMIPER | Semiperiphery | Snyder and Kick 1979 and Gasiorowski 1996 |
| + | PER | Periphery | Snyder and Kick 1979 and Gasiorowski 1996 |
| − | PA | Pacific Asia | |

Dependent variable: income inequality.

income-distribution cases occurred before 1980, the LDI for 1980 will most likely be used as the indicator. Since LDI is highly correlated with PR, the inclusion of LDI will reveal how sensitively the income-distribution data respond to past political conditions.

Democratic experience (DE) is constructed as in Muller's (1988) work: the number of years during which the country remains a democracy, up to the year in which the country's recent income data are collected. Weighted democratic experience (WDE) is the average number of years during which a country remains a democracy in the Gastil and Freedom House data sets from 1972 to the fourth year preceding the year in which the income data were measured. For instance, if the income data were collected in 1993, then WDE will be the average number of democratic years between 1972 and 1989. The robustness of the lags is tested in the next section to make sure that the result is not very sensitive to the lag structure. Thus WDE stands for the density of democratic effect, compared to DE, which indicates the number of democratic years since a nation's democratic inauguration.

The variable GDP reflects the recent development trajectory. It is real GDP per capita with a three-year lag preceding the year of recent income-distribution data. As in Bollen and Jackman 1985 and Muller 1988, $GDP^2$ is GDP squared, indicating the changing effect on income distribution of an increase or decrease in the level of GDP per capita. The percentage of population age 0 to 14 ($\text{POP}_{14}$) is available from the World Bank only for five-year intervals from 1960 to 1990. So the temporal design for this variable is as follows: If the recent income-distribution data were collected after 1990, $\text{POP}_{14}$ takes its 1985 value; if the recent income-distribution data were collected between 1985 and 1990, $\text{POP}_{14}$ takes its 1980 value. As income-distribution data collection is not confined by a five-year interval, the lag structure of $\text{POP}_{14}$ is more than five years in some cases.

## 9.4  Empirical Evidence

The specifications in the last section lead to the following model for the estimation of income inequality:

$$Y = \beta_0 + \beta_1 X + \beta_2 \text{ GDP} + \beta_3 \text{ GDP}^2 + \beta_4 \text{ PER} + \beta_5 \text{ SEMIPER}$$
$$+ \beta_6 \text{ POP}_{14} + \beta_7 \text{ PA} + \varepsilon$$

Here $Y$ is one of the four income-inequality indices discussed above, and $X$ stands for a variable from the set of political rights, the Liberal Democracy Index, the long-term democratic effect, and short-term democratic experience. GDP is real GDP per capita, $\text{GDP}^2$ is real GDP per capita squared, PER is a dummy variable taking a value of one for countries in the periphery area and zero otherwise; SEMIPER is a dummy variable that takes a value of one for countries in the semi-periphery and zero otherwise; $\text{POP}_{14}$ is the portion of those aged 0 to 14 in the population; PA is a dummy indicator for the seven Pacific Asian countries identified in the preceding section; and $\varepsilon$ is the error term. There are a total of 82 observations for the estimation of the Gini coefficient and 75 observations for the estimation of the MIDDLE, TOP, and RATIO indicators.[24]

To conserve space, table 9.7 reports the parameter estimates only for policy variables in the $X$ set of the above generic form of the model, namely, the variables for political systems. The four variables in $X$ are entered separately for each of the four income-distribution variables, with the rest of the equation kept the same. This results in a total of 16 equations. The first row for each policy variable is the parameter estimate of the given variable, the second is the standard error of the estimate, and the third is the $\bar{R}^2$ (adjusted $R^2$) for the equation containing the policy variable. The number of observations is indicated in the last row of the table.

**Table 9.7**
Summary of parameter estimates on political rights and democracy

| Variable | GINI | MIDDLE | TOP | RATIO |
|---|---|---|---|---|
| Weighted democratic experience | −6.313* | 0.031* | −0.054* | −1.746* |
| $\sigma$ | (2.796) | (0.013) | (0.024) | (0.565) |
| $\bar{R}^2$ | 0.391 | 0.532 | 0.418 | 0.285 |
| Democratic experience | −0.026 | 0.00019 | −0.00014 | −0.010 |
| $\sigma$ | (0.062) | (0.00029) | (0.00056) | (0.013) |
| $\bar{R}^2$ | 0.351 | 0.494 | 0.376 | 0.191 |
| Political rights | −7.267* | 0.022** | −0.050** | −1.590* |
| $\sigma$ | (3.467) | (0.017) | (0.033) | (0.786) |
| $\bar{R}^2$ | 0.386 | 0.503 | 0.396 | 0.231 |
| Liberal democracy | −0.042 | 0.00004 | −0.00006 | −0.0059 |
| $\sigma$ | (0.035) | (0.00017) | (0.00033) | (0.0079) |
| $\bar{R}^2$ | 0.362 | 0.491 | 0.376 | 0.190 |
| Total $N$ | 82 | 75 | 75 | 75 |

Dependent variables are given in the first row, and independent variables in the first column.
*Statistically significant at the 2.5% level, in a one-tailed test.
**Statistically significant at the 5% level, in a one-tailed test.
Standard errors in parentheses.

Of the four political-freedom or democracy variables, the best indicator for income inequality is weighted democratic experience, statistically significant at the 2.5% level across all four regressions.[25] The average value for political rights is statistically significant at the 2.5% level for two broad indicators of income inequality: the Gini coefficient and the ratio of the fifth quintile to the first and second quintiles. It is also statistically significant at the 5% level for the other two indicators of income distribution: MIDDLE and TOP.

The statistical evidence demonstrates that the degree of democracy, as measured by the political-rights indicator in the Gastil and Freedom House data, and the average number of years of democracy have a *negative* effect on income inequality. The *more* democratic the country and the *higher* the density of its democratic experience, the *lower* the overall income inequality, as measured by the Gini coefficient. All other policy variables consistently have the expected signs. *More* years of democracy and *higher* scores on liberal democracy tend to lead to a *lower* Gini coefficient, *higher* combined income shares of the third and fourth quintiles, a *lower* fifth quintile share, and a *lower* ratio of the fifth quintile to the first and second quintiles. Democratic experience and liberal democracy, however, are not statistically significant.

Generally, weighted democratic experience and political rights have better prediction accuracy than democratic experience and the liberal democracy index. They produce higher $\bar{R}^2$ measures than the other two alternative policy variables when estimating the same dependent variable with the same set of control variables controlled for. The $\bar{R}^2$ row indicates its highest level among the four regressions for the same dependent variable.

We see three potential reasons why the average number of years of democracy emerges as a strong indicator of income inequality. First, unlike the absolute number of years of democracy, it potentially fills the chronological space with the years of both democratic and non-democratic periods of each country, thus achieving a measure of the weighted totality of democratic experience. Second, unlike the years of democracy used by Muller (1988), it uses a shorter time period on the grounds that recent political experience matters, even though political institutions are path-dependent. Third, there may be a difference between democracy as a state and democracy as a degree. Income inequality can be effectively reduced only in countries that have reached and passed the threshold for achieving true democracy. Nondemocratic countries may not be able to develop sophisticated mechanisms to increase income equality. The empirical results seem to support this argument for the use of democracy as a state, which originated with Muller (1988).

Next I test the robustness of the intensity of democratic experience by using different lags as a regressor for the Gini coefficient, maintaining everything else as the same. Regression is run on the Gini coefficient with lags of zero through five for the weighted democratic-experience variable. The parameter estimates for all lags are statistically significant at the 2.5% level.[26] The results are presented graphically in figure 9.2.

Clearly, there is an increasing pattern in the values of the parameter estimates for weighted democratic experience, though the rising trend tends to flatten out when there is a greater lag. The underlying scenario is that when the lag increases, old democracies have more weight as new democracies—particularly those engendered in the Third Wave of democratization—fall out of the democracy group because they were not yet born. This produces a salient effect of high

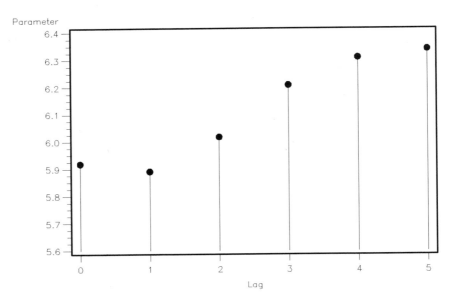

**Figure 9.2**
Lag structure and democratic density

democratic density versus low democratic density and intensifies the dampening impact of democracy on income inequality. Judging from the history of democracy in the post–World War II period, the overall democratic density (which is the average democratic density of all democratic countries at one point in time) becomes higher as we advance further into this period. We logically should expect an ascending trend of the parameter estimate for weighted democratic experience as its lag increases. However, it is important to notice that as the overall democratic density increases, the impact of democracy on income inequality increases, but diminishing returns to the negative effect of democracy on income inequality occur, as indicated by the declining rate of increase in the parameter estimate. A higher density of democratic experience will make the society more equal, though the reduction in income inequality lessens with each unit of increase in democratic density.

Income inequality appears to be influenced by the density of democratic experience. This finding has two implications when held next to Muller's (1988) result. On the one hand, democracy as a state seems to be a better indicator for income inequality than democracy as a degree, consistent with Muller's findings. On the other, a longer period of democracy is not found to be a significant factor in the reduction of income inequality; the number of years of democracy has virtually no explanatory power for income inequality. The latter result implies a modification of Muller's conclusions regarding democracy and income inequality. It is the density of democratic experience, rather than the number of years of democracy, that matters in the relationship between democracy and income inequality. In other words, we must qualify Muller's argument that a democracy needs to consolidate and requires a certain level of maturity, measured by years, for income inequality to be reduced.

The statistical information in table 9.7 is consistent with the democratic school of thought regarding democracy and income inequality, especially when overall income inequality is concerned. Compared with an autocracy, a nation that remains a democratic polity throughout the entire sample will have more than six points knocked off its Gini coefficient. Being a democracy for half of the sample time reduces the Gini coefficient by about three points, in comparison with being an autocracy for every year of the sample. All of this is consistent with the argument that democracy and political freedom lead to a reduction in income inequality, and is contrary to the argument that democracy increases the level of income inequality. The tenet of the authoritarian school cannot be sustained by the data.

The control variables seem to return meaningful results as well, as most take the signs predicted in table 9.6, though they are mostly insignificant.[27] Table 9.8 reports the regressions of weighted democratic experience on the four income-inequality indicators, with a view toward examining the effects of control variables.

Development tends to worsen income inequality, but the trend is slowed as the country moves toward full development. This result—as seen from the positive sign on GDP and the negative sign on GDP$^2$ in columns (1), (3), and (4), and the opposite signs in column (2), respectively—is consistent with Bollen and Jackman's and Muller's findings, though the effects here are far from statistically significant.

The world-system-position variables (PER, SEMIPER) have some effects on income inequalities, particularly in the cases of GINI and RATIO, the two broad indicators of income inequality. Both the periphery and semiperiphery areas tend to have higher levels of

**Table 9.8**
Regression of average democracy on the four indices of income inequality

|  | GINI | MIDDLE | TOP | RATIO |
|---|---|---|---|---|
| INTERCEPT | 38.915* | 0.382* | 0.411* | 4.585* |
|  | (8.808) | (0.043) | (0.083) | (1.910) |
| WDE | −6.313* | 0.031* | −0.053* | −1.746* |
|  | (2.796) | (0.013) | (0.024) | (0.565) |
| GDP | 0.368 | −0.00007 | 0.005 | 0.089 |
|  | (0.983) | (0.0046) | (0.009) | (0.204) |
| GDP$^2$ | −0.035 | 0.00016 | −0.0004 | −0.007 |
|  | (0.052) | (0.0002) | (0.0005) | (0.011) |
| SEMIPER | 7.392** | −0.029† | 0.047 | 1.434** |
|  | (4.349) | (0.020) | (0.039) | (0.894) |
| PER | 9.024* | −0.017 | 0.052† | 1.719** |
|  | (4.510) | (0.021) | (0.041) | (0.947) |
| POP$_{14}$ | −8.762 | −0.056 | 0.082 | −5.263 |
|  | (22.244) | (0.109) | (0.211) | (4.887) |
| PA | −9.832* | 0.022† | −0.067* | −2.234* |
|  | (3.359) | (0.016) | (0.030) | (0.699) |
| $\bar{R}^2$ | 0.391 | 0.532 | 0.418 | 0.285 |
| $\sigma$ | 6.943 | 0.031 | 0.060 | 1.394 |
| Total $N$ | 82 | 75 | 75 | 75 |

*Statistically significant at the 2.5% level, one-tailed test.
**Statistically significant at the 5% level, one-tailed test.
†Statistically significant at the 10% level, one-tailed test.
Standard errors in parentheses.

income inequality than the core states, which are industrialized countries. With everything else kept constant, a periphery country's Gini coefficient will be nine points higher than a core country; a semiperiphery country's Gini index will be seven points higher. Thus being situated in the periphery or semiperiphery is associated with undesirable income inequality. These countries typically have unequal income distributions manifested in a massive low-income class and a small, but dominant high-income group, in contrast to the core area, where the middle-income group has already emerged as a powerful political and economic actor. Percentage of population aged 0 through 14 is not significant in any equation.

Finally, the Pacific Asian countries do have low levels of income inequality relative to other states. With everything else kept constant, the Gini coefficient of a country in this group will be about 10 points lower than other countries' Gini indices. The Pacific Asian dummy variable is statistically significant across the four equations, which shows that it gives quite robust results. While Pacific Asian developing countries do not necessarily have a very strong middle class, there is evidence that their overall inequality is low. In other words, with or without a strong middle-income group, Pacific Asian societies are characterized by a certain degree of egalitarianism, supporting Root's observation that "the high performing East Asian economies grew while adhering to policies that reduced income inequality during growth" (1996, 153). The result also confirms the argument of Root (1996) and Campos and Root (1996) that these countries follow a "shared growth" strategy and adopt policies that significantly reduce income inequality, so that their growth-enhancing strategies can have broad national and social support.

The empirical results in this chapter have shed light on the debate between Bollen and Jackman (1985) on the one hand and Muller (1988) on the other. While Bollen and Jackman fail to find any statistical relationship between democracy and income distribution, Muller claims a positive effect of democracy on income equality. This chapter bears directly on this debate, using essentially the same models as in those two projects. However, the test conducted in this chapter was significantly wider and deeper in extent than these two well-known works, and the sample against which the hypothesis was tested was larger and of higher quality. The dependent variables included not only the Gini coefficient and upper-quintile income share, as used by Muller, and the ratio of the top-quintile income share to the bottom-quintile income share, as used by Bollen and Jackman, but also the middle quintile shares. The policy variable—democracy—takes several forms, including not only the years of democracy, used by Muller, and the level of democracy, used by Bollen and Jackman, but also weighted democratic experience, which measures the dynamic effect of democracy on income distribution. The findings show that neither Bollen and Jackman nor Muller is completely correct regarding democracy's effect on income distribution. Democracy does have a positive effect on income equality. However, such a positive effect is of a more imminent nature than suggested by Muller. Neither the democracy variable used by Muller nor the one used by Bollen and Jackman is statistically significant in this chapter's tests. Rather, it is the recent establishment of democracy that determines the level of income equality.

## 9.5 Summary and Policy Implications

This chapter studies one additional channel through which democracy is believed to enhance economic growth: the effect of democracy on income distribution. It has been found that democracy, particularly democratic experience, weighted by the years of a country in the data set, has a pronounced positive effect on income equality. In other words, the more years of recent democratic experience a country has, the more likely the country has a relatively low level of income inequality.

Chapter 4 finds a negative effect of income inequality on growth and also speculates that political freedom may affect economic growth through the channel of reducing income inequality. The finding in this chapter strongly supports this speculation.

The statistical results favor the democratic model of income inequality. New democracies can achieve a similar reduction in income inequality to older democracies, though it is also true that a sustainable democracy is more likely to have relative income equality than a democracy that occasionally breaks down. Another implication is that there may be a threshold effect of democracy on income equality. This speculation is derived from the empirical fact that income-inequality variables are less sensitive to degrees of democracy than to the discrete state of democracy. The theoretical basis of this finding may be that the democratic mechanisms necessary for creating a relatively equal society consistent with democratic principles are crucial for reducing income inequality. Quasi-democratic countries, although having relatively high scores on political rights, still lack these mechanisms, which exist only in fully democratic systems. Therefore, they are unable to achieve significant reductions in income inequality.

The skeptical school does not receive much support from the empirical findings in this chapter. Democracy has a negative effect on income inequality if the level of development is kept constant. Indeed, I took values of weighted democracy prior to the real GDP per capita data. While the signs on GDP and GDP$^2$ are consistent with the Kuznets (1955) thesis, they are not statistically significant. The world-system theory receives limited confirmation by the data. Income inequality tends to be higher in periphery countries than in semiperiphery and core countries.

This study found that democracy has a negative effect on income inequality independently of economic development. Perotti (1996) implies that it is difficult to separate the income effect from the democracy effect. Failure to differentiate the democracy effect from the income effect is due to failure to treat income distribution as endogenous, which is the reason that the reduced equation focusing on income distribution and growth fails to capture the main elements of the underlying political process affecting wealth distribution. The analysis in this chapter, however, fully endogenizes income distribution and reaches the conclusion that democracy does reduce income inequality. This study's implication for the fiscal policy model advanced by Alesina and Rodrik (1994) and Persson and Tabellini (1994) is that political mechanisms in democracies are likely to produce an equilibrium that diminishes income disparity, thus facilitating future economic growth.

As income distribution is one of the strongest political determinants of economic growth, the findings in this chapter on the relationship between democracy and income distribution have important policy implications. A democratic polity has a better chance of relieving income inequality than an autocracy does. One argument that has been made against democracy in terms of economic growth is that in a system of wealth transfer determined by voters, democracy deters investors from committing their capital. However, combining the findings in chapter 4 and chapter 9, we find that democracy actually promotes economic growth by leveling the ground of income distribution. In the short run, wealth transfer may reduce the incentives of investment; in the long run, sustainable growth cannot be achieved without relatively equal wealth distribution.

The remaining question regarding income inequality and democracy is one of reverse causation: does a reduction in income inequality lead to democracy? This chapter has operationalized a prior state of democracy to explain current income inequality, so a feedback effect from income inequality to democracy is excluded. However, it is plausible that income inequality has an adverse effect on transitions to democracy (Feng and Zak 1999, Zak and Feng 2003).

# 10            Political Freedom and Economic Freedom

*The personal right to acquire property, which is a natural right, gives to property, when acquired, a right to protection, as a social right.*

James Madison

As the title suggests, this is a study of the relationship between political freedom and economic freedom. While numerous well-supported hypotheses have been developed examining the relationships between political freedom and economic growth and between economic freedom and economic growth, the connection between the two freedoms remains ambiguous. Previous study of this relationship has yielded neither a theoretical nor empirical consensus. This chapter uses the Granger-causality procedure to examine the causal association between political freedom and economic freedom, with data spanning 20 years, from 1975 through 1995. The statistical results indicate that political freedom Granger-causes economic freedom, though the reverse is not supported. In addition, this chapter finds that both political and economic institutions are crucially influenced by their history, and that human capital accumulation and economic development positively influence both political democracy and economic freedom. Section 10.1 presents definitions and examples of political and economic freedom. Section 10.2 reviews the literature on this topic. Section 10.3 discusses the methodology used in this chapter. Section 10.4 reports the results of the statistical procedures. Section 10.5 presents a study of Indonesia, which is an interesting but controversial case concerning the causal relationship between political freedom and economic freedom.

## 10.1  Definitions and Examples

The sequence of political democratization and economic liberalization has been under a great deal of scrutiny since the end of the Cold War. Two paradigms in the literature are the former Soviet Union, where political democratization was launched without first engaging economic reforms, and the People's Republic of China, where economic liberalization has registered great success without substantial political reforms. While some scholars contend that political freedom is a prerequisite for economic prosperity, others maintain that strong political authorities capable of effectively relocating resources are required for developing countries to experience rapid economic growth (Sirowy and Inkeles 1990). A huge body of literature on institutions and growth has been produced; nonetheless, answers to some fundamental questions have been evasive: Is there a theory that explicitly relates economic freedom to political freedom? Is the former empirically distinguishable from the latter? And what is the causal relationship between the two?

The relationship between political freedom and economic freedom is fraught with a fundamental quandary. As Weingast points out, "The fundamental political dilemma of an economic system is this: A government strong enough to protect property rights and enforce contracts is also strong enough to confiscate the wealth of its citizens" (1995, 1). The protection of property rights, which is the centerpiece of economic freedom, requires a strong and efficient government. Weak governments are often the victims of riots, revolutions, and coups d'état, which often lead to violations of property rights and the destruction of property. However, a strong government possesses the ability to expropriate property from its citizens as a result of its capacity to maintain political and economic order. Classic examples of rapacious governments can be found in the Soviet Union after 1917, China after 1949, and North Korea today.

Gwartney, Lawson, and Block (1996) define the basic components of economic freedom as the protection of private property and freedom of its use and exchange. Individuals are said to have economic freedom if two conditions hold: (a) the property they acquire without the use of force, fraud, or theft is protected from physical invasion by others, and (b) they are free to use, exchange, or give their property to another as long as their actions do not violate the identical rights of others. Similarly, Levine defines economic freedom as liberty of commerce: "It is the liberty of individuals, and corporations, to own the nation's capital stock as their private property and use it to their advantage. Private ownership of society's productive resources is the hallmark of the kind of liberty political economists have claimed will lead to economic development" (1995, 3). By comparison, political freedom comprises various political rights and democratic procedures.[1] Weintraub offers examples for both kinds of freedom. "Economic opening means the ability to take private initiatives ... and a modest role for the state," whereas "political opening" means "such things as the ability of different groups to compete, raise funds, place items on the agenda, have an enlightened understanding of issues, access to media, voting equality at decisive stages, and peaceful transitions of power" (Weintraub 1991, 13).

Figure 10.1 plots economic freedom (Gwartney and Lawson 1997) against political rights (Freedom House 1996) for 13 countries for the year 1995. Both political freedom and economic freedom have been standardized to take values within a range from zero to one, with one as the freest. The size of the bubble in the figure represents the average of the two freedom values. At a particular historical

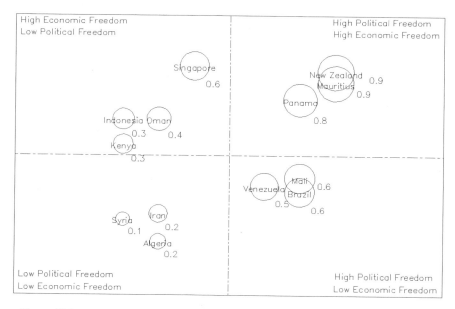

**Figure 10.1**
Coordinates of political and economic freedoms

moment, a country can *relatively* have a high level of economic freedom without much political freedom (e.g., Indonesia, Kenya, Oman,
and to some extent, Singapore), a high level of political freedom with
little economic freedom (e.g., Brazil, Mali, Venezuela, and some
Eastern European countries), a high level of both (e.g., New Zealand,
Mauritius, and Panama), or a low level of both (e.g., Iran, Algeria,
and Syria).

The focus of this chapter is on the dynamic relationship between
political freedom and economic freedom. A cross-country comparison, such as in figure 10.1, provides only a static interpretation of
political and economic freedom. It directly implies that some countries can be politically free but economically repressive, or politically
unfree but economically liberal. For instance, for the period immediately following World War II, many Third-World democracies
adopted economically restrictive policies, in part to protect certain
favored industries.[2] While these scenarios can be theoretically correct and actually do exist under certain historical circumstances, they
are not very interesting phenomena, as they understate the underlying dynamic change between the two kinds of freedom. Figure 10.1
implies that the cases in the northwest (second) and southeast
(fourth) quadrants are not stable. Those areas are what I call contradictions of freedoms. Historically, we have observed convergence
arising from contradictions of freedoms. For instance, with a relatively high level of economic freedom and a low level of political
freedom in the 1970s, South Korea eventually moved to a full
democracy in 1989; with a relatively high level of political freedom
and a low level of economic freedom in the early 1990s, the Eastern
European countries have since improved their economic freedom. It
is likely that political freedom without economic freedom, or economic freedom without political freedom, is but a false equilibrium
in the long run.

As the next section will explore, some scholars argue that the liberalization of the political order creates favorable conditions for economic freedom. When political rights and civil liberties are fully
respected and guaranteed, the rights to private property become a
corollary (Riker and Weimer 1993). However, other scholars maintain that economic freedom contributes to political freedom. Individual property rights, as well as the type of government per se,
result from the individual's need to protect his investments and from
the mutual recognition of such rights among individuals (Demsetz

1967, Libecap 1989, Weitzman 1993). Still others argue that both capitalism and democracy are influenced by a common philosophy of individual freedom, which boils down to the conclusion that it is impossible for people to adhere to economic and political philosophies that appear to be in opposition (Weitzman 1993). Furthermore, there is the notion that democracy and capitalism are fundamentally incompatible because of the contradictory underpinnings of the two systems (Verba 1991).

By contrast, other scholars assert that it is possible for a market economy to perform well under an authoritarian regime if its fiscal policies are sound (Gwartney, Lawson, and Block 1996), property rights are well protected (Knack and Keefer 1995, Zak 2000), sociopolitical instability is low (Venieris and Gupta 1983, Venieris and Stewart 1987, Venieris and Paupp 1996), or the government is efficient and capable (Organski 1996, Kugler and Arbetman 1997). Countries such as Taiwan and South Korea during the 1970s and most of the 1980s are classic examples supporting these arguments. Similarly, a country with a substantial amount of political freedom may still adopt politics and policies that conflict with economic freedom. This argument may find support in such cases as India, Israel, and Sweden, where political and civil liberties are present, but government policies—such as the levels of taxation, government spending, and regulation—nonetheless are often inconsistent with economic freedom (Gwartney, Lawson, and Block 1996). By contrast, Snider (1996) maintains that economic growth requires low transaction costs, and democracy is best suited to provide a political environment for minimizing these costs.

Clearly, the various theoretical arguments cited above lack a consensus as to the relationship between political freedom and economic freedom. Yet the existence of ambiguous theoretical conclusions should not prevent us from empirically investigating the causal relationship between the two kinds of freedom. Cross-country data are likely to either support or rebut the above arguments. Thus, theoretical ambiguity may be significantly reduced by an examination of the dynamics of political and economic freedom.

## 10.2   Literature Review

The relationship between liberty and property has yet to become an integral part of studies of the political and economic institutions.

Though a great deal of research has been conducted on the relationship between political freedom and growth and between economic
freedom and growth, little empirical investigation has been made
into the relationship between political freedom and economic freedom. Theoretically, scholars dealing with the evolution of institutions have emphasized the importance of endogeneity. Below,
substituting liberty for political freedom and property for economic
freedom, I cull some representative views regarding the relationship
between the two types of freedom.

*Liberty Follows Property*

Some philosophers and economists argue that it is the claimants
themselves who initiate private individual ownership (Demsetz
1967, Libecap 1989, Weitzman 1993). Weitzman writes, "The capitalist economy, because of its high degree of decentralization,
automatically builds in some countervailing power to check the
encroachment of the state" (1993, 313).

Levine (1995) regards liberty as endogenous to income, which
requires economic freedom. Therefore, according to Levine, economic freedom generates wealth, which gives rise to liberty. "The
theme centering on liberty speaks about our aspirations, individu-
ally and collectively, to assure the conditions needed to sustain our
independence of action and initiative. Liberty has to do with the
opportunities that society affords us to determine who we are and
how we will lead our lives. Wealth allows us to exercise our autonomy and individuality. With enough wealth to support our freedoms, we can take on the burden of responsibilities for our lives"
(Levine 1995, 3). For Levine, political freedom has its roots in wealth
accumulation made possible by economic freedom. In a nutshell,
Riker and Weimer (1993) offer three ways in which property rights
contribute to the establishment and consolidation of liberal political
institutions. First, property rights facilitate political compromise by
promoting the creation of wealth. Second, property rights provide a
focal point, thereby reducing the number of dimensions of policy
over which political systems must routinely make choices. Third,
property rights create wealth, which prevents the concentration of
political power in the hands of the state.

The view of the causal relationship between political freedom and
economic freedom is also influenced by the modernization thesis, as
advanced by Lipset (1959). The general overarching conclusion of

this thesis is that economic development leads to democracy, and the main reason for this denouement is twofold. As the economy grows, the middle class is enlarged and education increased. Both of the factors result in democratic political tolerance (Lipset 1959). Lipset (1959) additionally assumes that development requires the activity of private organizations, which constrain the autonomy of government. This view was stressed much earlier by Tocqueville (1835) and more recently by Putnam (1993), who argues that a penchant for civic activity intensified by involvement in development is a fundamental determinant for a well-functioning democratic government. Similarly, Huber, Rueschemeyer, and Stephens maintain that economic development will produce a "shift in the balance of class power" from the landlord class to the working class and the middle class, thereby leading to democracy (Huber, Rueschemeyer, and Stephens 1993, 74–75).

### Property Follows Liberty

In contrast, some political scientists and political economists believe that political authorities create the conditions required to accumulate private property. Riker and Weimer (1993) contend that the initial possessors of property cannot create a state to protect their property in society at large. "Rather, the strong preexisting state grants protection.... The origin of private property lies thus in the actions of political authority" (Riker and Weimer 1993, 92). Similarly, Olson (1993) argues that individual property rights are artifacts of a special set of government institutions; therefore, there is no right to property without a government. Riker and Weimer (1993) also demonstrate that in the long run, both political institutions and property rights are endogenous. While stable liberal political institutions facilitate the establishment of effective, credible property rights, the latter lend stability to liberal political institutions. Riker and Weimer (1993) propose that the political system first be studied as the independent variable, with property rights as the dependent variable, and then that the political system be treated as the dependent variable influenced by economic freedom in the long run. This argument suggests the existence of interactions, or a feedback mechanism, between political freedom and economic freedom.

Weintraub (1991) views political freedom and economic freedom as dynamically compatible and complementary, especially for transitional polities and economies. In particular, he advances the hypothesis that once a country opens its political system, economic freedom will follow. He reasons that a political opening cannot survive by itself. While not all market economies are democracies, every democracy has a market economy (Weintraub 1991, 13). Therefore, political reformers are expected to liberalize the economy in the interest of their own political survival.

### Property and Liberty Are Positively Correlated

Like Riker and Weimer, Denzau and North (1994) maintain that economic performance is a consequence of the institutional framework of the polity and the economy. However, unlike Riker and Weimer, they emphasize the idea that political freedom and the protection of property rights are both correlated with some shared values and common culture, and therefore are naturally compatible.[3] The presence of learning also creates path dependence in ideas and ideologies, and subsequently in institutions. This argument suggests that changes in or between political and economic institutions are likely to take the form of evolution rather than revolution.

There have been additional controversies in terms of the connection and compatibility between market and democracy. Scholars who argue for a positive correlation between the political system and the economic system cite shared values, common culture, and natural compatibility:

> The basic idea is that the essential philosophies of capitalism and democracy have so much in common that the human need for consistency consolidates them as one world view.... Both capitalism and democracy share the common philosophy of freewill of individual, imperfectability of human beings, primacy of private values and property.... There is a natural consistency between the political philosophy of democracy and the economic philosophy of capitalism, which, if it is long denied, causes tension that is eventually difficult to bear. (Weitzman 1993, 313–314)

### Property and Liberty Are Negatively Correlated

By contrast, some scholars argue the exact opposite. They claim that democracy and capitalism are incompatible, as their underlying principles run counter to each other:

> Democracy is based on a very clear principle: equality, on the notion that each individual is of equal worth. It is also based on the somewhat weaker

notion, which I think democrats accept, that not only is each individual of equal worth in terms of interests, each is equally competent to know what his or her own interests are and express them in the political process. This is reflected in such principles as "one person, one vote."

Capitalism ... rests in a way on inequality. It rests on the opportunity of individuals to make money and get ahead. And one of the greatest and most interesting problems in understanding modern democracies is the tension between these two systems side by side. The tension can be seen by the way in which people at both ends of the political spectrum look at democracy. For the right, democracy is the ultimate threat. It is a threat to their property, to what they think are their rights to be autonomous in the market, because the mass of people will vote in governments that will take away their rights. Looked from the left, capitalism is a threat to democracy in the opposite direction. Inequalities in wealth, inequalities in control over resources have a major effect in distorting the extent to which democracy is a system whereby each person has equal influence. (Verba 1991, 81)

In the same vein, Smith (1992) argues that the democratic regime strengthens the organized power of the working class. "The growth of trade unions and the political representation of worker interests can throw sands in the gears of the capitalist economy and this can produce a series of perverse macroeconomic outcomes, including relatively poor growth, high unemployment, and high inflation" (Smith 1992).

### Research Queries

These arguments above examine the long-term trend of political and economic development. This chapter, however, takes a different strategy when looking at the issue of political and economic freedom, emphasizing the *incremental* change in the relationship between the two and concentrating on the relationship between them as a dynamic statistical phenomenon.

I argue that a dynamic relationship exists between political freedom and economic freedom. The interesting and meaningful question should be, Does political freedom cause economic freedom, or is the causal relation the other way around? Despite the powerful and poignant theoretical arguments summarized earlier about the relationships between liberty and property, it is empirically important to ascertain the causality between political freedom and economic freedom. The empirical result will have enormous policy implications. What happens if a nation has a high level of economic freedom but an absence of political freedom? If it is found that political freedom causes economic freedom, then the answer will be that economic freedom without political freedom cannot be self-sustained in the long run. In the short term, economic freedom where political freedom is absent can be seriously distorted and serves the interests of the political elite only, which breeds political instability that eventually will deprive the nation of true economic freedom. On the other hand, if we find that economic freedom causes political freedom, then the above scenario may not happen. Therefore, it is crucial to identify the causal structure of the two kinds of freedom.

My objective, then, is to test the relationship between these two kinds of freedom. In particular, I intend to test the following hypotheses:

· Political freedom causes economic freedom.
· Economic freedom causes political freedom.
· There is a feedback effect between political freedom and economic freedom.

Testing these hypotheses should also provide some useful hints toward addressing the controversy on the compatibility between democracy and capitalism. If the two systems are not compatible, we likely will see opposite signs on the parameter estimates of political freedom and economic freedom. If they are compatible, we will see the same signs on the parameter estimates of political and economic freedom.

## 10.3   Method and Data

Granger (1969) has provided a useful definition of statistical causality that can be tested with standard time-series methods. Though it is assumed that the change in the dependent variable is caused by the change in the independent variables, the existence of a relationship between the dependent and independent variables may not prove the existence of causality or its direction. The intuition of the Granger test is that the past can cause the future, whereas the future cannot cause the past. Let $\Omega_t$ be the universe of information up to and including time period $t$. The Granger definition is then as follows: $X$ causes $Y$, given $\Omega_t$, if $Y_{t+1}$ can be better predicted using past $X$ ($X_s, s \leq t$) than by not using it. This entails a comparison of the forecasting ability of $\Omega_t$ with and without $X$. If $X_t$ significantly contributes to forecasting $Y_{t+1}$, then $X$ is said to *Granger-cause Y*.

This concept and test of causality conveniently help to infer the causality between political freedom and economic freedom. The procedure itself is also important; for Granger, noncausality is a necessary condition for strong econometric exogeneity (Sargent 1976, Sims 1972, Joerding 1986). Thus, if the evidence shows that political freedom Granger-causes economic freedom, then the idea that political institutions possess a higher degree of permanence than economic freedom is supported. If the reverse is true, then economic freedom will prove a powerful means toward improving political freedom. The test in the next section will check for Granger causality between political freedom and economic freedom, given information on past political and economic freedom, as well as past economic performance and education. The performance and education variables are included because a significant relationship has been found between the levels of per capita income and education on one hand and political development on the other (Lipset 1959).[4] Democracy may have an intrinsic value that is increasingly sought after as the income and education levels of populations rise. The level of GDP per capita, as established by Bilson (1982, 107–108), is the only statistically and substantively significant independent variable for democracy. Without these relevant control variables, the Granger test may produce a misleading result (Berndt 1991, 383).

Sargent's test for Granger causality is adopted because it is easy to implement and there is evidence that it has superior small-sample properties (Sargent 1976, Guilkey and Salemi 1982). The equation to be estimated is the following:

$$\text{PF}_t = \alpha + \beta(L)\text{EF}_{t-l} + \gamma(L)\text{PF}_{t-l} + \theta(L)\text{GDP}_{t-l} + \omega(L)\text{PRIMED}_{t-l}$$
$$+ \lambda(L)\text{GROWTH}_{t-l} + \varepsilon_t$$

In this equation $\beta(L)$, $\gamma(L)$, $\theta(L)$, $\omega(L)$, and $\lambda(L)$ are the parameter estimates and lag operators. For example,

$$\beta(L)\text{EF}_{t-l} = \sum_{l=1}^{m} \beta_l \text{EF}_{t-l}$$

Here PF stands for political freedom, EF stands for economic freedom, GDP is the real GDP per capita, GROWTH is the annual growth rate of GDP per capita, and PRIMED is the primary school enrollment rate. Then a standard $F$ test is conducted on the null hypothesis of Granger noncausality, i.e., $\beta_1 = \beta_2 = \cdots = \beta_m = 0$. Granger causality from political freedom to economic freedom is readily tested by replacing $\text{PF}_t$ with $\text{EF}_t$ as the dependent variable and testing $\gamma_1 = \gamma_2 = \cdots = \gamma_m = 0$. The use of lagged variables for growth, the size of the economy, and education helps reduce the reverse causality between them and political institutions.

This research will also directly test the notion of path dependence, initiated by David (1985), later studied by Arthur (1989), and significantly advanced by North (North 1990, 1996a, 1996b). Path dependence, which means nothing more than the idea that yesterday's choices are the initial starting point for today's, can be argued to be a fundamental determinant of long-term change. "What constrains the choices of the players is a belief system reflecting the past—the cultural heritage of a society—and its gradual alteration reflecting the current experiences as filtered by the belief system" (North 1996a, 13–14). If path dependence exists, we will expect to find that the lagged political-institution and economic-institution variables take a positive sign and are statistically significant. Though North has not made a fundamental distinction between political and economic institutions, it can be assumed that political institutions and economic institutions are closely related. Therefore, path dependence exists not only separately for political and economic institutions, but may also hold true between political institutions and economic institutions. That is, past political institutions may affect current economic institutions, and past economic institutions may affect current political institutions. A rejection of the null hypothesis of $\beta_1 = \beta_2 = \cdots = \beta_m = 0$ or $\gamma_1 = \gamma_2 = \cdots = \gamma_m = 0$ will corroborate cross-path dependence between political freedom and economic freedom.

To measure political freedom, I turn to the political-rights and civil-liberty variables of Gastil (various years) and Freedom House (various years) and the index for institutionalized democracy of Gurr (1990). For the measure of economic freedom, I utilize a composite index developed by Gwartney, Lawson, and Block (1996). The index has 17 components allocated to four major areas: money and inflation, government operations and regulations, takings and discriminatory taxation, and international exchange.[5] A 0-to-10 rating scale is used for each component in the index, with 10 representing the highest possible rating and 0 the lowest. Weights then are assigned to these preliminary values. Three kinds of weighting systems are utilized. The equal-impact system involves using a weight that is the inverse of the corresponding standard deviation, thus less weight is given to a component when it varies greatly across countries. This method results in each component exerting an equal impact on the index. The weights are also adjusted for differences in the variation of component ratings across countries. An alternative weight is to ask experts to provide estimates of the importance of each component, and to use this survey data as a basis for attaching weights. The third approach is to ask area specialists to rate countries and to run regressions using the economic data. If the predicted values of the subjective ratings are correct, then the parameter estimates are used as component weights.

Gwartney, Lawson, and Block recommend the second indicator because it reflects the collectively weighted assessment of various experts. The three indices have five observations for each country in the data set, for the years 1975, 1980, 1985, 1990, and 1995. The lack of annual observations for each country is somewhat compensated for by the relatively long time span of the data.[6]

## 10.4   Empirical Results

The results of Granger-causality tests depend on the choice of lag length. If the chosen lag length is less than the true lag length, the omission of the relevant lags may cause bias. If the chosen lag length is greater than the true lag length, the inclusion of irrelevant lags causes the estimates to be inefficient. Based on preliminary partial autocorrelation estimates, a first-order lag involving a five-year interval seems appropriate. However, tests using an additional lag involving a ten-year interval is also used and reported for comparison.

This study adopts alternative measures of political and economic freedom to compensate for measurement errors, which always exist in indexed variables.[7] The severity of these errors—that is, whether the results we arrive at are due to systematic measurement error—is always an issue. As such, the results reported below are "only useful to the extent that one has confidence in the reasonableness of the methods used by the collecting agency to measure the variable used in analysis" (Joerding 1986).

The correlation coefficients between the three economic-freedom indices are very high: 0.97 between $EF_1$ and $EF_2$, 0.97 between $EF_1$ and $EF_3$, and 0.91 between $EF_2$ and $EF_3$.[8] Similarly, the association of the two political-freedom indicators is quite strong, as the correlation coefficient is 0.87 between the political-rights, civil-liberties (PRCL) indicator and Gurr's institutionalized-democracy measure for the five-year interval. In contrast, political freedom and economic freedom are moderately associated. The correlation coefficient is 0.47 between PRCL and $EF_1$, 0.42 between PRCL and $EF_2$, and 0.53 between PRCL and $EF_3$. Almost identical statistics are obtained for institutionalized democracy (DEMOC) and the three measures of economic freedom. From this initial analysis I conclude that higher levels of political freedom tend to be associated with higher levels of economic freedom.

The results of the Granger-causality tests are reported in table 10.1. The Durbin–Watson statistic indicates no serial correlation in $\varepsilon_t$.[9] A further check was made by estimating an AR(1) process for the fitted residuals: I found that the estimated lag coefficient is insignificantly different from zero.

As political and economic institutions in developed countries may be different from those in developing countries (Kormendi and Meguire 1985), the Granger-causality test is applied to two samples.

**Table 10.1**
Granger-causality-test statistics

| Causal relationship | All countries | | Developing countries | |
|---|---|---|---|---|
| | Lag = 1 | Lag = 2 | Lag = 1 | Lag = 2 |
| PRCL to $EF_1$ | 5.616* | 5.269* | 3.185* | 6.762* |
| $EF_1$ to PRCL | 0.058 | 0.348 | 0.231 | 0.397 |
| PRCL to $EF_2$ | 4.424* | 4.842* | 4.272* | 8.325* |
| $EF_2$ to PRCL | 0.004 | 0.239 | 0.130 | 0.029 |
| PRCL to $EF_3$ | 5.050* | 4.119* | 2.096 | 2.163 |
| $EF_3$ to PRCL | 0.058 | 0.326 | 0.126 | 0.552 |
| DEMOC to $EF_1$ | 3.484* | 3.443* | 3.073* | 2.730 |
| $EF_1$ to DEMOC | 0.483 | 0.703 | 0.023 | 1.451 |
| DEMOC to $EF_2$ | 3.936* | 3.149* | 4.376* | 3.413* |
| $EF_2$ to DEMOC | 0.000 | 0.574 | 0.147 | 1.294 |
| DEMOC to $EF_3$ | 3.073* | 2.885 | 3.192* | 1.967 |
| $EF_3$ to DEMOC | 0.023 | 1.376 | 0.011 | 2.302 |

*Significant at the 0.05 error level.

One consists of all countries for which data are available; the other includes only developing countries for which data are available. Table 10.1 represents Granger-procedure results for both developed and developing countries. The existence of Granger causality is determined by the $F$ statistics for the test. An asterisk denotes that the null hypothesis of Granger noncausality is rejected at the 5% error level.

The results overwhelmingly demonstrate that political freedom Granger-causes economic freedom, though we cannot reject the null hypothesis that economic freedom has no effect on political freedom. The evidence is not very strong when using the third indicator for economic freedom. As this indicator involves utilizing some countries' information to predict other countries' economic status, systematic errors may have been built into this regression-generated variable. Overall, the result confirms some of the important arguments and assumptions made in the literature regarding the exogeneity of political institutions (Riker and Weimer 1993). Namely, political systems do evince a relatively permanent or semipermanent nature, and economic freedom is likely to be endogenous to political freedom. The difference in the testing statistics between developed and developing countries is not significant, indicating that the two groups of countries likely share the same pattern of causation between the two kinds of freedoms. Since Granger noncausality is a necessary condition for strong exogeneity, we have evidence that political institutions appear to be predetermined and influence economic institutions. However, the opposite is not likely to hold universally or in the short-run.

The regression results for PRCL and EF2 are reported in table 10.2.[10] Regressions for other measures of economic freedom and political freedom are highly consistent with the results in table 10.2. First, past institutions have a strong impact on current institutions; this is true of both political and economic systems. This result supports the path-dependence theory advanced by Denzau and North (1994) and North (1996a). Political and economic institutions *do* seem to have a self-sustaining force. They are more like organic structures that evolve and adapt themselves throughout history, rather than historical fixtures. However, it should be noted that it is not appropriate to study the separated effects of the different lags, owing to the potential problem of multicollinearity. Overall, we have evidence that the history of institutions is useful for understanding their current status.

**Table 10.2**
Regression results

|  | Political freedom | | Economic freedom | |
|---|---|---|---|---|
|  | (1) | (2) | (3) | (4) |
| INTERCEPT | 0.068** | 0.048 | 0.447* | 0.418** |
|  | (0.035) | (0.041) | (0.164) | (0.203) |
| PFLAG1 | 0.700** | 0.665* | 0.350** | 0.249 |
|  | (0.036) | (0.059) | (0.166) | (0.285) |
| PFLAG2 | — | 0.082 | — | 0.377 |
|  |  | (0.056) |  | (0.270) |
| EFLAG1 | −0.000 | −0.001 | 0.829* | 0.844* |
|  | (0.007) | (0.013) | (0.032) | (0.063) |
| EFLAG2 | — | 0.006 | — | −0.017 |
|  |  | (0.014) |  | (0.065) |
| GDP − 1 | 0.015* | 0.010* | 0.032** | 0.016 |
|  | (0.004) | (0.004) | (0.019) | (0.021) |
| GROWTH − 1 | 0.337 | 0.349 | −1.187 | −0.729 |
|  | (0.253) | (0.279) | (1.172) | (1.346) |
| EDU − 1 | 0.091* | 0.077* | 0.329** | 0.337** |
|  | (0.034) | (0.038) | (0.159) | (0.185) |
| $N$ | 378 | 278 | 371 | 277 |
| $\bar{R}^2$ | 0.760 | 0.777 | 0.715 | 0.731 |
| $\sigma$ | 0.159 | 0.152 | 0.735 | 0.730 |

*Significant at the 1% error level, one-tailed test.
**Significant at the 5% error level, one-tailed test.
Standard errors in parentheses.

Second, the coefficients of the first and second lags of economic freedom are not statistically significant in the political-freedom equation. The evidence of cross-path dependence from economic freedom to political freedom is not very strong, whereas the first lag of political freedom is statistically significant in the economic-freedom equation. After the path-dependence effect is controlled, it becomes more likely that past political freedom affects current economic freedom than that past economic freedom affects political freedom. These statistical results can be construed as a restatement of the results of the $F$-test in the Granger-causality procedure.

Third, previous levels of human-capital accumulation seem to exert a positive influence on economic freedom as well as on political freedom. The education variable is significant in all the regressions, corroborating Helliwell's (1994) argument that when a nation is better educated, its aspirations for democracy become stronger. Moreover, the finding regarding education in table 10.2 demonstrates that the accumulation of human capital can have a positive effect on economic freedom as well. There are many scenarios in which this may happen. An increase in knowledge leads to an increase in the protection of property rights, including intellectual property rights, and economic institutions are strengthened by the improvement of human capital. This may indicate that the need to protect intellectual property rights increases with an increase in human capital. Technological breakthroughs powered by innovations lead to an urgent need to protect intellectual property. In return, patents and other forms of protection provide incentives for further research and development. The feedback effects between the two related phenomena remain an interesting and important research topic.

Fourth, the lagged value of GDP per capita is found to have a significant positive impact on both political and economic freedom. Lipset (1959) argued that economic development is the most consequential factor for political democracy. Subsequently, numerous empirical studies have statistically established that economic development leads to democracy (Jackman 1973, Bollen and Jackman 1985, Helliwell 1994, Burkhart and Lewis-Beck 1994). Our result is consistent with the economic-development thesis. Similarly, I also found that the level of economic development enhances economic freedom. When a nation becomes richer, it will seek not only a higher level of political freedom but also a higher level of economic freedom. The need for property protection, like intellectual property rights, becomes more salient when more wealth is created. An important implication of the above results is that economic freedom tends to be better established where the nation's political system is more open and its levels of economic development and educational attainment are higher.

Fifth, economic growth holds an ambiguous sign for political freedom and economic freedom, though it is not statistically significant in either case. While growth tends to promote political freedom, its effect on economic freedom could be negative. Some scholars find that economic growth is likely to be conducive to political freedom (Bilson 1982; Bollen and Jackman 1985; Brunk, Caldeira, and Lewis-Beck 1987; Burkhart and Lewis-Beck 1994). Economic prosperity renders large sections of society politically— as well as economically—independent of the ruling class, thereby stimulating a demand for increased political freedom. Thus it is surprising to find that growth has a negative effect on economic freedom, although it is not statistically significant.

Finally, to check for a possible nonlinear effect of political freedom on economic freedom, I replaced the Gastil and Freedom House index with two dummy variables. If the index is between 0 and 0.33, the first dummy variable equals 1; otherwise it equals 0. If the index is larger than 0.33 and smaller than or equal to 0.67, the second dummy equals 1; otherwise it equals 0. If the index exceeds 0.67, then both dummy variables equal 0. Based on the means of the index within each group, a perfect linear relationship between political and economic freedom requires that the coefficient on the first dummy variable be twice as large as that on the second dummy. The estimated coefficients and standard errors (in parentheses) from equation 3 of table 10.2 are $-0.143$ (0.126) and $-0.080$ (0.108). Thus, the nations in the lowest political-freedom group have the lowest economic freedom, those in the middle political-freedom group have the next lowest economic freedom, and those ranked the highest in political freedom have the highest economic freedom. I tested the restriction that the coefficient on the first dummy doubles that on the second dummy with an $F$-test. The null hypothesis that there is no difference with the restriction cannot be rejected ($F = 0.018$, with 1,364 degrees of freedom). Hence, from all of the above analysis it is plausible that the relationship between political freedom and economic freedom is linear, and there is no need to use quadratic or other forms to take nonlinearity into account.

## 10.5   A Case Study: Indonesia

Indonesia offers an example in which a contradiction of political freedom and economic freedom led to economic and political crises. In Indonesia, the economy experienced rapid liberalization, and the market experienced substantial economic freedom. In 1995 Indonesia ranked 29th among 115 nations in terms of economic freedom, down from its place in 1985 (ranked 15th) and in 1990 (ranked 13th) (Gwartney and Block 1997, 116). In 1995 the level of economic freedom in Indonesia was still higher than that in Denmark, France, Italy, Spain, Sweden, Greece, India, Bangladesh, and Nepal; it was about the same level as in Belgium, Germany, Peru, Uruguay, and Oman.

Indonesia's potential gains of economic freedom, however, were compromised by its lack of political freedom. The nation is one of the few high-economic-freedom countries that are politically unfree, as defined by the Freedom House survey. The coexistence of economic freedom and political repression distorted market forces and increased transaction costs in the marketplace, leading to the country's economic debacle in 1997. This inconsistency between economic freedom and political repression is a major reason that Indonesia has metamorphosed from an apparently working market economy into an economic and political failure. Political repression in the country has eroded economic freedom and belied conditions needed for sustainable economic growth.

From the late 1980s to the early 1990s, the Indonesian government initiated significant economic liberalization, generating millions of jobs and delivering many Indonesian families out of poverty (Radelet 1999). As Johnson and Sheehy (1996) summarized, Indonesia reduced taxes, encouraged foreign trade, and stimulated foreign investment. The government recodified its foreign-investment laws to permit complete foreign ownership, opening many sectors to foreign investment, including electricity, telecommunications, shipping, airlines, railways, roads, and water supply. Before the late 1980s, no foreign banks had been granted a license since 1969, but this restriction was relaxed in the late 1980s. Prior to the Asian financial crisis in 1997, foreign banks were still regulated in Indonesia; however, they were allowed to operate through joint ventures with Indonesian domestic banks, bypassing government control (Johnson and Sheehy 1996).

One reason that the Indonesian economy was hit hard in the 1997 financial crisis was that a set of efficient, competitive mechanisms did not precede the opening of the country's financial markets. Capital liberalization before the establishment of sound domestic financial institutions will lead to inefficient allocation of resources, creating a situation called "perverse liberalization" (Willett and Auerbach 2002). For instance, capital inflows can cause serious damages to the recipient country's economy, generating market failures in which production factors are inefficiently allocated and policy failures in which the government is incapable of executing consistent and credible macroeconomic policies.[11]

In the context of the relatively open and free structure of the Indonesian economy, "Indonesia's regulatory environment is characterized by bribery, kickbacks, and corruption. Many regulations are applied arbitrarily, and bribes may be necessarily to receive an 'exemption' from a government regulation" (Johnson and Sheehy

1996, 169). Also, government regulation remained high in Indonesia. As Feng, Hsiang, and Lee (2002) note in their review, the Indonesian government continued to regulate the prices of certain "strategic" items (e.g., rice), using price ceilings or floors. The government also tried to protect the agricultural sector with subsidies. In addition, government enterprises were often protected from market competition. Indonesia did not establish a modern commercial code compatible with a market economy. "The legal structure provides public officials with too much arbitrary authority. When the discretion of government officials replaces the rule of law, the security of property rights is undermined and corruption (for example, bribes, selective enforcement of regulations, and favoritism) becomes a way of life" (Gwartney and Lawson 1997, 117). Finally, Indonesia had a very large black market prior to the onset of the financial crisis of 1997 (Johnson and Sheehy 1996).

In my view, a fundamental answer to the deterioration of Indonesia's economy lies in the contradiction between the country's liberalized economic policy and its fossilized political system. By the time of the 1997 financial crisis, which decimated the Indonesian economy and toppled its long-term dictator, Indonesia was enmeshed in an incongruity of fast economic liberalization and stalled political freedom. In a system characterized by perverse economic liberalization and lack of political freedom, the political elite has great opportunities to empower and enrich themselves by providing accesses to wealth to their family members, friends, supporters, and bribers. Without improvement in political freedom, economic liberalization eventually backfires, sending the economy into a downward spiral. "When the forces of reform hit up against the immovable object of political interests, reform makes a detour.... The reason for the foot-dragging is that reform has reached the point where the only interests left unchallenged are those close to the hearts of some very powerful people" (McBeth 1998, 128–129).

Compared to Hong Kong, Singapore, South Korea, Taiwan, Singapore, the Philippines, Malaysia, and Thailand, the group of the nations with which Indonesia was associated, Indonesia was the only full autocracy when the 1997 financial crisis occurred and was the one that was hit hardest by the crisis. In 1998 the Indonesian economy shrank over 13%, the worst among all the economies in the region. In 1999 and 2000, its recovery was the slowest. From 1998 to

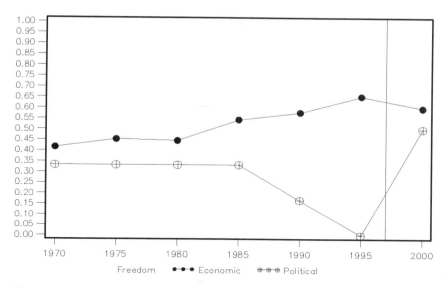

**Figure 10.2**
Political and economic freedom in Indonesia, 1970–2000

2000, its average annual inflation rate was 28.5%, far ahead of the second-place Philippines (6.8%) (Adams 2002).

Figure 10.2 plots the level of political freedom using the Freedom House data[12] and the level of economic freedom based on *Economic Freedom of the World* by Gwartney et al. (2002). Evidently, for most of the years for which we have data, political freedom and economic freedom diverged in Indonesia. It is difficult to interpolate the value of economic freedom for 1997, the year in which the financial crisis erupted in Asia, as the economic-freedom data uses a five-year interval. Nonetheless, we can infer from the general trends of the two series in figure 10.2 that in Indonesia, it is likely that economic freedom peaked and political freedom bottomed before 1997, when the financial crisis started to paralyze the country. Perverse financial liberalization leads to resource misallocation (Willett and Auerbach 2002). In my view, the lack of political openness provides special interests with rent-seeking opportunities, which cause bribery, corruption, and other forms of resource misallocation. Thus, political repression determines the sources of perverse liberalization. Without political freedom, economic liberalization will eventually backfire, creating conditions that lead to the abuse of economic power by the elite and special interests seeking to enrich themselves at the cost of national well-being. Political reform is required in a country such as Indonesia to increase the transparency and credibility of the government before the effects of perverse financial liberalization can be corrected.

## 10.6   Summary and Policy Implications

The finding in this chapter that Granger causality runs from political freedom to economic freedom is important in that it provides a unique contribution to our understanding of the relationship between political and economic systems and between political and economic systems and economic growth. The major conclusion in Barro (1996) is that "the advanced western countries would contribute more to the welfare of poor nations by exporting their economic systems, notably property rights and free markets, *rather than their political systems....* If economic freedom can be established in a poor country, then growth would be encouraged, and the country would tend eventually to become more democratic on its own. Thus in the long-run, the propagation of Western-style economic systems would also be the effective way to expand democracy in the world" (Barro 1996, 24; italics added). While the above evidence may hold in a single regression with both economic and political freedom indicators on the right-hand side of the equation, it will not hold if economic freedom is treated as endogenous to political freedom, as this study's findings suggest.

As has been discussed theoretically by Riker and Weimer (1993) and established empirically in this chapter, political systems may critically determine economic institutions. Maintaining economic freedom depends not only on a tradition of respect for property rights, but also on a political system consistent with economic freedom. While the direct effect of democracy on growth may be ambiguous, its indirect effects on growth can be immensely positive.[13] Numerous studies have found that secure property rights and other economic freedoms have a significantly positive impact on growth (Knack and Keefer 1995, Clague et al. 1995, Barro 1996, Zak 2000). What is missing, then, in this general relationship between economic freedom and economic growth is the role played by politics in securing and improving economic freedom. Empirical analysis performed on democracies may be misleading, because only the direct affect of democracy is studied, while the indirect effects of democracy on growth are either assumed or ignored. Political freedom may enhance growth by reducing political uncertainty, improving education, increasing investment, and narrowing income inequality. This chapter has presented some strong evidence that political freedom significantly contributes to economic growth through the channel of developing and maintaining economic freedom. While property rights may be protected in countries lacking political freedom, a democratic political system generally enhances economic freedom.

This chapter also shows that political institutions affect economic institutions over time while both political institutions and economic institutions evolve in a path-dependent manner. Thus, political elements are factored into economic institutions, which themselves evolve over time. The economic performance of such countries as Taiwan and South Korea was buttressed by an economic environment that has improved over time as the result of the evolution of both political and economic institutions.

Furthermore, the finding in this chapter that economic freedom does not Granger-cause political freedom is conditioned on lagged GDP per capita and lagged primary-school enrollments. I expect that economic freedom will affect political freedom positively and indirectly through its impact on education and economic development when these lagged conditions are replaced by their contemporaneous or leading effects. An increase in economic freedom will increase economic growth, thus enlarging the size of the economy. As table 10.2 demonstrates, the accumulation of wealth in the preceding period has a positive impact on political freedom in the current period. Hence, I expect to find a positive effect of economic freedom on political freedom through the channel of increased wealth. Similarly, since the economy increases as the result of economic freedom, there is a spillover effect relating economic freedom to education. Therefore, it is plausible that economic freedom is indirectly conducive to political freedom. The findings in this study are consistent with Fukuyama's (1993) observation on the indirect relationship between capitalism and democracy, in the sense that capitalism itself does not generate pressures for democracy yet is likely to generate the rapid socioeconomic change that favors the emergence of a stable democracy.

A major policy implication of this study is the importance of helping to establish democracy as the prevailing political order so as to facilitate worldwide economic development. In developing countries, including the Third World and former communist countries, a democratic system will be instrumental in creating and deepening economic freedom. Western countries should not only promote market economics in these nations, but also concurrently help develop political systems instrumental toward consolidating free-market economies.[14] This simultaneous approach is particularly important for those countries that do not have a tradition of economic freedom. It is imperative that they receive help to overcome the path-dependent negatives in order for their emerging market economies to develop. "Imported" democracy is a powerful policy instrument for establishing a political environment favorable to the creation and development of economic freedom, leading to economic growth. Beyond that, I agree with scholars (e.g., Lipset 1959; Brunk, Caldeira, and Lewis-Beck 1987; Burkhart and Lewis-Beck 1994) who advance the notion that in the long run, economic development will promote political freedom.

This study contributes to our understanding of the dynamic mechanisms of political and economic development. It identifies political freedom as an important determinant of—if not a necessary condition for—economic freedom. It traces the indirect effect of economic freedom on political freedom through the channels of education and wealth, although the direct effect of economic freedom on political freedom is inconclusive. Both forms of freedom were found to be path-dependent, though there is also cross-path dependence, particularly in the case of political freedom's impact on economic freedom. On the basis of these findings, one can predict that in the 21st century, nations will find themselves increasingly engaged in the interaction and interplay of the two forms of freedom. This is the key to the next stage of civilization and human development.

# 11

Births and Politics

*If government knew how, I should like to see it check, not multiply, the population. When it reaches its true law of action, every man that is born will be hailed as essential.*

Ralph Waldo Emerson

In this last thematic chapter in the book, our objective is to examine one more channel through which a political system may affect long-run economic growth: birth rates. In chapter 4, birth rates are identified as a negative determinant of economic growth. Przeworski et al. (2000) find that each additional child reduces the growth rate of per capita income by 0.43, implying that per capita income will double in 21 years in countries where a woman typically has two children, but will take 43 years in countries where a woman typically has six children (Przeworski et al. 2000, 259). This result was obtained without controlling such variables as political instability and policy uncertainty. The difference in growth rates could be significantly wider if estimation included the aforementioned variables. The established empirical fact is that an increase in birth rates decreases economic growth, regardless of religious or ideological preferences. If democracy is found to have an inhibiting effect on birth rates, then it promotes economic growth by reducing population growth. Population growth—like investment, education, income distribution, and property rights—falls under the influence of governmental policy and preference. As birth rates are one of the critical determinants of long-run growth, determining how politics affects population growth becomes crucial. The government can use its power to keep population growth low, enabling a poor nation to escape the poverty trap or a fast developing economy to maintain sustainable growth.

## 11.1 Literature Review

Two general approaches are utilized to examine the origins of fertility change. The modernization thesis argues that fertility reduction is a response to aspects of the modernization process (Thompson 1929, Notestein 1945). Therefore, fertility rates decline as an economy develops. Empirical studies lend support to this general relationship between development and demographic change (Demeny 1989, Bongaarts 1992). The modernization approach also inspired studies linking specific modernization policy or social conditions to demographic transition. Cowgill (1949), Freedman (1994), Kirk (1971), Nam and Philliber (1984), and Bongaarts (1992) examine the timing of changes and specific factors in modernizing societies undergoing demographic change.

By contrast, the political-institutionalization thesis maintains that the political system and governance make a difference in demographic transition. Works on politics and births—beginning with the work by Organski, Kugler, Johnson, and Cohen (1984)—demonstrate that government political capacity reduces birth rates. Przeworski, Alvarez, Cheibub, and Limongi (2000) find that population grows faster under an autocracy than under a democracy. These approaches to exploring demography transcend the economic and social variables typically utilized and found in the literature.

The central question in exploring the relationship between politics and birth rates is why and how political institutions matter. Knodel and van de Walle (1979) are correct in their assessment that while fertility declines occur under a wide variety of social, economic, and demographic conditions, a parsimonious theoretical explanation must start with political institutions and the role they play in the processes of economic development and modernization. This argument is consistent with those of Ness and Ando (1984) and Midgal (1988), who posit links between strong societies and declines in populations, of Rouyer (1987), who demonstrates that in the case of India, a particular population planning policy will succeed under a strong government and fail under a weak government, and of Wolf (1986) and Coale and Freedman (1993), who maintain that strong and effective government intervention in China has played a key role in reducing high levels of fertility.

Feng, Kugler, and Zak (2000) present a formal model that characterizes the political mechanisms of demographic change, establishing a critical link in economic development. They demonstrate that fertility decisions are determined by two fundamental political variables, political stability and political capacity, and by economic factors. Modeling a government's strategic multiobjective policy set, they derive a number of equilibrium conditions that enable poor nations to escape a poverty trap and successfully develop. The centerpiece of their model is public investment, through which political variables affect birth rates. Empirical tests for a sample of 109 countries from 1960 to 1990 provide strong support for the propositions of the formal model. In particular, they demonstrate that political stability and political capacity both lead to reduced birth rates, and they provide evidence that politics can be either a stimulant or a barrier to economic development. Feng, Kugler, and Zak (2001) incorporated political freedom into their original model and find that together with political stability and capacity, political freedom effectively reduces population growth.

While the theoretical arguments in Feng, Kugler, and Zak (2000, 2001) are embedded in the microfoundation of decision making by the government, firms, and individuals, they are consistent with the more parsimonious model in chapter 2. This model suggests that the three main aspects of political institutions—political freedom, political stability, and policy certainty—constitute the basic political environment for economic growth and socioeconomic development by conditioning and constraining an individual's economic decision to invest in reproducible capital in the marketplace. Economic activity (a function of the accumulation of reproducible capital) will also increase or decrease as a function of instability, polarization, and freedom. The three variables affect an individual's decision to consume now and save for the future, and can also explain an individual's decision to have children.

That political freedom reduces birth rates is intuitive. Various chapters in this book show that an increase in the level of political freedom or the degree of democracy has a positive effect on a wide range of factors that facilitate economic development. The enhancement of democratic values leads to a rise in investment, an increase in human capital formation, a decrease in wealth inequality, and the strengthening of property rights. All these activities permit choice in a society, moving resources in the direction of wealth accumulation. Birth rates decline when choice increases, which indicates that the most effective way of reducing population growth rates may reside not in political decrees or programs but in the freedoms offered in a democratic society, specifically, freedoms that increase the opportunities for female education and employment and for urbanization and migration from the countryside. One of the best ways to meet the challenge of population growth happens to be the easiest way, at least theoretically. That is, give political and economic freedom to the people, particularly women.

Political stability also reduces birth rates. As with decision making regarding investment and consumption, an agent examines the current and future political environments, particularly political stability, when making decisions regarding the number of children to have and the amount of goods to consume. Political instability contributes to a rise in fertility and birth rates for at least three reasons.

First, the prospect of political violence increases the probability that a child will die in violent times (e.g., as a result of poor sanitation or lack of medical services) and raises the insurance incentives of parenthood. Political instability also directly increases the risk of loss of life (e.g., in a revolution or coup d'état), which causes individuals to increase fertility levels to offset potential loss. Such decisions can also be made *ex post facto*, that is, when young lives are lost in political violence. In these situations, replacement immediately becomes an urgent need.

Second, political instability decreases the opportunity cost of raising children by disrupting the production process and lowering the present value of one's own future earnings. As a result, the relative cost of raising children is reduced, making raising a child a more attractive option than before. During the Cultural Revolution in China, the downward trend of births was interrupted and reversed. During this period, political chaos pushed up the number of pregnancies and births in China.

Third, in the case of a national program to reduce birth rates, a stable political regime is likely to have the capability to implement effective fertility policies, and an unstable political system is almost certainly doomed to see its family-planning policy stall.

Policy uncertainty also affects birth rates. The uncertainty resulting from potentially large policy swings between competing political parties that are drastically different in terms of ideology and representation always puts the country's future on hold. When investors withhold their investments in the face of mounting uncertainty, economic growth will decline, reducing the opportunity cost of raising children. Policy uncertainty is also related to the political capacity of government; a polity characterized by deep political divisions is synonymous with low political capacity. Various findings in the literature support the argument that higher government political capacity decreases birth rates.

In sum, all three political variables included in the theoretical model in chapter 2 have different implications for reductions in birth rates. Political freedom increases the menu of choices for society and leads to improved economic performance; increases in social and economic choices raises the opportunity costs of having children. Political stability provides a favorable political environment for economic development, which leads to lower birth rates. Policy certainty reduces market uncertainty and is also conducive to the effective execution of a government policy aimed at decreases in birth rates.

## 11.2   A Political-Economic Model

This chapter unites both the modernization thesis and political-institutionalization thesis into a political-economic theory of demographic transitions. The modernization process generates the need and desire for fertility reduction, and political institutions can either inhibit or promote decreases in human reproduction. Based upon the theoretical structure in chapter 2, the statistical models are these:

$$\text{TFR}_i = \alpha_0 + \alpha_1 \text{ FREEDOM}_i + \alpha_2 \text{ INSTABILITY}_i + \alpha_3 \text{ POLARIZATION}_i$$
$$+ \alpha_4 \text{ INCOME}_i + \varepsilon_i$$

$$\text{CBR}_i = \beta_0 + \beta_1 \text{ FREEDOM}_i + \beta_2 \text{ INSTABILITY}_i + \beta_3 \text{ POLARIZATION}_i$$
$$+ \beta_4 \text{ INCOME}_i + \nu_i$$

Here $i$ indicates the country. TFR is total fertility rates, and CBR is crude birth rates. The former is defined as the average stock of children for women in their reproductive years; the latter is defined as the number of births per thousand people. The source for TFR is the World Game Institute (1997), and the source for CBR is the World Bank's *World Development Indicators* (2000). FREEDOM is measured through political rights in the Freedom House data. INSTABILITY is political instability, measured through the probability function of irregular government change developed in this book. POLARIZATION is policy polarization or lack of policy certainty and is measured by the Gini coefficient. INCOME is real GDP per capita from *The Penn World Table* (Summers and Heston 1995, 2000, 2001).

For a proper measurement of population increase, the total fertility rate is a better variable than the crude birth rate. While the former is a stock variable, measuring the accumulation of children to a mother, the latter is a flow variable adjusted by the size of the population. As demographic structure varies from society to society and nation to nation, birth rates may not be directly comparable. A country with a sizable older population will, of course, tend to have a lower crude birth rate than a younger country.

Total fertility rates are standardized across younger and older societies by tabulating the number of children born to a mother, thus avoiding the problem caused by the demographic composition of the society. Total fertility rates do have one major limitation as a dependent variable. As a stock variable, it encompasses the entire reproductive period of a woman; this long span of time causes an endogeneity problem with the independent variables. In contrast, the crude birth rate takes a value for a certain year. The reverse causality problem can be easily neutralized by constraining the time frame of the independent variables to the passage of time prior to the year of the crude birth rate.

In this chapter I use both total fertility rates and crude birth rates as dependent variables. Consistent evidence from both variables will assist in evaluating my political theory of demographic change. In the analysis, CBR and TFR both take their 1995 values. The independent variables are averages for 1980–1995. I adopt a log-log model as previously specified (Feng, Kugler, and Zak 2000, 2001), though unlike previous works, here I utilize a cross-section research design, rather than panel data, as my focus is on cross-country variations.

On the basis of the theoretical predictions in chapter 2, I hypothesize the following relationships: birth and fertility rates (i) *decrease* when political freedom rises, (ii) *increase* when political instability increases, (iii) *increase* when policy polarization augments, and (iv) *decrease* when income per capita grows.

The first three hypotheses relate politics to births. Politics affects the incentive of child bearing by changing the opportunity cost of children. Political freedom widens political and economic choices for the society, indirectly increasing economic growth by keeping incomes growing, and individuals respond by spending more time working and having fewer children. Political instability weakens the economy, causing individual incomes to fall. As a result, the relative returns to work versus child rearing decreases, and so births increase. Also, political violence results in the loss of lives, accentuating the needs of human reproduction and replacement. Finally, when policy certainty is low, the investor tends to put his or her economic activities on hold and turn to other pursuits, including child bearing. Policy polarization also implies a government's inability to implement an effective family-planning policy. The fourth hypothesis is based upon the modernization thesis.[1] It is essential to include this variable as a control variable in a multivariate analysis of the effects of the political variables on birth rates, as the demography literature has identified economic development as the primary source of demographic transitions.

## 11.3  Empirical Results

All four explanatory variables in both regressions have the correct signs and are statistically significant in a one-tailed test, with the birth-rate model demonstrating slightly better estimates than the fertility-rate model. The strong results in both regressions lend substantial support to a political interpretation of demographic transitions. They confirm the implications that a nation can improve economic performance by politically influencing the nation's population size. In particular, the estimates show that birth rates decline as political freedom, political stability, and policy certainty increase. The modernization thesis of births also finds strong support in the sample, with per capita income a highly significant economic factor affecting births.

The estimates in table 11.1 show that political variables have sizable impacts on both fertility rates and birth rates. A 10% increase in political freedom will reduce fertility rates by 2.2% and birth rates by 1.6%. A 10% increase in polarization will increase fertility rates by

**Table 11.1**
Estimation of fertility and birth rates

|  | Unstandardized | | Standardized | |
| --- | --- | --- | --- | --- |
|  | TFR | CBR | TFR | CBR |
| Intercept | −0.238 | 1.784** | 0 | 0 |
|  | (1.117) | (0.930) |  |  |
| Political freedom | −0.220* | −0.160* | −0.333 | −0.272 |
|  | (0.005) | (0.039) |  |  |
| Political instability | 0.044** | 0.064* | 0.155 | 0.249 |
|  | (0.023) | (0.020) |  |  |
| Policy polarization | 0.443† | 0.480* | 0.142 | 0.170 |
|  | (0.286) | (0.238) |  |  |
| Real GDP per capita | −0.181* | −0.147* | −0.343 | −0.310 |
|  | (0.063) | (0.048) |  |  |
| $\bar{R}^2$ | 0.710 | 0.760 |  |  |
| $\sigma$ | 0.311 | 0.255 |  |  |
| N | 124 | 119 |  |  |

*Significant at the 0.025 error level, one-tailed test.
**Significant at the 0.05 error level, one-tailed test.
†Significant at the 0.10 error level, one-tailed test.
Numbers in parentheses are standard errors, corrected for heteroskedasticity.

4.4% and birth rates by 4.8%. A 10% increase political instability will increase fertility rates by 0.4% and birth rates by 0.6%. In contrast, the effect of GDP per capita on birth reduction is not as large as claimed by the modernization proponents. A 10% increase in real GDP per capita will reduce fertility rates by 1.8% and birth rates by 1.5%.

The last two columns display standardized parameter estimates that take the variances of both the dependent and independent variables into consideration and offers information on predictive importance, rather than causal importance. With predictive importance as the criterion, real GDP per capita is the most important variable affecting fertility and birth rates. However, political freedom remains a very important determinant. In terms of sampling variances, the difference in importance between GDP and political freedom is negligible. Political instability is also an important factor in predicting population increase, with significant variation from country to country. Where political instability is high, the number of births tends to be large. Finally, policy polarization has relatively weak predictive importance. The proxy for this variable, income distribution, does not vary much in comparison with political freedom and political instability. Altogether, political variables carry substantial weight in influencing birth and fertility rates.

These surprising results create an opportunity for politics to accelerate economic growth through management of population size. They also offer strong evidence that democracy promotes long-run growth through its impact on demographic transitions. Chapter 4 demonstrated that the birth rates have a significant negative effect on long-run growth, even in the same equation where the democracy variable is statistically insignificant, though the sign is correct. The combined results reveal that democracy promotes long-run growth through the indirect channel of influencing population growth.

The results here extend beyond what was found by Przeworski et al. (2000), who use a counterfactual method and find that population grows faster under an autocracy than under a democracy. The use of an incremental democracy variable in this chapter implies that any government can change its degree of political freedom and thereby reduce birth rates, with or without making a full transition to democracy.[2]

This chapter also demonstrates that politically stable nations with relatively homogenous policy preferences generate reductions in population growth and prompt output growth. This explains the anomaly in Przeworski et al.'s work whereby India was considered a democratic nation and China an autocracy (Przeworski et al. 2000, 65). Essentially the same birth-control program failed in India but succeeded in China. The next section offers a comparison of the two countries' demographic trends and political milieu.

## 11.4   A Case Study: China

One of every three babies in the world is born in India or China, with births in these two countries nearing 46 million in 1996 alone.[3] To overcome the enormous disadvantages of population pressure on sustainable economic development, each country launched birth-control programs. Figure 11.1 shows the crude birth rates (CBR), defined as births per thousand persons, in China and India for the period of 1960 to 1998. The birth rates data are from *Basic Data of China's Population*, compiled by Yao and Yin (1994) and China Population Information Center (1999). The Indian data are from the World Bank (2000).

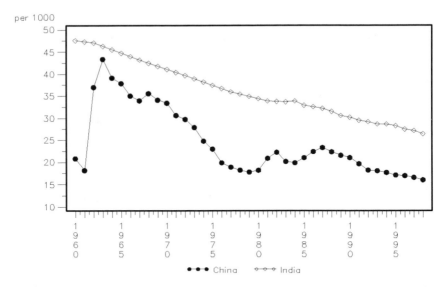

**Figure 11.1**
Crude birth rates of China and India, 1960–1998

Despite a clear downward trend in population growth, China and India demonstrate different patterns. The demographic decline in India is smoother than that in China. In China, crude birth rates declined from 37.97 in 1954 to 18.62 in 1961, increased rapidly in 1962, and peaked in 1963 (43.37). In the period from 1963 through 1971, the drop in population growth was stalled. The decline resumed after 1971. From 1977 to 1987, China's birth rates assumed a W shape, ranging from 17.82 in 1979 to 23.33 in 1987. From 1991 to 1998, it steadily declined to 16.03.

India's birth rates have followed a steadily declining trend, dropping from 47.48 in 1960 to 26.10 in 1999. Despite its steady decline in population growth, India has not been able to attain the decline in birth rates achieved in China. China's total fertility rate has already fallen below 2, whereas it has been projected that India will achieve the same level only by 2020.[4]

The long-term pattern of declining birth rates in the two countries can also be analyzed through the autoregressive method. The correlation between a given year's birth rate and that of the prior year is 0.999 for India, but only 0.885 for China. The R-square in an autoregressive model using the first-order lag is 0.998 for India, but 0.784

for China. These statistics indicate that India's birth rates can be easily predicted by themselves, while the prediction of China's birth rates requires inclusion of other factors.

The different patterns in demographic trends between China and India, in my view, can be accounted for by political and economic factors. While economic development and modernization power India's reductions in births rates, political stability and government capacity have largely influenced China's fertility transition. An economic process tends to generate a smooth decline in fertility and birth rates, whereas a political process underscored by political capacity and political instability is likely to produce more variance in the trend. The fluctuation in China's birth rates in figure 11.1 may well be a result of political processes in China. Below I focus on a political analysis of birth rates in China. For a comparative analysis of trends in birth rates in China and India, see Feng (2003).

Changes in China's birth and fertility rates have been ascribed to aspects of culture (Zhao 1997), the universal modernization process (Whyte and Parish 1984), sociological changes (Coale 1984, Poston 1992), and the political process (Wolf 1986; Feng, Kugler, and Zak 2000). I believe that each of the four approaches offers valid explanations of fertility transitions in China.

In this section I conduct a multivariate analysis of China's fertility and birth rates. The statistical model is based on the theory in chapter 2 as well as the analysis in section 11.2. In this model, the political-freedom variable is excluded. Polity's institutionalized-democracy index for China is zero for the entire period from 1960 to 1990. In terms of the political rights, Freedom House scores China 7 (the least free) for the 1972–1976 period, 6 for the 1977–1988 period, and 7 again for the 1989–1990 period. From 1960 to 1990, China's average political-rights score was 6.368, with a standard deviation 0.496. Despite the enormous political and social changes in the country since 1978, relative to its totalitarian regime during the Cultural Revolution, the democracy indices have yet to give China the credit it deserves. The lack of within-country variation in the time-series democracy data at the Polity project or Freedom House indicates that the democracy indices are not very useful for a within-country single time-series analysis, despite their contributions to cross-country aggregate studies.

In the model, I include several variables relevant to China's unique experience in birth control. Because of the role the Chinese government has played in the family-planning program in China, I include government capacity in the model. Wolf (1986) and Feng, Kugler, and Zak (2002) all emphasize the contributions to birth-rate reductions in China by a capable and strong government through a nationwide family-planning drive. I also include two variables for women's economic status and women's political status. The former is measured through the percentage of the female agricultural labor force in the national labor force. The higher the percentage is, the lower women's economic status stands in general. The latter is measured through the percentage of seats occupied by women in the National People's Congress. The higher the percentage is, the higher Chinese women's political status is. In addition, I include a dummy variable for family planning, another unique Chinese feature. Finally, I construct another dummy variable to isolate the Great Leap Forward era in China, which was an economic program overshadowed by a political agenda.

The model to be estimated in this section is the following:

$$R_i = \beta_0 + \beta_1 \text{ INSTABILITY}_i + \beta_2 \text{ POLARIZATION}_i + \beta_3 \text{ CAPACITY}_i$$

$$+ \beta_4 \text{ GDP}_i + \beta_5 \text{ AGRIW}_i + \beta_6 \text{ NPCW}_i + \beta_7 \text{ FAMILY}_i + \beta_8 \text{ GLF}_i + \varepsilon_i$$

Here $i$ indicates the year, $R$ stands for the fertility rate or birth rate. Political INSTABILITY is measured through the probability of irregular government change; policy POLARIZATION is measured by the Gini coefficient (Deininger and Squire 1996);[5] government CAPACITY is proxied by relative political extraction (Arbetman and Kugler 1996); and GDP is gross domestic product per capita, utilizing real GDP per capita (international prices) from Summers and Heston (2000). AGRIW denotes the female agricultural labor force as a percentage of the national labor force (World Game Institute 1997). NPCW stands for the percentage of seats occupied by women in the National People's Congress (Zheng 1995). FAMILY is a dummy variable that takes a value of one for the year 1970 and onward, and zero before 1970. It controls for the centralized program of birth control, which started to be implemented with conviction in 1970 (Wolf, 1986). Finally, GLF, standing for Great Leap Forward, is a dummy variable for the pre-1962 years. It contrasts the birth increase in 1962, which was related to the Great Leap Forward Movement and the first wave of birth-control programs by the government in 1962 (Wolf 1986).

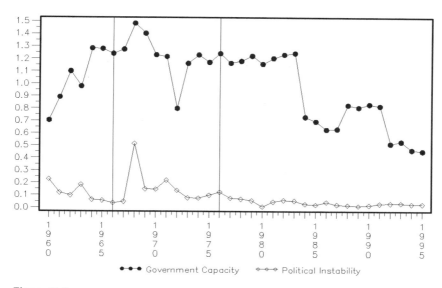

**Figure 11.2**
Government capacity and political instability in China, 1960–1995

Figure 11.2 shows the trends of political capacity and political instability in China.[6] Government capacity in China follows a unique pattern, as discussed in Feng and Li 1997. Political campaigns require that the Chinese government mobilize the society through centralization of power and control, while economic reform dictates that the Chinese government decentralize and reduce control, so that economic incentives can be brought into play. Government capacity rose during the Cultural Revolution (1966–1976), the renewal and consolidation of Deng's power (1976–1983), and the Tian An Men Square Incident (1989). It declined during periods of economic reconstruction in the early 1960s, the short-lived restoration of pre-Cultural Revolution "normalcy" (1972), and the consolidation of market reforms in the early and mid 1980s as well as the 1990s. Nonetheless, in most years, the Chinese government has been a strong one by the definition of relative government capacity, with a value of relative political extraction above one.

Political instability was relatively high in China during the 1960s through 1970s, with a peak formed in 1968. It is plausible that government capacity and political stability are endogenous to each other. While political instability weakens government authority, government capacity reduces political instability. In the Chinese context, political movements always generate chaos and instability, which require that the government exercise a high level of political control through increasing government capacity. The coexistence of relatively high political capacity and high birth rates during the Cultural Revolution years, seen from combining figure 11.1 and figure 11.2, can be misleading. Without political control, birth rates in China during the Cultural Revolution could have been much higher. The relationship between birth rates and government capacity in China must be studied while controlling political instability. From 1979 to 1987, China experienced profound change in its social, political, and economic arenas. To encourage market reforms, the government decentralized its power and lowered its political capacity. The decrease in government control may have caused the temporary rise in birth rates shown in figure 11.1.

Table 11.2 presents correlations. The correlation between crude birth rates and fertility rates are very strong: 0.96 between the national crude birth rates and the national fertility rates, alleviating

**Table 11.2**
Correlation coefficients

|        | CBR  | TFR_N | TFR_R | TFR_U | INST | RPE   | GDP   | GINI  | AGRIW | NPCW  |
|--------|------|-------|-------|-------|------|-------|-------|-------|-------|-------|
| CBR    | 1.00 | 0.96  | 0.89  | 0.95  | 0.38 | −0.36 | −0.75 | 0.34  | 0.79  | −0.83 |
| TFR_N  |      | 1.00  | 0.99  | 0.90  | 0.29 | −0.10 | −0.80 | 0.37  | 0.81  | −0.68 |
| TFR_R  |      |       | 1.00  | 0.86  | 0.19 | −0.09 | −0.77 | 0.39  | 0.78  | −0.62 |
| TFR_U  |      |       |       | 1.00  | 0.50 | −0.33 | −0.80 | 0.38  | 0.82  | −0.84 |
| INST   |      |       |       |       | 1.00 | −0.14 | −0.61 | 0.18  | 0.58  | −0.58 |
| RPE    |      |       |       |       |      | 1.00  | 0.05  | −0.08 | 0.03  | 0.47  |
| GDP    |      |       |       |       |      |       | 1.00  | −0.34 | −0.98 | 0.71  |
| GINI   |      |       |       |       |      |       |       | 1.00  | 0.30  | −0.29 |
| AGRIW  |      |       |       |       |      |       |       |       | 1.00  | −0.77 |
| NPCW   |      |       |       |       |      |       |       |       |       | 1.00  |

CBR: national crude birth rates (World Game Institute 1997). TFR_N: national total fertility rates (Yao and Yin 1994). TFR_R: rural total fertility rates (Yao and Yin 1994). TFR_U: urban total fertility rates (Yao and Yin 1994). INST: probability of political instability (irregular government change) (this book). RPE: relative political extraction (Arbetman and Kugler 1996). GDP: real GDP per capita (Summers and Heston 2000). GINI: Gini coefficient (Deininger and Squire 1996). AGRIW: female agricultural labor force (World Game Institute 1997). NPCW: the percentage of seats held by women in the National People's Congress (Zheng 1995).
$N = 31$

the concern about proxying total fertility rates with crude birth rates, which are more readily available from national statistics. The signs of the correlations between fertility rates and other variables are precisely as expected from earlier theoretical and empirical discussion: political instability and income inequality are positively related to fertility levels; government political capacity and GDP per capita are negatively related to fertility levels. Political instability is positively related to both birth rates and fertility rates; its connection with urban fertility rates is particularly salient (with a correlation coefficient of 0.50). Political instability seems to have a strong effect on city dwellers' fertility decisions. In the case of China, metropolitan areas are political epicenters; naturally, the impact of political instability is more pronounced in urban areas than rural areas. Similarly, the negative association between relative political capacity and urban fertility seems to be stronger than that between relative political capacity and rural fertility.

Strong correlations have been also found between the female agricultural labor force and fertility, and between the NPC women legislators and fertility. The female agricultural labor force is a proxy for women's economic status in the country, and the percentage of women legislators is a proxy for women's political status in the country. AGRIW is strongly positively correlated with fertility and birth rates (which makes sense, as a higher value of AGRIW indicates a lower degree in women's economic status), and the latter is strongly negatively correlated with fertility and birth rates. The relationship between the two kinds of status is high and negative, implying that an increase in women's political status is associated with an increase in women's economic status.

China's real national output per capita is positively related to women's representation in the legislature and negatively related to the female agricultural labor force as a ratio to the national labor force. In addition, real GDP per capita has a strong negative correlation with political instability, with a coefficient of $-0.61$, confirming the cross-country evidence that political instability has a negative impact on economic development.

The regression results are reported in table 11.3. The original data show some degree of higher-order serial correlation. The autoregressive error model of maximum likelihood (ML) is used to correct for autocorrelation. A backward elimination process screens out serial correlation beyond $\pm 0.10$, and ML estimation corrects

**Table 11.3**
Maximum likelihood estimation of an autoregressive model (1960–1990 China data)

| Variable | CBR (1) | Nat'l TFR (2) | Urban TFR (3) | Rural TFR (4) |
|---|---|---|---|---|
| Constant | 37.536 | 17.020 | 0.211 | −15.617 |
| | (63.198) | (12.438) | (13.887) | (15.158) |
| Instability | −1.816 | −0.090 | 1.231* | −0.339 |
| | (2.769) | (0.556) | (0.514) | (0.669) |
| Capacity | −5.912* | −0.825* | −0.373 | −0.893* |
| | (1.822) | (0.355) | (0.454) | (0.421) |
| Polarization | 22.28 | 7.442** | 3.193 | 5.268 |
| | (20.194) | (4.063) | (3.920) | (5.016) |
| GDP per capita | 1.111 | −0.458 | 0.350 | −1.403 |
| | (7.926) | (1.549) | (1.929) | (1.980) |
| NPC women | −0.749* | −0.105* | −0.207* | −0.081† |
| | (0.254) | (0.050) | (0.066) | (0.059) |
| Agri women | 3.029† | 0.823* | 0.207 | 0.829** |
| | (1.835) | (0.359) | (0.412) | (0.434) |
| Family planning | −4.1* | −0.451† | −1.007* | −0.332 |
| | (1.536) | (0.308) | (0.300) | (0.365) |
| Great Leap Forward | −5.056* | −2.841* | −2.208* | −3.020* |
| | (1.980) | (0.387) | (0.445) | (0.454) |
| A(9) | 0.774* | 0.817* | — | 0.830* |
| | (0.145) | (0.112) | | (0.113) |
| $\bar{R}^2$ | 0.967 | 0.973 | 0.925 | 0.965 |
| $\sigma$ | 1.865 | 0.364 | 0.423 | 0.42 |
| DW | 1.67 | 2.21 | 1.75 | 2.06 |

*Significant at the 0.025 error level, one-tailed test.
**Significant at the 0.05 error level, one-tailed test.
†Significant at the 0.10 error level, one-tailed test.
Standard errors in parentheses.

autocorrelation by internalizing the identified serial correlation in the model. The results in table 11.3 evidence a ninth-order correlation in three out of the four regressions.

The statistical results on China's time-series data are basically consistent with the previous analysis based on cross-country data and support the theoretical argument in the chapter 2. Political instability has a positive impact on urban births in China, while government capacity decreases the number of births in the countryside. Policy polarization also appears to have a positive effect on national fertility rates. Family planning imposed by the government has a positive effect on birth control, even after controlling for the modernization process (e.g., the female labor force in agriculture as a percentage of the total national labor force and real GDP per capita). The lower birth rates in China, particularly in the countryside, can largely be accounted for by a strong central government.

As expected, the dummy variable for the family-planning program has a significant negative effect on fertility and birth rates. The government imposed program is more effective in urban than rural areas. The decline in rural fertility seems to respond more to government political extractive power; the decline in urban fertility appears to result from the family-planning program. A feasible explanation is the political behavior of urban residents in the Chinese context. City dwellers were organized into *danwei*, which were working units that not only organized professional work but also administered political indoctrination. As a result, these individuals were used to following a government policy without requiring substantive enforcement by the central government. The rural population lacks political organization and responds less positively to the family-planning program while being sensitive to changes in government political capacity. To assure the success of birth control, the government has to increase its extractive capacity in the countryside. Evidence suggests that while the policy content is more important in urban areas, how the policy is carried out is more relevant in rural areas.

The political and economic status of women creates an additional distinction between urban and rural populations. The reduction in urban fertility responds more to political status; the reduction of rural fertility more to economic status. The parameter estimate for NPC women legislators is both larger in absolute value, and more significant, for urban fertility than for rural fertility.

In contrast, the parameter estimate for the female agricultural labor force is both larger in absolute value, and more significant, for rural fertility than for urban fertility. Again, a higher value for this variable (AGRIW) indicates a lower degree of women's economic status. Births respond positively to the lack of women's economic status.

These results once more confirm the view in this chapter that births will decline when women's political and economic status rises. Political and economic freedom is clearly an effective way to give women a wide range of career goals with adequate financial, spiritual, and emotional compensation.

Real GDP per capita has mixed signs and is not significant. One reason for its mixed signs and lack of significance is its high correlation with several variables: female agricultural labor force ($\rho = -0.98$), NPC women legislators ($\rho = 0.71$), and regime change probabilities ($\rho = -0.61$). The lack of significance of real GDP or the Gini coefficient cannot be interpreted as negating the modernization thesis, since they are significantly related to the empowerment and enrichment of women.

The analysis in this chapter does not claim that having a democratic government is the only response to birth reductions, as political stability and policy certainty are identified as other important determinants of population growth. Over the past three decades, China has achieved success in controlling population growth, thus facilitating its remarkable economic reform. It has done so, this study suggests, largely by maintaining a strong and capable government.

The analysis in this chapter implies, however, that the Chinese government has yet to claim an ultimate victory over population growth. There are two areas where opportunities and challenges coexist. First, politically stable democracies tend to have a smooth pattern of birth-rate reductions. Political freedom is an important determinant of birth rates, even for China. In the past, China has relied on its strong government capacity to achieve its policy objective of birth control. Political openness, as explained in this chapter, will provide an ultimate guarantee that China's population growth will be sustained. Open societies, combined with economic modernization, creates a context for steady declines in population growth. China does not yet have significant political competition or offer its population the ultimate political choices through free popular elections of the chief executive of the nation. Empirically, poorer regions tend to have higher birth rates. In China, poor people are also those that are politically disadvantaged. Political reforms will raise the political status of poor people, leading to a fundamental change in their political choices, which will in turn change their preferences about having children.[7]

Second, a major impediment to continued success in managing population growth is the widening gap in income. Both the cross-country analysis and the case study demonstrate that income inequality leads to an increase in birth and fertility rates. The survey data compiled by Deininger and Squire (1996) show that the Gini

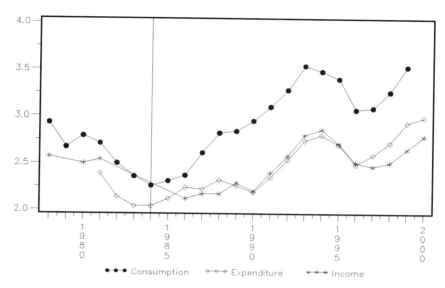

**Figure 11.3**
Ratio of urban to rural per-capita consumption, income, and living expenditures

coefficient has been steadily increasing in China since 1984 (Deininger and Squire 1996). The same trend can be also confirmed by data published by China's National Bureau of Statistics. Figure 11.3 plots the ratios of urban to rural per capita consumption, income, and living expenditures in current prices from 1978 to 2000. In the early years of economic reform, the disparity of wealth between China's rural and urban areas decreased. However, since 1984, wealth inequality between urban and rural residents has worsened.[8] The increase in income inequality will breed economic and political instability (Feng and Gizelis 2002) and, in the process, will translate into a stimulus for births, as the findings in this chapter reveals.

## 11.5  Summary and Policy Implications

This chapter demonstrates that democracy promotes long-run growth through an additional channel: birth-rate reduction. In addition, political stability and policy certainty also lead to a decline in birth rates, establishing a link between politics and growth through fertility decisions. Free, stable, and capable governments propel declines in fertility, setting the stage for sustained economic growth by increasing the transmission of human capital, raising productivity, and facilitating a demographic transition.

The major policy implication of this study is that a government with the aforementioned characteristics can initiate and carry out a fertility policy oriented toward economic growth. At the national level, such an approach is more effective than the alternative strategy of development, as characterized by the modernization thesis, which links births to the growth of the economy. While fertility and birth rates respond to economic development and modernization gradually, they can be shaped rapidly through political choices. For those countries trapped in the vicious cycle of accelerated increases in births and decreases in per capita physical- and human-capital accumulation, the role played by the government cannot be overstated. A government with the positive characteristics identified in this chapter can effectively administrate or facilitate population-growth control to power long-run sustainable economic development. The political thesis for controlling births provides a short cut for a developing nation to accelerate out of the poverty trap.

This chapter illustrates that certain political factors can liberate nations from poverty, implying that domestic political actors hold the key to a country's sustained development. Allowing populations to freely exercise their options, reducing income inequality, and mitigating political instability in developing countries produces long-run growth. While all societies make their own choices when it comes to forms of survival and development, prosperity beckons to those that are free, stable, and capable.

# 12 Conclusions

In his Nobel Prize lecture, Douglass C. North raises both the conundrums and the importance of politics in the course of economic development. "Polities significantly shape economic performance because they define and enforce the economic rules. Therefore, an essential part of development policy is the creation of polities that will create and enforce efficient property rights. However, we know very little about how to create such polities" (North 1996b, 353). Before we develop ways and means to create polities to enhance economic performance, we need to know what types of political systems provide desirable political and social conditions for economic and social development. This book has been devoted to discovering how politics affects economic performance. It examines the growth paths and political processes of nations, and relates various aspects of economic development—such as growth, investment, inflation, human capital, income distribution, property rights, and birth rates—to political institutions.

The statistical results of this book provide evidence that politics does matter for national economic growth and development. In particular, a political system characterized by freedom and stability is best suited to promoting a growth-oriented economic agenda. The effects of political institutions on growth more often than not are exercised through indirect, rather than direct, channels. For instance, democracy enhances growth by establishing and enforcing rules that protect property rights, promote general education, allow accumulation of private capital, reduce income inequality, and facilitate demographic transitions. Other aspects of political institutions—such as policy certainty, political stability, and government efficiency—have additional influences on growth and development. The best political infrastructure for growth is a system that is democratic, stable, and capable.

As a way of concluding this book, this chapter will focus and expand on the issues mentioned above. First, it will recapitulate the major findings in the book; it then will review some policy implications based upon these conclusions; and lastly, it will examine a few areas for future research on the political economy of growth.

## 12.1 Summaries of Major Findings

This book has tested various hypotheses relating political institutions to economic development and has produced a multitude of empirical results, of which the most important and salient can be summarized as follows.

The fundamental finding is that political institutions *do* matter in their influence on economic growth. Political repression, political instability, and policy uncertainty all define and constrain an individual's economic decisions in the marketplace. Therefore, they have pronounced dampening effects on a nation's economic development. Economic growth will be increased or decreased as a function of these three political variables, which constitute the basic political parameters for economic growth and socioeconomic development. Empirically, I found that political instability and policy uncertainty have significant negative effects on growth. The effect of democracy on growth is positive, but statistically insignificant. However, I argue that democracy affects growth through its impacts on political instability, policy uncertainty, investment, education, property rights, and birth rates.

While the direct effect of democracy on growth is ambiguous, its indirect effects on growth—through its impact on the probabilities of regular and irregular government changes—are positive. Major regular government change has a positive effect on growth, and regime change has a negative effect on growth; meanwhile, democracy has a positive impact on major regular government change and a negative impact on regime change. Overall, then, democracy indirectly promotes growth by inducing major regular government change and by inhibiting irregular government change.

Contrary to the view held by many scholars, this book finds no statistical evidence that a democracy is more likely than an autocracy to generate inflation. Indeed, democracies on average had lower inflation than autocracies during the period of 1970 through 1980. By contrast, the most significant political factor contributing to inflation is the likelihood of regime change, particularly for the period of 1980 through 1992. Moreover, the changeability of government political capacity, a separate indicator of political instability, was found to possess great potential for igniting inflation.

The degree of political democracy has a significant and positive impact on private investment. However, this effect attenuates after controlling for education. It is likely that democracy makes a contribution to physical capital formation through the channel of human capital accumulation. Political instability—amplified by the propensity for unconstitutional government change, the variability of government political capacity, variance in levels of political freedom, and deaths resulting from political events—has a very deleterious effect on private investment. In addition to domestic politics, some international factors also have an influence on domestic private investment. While economic sanctions have a negative effect on domestic private investment, international cooperation and trade have a positive relationship with domestic investment. The more cooperative the home country is toward others and the more cooperative other countries are toward the home country, the larger private domestic fixed-capital formation as a percentage of GDP.

Both the level and duration of democracy have an unmistakably propitious effect on education, even after controlling for the level of income. The data from 1960 to 2000 show that democracy has great potential for improving human capital in terms of completion of postsecondary education, though its effects on lower levels of education seem limited because universal education has already been adopted at the primary and secondary levels in many countries, democratic or autocratic. Political instability adversely affects human-capital formation, with its dampening effect felt more among the female population than the male population and more at the lower levels than at higher levels.

The density of democratic experience, defined as the average number of years of democracy for a country in the data set, was found to have a pronounced negative impact on income inequality. This negative effect of democracy on income inequality was independent of economic development. It holds true for various measures of income inequality, including the overall broad indicators (e.g., the Gini coefficient and the ratio of the fifth-quintile income share to the combined first- and second-quintile income shares) and indicators for particular income groups (e.g., the top-quintile income share and combined third- and fourth-quintile income shares).

The statistical results in this book indicate that political freedom Granger-causes economic freedom, but the reverse relationship is not supported. This finding contradicts the belief that economic freedom leads to political freedom. Rather, economic freedom can exist without immediately engendering political democracy. Additionally, both political and economic institutions were found to be influenced by their own past existence, and human-capital accumulation and economic development were found to positively influence both political democracy and economic freedom. The implication of this work is that while both economic freedom and political freedom are important to economic development, democratic institutions are instrumental in creating and deepening economic freedom, thus promoting economic growth.

The degree of democracy, or political freedom, also has a dampening effect on population growth. Since birth rates have been found as one of the most crucial negative factors for economic growth, this indirect effect of democracy on growth is especially important. Political stability and policy certainty also reduce birth rates. I argued that democracy leads to birth reductions not through coercion, but by way of opening choices—political, economic, and social—to the entire population, and particularly to women. Demographic change under these circumstances is more effective and brings more happiness to the society than a capable autocracy does. It is, however, a free, stable, and capable nation that can best use birth reductions as a short-cut to economic prosperity.

When discussing the impacts of democracy and other aspects of political institutions on growth, we should examine not only the direct effect of democracy but also the effects of democracy on other factors that may also affect growth.

Many of the second-order determinants of growth are also the developmental objectives of society. These determinants—which include education, equality, economic freedom, and women's social, economic, and political status—not only lead to the continued growth of the economy, but also represent some desired social objectives in and of themselves. The conditions that lead to their fulfillment are thus determinants of both economic growth and social development. Unless these channels are scrutinized and well understood, any conclusions on the roles played by political institutions in growth and development are premature and incomplete, if not misleading.

## 12.2  Some Policy Implications

A good number of policy-relevant implications have been revealed throughout this book. The most important lesson is that to have sustained and continued growth, a nation should maintain a stable political system, increase both political and economic freedom, and keep its government capable and efficient. It has generally been agreed that political stability and government efficiency stimulate economic growth. As indicated in this book, it is controversial as to whether a democracy has an advantage over an autocracy in the promotion of economic development. One oft-cited paradox is Singapore, which does not have a democratic political system by any criterion of liberal democracy but has been able to grow quickly and become the first of the Pacific Asian developing countries to join the ranks of the OECD.[1]

The Singapore experience raises the important question of whether a nation needs to improve political rights and civil liberties in order to foster economic development. Singapore perfectly satisfies the economic-freedom condition, but falls short in fulfilling the condition for political freedom. The tantalizing issue is whether a country with a high level of economic freedom can achieve a high level of growth in the absence of a high level of political freedom, and the Singapore case seems to give evidence for a positive answer. Other countries in the same region—Indonesia, South Korea, Malaysia, and Taiwan—also seem to support an affirmative answer. Before South Korea and Taiwan became democratic, their economies experienced stellar growth. Together, these countries created the so-called "governed-market" East Asian Model, which emphasizes state intervention to improve favorable market conditions and productivity.[2]

However, the Singapore paradox should be viewed as a counterfactual case. The essential question is, If Singapore had adopted a democratic system, would its economy have grown even faster than it did? From the evidence in this book, the answer is probably affirmative, but there are a few exceptional factors in the Singapore paradox. First and foremost, the nation already enjoyed high levels of economic freedom, private investment, human-capital accumulation, income equality, and political stability. Although any increase in political freedom should further improve these conditions for growth, the additional impetus for growth—as generated by improvement in the political infrastructure—should not be as crucial in Singapore as in a country without adequate economic endowment or political stability (for instance, some countries in sub-Saharan Africa, to be discussed below). That Singapore has already been equipped with high levels of second-order conditions favoring growth extenuates the exigencies of growth-enhancing democratic mechanisms. Given the favorable conditions for growth inherent in Singapore's human and physical capital, any additional increase in political rights may not increase the economy's growth rate by a large margin.

Second, given the small size of the country in terms of population and area (fewer than three million people on 246 square miles), the advantages of democracy may not be obvious. While it is efficient for a democracy to run a large country, where the aggregation and dissemination of information are complex and costly, the difference between democracy and autocracy may be insignificant when the country is small, particularly in terms of geographical size.

Third, it should be noted that the level of democracy in Singapore, while not high enough to be a liberal democracy, is neither very low. Though it has never been recognized as a "free" country in the Freedom House survey, it has been consistently ranked between four and five on a one to seven scale, with one representing the most free.[3]

Fourth, Singapore has been under pressure for national survival. Having seceded from the Federation of Malaya in 1965 after political and economic conflict with Malaysia, Singapore encountered the tremendous challenge of defining itself in the shadow of two much larger nations. One is China, a powerful neighbor with which Singapore shares the same race (more than 70% of Singapore's citizens are Chinese by extraction). The other is the Federation of Malaya, from which Singapore broke away. All of this is compounded by the extreme lack of natural resources in this city-state. The legitimacy of Singapore's leadership lies in the nation's growth-oriented economic performance,[4] for which the government has to hold itself accountable. Its cabinet members, among the highest paid in the world, are obliged to take a salary cut if the national economy does not perform well enough. Because of Singapore's small population and limited geographic area, its political system is deemed capable of efficiently dealing with the challenge of survival. Similarly, Taiwan and South Korea have faced crises of survival complicated by security concerns; both countries have to perform well economically to compensate for the weakness of their military positions. Given the relatively small area of both countries and the urgency of their survival, it is reasonable to expect that they would have strong, centralized governments efficient in developing the economy for the purpose of mere survival, if nothing else. These two countries have achieved a high degree of economic prosperity, although it took them a fairly long time to become democratic, in view of their levels of per capita income. All things considered, it might not be an accident that Singapore and other East Asian countries have adopted less-democratic political systems than those of Western countries.

Perhaps the real lesson we should learn from East Asia lies on the other side of the picture. Many nations are not endowed with some of the favorable conditions for growth, such as education, physical capital, income equality, and property rights. More important, perhaps, many nations are not faced with the survival crises typical of South Korea, Singapore, and Taiwan, where internal natural resources are limited and external military and political threats are enormous. For these countries, an improvement in the political hardware for growth becomes essential. Political reform leading to a greater level of openness can achieve efficient results in promoting economic performance. In fact, under certain circumstances, doing so is likely the only way out of their economic woes.

Africa provides a stark contrast to the countries of East Asia. "The real African economic problem," says L. R. Klein, a Nobel laureate in economics, "is the case of sub-Saharan Africa, the bulk of the African geographic area" (Klein 1993, 230). After comparing sub-Saharan Africa with Pacific Asia, Latin America, and the Middle East, Klein (1993) presents a list of major problems confronting the sub-Saharan economies. These include lack of an industrial base and institutional organizations, the prevalence of corruption, a shortfall of financial capital, inflation, high population growth, political instability, and an overall poor quality of life. While a great deal of research has been carried out to investigate the economic dimensions of the problem,[5] the amount of attention dedicated to examining the effect of political institutions on economic growth in sub-Saharan Africa has just started to increase.

In contrast to the crucial role played by the government in the economic success of Pacific Asian countries, "[the state] is part of the problem of economic stagnation in much of sub-Saharan Africa" (Sandbrook 1986). "Personal" rule, a particular mode of patrimonial governance prevailing in some sub-Saharan societies, permits the advancement of political insiders and leads to the misallocation of scarce public resources, thereby resulting in an interrelated downward spiral of political and economic deterioration (Sandbrook 1986, 319).

Bienen (1993) points out that sub-Saharan Africa differs from Latin America and the Middle East in its lack of a socially oriented political agenda. The most important single objective of the political elites in these nations is to maintain themselves in power and, perhaps, to favor a particular ethnic group.

One explanation for the lack of social movement in sub-Saharan Africa is that social relations in many African societies are communally based, rather than class-based. In Africa, the political elites are less constrained by social constituencies. Weak social and political resistance to power and rule has made it possible for sub-Saharan African "personal" regimes to render the majority of their people to a subsistence-level existence while providing rewards to the ethnic groups that form their support. Its "dynamism obeys imperatives emanating from the polity rather than from the economy" (Mouzelis 1994, 137). Not having to timely respond to economic crises, African political elites enjoy a high degree of autonomy in making policy (Gulhati 1991). Such unchecked statism is one of the true inhibiting factors in the development of a market economy in Africa.[6]

In this context, political democracy is crucial for sub-Saharan African countries, where the social constraints on government are weak. In a cross-sectional analysis of 40 sub-Saharan African countries, Feng (1996) found that an economy grows faster under a regime that enjoys a higher level of institutionalized democracy. He also found that a positive-feedback relationship exists between democracy and growth: Democracy promotes growth, and growth leads to a higher level of democratization. Furthermore, the duration of authoritarian rule decreases economic growth, while growth shortens the tenure of an autocratic government.[7] As we found in chapter 4, what sub-Saharan Africa needs is a political foundation for economic development. Botswana, as discussed in the beginning of this book, offers a brilliant example for fellow sub-Saharan African countries.

Despite all the appealing economic prospects of democracies, economic difficulties may create problems for new democracies. However, a reversal of the democratization processes can worsen, rather than solve, economic problems, as our data have shown that authoritarianism generally leads to lower, rather than higher, output. Since previous findings show that a democratic government is conducive to domestic private investment, human-capital formation, the rule of law, income equality, and reductions in births, a truly democratic government is capable of using all these means to increase growth.

Some transitional economies may encounter temporary difficulties resulting from the changes in political and economic structures typical of democratization and liberalization. Even though a nation has adopted a democratic political system and a market-oriented economy, its economy may initially fail miserably, with growth rates declining into the negative area, unemployment running high, and inflation rising unbridled. The most telling examples of this paradox are the nations of Eastern Europe and the former Soviet Union when they switched from communist regimes to democracy. It should be noted that for these countries, a distinction should be drawn between temporary crises caused by structural changes and long-term problems inherent in an inefficient structure. For the latter kind of problem, situations will deteriorate as the system ages and degenerates. Inveterate inefficiency rooted in existing political and economic mechanisms will cause a further downturn, compounding the dimensions of a catastrophe. However, the former kind of problem is of a temporary and transitional nature, as it is part of the investment cost for a better future.

A model by Przeworski (1991) implies that radical economic reform that fundamentally changes the price system will immediately lead to a lower level of consumption than would gradual economic reform that only modifies the system. As the structural revolution is completed, the consumption resulting from the radical approach will eventually surpass that of the gradual approach (Przeworski 1991). So what kinds of political configurations are likely to induce radical or gradual reforms?

According to Fish (1996), a political system that engages political reforms aimed at free and democratic elections tends to adopt and implement a radical approach of economic liberalization and privatization (e.g., the Czech Republic, Estonia, Hungary, Poland, Latvia,

and Lithuania). In contrast, countries that undertake little economic reform (e.g., Kazakhstan, Uzbekistan, Azerbaijan, Belarus,
and Turkmenistan) suffer from inflation, reduced income, and output no less severe than those countries adopting large-scale privatization. However, it is important to note that countries adopting
a radical approach in economic reform were more likely to recover
from inflation, unemployment, and shrinkage of the economy than
countries that maintained the status quo or undertook gradual
reforms.

Dillon and Wykoff (2002) argue that former communist countries
with previous experience with capitalism or where the communist
regime was the result of foreign invasion or domination are more
likely to have successful economic transitions toward capitalist
economies than otherwise. Their argument is clearly embedded in
path dependence. According to their theory, Estonia, the Czech
Republic, and Hungary should perform better in their transitions
than Russia, Bulgaria, and Slovakia. The empirics largely support
their predictions except in the case of Slovakia.

Fish's (1996) and Dillon and Wykoff's (2002) observations are
consistent with the theoretical implication of Przeworski's model
and the findings in chapter 10 of this book regarding political freedom and economic freedom, namely, that democratic reform leads to
economic liberalization and privatization. While radical economic
reform may suffer from temporal difficulties, its long-term prospects are bright. Figure 12.1 shows some trends in economic growth
among six former communist countries in East Europe, using the
data provided in Dillon and Wykoff 2002.

In the early stage of transitions from 1989 through 1993, all of these
countries experienced negative economic growth as the result of
converting from a centrally planned economy to a market-oriented
one after politically transitioning from totalitarianism to pluralism.
For this short period of time, the empirical data may support the
assertion that democracy leads to poor economic performance.

My point of departure from Fish (1996) and Dillon and Wykoff
(2002) is to emphasize long-term performance. Russia and Bulgaria
did experience greater economic difficulties than other countries in
the early stage of economic transformation; however, as long as they
maintain a political system that is in line with economic transitions, they will eventually overcome their historical path-dependent
obstacles. In the long run, political freedom in all these countries is

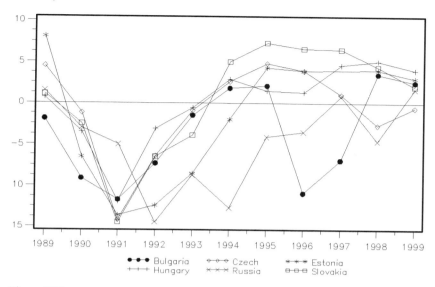

**Figure 12.1**
GDP-per-capita growth rate of six ex-communist states, 1989–1997

conducive to the consolidation and expansion of economic freedom, leading to recovery from temporary problems caused by the radical transition between the two types of economies.

Figure 12.2 plots chronological inflation data (Dillon and Wykoff 2002) for the same six countries. It indicates that since 1992, most of these countries have done well in reducing inflation, even Russia and Bulgaria.

In the formerly communist countries, deepening economic reforms requires a radical change in the way businesses are run. Three fundamental contradictions between reform and the status quo have been raised: reform conflicts with economic stability, with the emphasis on heavy industry, and with effective long-term economic development (Chen et al. 1988, 187). The solution to these contradictions involves devolution of power to individual enterprises and the use of spontaneous market mechanisms. This solution will lead to bankruptcies and massive layoffs, but these are needed to increase long-term efficiency. One complex and critical issue is the restructuring of state-owned enterprises (SOEs) in these transitional economies. As reform deepens, it becomes essential that market mechanisms be integrated into government economic policy. While

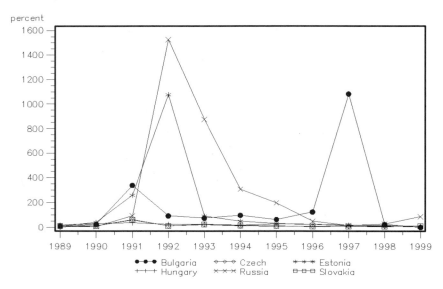

**Figure 12.2**
Inflation of six ex-communist states, 1990–1996

this will necessarily lead to bankruptcy, unemployment, and low growth for some time to come, the economy will eventually improve.

We need to examine the long-term trends of political and economic development in new democracies that have chosen to fundamentally change their economic systems. The political reforms that culminated in free elections in Russia and other East European countries are still a relatively recent phenomenon. It certainly takes more than the time that has elapsed since 1989 (when major political change was unleashed in Eastern Europe) to produce significantly improved and stable long-term economic performance. The circumstances under which political and economic reforms were undertaken indicate that the process of correcting all political, social, and economic misallocation and maladies inherent to a communist system is protracted, especially if we want to take the path-dependence argument seriously. It is necessary to study the political and economic development of these countries through a long-term aggregate model that looks at the secular trend of economic development far beyond the point at which political reforms were initially launched.

Next, suppose that we all agree that democracy is a good, rather than a bad. A relevant question is: How can we help manufacture this political product? This leads to the next section.

## 12.3   Related and Future Research

Formal and quantitative studies of democratic transitions and consolidations have increased over the past few years, but we are still in the infancy stage of understanding the mechanisms of democratic formation. Like the early studies on the effect of democracy on growth, the findings are ambiguous regarding the effect of economic development on democracy. The single most important thesis in this area is contained in the modernization argument attributed to Lipset (1959), which postulates that development or modernization is a requisite for democracy. Przeworski and Limongi (1997) and Przeworski, Alvarez, Cheibub, and Limongi (2000) find that development does not particularly contribute to democratic transitions, though it helps to sustain democratic consolidation.

The lack of support for the modernization thesis can be explained by the different ways of interpreting and subsequently testing the thesis. I believe that among a multitude of possible determinants for democratic transitions, it is not appropriate to view economic development as a prerequisite for democratic transitions. To hold that economic development must precede democracy confuses a necessary condition with a sufficient one. While development is a sufficient condition for democratic transitions—that is, as long as the economy expands, the likelihood of a democratic transition grows (Chen and Feng 1996b, 1999)—it is not a necessary condition for such a transition. Factors other than economic prosperity may contribute to such transitions. Some European nations, such as ancient Greece, began to practice democratic principles and democratic rule under a backward economy. Cross-country data show that a nation with a low level of income inequality stands a better chance of switching to democracy than a nation where income inequality is high, even when the former has a low level of development (Feng and Zak 1999). Furthermore, some scholars argue that cultures, traditions, and ideologies contribute to democratic transitions (Huntington 1993). Empirically, nations with some past democratic experience are more likely to make the transition to democracy than otherwise, while the threshold for a democratic transition in some

Muslim or Asian Pacific nations is relatively high, with all other factors kept constant (Feng and Zak 1999). Also, demographic transition may lead to a democratic transition. Reduction in birth rates has been found as a major determinant of democratic transitions (Feng, Kugler, and Zak 2000b). Finally, international actors can be instrumental in installing a democratic system on foreign soil, regardless of the latter's economic development and wealth distribution. In sum, while economic development is important for a democratic transition, other factors also foster conditions for such a transition.

As this book demonstrates, the level of economic development and the degree of democracy can reinforce each other. In addition to the indirect positive effects of democracy on economic growth, the latter promotes democratization and democratic transitions. The evidence shows that economic growth contributes to major regular government change and decreases political violence. Meanwhile, major regular government change promotes democratic values, whereas political violence tends to reduce democratic stability. Therefore, economic growth in the long run creates conditions for the peaceful evolution of an autocracy into a democratic state and facilitates the consolidation and expansion of a democratic political system.

One implication of the above analysis is that the effect of development on democracy should be studied together with all of the above-mentioned relevant variables. For instance, a poor, egalitarian society may stand a better chance of becoming democratic than a rich, unequal society. However, a rich, egalitarian society has a better prospect of a democratic transition than a poor, egalitarian society. It is essential to include an income-distribution variable while estimating the effect of development on democratic transitions. Other relevant control variables include culture, demography, education, and international influence.

Despite an increasing number of empirical works on democratic transitions, "theoretical models of the effect of prosperity on democracy are not well developed" (Barro 1997, 51). Few studies have both formalized and statistically tested the dynamics of democratic transitions. In the future, I expect to see a rise in efforts to establish a general equilibrium model that weaves in the factors for democratic transitions mentioned above.

The measurement of democracy is one essential methodological area of research that requires a great deal of further improvement.

The degree of liberal and institutional democracy as measured in the Gastil/Freedom House survey and Polity data lacks sufficient within-country variation. This work has implied that the indicators of political freedom or institutionalized democracy fall short of reflecting subtle changes in partisan politics in such countries as Singapore or substantial dynamic changes in such countries as China. For instance, despite the change in popular support for the People's Action Party (PAP) in Singapore, as indicated in the PAP's share of the popular vote received over the years, the change in the measures of political rights and institutionalized democracy has been small and very often absent. In China today, citizens can openly criticize government leaders without being arrested, and hundreds of thousands of people go to church on Sundays. Yet in 2002 it received from Freedom House (2002) the most repressive score on political rights, the same score it received during the Cultural Revolution years, and the second most repressive score on civil liberties, the same score it received in 1977.

Understandably, the ratings at Freedom House are based on the country's procedures and laws regarding democratic elections and freedoms. The governing party in China has yet to allow significant partisan competition for the national government in free elections, depoliticize the military, and completely open up mass media. On those grounds, China remains an authoritarian society. However, as with China's economic reforms, which originated in the countryside in the late 1970s, China is experimenting with democratic politics at the levels of villages and towns, where some officials are directly elected by secret ballots. Village democracy, as it is called, may be an important milestone in Chinese history, pointing to a new political system characteristic of a liberal democracy. Yet village democracy is not on Freedom House's radar screen. To catch important directional changes in the political landscape, the measure of democracy needs to be sensitive to dynamic nuances that have significant implications for future fundamental change, although they do not meet the rating criteria based on today's laws and procedures.

The lack of within-country variation in the measure of political freedom and democracy causes immediate difficulties for the study of the dynamic relationship between political and economic development within a country using short-term observations such as annual data. While this deficiency should not seriously affect aggregate cross-country studies (which analyze the means of data over a

long period of time), it is important to identify the dynamic mechanisms subsumed under long-term relationships, a study that requires
an improved measure of political systems so that subtle political
changes can be captured within a country.

Political scientists may well take some cues from how economic
indictors, such as the consumer-confidence index and the index of
consumer sentiment, are developed. The political and social data on
elections and other political events should be combined with survey
data to produce a time series of indicators for political democracy
and political stability. Such indictors should also have a range of
variation to reflect dynamic changes. Furthermore, these indicators
should not be close-ended. In more than one sense, democracy is not
an end in itself. History does not end with democracy; it witnesses
an ongoing process of continually improving democracy. Not only is
this true in nations that recently became democracies, but it also
applies to democratic states that were established a long time ago.
Refining our measures of democracy depends on our ongoing learning of what democracy is and should be, and it will lead to an
improved understanding of political systems in terms of both their
determinants and derivatives.

Another important area of further substantive research lies in
the relationship of social changes (e.g., fertility, mortality, life expectancy, and migration) and of environmental protection to political
and economic development. Economic growth is certainly the most
important indicator of a nation's development performance; nonetheless, it may not be the only indicator. Economic development,
which implies the expansion of a nation's income level, is only one
factor in the utility function of human welfare. In addition, human
welfare depends on other dimensions of the quality of life, such as
life expectancy, infant mortality, crime reduction, and the preserva-
tion of valuable natural resources.

What are the determinants of these aspects of life? Is economic
growth or the level of economic development the major determinant of the quality of life? Are there any government policies whose
primary object is to improve the quality of life, yet that does not do
so through economic development? What kind of political institutional framework is best not only to promote economic growth, but
also to reduce crime rates, improve life expectancy, and protect the
environment?

These are important questions. To the extent that economic growth is the dominant factor in improving infant mortality or life expectancy, government policies should be designed to achieve maximum economic growth. Determinants conducive to economic growth—such as education, private investment, and the rule of law—will also likely enhance life expectancy and the general quality of life. However, if some factors can explain these capabilities beyond what can be explained by economic growth, then we need to know what they are. In the case in which policy variables have opposite effects on the quality of life and economic growth, a government has to provide a balance among policies that improve the quality of life and policies that promote economic growth.

The relationship between economic growth and environmental protection is one example that holds much interest for many people. At issue is the long-term growth rate, which maximizes a utility function of both current income and future wealth as constrained by environmental protection. The depletion of natural resources may give us the best growth today, but very little for tomorrow. Sustainable development depends on the allocation of resources so that future benefits are guaranteed.

Furthermore, as democracy leads to an improved quality of life—including better education, a safer investment environment, higher income levels, and longer life expectancies—individuals may want to legally or illegally emigrate from an autocracy to a democracy. All this has profound consequences on the hosting democracy. Its life quality and output per capita may decline as the result of certain patterns of immigration. Dependent upon the heterogeneity of the skill sets of the individual, the recipient country (democracy) and the sender country (autocracy) are both affected by the individual's decision to stay or leave, in terms of the level of income as well as the autocracy's prospects of becoming a democracy (Zak, Feng, and Kugler 2001).

Finally, the relationship between democracy and regional integration is an important area of further study. Feng and Genna (2003) find that the homogeneity of domestic economic institutions and the process of regional integration reinforce each other in a comparative analysis of various regional blocs in the world, including the Andean Common Market, the Association of Southeast Asian Nations, the Central African Customs and Economic Union, the Central American Common Market, the European Union, the Forum for Asia-Pacific

Economic Cooperation, the North American Free Trade Association, and the Southern Cone Common Market. The most successful case of integration, the European Union, does evince a pattern of positive interaction between the two variables, while less successful cases, found in Latin America, are lacking in this mechanism of mutual influence. It may not be coincidental that the most democratic group of the above is the European Union, which is also the most successful integrator. Two issues of interest arise. First, in addition to the homogeneity of economic institutions as studied by Feng and Genna (2003), the convergence of political institutions across the member states of a regional bloc may also be important for the ultimate phase of political and economic integration of the group. Therefore, the NAFTA countries hold much greater promise than the APEC countries in terms of the completion of their integration process, as the former are politically far more homogenous than the latter. Second, the leading democratic nation or nations in the region exert a dynamic effect on the democratization of others in the group. The United States and major Western European countries have all played such a role in promoting democratization in other member states such as Mexico and some Southern and Eastern European countries. These two related arguments, if true, hold great policy implications for the world. The democratic peace literature as discussed elsewhere in the book demonstrates that democracies seldom fight each other. Regional integration driven by a convergence toward democracy may also reduce economic transaction costs across various regional blocs and ultimately promote economic globalization. Peace and prosperity will be thus intertwined and strengthened in worldwide political and economic integration powered by democracy.

The current literature has yet to produce clear evidence for any of the relationships discussed in this section. It is imperative that we carry this research further.

# Appendix 3.A: Political-Rights and Civil-Liberties Indices

## Political rights

- Chief authority recently reelected by a meaningful process.
- Legislature recently elected by a meaningful process.
- Fair election laws, campaigning opportunity.
- Fair reflection of voter preference in distribution of power.
- Multiple political parties.
- Recent shifts in power through elections.
- Significant opposition vote.
- Freedom from military or foreign control.
- Major groups allowed reasonable self-determination.
- Decentralized political power.
- Informal consensus, de facto opposition power.

## Civil liberties

- Media/literature free of political censorship.
- Open public discussion.
- Freedom of assembly and demonstrations.
- Freedom of political organization.
- Nondiscriminatory rule of law in politically relevant cases.
- Free from unjustified political terror or imprisonment.
- Free trade unions or peasant cooperatives.
- Free businesses or cooperatives.
- Free professional or other private organizations.

- Free religious institutions.
- Personal social rights.

Source: Gastil and Freedom House; see Burkhart and Lewis-Beck 1994, 908.

The operational indicator of democracy in Polity II is derived from a coding of the competitiveness of political participation, the openness of executive recruitment, and constraints on the chief executive. The democracy indicator is an additive 10-point scale, constructed for the traits that are conceptually associated with democracy. The indicator uses the following weights.

### Scale Weight for Coding Authority

### Competitiveness of political participation

| | |
|---|---|
| Competitive | 3 |
| Transitional | 2 |
| Factional | 1 |
| Other | 0 |

### Competitiveness of executive recruitment

| | |
|---|---|
| Election | 2 |
| Transitional | 1 |
| Other | 0 |

### Openness of executive recruitment

| | |
|---|---|
| Dual election | 1 |
| Open | 1 |
| Other | 0 |

### Constraints on chief executive

| | |
|---|---|
| Executive parity or subordination | 4 |
| (Intermediate category) | 3 |

Substantial limitations            2

(Intermediate category)            1

## Definitions of the Terms Used Above

### Competitiveness of political participation

*Competitive* There are relatively stable and enduring political groups, which regularly compete for political influence at the national level. Competition among them seldom causes widespread violence or disruption. Very small parties or political groups may be restricted in the *competitive* pattern.

*Transitional* Any transitional arrangements from factional patterns to fully competitive patterns, or vice versa. Transitions to *competitive* are not complete until a national election is held on a fully competitive basis.

*Factional* Polities with factional or restricted patterns of competition.

### Competitiveness of executive recruitment

*Election* Chief executives are typically chosen in or through competitive elections matching two or more major parties or candidates (elections may be popular or by an elected assembly).

*Transitional* Transitional arrangements between selection (ascription/designation) and competitive election.

### Openness of executive recruitment

*Dual election* Hereditary succession plus electoral selection of an effective chief minister.

*Open* Chief executives are chosen by elite designation, competitive election, or transitional arrangements between designation and election.

### Constraints on chief executive

*Executive parity or subordination* Accountability groups have effective authority equal to or greater than the executive in most areas of activity. Examples of evidence:

• A legislature, ruling party, or council of nobles initiates much or more important legislation.

• The executive (president, premier, king, cabinet, or council) is chosen by the accountability group and depends on its continued support to remain in office (as in most parliamentary systems).

• In multiparty democracies, there is chronic cabinet instability.

*Substantial limitations on executive authority* The executive has more effective authority than any accountability group but is subject to substantial constraints from such groups. Examples:

• A legislature or party council often modifies or defeats executive proposals for action.

• A council or legislature sometimes refuses funds to the executive.

• The accountability group makes important appointments to administrative posts.

• The legislature does not permit the executive to leave the country.

Source: Gurr, Jaggers, and Moore 1990.

# Appendix 4.A:  A Brief Review of the Literature on Democracy, Stability, and Growth

## Democracy and Growth

Two overarching themes in the study of the political economy of growth are the relationships between democracy and growth and between political stability and growth. Huntington (1987) and Sirowy and Inkeles (1990) discuss three schools of thought on the first relationship. The "conflict school" argues that democracy hinders economic growth, particularly in less developed countries (LDCs).[1] These scholars offer three assumptions to support this claim: that there are "dysfunctional consequences" of "premature" democracy upon growth; that democratic regimes are unable to implement those policies necessary for rapid growth; and that in the present world-historical context, democracy is incapable of pervasive state involvement in the development process (Sirowy and Inkeles 1990, 129). Additionally, it has been argued that a nation's rapid growth requires autocratic control and reduced freedom, and that developing countries, in particular, cannot achieve rapid economic growth without a strong centralized government (Johnson 1964, Moore 1966, Gerschenkron 1962, O'Donnell 1973, Marsh 1979, Donnelly 1984, MacIntyre 1996).

The case of South Korea conveniently supports this view. Though Fukuyama himself may not be of this school of thought, he points out that "democracies tend to transfer wealth from rich to poor in the interests of social equality, to protect or subsidize failing industries, to spend more on social services than investment, and the like. The military regime in South Korea accelerated economic growth by suppressing strikes and holding down wages and consumption; the transition to democracy in 1987 led to a wave of labor unrest and rapidly rising wages that ultimately reduced Korea's international competitiveness" (Fukuyama 1993, 99). Despite pressures from labor organizations, the democratically elected South Korean government has taken austere measures, including curtailing workers' benefits, so as to reverse the decline of its economic power. The largest labor strike in South Korea's history erupted in December 1996 in reaction to a bill passed by the legislature ending the security of lifetime employment for Korean workers. The law was intended to increase the efficiency and competitiveness of South Korean industries. Such efforts were much needed. Previously a large net exporter, South Korea ran a trade deficit of 20 billion U.S. dollars in 1996, twice that of 1995.

In contrast, the "compatibility school" of thought sharply objects to the assumptions of the "conflict school," and contends that democracy enhances economic growth. Proponents of the compatibility school argue that democratic governments in less developed countries are best suited to foster sustained and equitable economic development. They maintain that democratic processes, as well as the existence and exercise of fundamental civil liberties and political rights, generate the social conditions most conducive to economic development. Political and economic freedom enhances property rights and market competition, thus promoting economic growth (Smith 1937, Hayek 1944, Lipset 1959, Friedman 1961, Mises 1981, Riker and Weimer 1993, Bueno de Mesquita et al. 2003).

Finally, according to the "skeptical" perspective, there is no systematic relationship between democracy and economic development (Pye 1966, McKinlay and Cohan 1975). The proponents of this school maintain that having a democratic government alone means very little for economic growth. Instead, the focus should be placed on institutional structures (e.g., two-party versus multiparty systems) and government development strategies (e.g., import substitution versus export promotion), which may vary independently of the democratic character of a political system. This perspective's skepticism also includes the idea that different political systems are capable of adopting the same economic policy, suggesting that the effects of political systems on growth are negligible.

Until recently, despite fertile theoretical literature on the subject, cross-national quantitative efforts at testing the various hypotheses fell short in their attempt to produce clear empirical evidence (Sirowy and Inkeles 1990, 150, Przeworski and Limongi 1993, 64). Some empirical studies have found no significant relationship between economic growth and regime type (Kohli 1986, Marsh 1988), while others have established a strong impact of democracy on growth (Scully 1988, Grier and Tullock 1989, Chen and Feng 1996, Leblang 1997, Feng 1997a, Przeworski et al. 2000,[2] Bueno de Mesquita et al. 2003). Yet others have ascertained only a weak positive effect of freedom on growth (Kormendi and Meguire 1985, Pourgerami 1992), or even a negative influence of freedom on growth (Przeworski 1966, Adelman and Morris 1967, Huntington and Dominguez 1975, Marsh 1979, Weede 1983, Landau 1986). Several regional studies focusing on developing countries have also produced ambiguous findings.[3]

### Political Stability and Growth

Like the study of democracy and growth, the study of political stability and growth has yielded contradictory findings. Alesina, Özler, Roubini, and Swagel (1996) find that countries with a high incidence of government collapse also have low economic growth, though they also find that low economic growth does not affect political instability. Londregan and Poole (1990), on the other hand, do not find evidence for reduced growth as a consequence of increased political instability; instead, they infer that low economic growth increases political instability. In addition, some studies that use single-equation estimation see low economic growth as a result of political turbulence (Barro 1991, Siermann 1998).

In the study of political stability and economic performance, regime change and government change are typically confounded.[4] For instance, no distinction is made between a military coup d'état and an election change whereby one party succeeds another in office (Alesina et al. 1996, Cukierman, Edwards, and Tabellini 1992). By contrast, Sanders (1981) identifies two major dimensions of political instability: regime change (changes in regime norms, changes in types of party systems, changes in military-civilian status) and government change (changes in the effective executive or cabinet). In his analysis, Sanders finds that freedom contributes to regime-change instability, and economic development inhibits regime-change instability, although freedom and development have much less of an effect on government-change instability. This definition of political instability provides two mutually exclusive subsets of political change that may have different impacts on economic growth. Moreover,

Sanders's empirical results imply that a study of political instability and growth will be theoretically meaningless and will probably lead to confusing and ambiguous empirical conclusions unless political instability is differentiated accordingly. Major political instability (such as a successful coup d'état) or minor political instability (such as a government change involving the same party) will have different consequences for growth.

| Code | Interaction | Weight | SD |
|------|-------------|--------|-----|
| 223 | Military attack, assault | −10.0 | 0.0 |
| 211 | Seize position or possessions | −9.2 | 0.7 |
| 222 | Nonmilitary destruction/injury | −8.7 | 0.5 |
| 221 | Nonmilitary destructive action | −8.3 | 0.6 |
| 182 | Armed-force mobilization, exercises, display; military buildup | −7.6 | 1.2 |
| 195 | Break in diplomatic relations | −7.0 | 1.3 |
| 173 | Threat with force specified | −7.0 | 1.1 |
| 174 | Ultimatum, threat with negative sanction and time limit | −6.9 | 1.4 |
| 172 | Threat with specific negative nonmilitary sanction | −5.8 | 1.9 |
| 193 | Reduce or cut off aid or assistance; act to punish/deprive | −5.6 | 1.4 |
| 181 | Nonmilitary demonstration, walk out | −5.2 | 2.1 |
| 201 | Order person or personnel out of country | −5.0 | 1.7 |
| 202 | Expel organization or group | −4.9 | 1.4 |
| 150 | Issue order or command, insist, demand compliance | −4.9 | 1.7 |
| 171 | Threat without specific negative sanction | −4.4 | 1.5 |
| 212 | Detain or arrest person(s) | −4.4 | 2.3 |
| 192 | Reduce routine international activity; recall officials | −4.1 | 1.2 |
| 112 | Refuse; oppose; refuse to allow | −4.0 | 1.5 |
| 111 | Turn down proposal; reject protest, demand, threat | −4.0 | 1.5 |

| Code | Interaction | Weight | SD |
|------|-------------|--------|-----|
| 194 | Halt negotiation | −3.8 | 0.9 |
| 122 | Denounce; denigrate; abuse | −3.4 | 1.1 |
| 160 | Give warning | −3.0 | 1.3 |
| 132 | Issue formal complaint or protest | −2.4 | 0.9 |
| 121 | Charge; criticize; blame; disapprove | −2.2 | 1.3 |
| 191 | Cancel or postpone planned event | −2.2 | 1.5 |
| 131 | Make informal complaint | −1.9 | 0.6 |
| 063 | Grant asylum | −1.1 | 2.5 |
| 142 | Deny an attributed policy, action, role, or position | −1.1 | 1.0 |
| 141 | Deny an accusation | −0.9 | 1.3 |
| 023 | Comment on situation | −0.2 | 0.5 |
| 102 | Urge or suggest action or policy | −0.1 | 1.5 |
| 021 | Explicitly decline to comment | −0.1 | 0.6 |
| 094 | Request action; call for | −0.1 | 1.0 |
| 025 | Explain or state policy; state future position | 0.0 | 0.0 |
| 091 | Ask for information | 0.1 | 0.4 |
| 011 | Surrender; yield to order; submit to arrest | 0.6 | 7.2 |
| 012 | Yield position; retreat; evacuate | 0.6 | 6.6 |
| 031 | Meet with; send note | 1.0 | 0.9 |
| 095 | Entreat; plead; appeal to; beg | 1.2 | 1.8 |
| 101 | Offer proposal | 1.5 | 1.9 |
| 061 | Express regret; apologize | 1.8 | 1.5 |
| 032 | Visit; go to | 1.9 | 2.4 |
| 066 | Release and/or return persons or property | 1.9 | 2.7 |
| 013 | Admit wrongdoing; apologize; retract statement | 2.0 | 2.2 |
| 062 | Give state invitation | 2.5 | 2.7 |
| 054 | Assure; reassure | 2.8 | 2.2 |
| 033 | Receive visit; host | 2.8 | 3.0 |
| 065 | Suspend sanctions; end punishment; call truce | 2.9 | 3.6 |
| 082 | Agree to future action or procedure, to meet, or to negotiate | 3.0 | 2.5 |

| Code | Interaction | Weight | SD |
|------|-------------|--------|-----|
| 092 | Ask for policy assistance | 3.4 | 1.1 |
| 093 | Ask for material assistance | 3.4 | 2.4 |
| 041 | Praise; hail; applaud; extend condolences | 3.4 | 2.1 |
| 042 | Endorse other's policy or position; give verbal support | 3.6 | 1.8 |
| 053 | Promise other future support | 4.5 | 1.6 |
| 051 | Promise own policy support | 4.5 | 1.7 |
| 052 | Promise material support | 5.2 | 1.5 |
| 064 | Grant privilege, diplomatic recognition, de facto relations | 5.4 | 1.4 |
| 073 | Give other assistance | 6.5 | 1.9 |
| 081 | Make substantive agreement | 6.5 | 1.4 |
| 071 | Extend economic aid; give, buy, sell, loan, borrow | 7.4 | 1.0 |
| 072 | Extend military assistance | 8.3 | 0.9 |

Source: Goldstein 1992

| Country | Obs | Gini (mean) | SD | B&J | Muller |
|---|---|---|---|---|---|
| United Kingdom | 31 | 25.98 | 2.61 | Y | Y |
| Spain | 8 | 26.25 | 1.85 | Y | Y |
| Belgium | 4 | 27.01 | 0.88 | N | Y |
| Luxembourg | 1 | 27.13 | | N | N |
| Netherlands | 12 | 28.59 | 0.95 | Y | Y |
| Rwanda | 1 | 28.90 | | N | N |
| Taiwan | 26 | 29.62 | 1.53 | Y | Y |
| Finland | 12 | 29.93 | 2.17 | Y | N |
| Nepal | 1 | 30.06 | | N | N |
| Germany | 7 | 31.22 | 1.71 | Y | Y |
| Canada | 23 | 31.27 | 1.67 | Y | Y |
| Pakistan | 9 | 31.50 | 0.86 | Y | N |
| Sweden | 14 | 31.74 | 1.48 | Y | Y |
| Denmark | 4 | 32.08 | 1.26 | Y | N |
| India | 31 | 32.55 | 2.06 | Y | Y |
| Indonesia | 11 | 33.49 | 2.17 | Y | Y |
| South Korea | 14 | 34.19 | 2.63 | Y | Y |
| Norway | 9 | 34.21 | 2.90 | Y | Y |
| New Zealand | 12 | 34.36 | 2.90 | Y | Y |
| Greece | 3 | 34.53 | 1.07 | N | N |
| Japan | 23 | 34.82 | 1.35 | Y | Y |
| Italy | 15 | 34.93 | 2.61 | Y | Y |
| Portugal | 4 | 34.95 | 2.93 | N | Y |
| Ghana | 4 | 35.13 | 1.42 | N | N |

| Country | Obs | Gini (mean) | SD | B&J | Muller |
|---|---|---|---|---|---|
| United States | 45 | 35.28 | 1.29 | Y | Y |
| Bangladesh | 10 | 35.83 | 1.63 | N | N |
| Ireland | 3 | 36.31 | 2.12 | N | Y |
| Uganda | 2 | 36.89 | 5.50 | Y | N |
| Australia | 9 | 37.88 | 3.08 | Y | Y |
| Egypt | 4 | 38.00 | 4.32 | Y | Y |
| Mauritius | 3 | 38.47 | 1.57 | N | N |
| Nigeria | 3 | 38.55 | 2.27 | N | N |
| Sudan | 1 | 38.72 | | Y | Y |
| Algeria | 1 | 38.73 | | N | N |
| Ivory Coast | 4 | 39.18 | 1.86 | Y | Y |
| Jordan | 3 | 39.19 | 2.67 | N | N |
| Morocco | 2 | 39.20 | 0.01 | Y | N |
| Singapore | 6 | 40.12 | 1.81 | N | N |
| Tanzania | 3 | 40.37 | 3.18 | N | Y |
| Sri Lanka | 9 | 41.71 | 6.10 | Y | Y |
| Bolivia | 1 | 42.04 | | Y | Y |
| Jamaica | 9 | 42.17 | 3.02 | Y | N |
| Tunisia | 5 | 42.51 | 1.41 | Y | Y |
| Mauritania | 1 | 42.53 | | N | N |
| Ecuador | 1 | 43.00 | | Y | N |
| France | 7 | 43.11 | 6.07 | Y | Y |
| Iran | 5 | 43.23 | 1.41 | N | Y |
| Madagascar | 1 | 43.44 | | Y | N |
| Venezuela | 9 | 44.42 | 4.27 | Y | Y |
| Thailand | 8 | 45.48 | 3.78 | Y | Y |
| Bahamas | 11 | 45.77 | 4.10 | N | N |
| Costa Rica | 9 | 46.00 | 2.97 | Y | Y |
| Trinidad | 4 | 46.21 | 3.79 | Y | Y |
| Peru | 4 | 46.34 | 5.86 | Y | Y |
| Seychelles | 2 | 46.50 | 0.71 | N | N |
| Dominican Republic | 4 | 46.94 | 3.35 | Y | N |
| Barbados | 2 | 47.18 | 2.38 | N | Y |
| Philippines | 7 | 47.62 | 2.46 | Y | Y |

| Country | Obs | Gini (mean) | SD | B&J | Muller |
|---|---|---|---|---|---|
| El Salvador | 1 | 48.40 | | Y | Y |
| Cameroon | 1 | 49.00 | | N | N |
| Nicaragua | 1 | 50.32 | | N | Y |
| Malaysia | 6 | 50.36 | 1.96 | Y | Y |
| Turkey | 3 | 50.36 | 5.98 | Y | Y |
| Zambia | 2 | 50.56 | 0.63 | N | N |
| Guyana | 2 | 51.49 | 6.60 | N | N |
| Colombia | 7 | 51.51 | 2.68 | Y | Y |
| Chile | 5 | 51.84 | 5.76 | Y | Y |
| Panama | 4 | 52.43 | 5.01 | Y | Y |
| Senegal | 1 | 54.12 | | Y | Y |
| Botswana | 1 | 54.21 | | N | N |
| Kenya | 1 | 54.39 | | Y | Y |
| Honduras | 7 | 54.49 | 3.63 | Y | Y |
| Mexico | 9 | 54.59 | 2.92 | Y | Y |
| Central African Rep. | 1 | 55.00 | | N | N |
| Guatemala | 3 | 55.68 | 5.18 | N | Y |
| Lesotho | 1 | 56.02 | | N | N |
| Guinea Bissau | 1 | 56.12 | | N | N |
| Zimbabwe | 1 | 56.83 | | N | Y |
| Brazil | 14 | 57.84 | 2.92 | Y | Y |
| Sierra Leone | 1 | 60.79 | | Y | Y |
| Gabon | 2 | 61.23 | 2.76 | Y | Y |
| South Africa | 1 | 62.30 | | N | Y |

Obs: Number of observations.
Y: Included in Bollen and Jackson's or Muller's sample.
N: Not Included in Bollen and Jackson's or Muller's sample.

# Appendix 10.A:
# Measures of Economic
# Freedom

**Money and inflation (protection of money as a store of value and medium of exchange)**

· Average annual growth rate of the money supply during the last five years minus the potential growth rate of real GDP.

· Standard deviation of the annual inflation rate during the last five years.

· Freedom of citizens to own a foreign-currency bank account domestically.

· Freedom of citizens to maintain a bank account abroad.

**Government operations and regulations (freedom to decide what is produced and consumed)**

· Government general-consumption expenditures as a percent of GDP.

· The role and presence of government-operated enterprises.

· Price controls—the extent to which businesses are free to set their own prices.

· Freedom of private businesses and cooperatives to compete in markets.

· Equality of citizens under the law and access of citizens to a non-discriminatory judiciary.

· Freedom from government regulations and policies that cause negative real interest rates.

**Takings and discriminatory taxations (freedom to keep what you earn)**

· Transfers and subsidies as a percent of GDP.

· Top marginal tax rate.

· The use of conscripts to obtain military personnel.

**Restraints on international exchange (freedom of exchange with foreigners)**

• Taxes on international trade as a percent of exports plus imports.

• Difference between the official exchange rate and the black-market rate.

• Actual size of trade sector compared to the expected size.

• Restrictions on the freedom of citizens to engage in capital transactions with foreigners.

Source: Gwartney, Lawson, and Block 1996, 16.

# Notes

## Chapter 1

1. Additionally, works utilizing the median-voter theorem imply that there might be an incentive to expropriate capital in a democracy. This will be reviewed in chapters 2, 7, and 9.

2. First, these factors, influenced by democracy, have been found to affect growth. A misspecification problem occurs when these relevant variables are excluded in the growth equation. Growth is not entirely determined by democracy, and the exclusion of relevant control variables will bias the final results. Second, many of these variables, in addition to being determinants of growth, are desired social goals to be achieved for their own sake. For instance, education and income equality have their own intrinsic values. They are means to economic growth, but they also perform the invaluable function of achieving intellectual growth and/or increasing social equality.

3. Relative to GDP per capita, standards of living might be more appropriately measured by GNP per capita, which adjusts the former to remove net factor payments to foreigners, or by sustainable consumption levels. Since GDP is widely used and the international differences in the rates of growth of per capita GDP and GNP are highly correlated over the period of analysis, GDP is used in this study. In addition to the growth rate of per capita GDP or GNP, the developmental goals of any country may include improvements in the living standard, health, education, employment, control of inflation, foreign debts, etc. (Firebaugh and Beck 1994).

4. *The Penn World Table (Mark 6)* uses the same method as in Summers and Heston 1995. They extend the last year from 1992 in *PWT 5.6* to 1996 in *PWT 5.7* and 1998 in *PWT 6.0*.

5. Internet source: http://www.pbs.org/wgbh/commandingheights/shared/pdf/ess_dependencia.pdf.

6. It should be understood that steady-state growth is a useful concept only in understanding economic growth; in reality, it is rather difficult to determine if steady-state growth has been obtained.

7. The main reason for this phenomenon in neoclassical growth models is diminishing returns to reproducible capital. Poor countries tend to have low ratios of capital to labor and, consequently, have high marginal products of capital; therefore, they tend to grow at relatively high rates.

8. In contrast, Easton distinguishes the structure of norms from the structure of behavior. "If the parts of [institutions] we wish to refer to are the norms, or rules and regulations, we have a normative structure. If, however, the parts are the behavior of the participants, we have structures of behavior" Easton (1990, 59). While I agree with Easton that it is a weakness to confound different kinds of structures, as long as it is possible to identify which part of the political environment is characterized by the structure of norms and which part by the structure of behavior, it is convenient to use *political institutions* to refer to both the rules of the game (as North does) and institutionalized behavior (as Easton does).

9. Works such as Robert Bates 1989, Haggard and Kaufman 1989, and Remmer 1990 provide excellent insights into country-specific policy operations.

## Chapter 2

1. The model appears in Chen and Feng 1996. This chapter extends discussions to present full implications. A short-run model using the same logic can be found in Feng and Chen 1996.

2. For political scientists who need a quick introduction to endogenous growth theory and theory of reproducible capital, see Feng 2001c.

3. Since the individual is already living in the current period, $\tau$ does not enter the calculation of consumption during the current period. It is the future period about which the individual is concerned when making an investment decision.

4. In this model, $\tau$ is exogenously given. In a general equilibrium model in which the political equilibrium is endogenously determined, the government's policy is determined by the median voter's preference toward the regulatory policy. (See Chen and Feng 1999.)

5. In very repressive societies, $\tau$ may well be over one, implying that an investor may lose all his investment and in addition may lose more through suffering physically, mentally, and financially for being an erstwhile capitalist. To simplify the model, I make $\tau = (-\infty, 1)$.

6. It is assumed that $w_{t-1} = w_t = w$ and $r_{t-1} = r_t = r$ for all $t$. Therefore, $g$ is the common steady-state growth rate of capital accumulation, output, and consumption.

7. The standardized coefficient estimates the predictive importance of the independent variables. It takes into account the variation of the independent variable in the sample by multiplying the parameter estimate by the ratio of the standard deviation of the independent variable over the standard deviation of the dependent variable.

8. Roemer (1995) uses a deductive model to show that potential government change in a democratic political system creates uncertainty because of the difference in policy between political parties. The difference in policy between incoming and outgoing parties of an unconstitutional government change should be even larger, thus creating a higher level of uncertainty.

9. After months of delicate and tactical negotiations by the government and the release of most hostages, the remaining 72 hostages were secured in a surprise raid on April 23, 1997, by army commandos, who killed all the Tupac Amaru personnel on the premises. Political uncertainty and violence intensified by political polarization foreshadowed Fujimori's downfall.

10. See appendix 4.A for a review of the debate on democracy and growth.

11. The above growth rates are based on real income by using purchasing power parity (Summers and Heston 2001).

12. Government crises are defined as any rapidly developing situation that threatens to bring the downfall of the present regime, excluding situations of revolt intended to overthrow the government. Revolutions are defined as any illegal or forced change in the top governmental elite, any attempt at such a change, or any successful armed rebellion whose aim is independence from the central government. Assassinations are defined as any politically motivated murder or attempted murder of a high-level government official or politician (Banks 1979, 25).

13. In a recent book, Easterly (2001) demonstrates that despite foreign aid, physical capital, human capital, and population policy, sub-Saharan economies have failed; the reason for their failure, he asserts, lies in the application of economic principles to practical policy work. My argument, as in chapter 4, is that certain political factors—particularly political freedom and policy certainty—are the fundamental determinants for economic performance in sub-Sahara.

14. Juhyeon Park has collected the data and helped provide this case study.

15. Under the Treaty of Nanking (now known as Nanjing) in 1842, which ended the First Opium War, Hong Kong was ceded to the British in perpetuity. After a second conflict in 1860, Great Britain acquired Kowloon and Stonecutters Island, and in 1898 it obtained the New Territories under a 99-year lease.

16. Case's (1995) study of Malaysia provides an example of a stable government in an environment of ethnic and religious polarization.

17. For background information on Colombia and Venezuela, see Karl 1991.

## Chapter 3

1. Other well-cited definitions of democracy include Dahl (1971), who prefers to use the term *polyarchies* for a political system that is close to the ideal prototype of democracy, which is "completely or almost completely responsive to its citizens" (Dahl 1971, 2). Almond and Verba define democracy as the "diffusion of influence over political decisions" (1963, 351).

2. Arthur S. Banks's time-series data contain variables that measure procedural democracy, and therefore are said to have a bias for Eastern European countries, which, during the Cold War period, had periodic elections (at least in appearance) (Bollen 1993).

3. It should be noted that Raymond D. Gastil and his associates compiled the data for the period of 1973–1989. Freedom House has continued the series since 1990.

4. The disadvantage in using these variables occurs in the investigation of democratic transitions, specifically, when we have to pin down a cutoff point in a transition to democracy. In this case, a dichotomous variable that differentiates democracies from nondemocracies is a better choice for the dependent variable than these continuous indices, as the issue is a categorical transition from one state to another.

5. The opposite of the probability of government change is government durability, which implies the stability and efficacy of a government (Powell 1986).

6. Easton (1965) provides a useful analytical framework of regime change and government change, distinguishing three levels of political structures: political authorities, regimes, and political communities. Political authorities are the incumbents in political office or the pool of political elites from which government leaders are chosen. In this chapter, political authorities are conveniently defined as the government. A regime is the institutions, rules, and arrangements related to the selection and operation of government. Finally, a political community comprises the historical values and tradition that transcend and encompass the political offices of the nation. Examples include characterizations and categorizations based on religion, ethnicity, or nationality. For instance, political communities can be identified as "Catholic" or "Japanese" (Easton 1965, 177; Sanders 1981, 68).

7. For instance, Raymond Gastil and Freedom House list 40 polities for more than one hundred countries and regions between 1978 and 1990. (Gastil 1978–1989; Freedom House 1990).

8. Assassinations were used to proxy policy uncertainty in Chen and Feng 1996. Assassinations, strikes, riots, and revolutions were used in Feng and Chen 1996. Revolutions were used to measure policy polarization in Feng 2000a.

9. For a nontechnical exposition, see Bueno de Mesquita and Root 2000. For a formal model and statistical testing, see Bueno de Mesquita et al. 2003.

10. From 1960 to 1978, Zimbabwe was ranked 7 on a 0-to-10 scale, with 10 indicating the freest in the Polity data. Since 1987, Zimbabwe has received 0 on the Institutionalized Democracy index. The average democracy score for Zimbabwe during the period of 1960 through 1998 is 4.28, still high compared to many other sub-Saharan African countries. The average score on Institutonalized Democracy for all of sub-Sahara Africa for this period is 1.60 ($N = 1,542$).

## Chapter 4

1. For a detailed discussion of these problems, see Barro 1997, 36–42. Barro also finds that, except for the level of GDP per capita, in which a measurement error looms large, most of the other variables yield essentially similar results to these from the cross-sectional data only.

2. See Haggard and Kaufman 1995, 10. In their study of government stability and outcomes of international conflict, Bueno de Mesquita and Siverson (1995) show that the former is endogenous and pervious to the latter.

3. Growth rate is calculated from real GDP per capita in *The Penn World Table* 5.6 and 5.7 (Summers and Heston). Of the three versions, 5.6 (1995), 5.7 (2000), and 6.0 (2001), 5.6 covers more countries than 5.7 and 6.0. Of a set of 136 countries that have missing values in at least one and at most two of the three versions, 5.6 misses 3 countries, 5.7 misses 19, and 6.0 misses 17. In terms of time series, 5.6 covers 1950–1992, 5.7 covers 1950–1996, and 6.0 covers 1950–1998. As the growth period under study is 1960–1995 and because I would like to include all the countries in the data set possible, I combine data from versions 5.6 and 5.7.

4. It is plausible that growth leads to a decrease in income inequality in terms of the Kuznets Curve. To test the effect of income inequality on growth in the context of reverse causality, I ran a simultaneous-equations system, holding both growth and

income inequality endogenous. The result from the simultaneous system is consistent with equations (6) of table 4.3.

5. For the theoretical argument, see Lucas 1988; Romer 1986, 1990; and Young 1992. For empirical works, see Levine and Renelt 1992, Barro 1991, and Young 1992.

6. For example, Kormendi and Meguire (1985) find that inflation negatively impacts growth, and Schneider and Frey (1985) establish that inflation has a negative effect on foreign direct investment.

7. The formula is $(p_t - p_{t-1})/p_{t-1}$, where $p$ is the GDP deflator.

8. This indicator is based on fifteen categories of economic freedom and political rights. These fifteen categories are freedom of the foreign-currency regime, freedom from military draft, freedom of property, freedom of movement, freedom of information, Gastil's civil rights index, the Gastil-Wright classification of economic-system type, freedom of the print media, freedom of the broadcast media, freedom of internal travel, freedom of external or foreign travel, freedom of peaceful assembly, freedom from work permits, freedom from search without a warrant, and freedom from arbitrary seizure of property (Scully 1992).

9. While the ICRG indicator is based on political-risk criteria, such as government corruption, law and order, quality of bureaucracy, as well as financial-risk criteria, such as repudiation of contracts by governments and expropriation, the BERI indicator attempts to measure cross-country political environments for business activities through the risk of nationalization, government efficiency in business transactions, contract enforceability, and the quality of the communications and transportation infrastructure.

10. This variable is defined to be the ratio of noncurrency money to the total money supply, i.e., $(M2 - C)/M2$, where M2 is the conventional broad measure of the money supply, and C represents the amount of currency held outside banks. According to Clague et al., this variable provides an objective standard of the strength of a country's economic institutions. A higher level of CIM in a nation is associated with a larger amount of money in less liquid form, indicating a "transaction-friendly" environment (Clague et al. 1995).

11. The political-rights index of Freedom House is used for democracy. The institutionalized-democracy index in the Polity data yields comparable results.

12. Culture may be a factor. Also, an export-oriented economy could be a defining characteristic for Pacific Asia. However, when exports are included in regression (12), PACIFIC ASIA is still significant.

## Chapter 5

1. For a quick review on this topic, see Kugler and Feng 1999.

2. This is another reason that the aggregate long-term approach is adopted here.

3. A fast growing subfield in political science is the study of elections and economies in democracies. For a survey, see Lewis-Beck 1988. For examples of empirical works, see MacKuen, Erikson, and Stimson 1992; Price and Sanders 1993; Powell and Whitten 1993; Hallar and Norpoth 1994; Clarke and Stewart 1995; Sanders 1995.

4. The potential short-run negative effect of growth on democracy may be evidenced by a negative correlation between growth and civil liberties in the short-run (annual) data (1978–1990) for four Asian countries considered to have neoauthoritarian governments: Singapore, Malaysia, South Korea, and Taiwan. The Pearson coefficient is $-0.305$ ($N = 52$). By comparison, the Pearson coefficient for the whole sample is $-0.133$ ($N = 1,666$).

5. For other statistical, as well as software-operation, references, see SAS Institute 1993, 815–868.

6. The historical period selected for study may determine statistical results under the same model, as the parametric structure can change over time or between different waves of democratization.

7. The one variable not included here was crude birth rates. As found in chapter 4, a high correlation ($-0.80$) exists between crude birth rates and primary-school enrollment rates.

8. The 1960 primary-school-enrollment rate was used because this variable indicates human-capital formation in the future. The period of fifteen years from 1960 to 1975 allows sufficient time for primary education to bear fruit. It can be argued that the great increases in spending in Latin America came during the mid-1960s, often in autocracies, and therefore, by measuring education level in 1960, instead of in 1975, the regression is biased against autocracies. However, this design may actually favor autocracies, as the effect of increased education on growth in Latin America during the mid-1960s will be absorbed into the political-freedom variable, thus giving credit to autocracies. I did, however, try the enrollment rates in later years (e.g., 1970) and the statistical results did not change.

9. Statistically, they ensure that the 3SLS system is identified.

10. The two cultural variables also help to specify the equation where they are excluded.

11. Not all of these countries are in the final sample, as there may be missing values for them in other variables.

12. The derivation from table 5.2 is $0.056 = (1)(-0.066) + (-2.444)(-0.016) + (1.360)(0.061)$. While the first term on the right-hand side of the equation is the direct effect, the second is the indirect effect through the inhibition of irregular change, and the third is the indirect effect through the promotion of regular change. Note that the effect of democracy on growth through minor regular change is positive but insignificant, though minor regular change has a positive effect on growth. Other channels were excluded to retain trackability.

13. This finding is consistent with Dalton's observation regarding advanced industrialized democracies. In these countries, "Contemporary publics have raised their expectations of government: they are more demanding of politicians and their governments. Furthermore, an increasingly critical media and more open public discussion of government reinforces public doubts about the political process.... The public's expanding issue interests involved governments in new political controversies. In addition to ensuring the economic and physical well-being of their citizens, governments now were expected to protect the quality of the environment, guarantee consumer rights, arbitrate moral issues, assure equality for minorities and women, and deal with many other new political concerns" (Dalton 1996, 261, 275).

14. For a system where all political-instability variables (endogenous as well as predetermined) are excluded, the parameter estimates for growth, initial development and education in the democracy equation would be positive and significant.

Parameter standard

| Variable | Estimate | Error | Prob $> |t|$ |
|---|---|---|---|
| INTERCEPT | 0.127 | 0.163 | 0.438 |
| GROWTH | 3.251 | 1.360 | 0.019 |
| GDP$_{75}$ | 0.064 | 0.012 | $< .0001$ |
| PRIM$_{60}$ | 0.210 | 0.129 | 0.109 |
| ISLAM | $-0.097$ | 0.069 | 0.1640 |
| CONFUCIAN | $-0.286$ | 0.118 | 0.0176 |
| GINI | 0.149 | 0.305 | 0.6446 |

# Chapter 6

1. For insights into the rationales and behavior of political authorities to keep office, see Bueno de Mesquita and Siverson 1997 and Bueno de Mesquita et al. 2003.

2. Under the circumstances, inflation is held as necessary for growth. One example of this more balanced view is as follows. "Is inflation a social evil? To the extent that it is caused by the abuse of seigniorage rights by the government, it goes counter to our notion of justice. Inflation can cause a massive redistribution of wealth from the creditors to the debtors. This too defies our sense of justice. Inflation causes further inconveniences and nuisances to all. In this sense also it is an evil. But if today's high productivity and expanded economic democracy were made possible by the constant growth of monetary debt, and if the loosening effect of inflation has been instrumental in fostering economic minds and activities in general, and if the alternative were a return to the family capitalism of past centuries, a mild or sporadic inflation may well have been a price worth paying" (Nagatani 1989, 151, 152).

3. Also see Korpi 1983 and Stephens 1979.

4. In the third case, the government orders or persuades the central bank to purchase government securities with checks drawn from accounts specifically created by the central bank to allow the checks to clear.

5. As Mumper and Uslaner argue, the crucial inflationary time lag occurs because monetary expansion can give output employment a short-run boost of the Keynesian type. If there were no such lag, there would be an immediate cost to all government spending, whether financed by taxes, borrowing from the public, or monetary expansion (Mumper and Uslaner 1982, 109).

6. For the concept of the median citizen, see Chen and Feng 1999.

7. Industrial and agricultural interests favored inflation, as they had borrowed a great deal of capital to start their operations, and would form alliances with organized labor to press for inflationary policies. Once inflation had lessened the burden of debts incurred by industry and agriculture, these interests then preferred to have prices stabilized so that they might continue production with less economic uncertainty. In this pursuit, they would ally with commercial banks and impose the costs of deflation on

their former allies, organized labor. In democracies where the middle class was substantial, the shifting coalitions and the subsequent policy change from inflation to deflation were accomplished through democratic elections that excluded organized labor (e.g., Portugal from 1976 to 1978). In nondemocracies where the middle class was strong (such as Italy in 1922, Spain in 1923, and Portugal in 1926), this shift was accomplished through authoritarian means. As implied here, inflation is likely to occur as a consequence of a combination of two factors: a weak middle class and late industrialization (e.g., Chile from 1970 to 1973). See Kurth 1982 for further analysis.

8. Since Cagan's (1956) study of post–World War I German inflation, the conventional criterion for hyperinflation has been price increases of around 50% per month.

9. For instance, see Alwyn Young's (1992) contrast of investment patterns between Hong Kong and Singapore. While growth in Hong Kong tends to be generated by human capital, growth in Singapore is more of the result of savings required by the government.

10. I used inflation to create the political-instability variables in chapter 3. To test the validity problem caused by the use of inflation to estimate instability, I created a new set of instability variables without using inflation. Then I correlated the new political-instability variables and inflation. The new correlations between inflation (GDP), on the one hand, and irregular change, major and minor regular change, on the other, are 0.085, 0.117, and 0.036, respectively; between inflation (CPI) and the types of change, the correlations are 0.087, 0.096, and 0.038. Since the original instability variables were used throughout the book, they are used in this chapter for the sake of consistency. The use of new instability variables constructed without inflation does not qualitatively change any statistical results in this chapter.

11. The relationship between regime type and government capacity can be examined through the use of $\chi^2$ statistics. The regime type is based upon the categorical data compiled by Gasiorowski (1996) on regime type. The null hypothesis of independence between the variables cannot be rejected even at the 20% level, which provides some evidence that the democratic nature of a government and its political capacity are quite orthogonal.

12. Both Edwards and Tabellini (1991a) and Alcazar (1997) used the GDP measures. While Edwards and Tabellini used the urbanization variable, Alcazar used the fiscal-deficit data.

13. Protoparadakis and Siegal (1987) conclude that there is little evidence that government-debt growth leads to money growth or inflation. The limitations of their study are that in a longer period of time than their time series, a relationship between government debt and inflation may appear, and that only 10 developed countries, and no less-developed countries, were studied.

## Chapter 7

1. In the literature, the average share of investment in GDP has been found to be one of the most robust and important determinants for average economic-growth rates (Levine and Renelt 1992).

2. Also see chapter 9 of this book, which deals with democracy and income distribution.

3. The impact of different forms of uncertainty on private investment has been discussed by Servén and Solimano (1993), Rodrik (1991), Aizenman and Marion (1993), Price (1995), and Brunetti and Weder (1998).

4. For instance, while Polachek (1992), Pollins (1989), and Sayrs (1989) examine the effect of bilateral conflict on dyadic trade, Gasiorowski (1986) and Mansfield (1992) study trade and interstate conflict at an aggregated level, and Gowa and Mansfield (1993) and Feng (1994, 2000c) investigate the impact of alliance structures on trade. In addition, Nigh (1984) and Oneal (1994) study bilateral security conflicts and regime types as determinants of foreign direct investment.

5. The 42 developing countries are Argentina, Bangladesh, Bolivia, Brazil, Chile, Colombia, Costa Rica, Dominican Republic, Ecuador, El Salvador, Ethiopia, Fiji, Guatemala, Guyana, Haiti, India, Indonesia, Ivory Coast, Kenya, South Korea, Malawi, Malaysia, Mauritius, Mexico, Nepal, Nigeria, Pakistan, Papua New Guinea, Paraguay, Peru, the Philippines, Portugal, Singapore, Sri Lanka, Tanzania, Thailand, Tunisia, Turkey, Uruguay, Venezuela, Zambia, and Zimbabwe. Of them, Fiji and Guyana do not have data for the other variables in the regressions, thus reducing the number of cross-country observations in regressions to 40.

6. The two indices are summed according to the following formula: $(14 - (\text{POLITICAL RIGHTS} + \text{CIVIL LIBERTIES}))/12$.

7. Pastor and Hilt (1993) take the former view, while Taylor (1988) and Greene and Villanueva (1990) argue for the latter.

8. The events are weighted following the work of Goldstein (1992).

9. Quinn and Inclan (1997) and Garrett (1995, 1998) imply that financial liberalization, another indicator of globalization, may lead to a decrease in domestic investment as the result of international diversification of an investment portfolio. Feng (2001a) found evidence that financial liberalization may both promote and inhibit domestic capital formation.

10. The inclusion of the communist countries would probably counter this result as, typically, freedom was low and education relatively high in these countries; at the same time, private investment remained zero.

11. See Khan and Reinhart 1990; Firebaugh 1992; Borensztein, Gregorio, and Lee 1994. Foreign direct investment has been identified as a major stimulant for economic growth. For instance, in comparing the effects of domestic and foreign direct investments, Firebaugh (1992) finds that though homegrown capital outperforms imported capital in generating economic growth, both have a positive impact on the economic growth of the recipient country. By contrast, Borensztein, Gregorio, and Lee (1994) suggest that foreign direct investment is an important vehicle for the development and proliferation of technology, contributing relatively more than domestic investment to growth. Amirahmadi and Wu (1994) link a shortage of foreign investment to decline of the economy.

12. See, e.g., Schneider and Frey 1985; Adij, Ahn, Holsey, and Willett 1997; and Wei 1997a, 1997b. Besides, the results in Amirahmadi and Wu 1994 indicate that the level of economic development, credit rating, technological infrastructure, institutional environment, and political stability are among the factors conducive to foreign indirect investment.

13. The amount of foreign direct investment is in U.S. dollars. As in previous studies, lagged values for independent variables are used to alleviate the endogeneity problem.

14. See the discussion in Singh and Gupta 1997.

15. See the discussion in Adij, Ahn, Holsey, and Willett 1997.

16. The developed countries accounted for 97% of all foreign direct investment out-flows in the 1980s, while accounting for 83% of the inflows in the 1985–1990 period (Wei 1995).

17. It has also been found that foreign direct investment by the United States has performed better in developed democracies, though the rates of return may have been higher in autocracies. See Oneal 1994.

18. For the debate, see the discussion in Servén and Solimano 1993.

19. For a mathematical model, see Chen and Feng 1999.

20. For theoretical arguments, see Lake 1992, Dixon 1994. For empirical evidence, see Ray 1995 and Russett 1995.

## Chapter 8

1. Romer makes a distinction between human capital and ideas. For him, the former is an extension of the economics of objects and cannot capture the essence of the economics of ideas, which involves "the production and exploitation of the kind of knowledge that lets Frito-Lay keep the right quantity of food on the shelves of thousands of geographically dispersed stores" (Romer 1993, 551).

2. Formally, this is tantamount to an $AK$ model in which $Y = AK$, where $Y$ is output, and $K$ is human and nonhuman capital. $A$ is the parameter. This theoretical structure implies that output is proportional to the stock of human and physical capital goods, and can be accumulated without bound.

3. For a summary, see Sarup 1982, 46.

4. For other measurements on educational attainment, see Psacharopoulos and Aria-gada 1986a, 1986b; Kaneko 1986; Lau, Jamison, and Louat 1991; and Kyriacou 1991.

5. Barro and Lee (1993) use 30 countries for a sensitivity test of the accuracy of their estimation. It is not clear which 30 countries are included nor how their survey results are related to the countries that tend to overestimate their enrollment rates, as reported by Chapman and Boothroyd (1988), or to the countries where absenteeism is serious, as found by Fredriksen (1991).

6. Bob Anderson, a consultant with the California Department of Education, as quoted by Ana Menendez (1996).

7. A polity is defined as a democracy if the sum of the political-rights and civil-liberties scores is 5 or less, a hybrid if the sum is larger than 5 but less than or equal to 11, and an autocracy if the sum is higher than 11.

8. In the case of average number of school years and national percentage of educated people with college degrees, reverse causality may be an issue, as it is plausible that

earlier education may affect the type of political system. Differentiating the data or using growth rates in education may alleviate the problem. But unlike economic growth, growth rates for education tend to be bounded.

9. Given how educational attainment is measured, a most serious implication for statistical testing is reverse causation. Both the average number of years of schooling and the percentage of the total population with a college education represent human capital formation over a long period of time. Learning is a lifelong pursuit of knowledge. The averaged data on years of schooling in 1985 include, for instance, septuagenarians who started their schooling more than six decades ago, as well as fresh college graduates. While a political-institution variable dating back to the beginning of the century is able to control for the political environment of learning for septuagenarians, it is almost irrelevant for the educational experience of the newly graduated.

10. In terms of educational quantity, the negative consequences of political instability are felt more at the primary level than at higher levels. Regression results are available upon request.

## Chapter 9

1. Also see Lipset 1959 and Lenski 1966.

2. Alesina and Rodrik (1994) assume that the consequences fall on public investment, while Perotti (1993) and Persson and Tabellini (1994) assume they occur through redistribution.

3. For similar results, also see Gupta 1990, Venieris and Gupta 1986, and Zak 1997.

4. The effect of income equality on growth through education is reduced if controlled by fertility, which reflects income distribution, in the same model (Perotti 1996, 180).

5. The former seven articles are Cutright 1967; Hewitt 1977; Stack 1979, 1980; Weede and Tiefenbach 1981; Weede 1982; Muller 1988. The latter five are Jackman 1975, Rubinson and Quinlan 1977, Bollen and Grandjean 1981, Kohli et al. 1984, and Bollen and Jackman 1985.

6. Also see Lenski 1966.

7. The empirical analysis in Bollen and Jackman 1985 confirms the difference between the household survey data and the individual survey data; the household survey data do represent a lesser degree of income inequality.

8. This problem can be assumed away, as wealth distribution is highly correlated with and monotonically increasing with income distribution.

9. Muller (1988) garnered 55 cases of income-inequality data, but used only 50 cases of income data in his regressions for a lack of political and economic variables.

10. One of the 82 countries in the sample, Sudan, does not have the observations for real GDP per capita in the Summers and Heston data. Its income-distribution survey occurred in 1968. Its initial real GDP per capita was then estimated from Barro and Wolf's (1989) cross-country data. The closest lagged data point to 1968 in Barro and Wolf's data is the 1965 real GDP per capita. The estimation equation, based on an OLS regression between the real GDP per capita in Summers and Heston's data and in Barro and Wolf's data, is given as $GDP_{sh} = 81.863 + 1257.337\ GDP_{65}$ ($\bar{R}^2 = 0.972$,

$N = 111$). The selection criterion is that countries selected are not communist or former communist countries (which excludes China, Hungary, Poland, and Yugoslavia, as well as others in this category), have data on political freedom (which excludes Hong Kong and Puerto Rico), and have valid information on whether the income is gross or net (which excludes Fiji and Niger). This results in 82 observations.

11. The liberal-democracy index by Bollen (1980, 1990, 1993) is only available for 1960, 1965, and 1980.

12. According to Muller (1988), the United States was inaugurated as a democracy in 1870, whereas Germany's democratic phase began in 1949.

13. Larry Sirowy and Alex Inkeles write, "Clearly the efforts of Bollen and Jackman and Muller are superior to the others in terms of such considerations as their sample composition, assessment of simultaneity, and controls for the source of income data" (1990, 151).

14. The missing values in Bollen's data are estimated from the political-rights variable in Gastil's data. The estimation equation is Liberal Democracy Index (LDI) = $112 - 15.203 \times$ Political Rights ($\bar{R}^2 = 0.823$, $N = 92$).

15. Bollen and Jackman (1989) hold that democracy should be measured ordinally, rather than dichotomously, so as to avoid blurring the distinction between borderline cases.

16. Two countries have not been surveyed by Gastil or Freedom House the year they were surveyed by the World Bank for income-distribution data: Morocco and Sierra Leone. The political-rights data were collected starting in 1972, but the latest possible income-distribution data for Morocco and Sierra Leone were both in 1968, for when political-rights data are lacking. Political rights data were estimated for these two countries with the indicator for institutionalized democracy in the Polity III data by Gurr and associates (1990), which covers these two countries for before 1968. The estimation equation is Political Rights = $6.1045 - 0.4685 \times$ DEMOC ($\bar{R}^2 = 0.775$, $N = 2,604$).

17. Hong Kong may be an economic democracy, considering that Gwartney, Lawson, and Block (1996) record it as having the highest economic freedom in the world for 1993–1995. However, there is some difference between political freedom and economic freedom, which should be separated. See chapter 10 for a special treatment of these two kinds of freedom.

18. For theoretical arguments, see Kuznets 1955, 1963; Lenski 1966. For empirical evidence, see Paukert 1973, Ahluwalia 1976, and Weede 1980. The omission of this non-linear relationship affects research in the 1970s before Weede (1980) called attention to it (Muller 1988, 52).

19. For the bivariate model, the $\bar{R}^2 = 0.106$ and $\sigma = 8.602$; for the trivariate model, the $\bar{R}^2 = 0.107$ and $\sigma = 8.598$.

20. As Perotti (1996) notes, inequality is lower among retirees, but so is their average income. He finds that the effect of population share on income inequality is negative for these aged 65 or over.

21. Taiwan does not have population statistics in the World Bank's data. The population aged fourteen or under as a ratio to the total population in Taiwan is obtained from the Department of Budget, Accounting, and Statistics, Taiwan Provincial Government, Republic of China (1994).

22. According to Immanuel Wallerstein, the semiperipheral areas are in between the core and the periphery on a series of dimensions, such as the complexity of economic activities, the strength of the state machinery, cultural integrity, etc. They can be an early version of a core state or the result of degeneration of a core state (Wallerstein 1974, 349).

23. Mark J. Gasiorowski has kindly made available his data on the periphery and semiperiphery. Seven countries were not included in his data set: Bahamas, Barbados, Botswana, Guinea Bissau, Guyana, Mauritius, and Seychelles. In accordance with the classification method in Snyder and Kick 1979 and in comparison with the classification in Gasiorowski's data, these countries are classified as periphery areas.

24. Six of the 82 countries covered in the Gini data (Cameroon, Central African Republic, Egypt, Seychelles, Tanzania, and Iran) do not have observations for the three income-share indicators. Additionally, Guyana's observation for income share occurred in 1955, prior to its independence.

25. The results are collectively stronger than those obtained by Muller (1988), where the significance level was set to 5% at one tail, which requires $t$-statistics to be larger than 1.675 ($N = 50$) to be significant. The 2.5% error level in a one-tailed test, as in this chapter, would require $t$-statistics to be larger than 1.992 ($N = 75$) to be significant.

26. The parameter estimates and their standard errors for lags 0 through 5 are $-5.919$ (2.908), $-5.891$ (2.821), $-6.018$ (2.809), $-6.029$ (2.806), $-6.310$ (2.800), and $-6.340$ (2.795), respectively.

27. Dummy variables to differentiate household income from individual income and to differentiate the income method from the expenditure method have also been included in this analysis; in neither case is the dummy variable statistically significant.

## Chapter 10

1. For instance, Bollen (1993) defines political freedom in terms of liberal democracy as a function of political liberties and democratic rule.

2. I owe a reviewer for this observation.

3. The same notion was summarized by Weitzman (1993).

4. Additionally, Helliwell suggests that there "appear to be no clearly defined thresholds or prerequisites—just a strong tendency—for democracy to become the chosen and maintained form of government as countries get richer and as education levels increase" (1994, 246).

5. These categories do not directly represent economic freedom as defined by Gwartney, Lawson, and Block (1996). Rather, they are inferences of economic freedom characterized by the protection of property rights and the freedom of exchange of private goods. See appendix 10.A for details.

6. Gwartney et al. (2002) have updated the five-year-interval economic-freedom index to 2000. However, since Gwartney et al. (1995), they have given up the three indices to settle on only one index. To test the robustness of the findings in this chapter, I utilize the three indices in Gwartney et al. (1995), which means that the data series has to end in 1995.

7. Bollen (1993) discusses this problem in detail.

8. One concern I have about the data is that various democracy indices lack within-country variation, as discussed in chapter 12. However, this problem should be alleviated by two factors. First, cross-sectionally, there is a great deal of variance in those indices. Second, by design and necessity, the data economic freedom and political freedom occur at five-year intervals. The means and standard deviations of the variables are reported here ($N = 461$):

| Variable | Mean | SD | Min | Max |
|----------|------|------|------|------|
| PRCL | 0.565 | 0.328 | 0 | 1 |
| DEMOC | 0.492 | 0.435 | 0 | 1 |
| Index1 | 0.455 | 0.145 | 0.09 | 0.85 |
| Index2 | 0.451 | 0.135 | 0.08 | 0.85 |
| Index3 | 0.440 | 0.180 | 0.06 | 0.91 |

9. The null hypothesis of no autocorrelation cannot be rejected at the 20% error level. Even though the data are cross-sectional, the Durbin statistic will be seen to provide some useful evidence for model specification (Berndt 1996, 92–93).

10. An early examination shows that there is no autocorrelation within the statistical model. As long as the regressor is asymptotically uncorrelated with the disturbance, ordinary least-squares estimation is consistent even if the regressor is stochastic (Greene 1993, 419–420).

11. For a review of the sequence of liberalization of the current account, the capital account, and domestic financial markets, see Wihlborg and Willett 1997 and Feng 2000b.

12. As the political rights data started in 1972–1973 in the Freedom House data, I estimated the political-rights level for Indonesia in 1970 to be 5, on the basis of the Freedom House data. In figure 10.2, political freedom = $(7 - $ political rights$)/6$, and economic freedom = the original value of economic freedom divided by 10.

13. I originally argued that democracy has indirect effects on growth (Feng 1997a). There I found that democracy is likely to have a positive effect on growth by substantially reducing the probability of irregular government transfers and increasing the probability of major regular government change.

14. Barkley and McMillan (1994) have found that the presence of political freedom increases the responsiveness of labor migration to economic incentives in 32 African nations. The effect of price signals on migration was conditional on the degree of political rights and civil liberties.

## Chapter 11

1. Thompson (1929) and Notestein (1945) were among the first to propose that with economic development, societies will experience a reduction in birth rates, which has been verified empirically by Sinding, Ross, and Rosenfeld (1994); Freedman (1994); Camp (1993); and Bongaarts, Mauldin, and Phillips (1990); among others.

2. For a detailed discussion of Przeworski et al. (2000), see Yi Feng 2001b.

3. See     http://216.239.37.100/search?q=cache:r9-SaI4Oi9cC:www.census.gov/ipc/ prod/wp96/wp96033.pdf+taiwan+fertility+rates&hl=en.

4. See     http://216.239.37.100/search?q=cache:r9-SaI4Oi9cC:www.census.gov/ipc/ prod/wp96/wp96033.pdf+taiwan+fertility+rates&hl=en.

5. Deininger and Squire's (1996) data on income distribution do not have data on China prior to 1982. Therefore, the pre-1982 Gini coefficient data were estimated through cross-country time-series data using real GDP per capita, real GDP per capita squared, and regional dummy variables.

6. Political instability was multiplied by two to increase readability. The data on China's probability of irregular government change are missing for the years 1968–1972, one of the most politically turbulent periods in China's recent history. Though the missing data were estimated through the autoregressive method, it would be difficult to restore the true probabilities of political instability for that period. Since political instability was high during the beginning of the Cultural Revolution, the estimated data may well underestimate the true probability for the period, which also evidenced a rise in birth and fertility rates.

7. As Shirk (1993) observed, limited political openness in China started with the provincial governments' cultivating and expanding their power base greatly as the result of economic reforms. Similarly, Montinola, Qian, and Weingast (1995) conclude that the Chinese provinces take a form of economic federalism in which they compete and learn from each other. The recent development of rural elections paves the way for future political reforms that will eventually adopt political elections at the national level.

8. As Johnson (2000) discusses, three major factors have adversely affected China's rural incomes: restrictions on rural-to-urban migration, lack of rural education, and urban bias in the allocation of investment and credit.

# Chapter 12

1. Larry Diamond has made me think about whether not Singapore needed liberal democracy for its capitalist economy.

2. Such a model invariably leads to the government's selection of "leading" industries, which are often export-oriented, for favorable treatment, along with its provision of public information and its encouragement of such social movements as education and saving (Wade 1990, 1993).

3. Huntington (1991) might label countries in this category as "a democracy without turnover," and Diamond (1997) "a pseudodemocracy." These countries, like Mexico under the Institutional Revolutionary Party (PRI) and Singapore under the People's Action Party (PAP), typically get a combined score for political rights and civil liberties higher than or equal to 5 but lower than 11 in the Gastil and Freedom House annual surveys of democracy.

4. For some excellent reviews and essays on political legitimacy in Pacific Asia, see Alagappa 1995.

5. For example, on trade, finance, and investment, see Wheeler 1984, Devarajan and De Melo 1987, and Levy 1988, respectively.

6. See Bartlett 1989. It has long been argued that capitalism failed to develop in sub-Saharan Africa for two main reasons: the communal African society, which makes the security of property rights difficult, and colonialism. Empirically, it has been found that there was significant, indigenous precolonial market activity, and the aftermath of colonial rule can be related to statism.

7. This study covers 40 sub-Saharan African countries for which we have complete data for the period of 1960–1992. They are Angola, Benin, Botswana, Burkina Faso, Burundi, Cameroon, the Central African Republic, Chad, Congo, Ethiopia, Gabon, Gambia, Ghana, Guinea, Ivory Coast, Kenya, Lesotho, Liberia, Madagascar, Malawi, Mali, Mauritania, Mauritius, Mozambique, Niger, Nigeria, Rwanda, Senegal, Sierra Leone, Somalia, South Africa, Sudan, Swaziland, Tanzania, Togo, Tunisia, Uganda, Zaire, Zambia, and Zimbabwe.

## Appendix 4.A

1. Some scholars of Latin American politics have particularly favored this school of thought. For a review of variations on the argument that democracy has failed to achieve economic growth in Latin America, see Cohen 1994, 23–32.

2. Przeworski et al. find that democracy has a positive effect on the growth rate of income per capita, though not on the growth rate of total income.

3. For instance, in studies of Latin American countries, the following works have produced different evidence. Remmer (1990) finds that, though a democracy performs better than an autocracy in terms of economic growth, the difference between them is not statistically significant. Feng (1995) finds that a democracy grows significantly faster than an autocracy. Sloan and Tedin (1987) find that bureaucratic-authoritarian regimes do better than democracy, and traditional dictatorships do worse.

4. Easton makes a distinction between "political authorities" and "regimes." *Political authorities* or *government* refers to a set of decision makers who determine, and are seen to determine, policy during any given time period; *regime* is defined as the legal and informal rules that govern the resolution of conflict within a system (Easton 1965, 177).

# References

Adams, F. Gerard. 2002. "The East Asian Crisis and Recovery: A Reappraisal." In *Managing Economic Development in Asia*, ed. Thomas K. Liou, pp. 261–288. Westport, Conn.: Praeger.

Adelman, Irma, and Cynthia Morris. 1967. *Society, Politics, and Economic Development.* Baltimore: Johns Hopkins University Press.

Adij, Slamet Seno, Y. S. Ahn, Cheryl M. Holsey, and Thomas D. Willett. 1997. "Political Capacity, Macroeconomic Factors, and Factor Flows." In *Political Capacity and Economic Behavior*, ed. Marina Arbetman and Jacek Kugler, pp. 127–148. Boulder, Colo.: Westview Press.

Aghion, Philippe, and Patrick Bolton. 1990. "Government Domestic Debt and the Risk of Default: A Political Economic Model of the Strategic Role of Debt." In *Public Debt Management: Theory and History*, ed. Rudiger Dornbusch and Mario Draghi, pp. 315–345. New York: Cambridge University Press.

Ahluwalia, Montek S. 1976. "Inequality, Poverty, and Development." *Journal of Development Economics* 3: 307–342.

Aizenman, Joshua. 1992. "Competitive Externalities and the Optimal Seigniorage." *Journal of Money, Credit, and Banking* 24: 61–71.

Aizenman, Joshua, and Nancy P. Marion. 1993. "Macroeconomic Uncertainty and Private Investment." *Economics Letters* 41: 201–210.

Alagappa, Muthiah. 1995a. "The Anatomy of Legitimacy." In *Political Legitimacy in Southeast Asia: The Quest for Moral Authority*, ed. Muthiah Alagappa, pp. 11–30. Stanford: Stanford University Press.

Alagappa, Muthiah. 1995b. "The Base of Legitimacy." In *Political Legitimacy in Southeast Asia: The Quest for Moral Authority*, ed. Muthiah Alagappa, pp. 31–53. Stanford: Stanford University Press.

Alagappa, Muthiah. 1995c. "Contestation and Crisis." In *Political Legitimacy in Southeast Asia: The Quest for Moral Authority*, ed. Muthiah Alagappa, pp. 54–68. Stanford: Stanford University Press.

Alcazar, Lorena. 1997. "Political Constraints and the Use of Seigniorage." In *Political Capacity and Economic Behavior*, ed. Marina Arbetman and Jacek Kugler, pp. 79–96. Boulder, Colo.: Westview Press.

Alesina, Alberto, and A. Drazen. 1989. "Why are Stabilizations Delayed? A Political Economic Model." Working paper no. 3053. National Bureau of Economic Research.

Alesina, Alberto, and Dani Rodrik. 1991. "Distributive Politics and Economic Growth." Working paper no. 3668. National Bureau of Economic Research.

Alesina, Alberto, Şule Özler, Nouriel Roubini, and Philip Swagel. 1996. "Political Instability and Economic Growth." *Journal of Economic Growth* 1: 189–212.

Alesina, Alberto, and Roberto Perotti. 1996. "Income Distribution, Political Instability, and Investment." *European Economic Review* 40: 1203–1228.

Alesina, Alberto, and Dani Rodrik. 1994. "Distributive Politics and Economic Growth." *Quarterly Journal of Economics* 109: 465–490.

Alesina, Alberto, and Guido Tabellini. 1990. "A Positive Theory of Fiscal Deficit and Government Debt." *Review of Economic Studies* 57: 403–414.

Allison, Paul D. 1978. "Measures of Inequality." *American Sociological Review* 43: 865–880.

Al-Marhubi, Fahim. 1997. "Political Capacity and Economic Determinants of Inflation." In *Political Capacity and Economic Behavior*, ed. Marina Arbetman and Jacek Kugler, pp. 67–78. Boulder, Colo.: Westview Press.

Almond, Gabriel A., and Sidney Verba. 1963. *The Civic Culture: Political Attitudes and Democracy in Five Nations.* Princeton: Princeton University Press.

Alston, Lee J., Thráinn Eggertsson, and Douglass C. North, eds. 1996. *Empirical Studies in Institutional Change.* New York: Cambridge University Press.

Amirahmadi, Hoosahang, and Weiping Wu. 1994. "Foreign Direct Investment in Developing Countries." *Journal of Developing Areas* 28: 167–190.

Arbetman, Marina, and Jacek Kugler, eds. 1997. *Political Capacity and Economic Behavior.* Boulder, Colo.: Westview Press.

Arbetman, Marina, and Jacek Kugler. 1995. "The Politics of Inflation: An Empirical Assessment of the Emerging Market Economies." In *Establishing Monetary Stability in Emerging Market Economies*, ed. Thomas D. Willett, Richard C. K. Burdekin, Richard J. Sweeney, and Clas Whilborg, pp. 81–100. Boulder, Colo.: Westview Press.

Arbetman, Marina, Jacek Kugler, and A. F. K. Organski. 1997. "Political Capacity and Demographic Change." In *Political Capacity and Economic Behavior*, ed. Marina Arbetman and Jacek Kugler, pp. 193–220. Boulder, Colo.: Westview Press.

Arrow, Kenneth J. 1962. "The Economic Implications of Learning by Doing." *Review of Economic Studies* 29: 155–173.

Arthur, Brian. 1989. "Competing Technologies, Increasing Returns, and Lock-In by Historical Events." *Economic Journal* 99: 116–131.

Baer, Werner. 1991. "Social Aspects of Latin American Inflation." *Quarterly Review of Economics and Business* 31: 45–57.

Balassa, Bela. 1991. *Economic Policies in the Pacific Area Developing Countries.* New York: New York University Press.

Banaian, King, Leroy O. Laney, John McArthur, and Thomas D. Willett. 1988. "Subordinating the Fed to Political Authorities Will Not Control Inflationary Tendencies." In *Political Business Cycles: The Political Economy of Money, Inflation, and Unemployment*, ed. Thomas D. Willett, pp. 490–508. Durham: Duke University Press.

Banks, Arthur S. 1970. *Political Handbook of the World*. New York: McGraw-Hill.

Banks, Arthur S. 1971. *Cross-National Time-Series Data Archive User's Manual*. Binghamton, N.Y.: SUNY Binghamton.

Banks, Arthur S. 1979. *Manual for Cross-National Time-Series Data*. Binghamton, N.Y.: SUNY Binghamton.

Banks, Arthur S. 1999. *Cross-National Time-Series Data*. Binghamton, N.Y.: SUNY Binghamton.

Barkley, Andrew P., and John McMillan. 1994. "Political Freedom and the Response to Economic Incentives: Labor Migration in Africa, 1972–1987." *Journal of Development Economics* 45: 393–406.

Barro, Robert J. 1991. "Economic Growth in a Cross-Section of Countries." *Quarterly Journal of Economics* 106: 408–443.

Barro, Robert J. 1996. "Democracy and Growth." *Journal of Economic Growth* 1: 1–28.

Barro, Robert J. 1997. *Determinants of Economic Growth: A Cross-Country Empirical Study*. Cambridge: MIT Press.

Barro, Robert J., and Jong-Wha Lee. 1993. "International Comparisons of Educational Attainment." *Journal of Monetary Economics* 32: 363–394.

Barro, Robert J., and Jong-Wha Lee. 2000. "International Comparisons of Educational Attainment: Updates and Implications." Manuscript. Harvard University.

Barro, Robert J., and Holger C. Wolf. 1989. *Data Appendix for Economic Growth in a Cross Section of Countries*. Cambridge, Mass.: National Bureau of Economic Research.

Bartlett, Bruce. 1989. "The State and the Market in Sub-Saharan Africa." *World Economy* 12: 293–314.

Bates, Robert H. 1989. *Beyond the Miracle of the Market: The Political Economy of Agrarian Development in Kenya*. Cambridge: Cambridge University Press.

Bates, Robert H. 1996. "Letter from the President: The Death of Comparative Politics?" *APSA-CP Newsletter* 7: 2.

Bates, Robert H. 2001. *Prosperity and Violence: The Political Economy of Development*. New York: W. W. Norton & Company.

Becker, Gary S., Kevin M. Murphy, and Robert Tamura. 1990. "Human Capital, Fertility, and Economic Growth." *Journal of Political Economy* 98: S12–S37.

Becker, Gary S., and N. Tomes. 1979. "An Equilibrium Theory of the Distribution of Income and Inter-generational Mobility." *Journal of Political Economy* 87: 1153–1189.

Beitz, Charles R. 1982. "Democracies in Developing Societies." In *Freedom in the World: Political Rights and Civil Liberties*, ed. Raymond Gastil, pp. 145–166. New York: Freedom House.

Benhabib, Jess, and Mark M. Spiegel. 1994. "The Role of Human Capital in Economic Development: Evidence from Aggregate Cross-Country Data." *Journal of Monetary Economics* 34: 143–173.

Berndt, Ernst R. 1991. *The Practice of Econometrics: Classic and Contemporary*. New York: Addison Wesley.

Berry, Brian. 1970. *Economists, Sociologists, and Democracy*. London: Collier-Macmillan.

Berryman, Phillip. 1984. *The Religious Roots of Rebellion*. Maryknoll, N.Y.: Orbis Books.

Bienen, Henry. 1993. "Leaders, Violence, and the Absence of Change in Africa." *Political Science Quarterly* 108: 271–282.

Bilson, John F. O. 1982. "Civil Liberty: An Econometric Investigation." *Kyklos* 35: 94–114.

Bollen, Kenneth A. 1980. "Issues in the Comparative Measurement of Political Democracy." *American Sociological Review* 45: 567–591.

Bollen, Kenneth A. 1990. "Political Democracy: Conceptual and Measurement Traps." *Studies in Comparative International Development* 25: 7–24.

Bollen, Kenneth A. 1993. "Liberal Democracy: Validity and Method Factors in Cross-National Measures." *American Journal of Political Science* 37: 1207–1230.

Bollen, Kenneth A., and Burke D. Grandjean. 1981. "The Dimension(s) of Democracy: Further Issues in the Measurement and Effects of Political Democracy." *American Sociological Review* 46: 651–659.

Bollen, Kenneth A., and Robert W. Jackman. 1985. "Political Democracy and the Size Distribution of Income." *American Sociological Review* 50: 438–457.

Bollen, Kenneth A., and Robert W. Jackman. 1989. "Democracy, Stability, and Dichotomies." *American Sociological Review* 54: 612–621.

Bongaarts, J. 1992. "The Supply-Demand Framework for the Determinants of Fertility." Working paper no. 44. Research Division of the Population Council, New York.

Bongaarts, J., W. P. Mauldin, and J. F. Phillips. 1990. "The Demographic Impact of Family Planning Programs." *Studies in Family Planning* 21: 299–310.

Borensztein, Eduardo, José De Gregorio, and Jong-Wha Lee. 1994. "How Does Foreign Direct Investment Affect Economic Growth?" Working paper. International Monetary Fund.

Bowen, Howard R. 1977. *Investment in Learning: The Individual and Social Value of American Higher Education*. San Francisco: Jossey-Bass.

Bowles, Samuel, and Herbert Gintis. 1976. *Schooling in Capitalist America*. London: Routledge and Kegan Paul.

Brunetti, Aymo, and Beatrice Weder. 1998. "Investment and Institutional Uncertainty: A Comparative Study of Different Uncertainty Measures." *Weltwirtschaftliches Archiv* 134: 513–533.

Brunk, Gregory G., Gregory A. Caldeira, and Michael S. Lewis-Beck. 1987. "Capitalism, Socialism, and Democracy: An Empirical Inquiry." *European Journal of Political Research* 15: 459–470.

Buchanan, James M., and Richard E. Wagner. 1977. *Democracy in Deficit: The Political Legacy of Lord Keynes*. New York: Academic Press.

Bueno de Mesquita, Bruce, and David Lalman. 1992. *War and Reason*. New Haven: Yale University Press.

Bueno de Mesquita, Bruce, and Hilton L. Root. 2000. "When Bad Economics Is Good Politics." In *Governing for Prosperity*, ed. Bruce Bueno de Mesquita and Hilton L. Root, pp. 1–16. New Haven: Yale University Press.

Bueno de Mesquita, Bruce, and Randolph M. Siverson. 1995. "War and the Survival of Political Leaders: A Comparative Study of Regime Types and Political Accountability." *American Political Science Review* 89: 841–855.

Bueno de Mesquita, Bruce, and Randolph M. Siverson. 1997. "Nasty or Nice: Political Systems, Endogenous Norms, and the Treatment of Adversaries." *Journal of Conflict Resolution* 41: 175–199.

Bueno de Mesquita, Bruce, Alstair Smith, Randolph M. Siverson, and James D. Morrow. 2003. "Logic of Political Survival." Manuscript.

Burkhart, Ross E. 1998. "Measuring Political Freedom." Working paper. Department of Political Science, University of Iowa.

Burkhart, Ross E., and Michael S. Lewis-Beck. 1994. "Comparative Democracy: The Economic Development Thesis." *American Political Science Review* 88: 903–910.

Cagan, Phillip. 1956. "The Monetary Dynamics of Hyperinflation." In *Studies in the Quantity Theory of Money*, ed. Milton Friedman, pp. 25–117. Chicago: University of Chicago Press.

Calvert, Randall L. 1994. "Explaining Social Order: Internalization, External Enforcement, or Equilibrium?" Manuscript. Department of Political Science, University of Rochester.

Camp, S. L. 1993. "Population: The Critical Debate." *Foreign Policy* 90: 126–144.

Campos, Jose Edgardo, and Hilton L. Root. 1996. *The Key to the Asian Miracle: Making Shared Growth Credible*. Washington, D.C.: Brookings Institution.

Carceles, C. 1990. "World Literacy Prospects at the Turn of the Century: Is the Objective of Literacy for All by Year 2000 Statistically Plausible?" *Comparative Education Review* 34: 4–20.

Carmen, Raff. 1996. *Autonomous Development: Humanizing the Landscape: An Excursion into Radical Thinking and Practice*. London: Zed Books.

Case, William. 1995. "Malaysia: Aspects and Audiences of Legitimacy." In *Political Legitimacy in Southeast Asia*, ed. Muthiah Alagappa, pp. 69–107. Stanford: Stanford University Press.

Casper, Gretchen, and Michelle M. Taylor. 1996. *Negotiating Democracy: Transitions from Authoritarian Rule*. Pittsburgh: University of Pittsburgh Press.

Chapman, D. W., and R. A. Boothroyd. 1988. "Threats to Data Quality in Developing Country Settings." *Comparative Education Review* 32: 416–429.

Chen, Baizhu, and Yi Feng. 1996. "Some Political Determinants of Economic Growth." *European Journal of Political Economy* 12: 609–627.

Chen, Baizhu, and Yi Feng. 1996b. "Economic Development, Political Cost, and Democratic Transition: Theory, Statistical Testing, and a Case Study." *Journal of Economic Development* 21: 185–220.

Chen, Baizhu, and Yi Feng. 1997. "Determinants of Survival-Related Capabilities." In *Rethinking Development in Asia and Latin America*, ed. James McGuire, pp. 52–57. Los Angeles: Pacific Council.

Chen, Baizhu, and Yi Feng. 1999. "Political Regime Change and Economic Development: A Formal Model." *Social Choice and Welfare* 16: 1–16.

Chen, Yizi, Wang Xiaoqiang, et al. 1988. "Reform: Results and Lessons from the 1985 CESRRI Survey." In *Chinese Economic Reform: How Far, How Fast?* ed. Bruce L. Reynolds, pp. 172–188. New York: Academic Press.

China Population Information Center. 1999. *Population and Family Planning Key Data Manual*. Beijing: State Commission of Family Planning.

China State Statistics Bureau. 1993. *China Statistical Yearbook*. Beijing: China Statistics Press.

Chirot, Daniel. 1977. *Social Change in the Twentieth Century*. New York: Harcourt Brace Jovanovich.

Chu, Yun-han. 1996. "Taiwan's Unique Challenge." *Journal of Democracy* 7: 69–82.

Clague, Christopher, Philip Keefer, Stephen Knack, and Mancur Olson. 1995. "Contract-Intensive Money: Contract Enforcement, Property Rights, and Economic Performance." Working paper. Center for Institutional Reform and the Informal Sector.

Clarke, Harold D., and Marianne C. Stewart. 1995. "Economic Evaluations, Prime Ministerial Approval, and Government Party Support: Rival Models Considered." *British Journal of Political Science* 25: 145–170.

Coale, Ansley J. 1984. *Rapid Population Change in China, 1952–1982*. Washington, D.C.: National Academic Press.

Coale, Ansley J., and Ronald Freedman. 1993. "Similarities in the Fertility Transition in China and Three Other East Asian Populations." In *The Revolution in Asian Fertility*, ed. Richard Leete and Iqbal Alam, pp. 208–238. Oxford: Clarendon Press.

Cohen, Youssef. 1994. *Radical Reformers and Reactionaries: The Prisoner's Dilemma and the Collapse of Democracy in Latin America*. Chicago: University of Chicago Press.

Coverdale, John F. 1982. "Inflation and Democratic Transition in Spain." In *The Politics of Inflation: A Comparative Analysis*, ed. Richard Medley, pp. 225–241. New York: Pergamon Press.

Cowgill, C. P. 1949. "The Theory of Population Growth Cycles." *American Journal of Sociology* 55: 163–170.

Crystal, Jonathan. 1994. "The Politics of Capital Flight: Exit and Exchange Rates in Latin America." *Review of International Studies* 20: 131–147.

Cukierman, Alex, Sebastian Edwards, and Guido Tabellini. 1992. "Seigniorage and Political Instability." *American Economic Review* 82: 537–555.

Cutright, Phillips. 1967. "Inequality: A Cross-National Analysis." *American Sociological Review* 32: 562–578.

Dahl, Robert A. 1971. *Polyarchy: Participation and Opposition*. New Haven: Yale University Press.

Dahl, Robert A. 1989. *Democracy and Its Critics*. New Haven: Yale University Press.

Dalton, Russell J. 1996. *Citizen Politics: Public Opinion and Political Parties in Advanced Industrial Democracies*. 2nd ed. Chatham, N.J.: Chatham House.

David, Paul A. 1985. "Clio and the Economics of Qwerty." *American Economic Review* 75: 332–337.

De Long, J. Bradford, and Lawrence H. Summers. 1993. "How Strongly Do Developing Economies Benefit from Equipment Investment?" *Journal of Monetary Economics* 32: 395–415.

Deininger, Klays, and Lyn Squire. 1996. "A New Data Set Measuring Income Inequality." *World Bank Economic Review* 10: 565–591.

Demeny, P. 1989. "World Population Growth and Prospects." Working paper no. 4. Research Division, Population Council.

Demsetz, Harold. 1967. "Toward a Theory of Property Rights." *American Economic Review* 57: 347–359.

Denzau, Arthur T., and Douglass C. North. 1994. "Shared Mental Models: Ideologies and Institutions." *Kyklos* 47: 3–31.

Devarajan, Shantayana, and Jamie De Melo. 1987. "Evaluation Participation in African Monetary Unions: A Statistical Analysis of the CFA Zones." *World Development* 15: 483–496.

Diamond, Larry. 1997. *Prospects for Democratic Development in Africa*. Hoover Essays in Public Policy, no. 74. Stanford: Hoover Institution Press.

Diaz-Alejandro, Carlos F. 1970. *Essays on the Economic History of the Argentine Republic*. New Haven: Yale University Press.

Dillon, Patricia, and Frank C. Wykoff. 2002. *Creating Capitalism: Transition and Growth in Post-Soviet Europe*. Cheltenham, UK: Edward Elgar Publishing.

Dixit, Avinash K. 1989. "Entry and Exit Decisions under Uncertainty." *Journal of Political Economy* 97: 620–638.

Dixon, William. 1994. "Democracy and Peaceful Settlement of International Conflict." *American Political Science Review* 88: 14–32.

Donnelly, Jack. 1984. "Human Rights and Development: Complementary or Competing Concerns?" *World Politics* 36: 255–283.

Dornbusch, Rudiger, and Sebastian Edwards. 1991. *The Macroeconomics of Populism in Latin America*. Chicago: University of Chicago Press.

Doyle, Michael W. 1983. "Kant, Liberal Legacies, and Foreign Affairs." *Philosophy and Public Affairs* 12: 205–235.

Doyle, Michael W. 1986. "Liberalism and World Politics." *American Political Science Review* 84: 1151–1161.

Easterlin, Richard A. 1981. "Why Isn't the Whole World Developed?" *Journal of Economic History* 41: 1–17.

Easterly, W. 2001. *The Elusive Quest for Growth: Economists' Adventures and Misadventures in the Tropics*. Cambridge: MIT Press.

Easterly, W., and S. Rebelo. 1993. "Fiscal Policy and Economic Growth: An Empirical Investigation." *Journal of Monetary Economics* 32: 41–458.

Easton, David. 1965. *A Systems Analysis of Political Life*. New York: Wiley.

Easton, David. 1990. *The Analysis of Political Structure*. New York: Routledge.

Edwards, Sebastian, and Guido Tabellini. 1991a. "Political Instability, Political Weakness, and Inflation: An Empirical Analysis." Working paper no. 3721. National Bureau of Economic Research.

Edwards, Sebastian, and Guido Tabellini. 1991b. "Explaining Fiscal Policies and Inflation in Developing Countries." *Journal of International Money and Finance* 10: 16–33.

Ember, Carol R., Melvin Ember, and Bruce Russett. 1992. "Peace between Participatory Polities: A Cross-Cultural Test of the 'Democracies Rarely Fight Each Other' Hypothesis." *World Politics* 44: 573–599.

Encyclopedia Britannica. 1994. "Comparative National Statistics." In *Britannica Book of the Year*, pp. 783–785. Chicago: Encyclopedia Britannica.

Evans, Peter. 1979. *Dependent Development: The Alliance of Multinational, State, and Local Capital in Brazil*. Princeton: Princeton University Press.

Feng, Yi. 1992. *District Data Report*. Rochester, N.Y.: City School District.

Feng, Yi. 1994. "Trade, Conflict, and Alliances: An Empirical Study." *Peace and Defence Economics* 5: 301–313.

Feng, Yi. 1995. "Regime, Polity, and Economic Performance: The Latin American Experience." *Growth and Change* 26: 77–104.

Feng, Yi. 1996. "Democracy and Growth: The Sub-Saharan African Case, 1960–1992." *Review of Black Political Economy* 25: 93–123.

Feng, Yi. 1997a. "Democracy, Political Stability, and Economic Growth." *British Journal of Political Science* 27: 391–418.

Feng, Yi. 1997b. "Economic Reform in China: Logic and Dynamism." *International Interactions* 23: 315–332.

Feng, Yi. 2000a. "Political Institutions, Economic Growth, and Democratic Evolution: The Pacific Asian Scenario." In *Governing for Prosperity*, ed. Bruce Bueno de Mesquita and Hilton L. Root, pp. 172–208. New Haven: Yale University Press.

Feng, Yi. 2000b. "Capital Account Liberalization: Sequencing and Implications." In *Financial Market Reform in China: Progress, Problems, and Prospects*, ed. B. Chen, J. Kimball Dietrich, and Yi Feng, pp. 87–108. Boulder: Colo.: Westview Press.

Feng, Yi. 2000c. "Measuring International Conflict: Constructing a Time-Series Cross-Country Data Set." *International Interactions* 26: 287–319.

Feng, Yi. 2000d. "Provincial Distribution of Direct Foreign Investment in China: 1992–1996: A Pooled Time-Series Empirical Study." In *Financial Market Reform in China: Progress, Problems, and Prospects*, ed. B. Chen, J. Kimball Dietrich, and Yi Feng, pp. 401–424. Boulder: Colo.: Westview Press.

Feng, Yi. 2001a. "Political Institutions and Private Investment: A Study of Developing Countries." *International Studies Quarterly* 45: 271–294.

Feng, Yi. 2001b. "Politics and Development." *Journal of Democracy* 12: 170–174.

Feng, Yi. 2001c. "Endogenous Growth Theory." In *Routledge Encyclopedia of International Political Economy*, ed. R. J. Barry Jones, pp. 438–440. London: Routledge.

Feng, Yi. 2003. "Political Capacity and Demographic Change: A Study of China with a Comparison to India." In *Urban Transformation in China: Theory, Evidence, and Policy*, ed. Aimin Chen and Kevin Zhang. Ashgate Publishers. Forthcoming.

Feng, Yi, and Baizhu Chen. 1996. "Political Environment and Economic Growth." *Social and Economic Studies* 45: 77–105.

Feng, Yi, and Baizhu Chen. 1997. "Government Capacity and Private Investment: A Study of Developing Countries." In *Political Capacity and Economic Behavior*, ed. Marina Arbetman and Jacek Kugler, pp. 97–108. Boulder, Colo.: Westview Press.

Feng, Yi, and Gaspare Genna. 2003. "Regional Integration and Domestic Institutional Compatibility: A Comparative Analysis of Regional Integration in the Americas, Pacific Asia, and Western Europe." *Review of International Political Economy*. Forthcoming.

Feng, Yi, and Ismene Gizelis. 2002. "Building Political Consensus and Distributing Resources: A Trade-Off or a Compatible Choice?" *Economic Development and Cultural Change* 51: 217–236.

Feng, Yi, Ismene Gizelis, and Jae Hoon Lee. 2002. "Managing Economic Development in the Presence of Ethnic Diversity: The Malaysian Experience." In *Managing Economic Development in Asia*, ed. Thomas K. Liou, pp. 209–238. Westport, Conn.: Praeger.

Feng, Yi, and Antonio Hsiang. 1998. "Developmental Experience and Issues in Latin America." In *The Handbook of Economic Development*, ed. K. T. Liou, pp. 523–550. New York: Marcel Dekker.

Feng, Yi, Antonio Hsiang, and Jae Hoon Lee. 2002. "Indonesian Economic Crisis: The Contradictions of Freedoms." In *Managing Economic Development in Asia*, ed. Thomas K. Liou, pp. 187–208. Westport, Conn.: Praeger.

Feng, Yi, and Jieli Li. 1997. "Internal Constraints and International Competitiveness: A Research Note on China." *Journal of Contemporary China* 6: 377–387.

Feng, Yi, and Paul J. Zak. 1999. "Determinants of Democratic Transitions: Theory and Empirical Evidence." *Journal of Conflict Resolution* 42: 162–177.

Feng, Yi, Paul J. Zak, and Jacek Kugler. 2000a. "The Politics of Fertility and Economic Development." *International Studies Quarterly* 44: 667–693.

Feng, Yi, Paul J. Zak, and Jacek Kugler. 2000b. "Demography, Democracy, and Development." Paper presented at the annual meeting of the American Political Science Association, Washington, D.C., August 31–September 1.

Feng, Yi, Paul J. Zak, and Jacek Kugler. 2001. "The Path to Prosperity: A Political Model of Demographic Change." Working paper. Claremont Graduate University.

Feng, Yi, Jacek Kugler, and Paul Zak. 2002. "Population Growth, Urbanization, and the Role of the Government: A Political Economic Model of Demographic Change and the Evidence from China." *Urban Studies*. Forthcoming.

Firebaugh, Glen. 1992. "Growth Effects of Foreign and Domestic Investment." *American Journal of Sociology* 98: 105–130.

Firebaugh, Glenn, and Frank D. Beck. 1994. "Does Economic Growth Benefit the Masses? Growth, Dependence, and Welfare in the Third World." *American Sociological Review* 59: 631–653.

Fish, M. Steven. 1996. "Democracy, Elections, and Economic Reform in the Post-socialist World." Paper presented at the annual meeting of the American Political Science Association, San Francisco, August 29–September 1.

Fletcher, Matthew, and Julian Gearing. 1996. "Now It's Up to Him: With Chavalit Poised to Take His Dream Job, the Economy Is the First Priority." *Asia Week*, November 29, pp. 20–22.

Foucault, Michel. 1977. *Discipline and Punish*. New York: Pantheon.

Foxley, A., M. S. MacPherson, and G. O'Donnell. 1986. *Development, Democracy, and the Art of Trespassing: Essays in Honor of A. O. Hirschman*. Notre Dame: University of Notre Dame Press.

Fredriksen, B. 1991. "An Introduction to the Analysis of Student Enrollment and Flow Statistics." Report no. PHREE/91/39. Washington, D.C.: Population and Human Resources Department, World Bank.

Freedman, L. P. 1994. "Family Planning as an Instrument of Empowerment." *International Family Planning Perspectives* 20: 31–33.

Freedom House. 1990. "Tables of Independent States: Comparative Measures of Freedom." *Freedom at Issue* 112: 18–19.

Freedom House. 1991. "Tables of Independent States: Comparative Measures of Freedom." *Freedom Review* 22: 17–18.

Freedom House. 1992. "Tables of Independent States: Comparative Measures of Freedom." *Freedom Review* 23: 17–18.

Freedom House. 1993. "Tables of Independent States: Comparative Measures of Freedom." *Freedom Review* 24: 15–16.

Freedom House. 1994. "Tables of Independent States: Comparative Measures of Freedom." *Freedom Review* 25: 14–15.

Freedom House. 1995. "Tables of Independent States: Comparative Measures of Freedom." *Freedom Review* 26: 15–16.

Freedom House. 1996a. "Tables of Independent States: Comparative Measures of Freedom." *Freedom Review* 27: 16–17.

Freedom House. 1996b. "Freedom House Reports Highest Number of Free Countries Ever." *Freedom House News*, December 18, p. 3.

Freedom House. 1997a. "Tables of Independent States: Comparative Measures of Freedom." *Freedom Review* 28: 12–13.

Freedom House. 1997b. "Survey Methodology." *Freedom Review* 28: 8–11.

Freedom House. 2002. "The World's Most Repressive Regimes." Internet: http://www.freedomhouse.org/research/mrr2002.pdf.

Friedman, Milton. 1956. "The Quantity Theory of Money: A Restatement." In *Studies in the Quantity Theory of Money*, ed. Milton Friedman, pp. 3–21. Chicago: University of Chicago Press.

Friedman, Milton. 1960. *A Program for Monetary Stability*. New York: Fordham University Press.

Friedman, Milton. 1961. "Capitalism and Freedom." *New Individualist Review* 1: 3–10.

Friedman, Milton. 1977. "Inflation and Unemployment." *Journal of Political Economy* 85: 451–472.

Fukuyama, Francis. 1993. "Capitalism and Democracy: The Missing Link." In *Capitalism, Socialism, and Democracy Revisited*, ed. Larry Diamond and Marc F. Plattner, pp. 94–104. Baltimore: Johns Hopkins University Press.

Fuller, Fuller, and Richard Rubinson. 1992. "Does the State Expand Schooling? Review of the Evidence." In *The Political Construction of Education: The State, School Expansion, and Economic Change*, ed. Bruce Fuller and Richard Rubinson, pp. 1–17. New York: Praeger.

Furubotn, Eirik, and Rudolf Richter. 1997. *Institutions and Economic Theory: The Contribution of the New Institutional Economics*. Ann Arbor: University of Michigan Press.

Galor, Oded, and Joseph Zeira. 1993. "Income Distribution and Macroeconomics." *Review of Economic Studies* 60: 35–52.

Galor, Oded, and H. Zhang. 1993. "Fertility, Income Distribution, and Economic Growth: Theory and Cross-Country Evidence." Manuscript. Brown University.

Garrett, Geoffrey. 1995. "Capital Mobility, Trade, and the Domestic Politics of Economic Policy." *International Organization* 49: 657–687.

Garrett, Geoffrey. 1998. *Partisan Politics in the Global Economy*. New York: Cambridge University Press.

Gasiorowski, M. J. 1986. "Economic Interdependence and International Conflict: Some Cross-National Evidence." *International Studies Quarterly* 30: 39–57.

Gasiorowski, Mark J. 1995. "Economic Crisis and Political Regime Change: An Event History Analysis." *American Political Science Review* 89: 882–897.

Gasiorowski, Mark J. 1996. "An Overview of the Political Regime Change Data set." *Comparative Political Studies* 29: 469–483.

Gastil, Raymond D. 1978–1990. *Freedom in the World*. Westport, Conn.: Greenwood Press.

Gastil, Raymond D. 1983. "Table of Independent Nations: Comparative Measures of Freedom." *Freedom at Issue* 70: 8–9.

Gastil, Raymond D. 1984. "Table of Independent Nations: Comparative Measures of Freedom." *Freedom at Issue* 76: 8–9.

Gastil, Raymond D. 1985. "Table of Independent Nations: Comparative Measures of Freedom." *Freedom at Issue* 82: 8–9.

Gastil, Raymond D. 1986. "Table of Independent Nations: Comparative Measures of Freedom." *Freedom at Issue* 88: 8–9.

Gastil, Raymond D. 1987. "Table of Independent Nations: Comparative Measures of Freedom." *Freedom at Issue* 94: 24–25.

Gastil, Raymond D. 1988. "Table of Independent Nations: Comparative Measures of Freedom." *Freedom at Issue* 100: 26–27.

Gastil, Raymond D. 1989. "Table of Independent Nations: Comparative Measures of Freedom." *Freedom at Issue* 106: 52–53.

Gaubatz, Kurt T. 1996. "Democratic States and Commitment in International Relations." *International Organization* 50: 109–139.

Gerschenkron, Alexander. 1962. *Economic Backwardness in Historical Perspective: A Book of Essays.* Cambridge: Harvard University Press.

Gildea, Robert. 1983. *Education in Provincial France, 1800–1914.* Oxford: Oxford University Press.

Gillespie, Charles Guy. 1991. *Negotiating Democracy: Politicians and Generals in Uruguay.* Cambridge: Cambridge University Press.

Goldstein, Joshua S. 1992. "A Conflict-Cooperation Scale for WEIS Events Data." *Journal of Conflict Resolution* 36: 369–385.

Goldthorpe, John H. 1978. "The Current Inflation: Toward a Sociological Account." In *The Political Economy of Inflation*, ed. Fred Hirsch and John H. Goldthorpe, pp. 186–213. London: Martin Robertson.

Goldthorpe, John H. 1987. "Problems of Political Economy after the Postwar Period." In *Changing Boundaries of the Political: Essays on the Evolving Balance between the State and Society, Public and Private in Europe*, ed. Charles S. Maier, pp. 363–407. Cambridge: Cambridge University Press.

Gowa, J. 1994. *Allies, Adversaries, and International Trade.* Princeton: Princeton University Press.

Gowa, J., and Edward D. Mansfield. 1993. "Power Politics and International Trade." *American Political Science Review* 87: 408–420.

Granger, C. W. J. 1969. "Investigating Causal Relations by Econometric Methods and Cross-Spectral Methods." *Econometrica* 37: 424–438.

Green, Andy. 1990. *Education and State Formation: The Rise of Education Systems in England, France, and the USA.* New York: St. Martin's Press.

Greene, Joshua, and Delano Villanueva. 1990. "Private Investment in Developing Countries: An Empirical Analysis." Working paper. International Monetary Fund.

Greene, William H. 1993. *Econometric Analysis.* 2nd ed. New York: Macmillan.

Gregorio, José De. 1993. "Inflation, Taxation, and Long-Run Growth." *Journal of Monetary Economics* 31: 271–298.

Grier, Kevin B., and Gordon Tullock. 1989. "An Empirical Analysis of Cross-National Economic Growth: 1951–1980." *Journal of Monetary Economics* 24: 259–276.

Grilli, Vittorio, Donato Masciandaro, and Guido Tabellini. 1991. "Political and Monetary Institutions and Public Financial Policies in the Industrial Countries." *Economic Policy* 13: 341–392.

Guilkey, David K., and Michael K. Salemi. 1982. "Small Sample Properties of Three Tests for Granger-Causal Ordering in a Bivariate Stochastic System." *Review of Economics and Statistics* 64: 668–680.

Gulhati, Ravi. 1991. "Who Makes Economic Policy in Africa and How?" *World Development* 18: 1147–1161.

*Guoji ribao.* 1997. "'The People Have Vetoed Western Democracy,' Declared Goh after Winning the Election." *Guoji ribao*, January 4, A2.

Gupta, Dipak K. 1990. *The Economics of Political Violence.* New York: Praeger.

Gurr, Ted Robert, Keith Jaggers, and Will H. Moore. 1990. "The Transformation of the Western State: The Growth of Democracy, Autocracy, and State Power Since 1800." *Studies in Comparative International Development* 25: 73–108.

Gurr, Ted Robert. 1990. *Polity II: Political Structures and Regime Change, 1800–1986.* Ann Arbor, Mich.: Inter-university Consortium for Political and Social Research.

Gwartney, James D., and Robert Lawson. 1997. *Economic Freedom of the World: 1977.* Vancouver, B.C.: Fraser Institute.

Gwartney, James D., Robert Lawson, and Walter Block. 1996. *Economic Freedom of the World: 1975–1995.* Vancouver, B.C.: Fraser Institute.

Gwartney, James D., and Robert Lawson. 2002. *Economic Freedom of the World: Annual Report 2002.* Internet: http://www.cato.org/economicfreedom/.

Haggard, Stephen, and Robert R. Kaufman. 1989. "Economic Adjustment in New Democracies." In *Fragile Coalitions: The Politics of Economic Adjustment*, ed. Joan Nelson, pp. 57–77. New Brunswick, N.J.: Transaction Books.

Haggard, Stephen, and Robert R. Kaufman. 1995. *The Political Economy of Democratic Transitions.* Princeton: Princeton University Press.

Hallar, H. Brandon, and Helmut Norpoth. 1994. "Let the Good Times Roll: The Economic Expectations of U.S. Voters." *American Journal of Political Science* 38: 625–650.

Harmel, Robert. 1980. "Gurr's 'Persistence and Change' Revisited: Some Consequences of Using Different Operationalizations of 'Change of Policy'." *European Journal of Political Research* 8: 189–214.

Hayek, Friedrich A. von. 1944. *The Road to Serfdom.* Chicago: University of Chicago Press.

Hayek, Friedrich A. von. 1959. "Unions, Inflation, and Profits." In *The Public Stake in Union Power*, ed. Philip D. Bradley, pp. 46–62. Charlottesville: University of Virginia Press.

Hayek, Friedrich A. von. 1960. *The Constitution of Liberty.* London: Routledge & Kegan Paul.

Hayek, Friedrich A. von. 1976. *Law, Legislation, and Liberty.* Vol. 2. London: Routledge & Kegan Paul.

Helliwell, John F. 1994. "Empirical Linkages between Democracy and Economic Growth." *British Journal of Political Science* 24: 225–248.

Hewitt, Christopher. 1977. "The Effect of Political Democracy and Social Democracy on Equality in Industrial Societies: A Cross-National Comparison." *American Sociological Review* 42: 450–464.

Hirsch, Fred. 1976. *Social Limits to Growth*. Cambridge: Harvard University Press.

Hirsch, Fred. 1978. "The Ideological Underlay of Inflation." In *The Political Economy of Inflation*, ed. Fred Hirsch and John H. Goldthorpe, pp. 263–284. London: Martin Robertson.

Holmes, Brian. 1985. "Equality and Freedom in Education." In *Equality and Freedom in Education: A Comparative Study*, ed. Brian Holmes, pp. 209–252. London: George Allen & Unwin.

Huber, Evelyne, Dietrich Rueschemeyer, and John D. Stephens. 1993. "The Impact of Economic Development on Democracy." *Journal of Economic Perspectives* 7: 71–85.

Hufbauer, Gary Clyde, Jeffrey J. Schott, and Kimberly Ann Elliott. 1990. *Economic Sanctions Reconsidered: History and Current Policy*. 2nd ed. Washington, D.C.: Institute for International Economics.

Huntington, Samuel P. 1968. *Political Order in Changing Societies*. New Haven: Yale University Press.

Huntington, Samuel P. 1984. "Will More Countries Become Democratic?" *Political Science Quarterly* 99: 193–218.

Huntington, Samuel P. 1987. "The Goals of Development." In *Understanding Political Development*, ed. Myron Weiner and Samuel P. Huntington, pp. 3–32. Boston: Little, Brown.

Huntington, Samuel P. 1991. "Democracy's Third Wave." *Journal of Democracy* 2: 12–34.

Huntington, Samuel P. 1993. "Clashes of Civilizations?" *Foreign Affairs* 72: 22–49.

Huntington, Samuel P., and Jorge I. Dominguez. 1975. "Political Development." In *Handbook of Political Science*, vol. 3, *Macropolitical Theory*, ed. F. I. Greestein and N. W. Polsby, pp. 1–114. Reading, Mass.: Addison-Wesley.

Huntington, Samuel P., and Joan Nelson. 1976. *No Easy Choice: Political Participation in Developing Countries*. Cambridge: Harvard University Press.

Hyland, James L. 1995. *Democratic Theory: The Philosophical Foundations*. Manchester: Manchester University Press.

International Reports, Inc. Various years. *International Country Risk Guide*. New York: International Reports, Inc.

Jackman, Robert W. 1973. "On the Relationship of Economic Development to Political Performance." *American Journal of Political Science* 17: 611–621.

Jackman, Robert W. 1975. *Politics and Social Equality: A Comparative Analysis*. New York: Wiley.

Jaggers, Keith, and Ted Robert Gurr. 1995. "Transition to Democracy: Tracking the Third Wave with Polity III Indicators of Democracy and Autocracy." *Journal of Peace Research* 32: 469–482.

Joerding, Wayne. 1986. "Economic Growth and Defense Spending." *Journal of Development Economics* 21: 35–40.

Johnson, B. T., and T. P. Sheehy. 1996. *1996 Index of Economic Freedom.* Washington, D.C.: Heritage Foundation.

Johnson, D. Gale. 2000. "Reducing the Urban-Rural Income Disparity." Paper no. 00–07, November 6. Office of Agricultural Economics Research, University of Chicago.

Johnson, Harry G. 1972. *Inflation and the Monetarist Controversy.* Amsterdam: North-Holland.

Johnson, John W. 1964. *The Military and Society in Latin America.* Stanford: Stanford University Press.

Kaneko, M. 1986. "The Educational Composition of the World Population: A Database." Report no. EDT 29. Washington, D.C.: Education and Training Department, World Bank.

Karl, Terry. 1986. "Petroleum and Political Pacts: The Transition to Democracy in Venezuela." In *Transitions from Authoritarian Rule: Latin America,* ed. Guillermo O'Donnell, Philippe C. Schmitter, and Laurence Whitehead, pp. 196–219. Baltimore: Johns Hopkins University Press.

Karl, Terry. 1991. "Getting to Democracy." In *The Transition to Democracy: Proceedings of a Workshop,* ed. Commission on Behavioral and Social Sciences and Education, National Research Council, pp. 29–40. Washington, D.C.: National Academy Press.

Katona, George. 1980. "How Expectations Are Really Formed." *Challenge* 23: 32–35.

Kaufman, Robert R. 1979. "Industrial Change and Authoritarian Rule in Latin America: A Concrete Review of the Bureaucratic-Authoritarian Model." In *The New Authoritarianism in Latin America,* ed. David Collier, pp. 165–253. Princeton: Princeton University Press.

Kaufman, Robert R. 1986. "Liberalization and Democratization in Latin America: Perspectives from the 1970s." In *Transitions from Authoritarian Rule: Latin America,* ed. Guillermo O'Donnell, Philippe C. Schmitter, and Laurence Whitehead. Baltimore: Johns Hopkins University Press.

Kennedy, Peter. 1996. *A Guide to Econometrics.* Cambridge: MIT Press.

Keohane, Robert O. 1984. *After Hegemony: Cooperation and Discourse in the World Political Economy.* Princeton: Princeton University Press.

Kerr, Clark, John T. Dunlop, Frederick Harbison, and Charles Myers. 1969. *Industrialism and Industrial Man: The Problems of Labor and Management in Economic Growth.* New York: Oxford University Press.

Khan, M., and Carmen M. Reinhart. 1990. "Private Investment and Economic Growth in Developing Countries." *World Development* 18: 19–27.

Kim, Kyong-dong. 1991. "Sociocultural Developments in the Republic of Korea." In *Democracy and Development in East Asia: Taiwan, South Korea, and the Philippines,* ed. Thomas W. Robinson, pp. 137–154. Washington, D.C.: American Enterprise Institute Press.

Kim, Kyung-won. 1993. "Marx, Schumpeter, and the East Asian Experience." In *Capitalism, Socialism, and Democracy Revisited*, ed. Larry Diamond and Marc F. Plattner, pp. 11–25. Baltimore: Johns Hopkins University Press.

Kirk, Dudley. 1971. "A New Demographic Transition?" In *Rapid Population Growth*. Washington D.C.: National Academy of Sciences.

Klein, Herrert S. 1992. *Bolivia: The Evolution of a Multi-ethnic Society*. New York: Oxford University Press.

Klein, L. R. 1993. "African Economic Development: Situations and Prospects." *South African Journal of Economics* 61: 229–238.

Knack, Stephen, and Phillip Keefer. 1995. "Institutions and Economic Performance: Cross-Country Tests Using Alternative Institutional Measures." *Economics and Politics* 7: 207–227.

Knodel, J., and E. van de Walle. 1979. "Lessons from the Past: Policy Implications of Historical Fertility Studies." *Population and Development Review* 5: 217–245.

Kohli, Atul, Michael F. Altfeld, Saideh Lotflan, and Russell Morden. 1984. "Inequality in the Third World: An Assessment of Competing Explanations." *Comparative Political Studies* 17: 283–318.

Kohli, Atul. 1986. "Democracy and Development." In *Development Strategies Reconsidered*, ed. John Lewis and Valeriana Kallab, pp. 153–182. New Brunswick, N.J.: Transaction Books.

Kormendi, Roger C., and Philip G. Meguire. 1985. "Macroeconomic Determinants of Growth: Cross-Country Evidence." *Journal of Monetary Economics* 16: 141–163.

Korpi, Walter. 1983. *The Working Class in Welfare Capitalism: Work, Unions, and Politics in Sweden*. London: Routledge & Kegan Paul.

Kugler, Jacek, and Marina Arbetman. 1997. "Relative Political Capacity: Political Extraction and Political Reach." In *Political Capacity and Economic Behavior*, ed. Marina Arbetman and Jacek Kugler, pp. 11–46. Boulder, Colo.: Westview Press.

Kugler, Jacek, and Yi Feng. 1999. "Explaining and Modeling Democratic Transitions." *Journal of Conflict Resolution* 42: 139–146.

Kurth, James. 1982. "Economic Sectors and Inflationary Policies: The Politics of Inflation in Historical Perspective." In *The Politics of Inflation: A Comparative Analysis*, ed. Richard Medley, pp. 44–64. New York: Pergamon.

Kuznets, Simon. 1955. "Economic Growth and Income Inequality." *American Economic Review* 45: 1–28.

Kuznets, Simon. 1963. "Quantitative Aspects of the Economic Growth of Nations. VIII: Distribution of Income by Size." *Economic Development and Cultural Change* 11: 1–80.

Kyriacou, George A. 1991. "Level and Growth Effects of Human Capital: A Cross-Country Study of the Convergence Hypothesis." New York University Economic Research Report.

Lake, David A. 1992. "Powerful Pacifists: Democratic States and War." *American Political Science Review* 86: 24–37.

Landau, Daniel. 1986. "Government and Economic Growth in the LDCs: An Empirical Study for 1960–1980." *Economic Development and Social Change* 35: 35–76.

Lau, Lawrence J., Dean T. Jamison, and F. Louat. 1991. "Education and Productivity in Developing Countries: An Aggregate Production Function Approach." Report no. WPS 612. Washington, D.C.: World Bank.

Leblang, David A. 1997. "Political Democracy and Economic Growth: Pooled Cross-Sectional and Time-Series Evidence." *British Journal of Political Science* 27: 453–472.

Leijonhufvud, Axel. 1992. "High Inflations and Contemporary Monetary Theory." *Economic Notes* 21: 211–224.

Lenski, Gerhard. 1966. *Power and Privilege: A Theory of Social Stratification*. New York: McGraw-Hill.

Levine, David. 1995. *Wealth and Freedom: An Introduction to Political Economy*. Cambridge: Cambridge University Press.

Levine, Ross, and David Renelt. 1992. "A Sensitivity Analysis of Cross-Country Growth Regressions." *American Economic Review* 82: 942–963.

Levine, Ross, and Sara Zervos. 1993. "What We Have Learned about Policy and Growth from Cross-Country Regressions." *American Economic Review* 83: 426–430.

Levy, Victor. 1988. "Aid and Growth in Sub-Saharan Africa: The Recent Experience." *European Economic Review* 32: 1777–1795.

Lewis-Beck, Michael S. 1988. *Economics and Elections: The Major Western Democracies*. Ann Arbor: University of Michigan Press.

Libecap, Gary D. 1989. *Contracting for Property Rights*. Cambridge: Cambridge University Press.

Lijphart, Arend. 1980. "The Structure of Inference." In *The Civic Culture Revisited*, ed. Gabriel A. Almond and Sidney Verba, pp. 37–56. Boston: Little, Brown.

Lipset, Seymour M. 1959. "Some Social Requisites of Democracy: Economic Development and Political Development." *American Political Science Review* 53: 69–105.

Lipset, Seymour M. 1960. *Political Man*. Garden City, N.Y.: Anchor Books.

Londregan, John B., and Keith T. Poole. 1990. "Poverty, the Coup Trap, and the Seizure of Executive Power." *World Politics* 32: 151–183.

Londregan, John B., and Keith T. Poole. 1996. "Does High Income Promote Democracy?" *World Politics* 49: 1–30.

Lovett, William A. 1982. *Inflation and Politics: Fiscal, Monetary, and Wage-Price Discipline*. Lexington, Mass.: D. C. Heath.

Lucas, Robert E. 1988. "On the Mechanics of Economic Development." *Journal of Monetary Economics* 22: 3–42.

MacIntyre, Andrew. 1996. "Democracy and Markets in Southeast Asia." In *Constructing Democracy and Markets: East Asia and Latin America*, ed. International Forum for Democratic Studies and Pacific Council on International Policy, pp. 39–47. Los Angeles: Pacific Council.

MacKuen, Michael B., Robert S. Erickson, and James S. Stimson. 1992. "Peasants or Bankers? The American Electorate and the U.S. Economy." *American Political Science Review* 86: 597–611.

Mankiw, N. Gregory, David Romer, and David N. Weil. 1992. "A Contribution to the Empirics of Economic Growth." *Quarterly Journal of Economics* 107: 407–437.

Mansfield, E. D. 1992. "The Concentration of Capabilities and International Trade." *International Organization* 46: 731–763.

Mao, Zedong. 1966. "An Analysis of Classes in China." In Mao Zedong, *Selected Works by Mao Zedong*, vol. 1, pp. 1–11. Beijing: People's Press.

Margolis, Michael. 1979. *Viable Democracy*. New York: St. Martin's Press.

Marks, Gary. 1992. "Rational Sources of Chaos in Democratic Transition." *American Behavioral Scientist* 35: 397–421.

Marsh, Robert M. 1979. "Does Democracy Hinder Economic Development in the Latecomer Developing Nations?" *Comparative Social Research* 2: 215–248.

Marsh, Robert M. 1988. "Sociological Explanations of Economic Growth." *Studies in Comparative International Development* 23: 41–76.

Mauro, Paulo. 1995. "Corruption and Growth." *Quarterly Journal of Economics* 110: 681–172.

Maxfield, Sylvia. 1990. *Governing Capital: International Finance and Mexican Politics.* Ithaca: Cornell University Press.

McBeth, J. 1998. "Dept. of Connections." In *Crash of '97: How the Financial Crisis is Reshaping Asia*, ed. Dan Biers, pp. 128–134. Hong Kong: Review Publishing Co.

McHenry, Dean E., Jr. 2000. "Is the Quantitative Study of Democracy in Africa Empirical? An Assessment of Data Sets." *Journal of Democracy* 11: 168–185.

McKinlay, Robert D., and A. S. Cohan. 1975. "A Comparative Analysis of the Political and Economic Performance of Military and Civilian Regimes: A Cross-National Aggregate Study." *Comparative Politics* 8: 1–30.

McMahon, W. W. 1987. "Student Labor Market Expectations." In *Economics of Education: Research and Studies*, ed. George Psacharopoulos, pp. 182–186. Oxford: Pergamon Press.

McMillan, Carl. 1995. "Foreign Direct Investment in Eastern Europe: Harnessing FDI to the Transition from Plan to Market." In *Foreign Direct Investment in a Changing Global Political Economy*, ed. Steve Chan, pp. 127–149. New York: St. Martin's Press.

Meltzer, Allan H., and S. F. Richard. 1981. "A Rational Theory of the Size of the Government." *Journal of Political Economy* 89: 914–927.

Menendez, Ana. 1996. "Raising the Bar in California Schools." *Orange County Register*, December 22, News 1.

Midgal, J. S. 1988. *Strong Societies and Weak States: State-Society Relations and State Capacities in the Third World.* Princeton: Princeton University Press.

Mises, Ludwig von. 1981. *Socialism: An Economic and Sociological Analysis.* Indianapolis: Liberty Classics.

Montinola, Gabriella, Yingyi Qian, and Barry R. Weingast. 1995. "Federalism, Chinese Style: The Political Basis for Economic Success in China." *World Politics* 48: 50–81.

Moore, Barrington, Jr. 1966. *Social Origins of Dictatorship and Democracy*. Boston: Little, Brown.

Morell, David, and Chai-anan Samudavanija. 1981. *Political Conflict in Thailand: Reform, Reaction, and Revolution*. Cambridge, Mass.: Oelgeschlager, Gunn, and Hain, Publishers.

Mouzelis, Nicos. 1994. "The State in Late Development: Historical and Comparative Perspectives." In *Rethinking Social Development: Theory, Research, and Practice*, ed. David Booth, pp. 126–151. Harlow: Longman.

Muller, Edward. 1988. "Democracy, Economic Development, and Income Inequality." *American Sociological Review* 53: 50–68.

Mumper, Michael J., and Eric M. Uslaner. 1982. "The Bucks Stop Here: The Politics of Inflation in the United States." In *The Politics of Inflation: A Comparative Analysis*, ed. Richard Medley, pp. 104–126. New York: Pergamon Press.

Nagatani, Keizo. 1989. *Political Macroeconomics*. Oxford: Clarendon Press.

Nam, C. B., and S. G. Philliber. 1984. *Population: A Basic Orientation*. Englewood Cliffs, N.J.: Prentice-Hall.

Neher, Clark. 1992. "Political Succession in Thailand." *Asian Survey* 32: 585–605.

Nelson, Joan. 1987. "Political Participation." In *Understanding Political Development: An Analytic Study*, ed. Myron Weiner and Samuel P. Huntington, pp. 103–159. Boston: Little, Brown.

Ness, G., and H. Ando. 1984. *The Land Is Shrinking: Population Planning in Asia*. Baltimore: John Hopkins University Press.

Newman, Barbara, and Randall J. Thompson. 1989. "Economic Growth and Social Development: A Longitudinal Analysis of Causal Priority." *World Development* 17: 461–471.

Nigh, Douglass. 1984. "The Effect of Political Events on United States Direct Foreign Investment: A Pooled Time-Series Cross-Sectional Analysis." *Journal of International Business Studies* 16: 1–17.

Nordlinger, Eric. 1977. *Soldiers in Politics: Military Coups and Governments*, Englewood Cliffs, N.J.: Prentice-Hall.

North, Douglass C. 1988. *Structure and Change in Economic History*. New York: W. W. Norton.

North, Douglass C. 1990. *Institutions, Institutional Change, and Economic Performance*. New York: Cambridge University Press.

North, Douglass C. 1996a. "Some Fundamental Puzzles in Economic History/ Development." Working paper. The Von Gremp Workshop in Entrepreneurial History, UCLA.

North, Douglass C. 1996b. "Epilogue: Economic Performance through Time." In *Empirical Studies in Institutional Change*, ed. Lee J. Alston, Thráinn Eggertsson, and Douglass C. North, pp. 342–356. New York: Cambridge University Press.

North, Douglass C., William Summerhill, and Barry R. Weingast. 2000. "Order, Disorder, and Economic Change: Latin America versus America." In *Governing for Prosperity*, ed. Bruce Bueno de Mesquita and Hilton L. Root, pp. 17–58. New Haven: Yale University Press.

Notestein, F. 1945. "Population: The Long View." In *Food for the World*, ed. T. W. Schultz, pp. 36–57. Chicago: Chicago University Press.

Obstfeld, Maurice. 1991. "A Model of Currency Depreciation and the Debt-Inflation Spiral." *Journal of Economic Dynamics and Control* 15: 151–177.

Ockey, James. 1996. "Thai Society and Patterns of Leadership." *Asian Survey* 36: 345–360.

O'Donnell, Guillermo. 1973. *Modernization and Bureaucratic-Authoritarianism: Studies in South American Politics*. Berkeley: Institute of International Studies, University of California.

O'Donnell, Guillermo. 1978. "Reflections on the Patterns of Change in the Bureaucratic Authoritarian State." *Latin American Research Review* 13: 3–38.

O'Donnell, Guillermo, and Philippe C. Schmitter. 1986. "Tentative Conclusions about Uncertain Democracies." In *Transitions from Authoritarian Rule*, ed. Guillermo O'Donnell, Philippe G. Schmitter, and Laurence Whitehead, pp. 3–78. Baltimore: Johns Hopkins University Press.

Olson, Mancur. 1982. *The Rise and Decline of Nations: Economic Growth, Stagflation, and Social Rigidities*. New Haven: Yale University Press.

Olson, Mancur. 1993. "Dictatorship, Democracy, and Development." *American Political Science Review* 87: 567–576.

Oneal, John R. 1994. "The Affinity of Foreign Investors for Authoritarian Regime." *Political Research Quarterly* 47: 565–588.

Organski, A. F. K. 1996. "Theoretical Link of Political Capacity to Development." In *Political Capacity and Economic Behavior*, ed. Marina Arbetman and Jacek Kugler, pp. 47–66. Boulder, Colo.: Westview Press.

Organski, A. F. K., and Jacek Kugler. 1980. *The War Ledger*. Chicago: University of Chicago Press.

Organski, A. F. K., Jacek Kugler, Timothy Johnson, and Youssef Cohen. 1984. *Births, Deaths, and Taxes*. Chicago: University of Chicago Press.

Özler, Şule, and Dani Rodrik. 1992. "External Shocks, Politics, and Private Investment." *Journal of Development Economics* 39: 141–162.

Paarlberg, Don. 1993. *An Analysis and History of Inflation*. Westport, Conn.: Praeger.

Pastor, Manuel, Jr., and Eric Hilt. 1993. "Private Investment and Democracy in Latin America." *World Development* 21: 489–507.

Pastor, Manuel, Jr., and Jae Ho Sung. 1995. "Private Investment and Democracy in Developing Countries." *Journal of Economic Issues* 29: 223–243.

Paukert, Felix. 1973. "Income Distribution at Different Levels of Development: A Survey of Evidence." *International Labour Review* 108: 97–125.

Peacock, Alan T., and Martin Riketts. 1978. "The Growth of the Public Sector and Inflation." In *The Political Economy of Inflation*, ed. Fred Hirsch and John H. Goldthorpe, pp. 117–136. London: Martin Robertson.

Perotti, Roberto. 1991. "Income Distribution, Politics, and Growth." *AEA Papers and Proceedings* 82: 311–316.

Perotti, Roberto. 1993. "Political Equilibrium, Income Distribution, and Growth." *Review of Economic Studies* 60: 755–776.

Perotti, Roberto. 1996. "Growth, Income Distribution, and Democracy: What the Data Say." *Journal of Economic Growth* 1: 149–187.

Persson, Torsten, and Guido Tabellini. 1990. "Politico-economic Equilibrium Growth: Theory and Evidence." Manuscript.

Persson, Torsten, and Guido Tabellini. 1994. "Is Inequality Harmful for Growth? Theory and Evidence." *American Economic Review* 84: 600–621.

Persson, Torsten, and Lars E. O. Svensson. 1989. "Why Would a Stubborn Conservative Run a Deficit?" *Quarterly Journal of Economics* 104: 325–346.

Pfeffermann, Guy P., and Andrea Madarassy. 1991. "Trends in Private Investment in Developing Countries." International Financial Corporation discussion paper no. 11. Washington, D.C.: World Bank.

Pindyck, Robert S. 1993. "Irreversibility, Uncertainty, and Investment." In *Striving for Growth after Adjustment: The Role of Capital Formation*, ed. Lius Servén and Andrés Solimano, pp. 31–80. Washington, D.C.: International Bank for Reconstruction and Development.

Polachek, S. W. 1992. "Conflict and Trade: An Economics Approach to Political International Interactions." In *Economics of Arms Reduction and the Peace Process*, ed. W. Isard and C. H. Anderton, pp. 89–120. Amsterdam: Elsevier Science Publishers.

Pollins, B. M. 1989. "Does Trade Still Follow the Flag?" *American Political Science Journal* 83: 465–490.

Pomfret, Richard. 1994. "Foreign Direct Investment in a Centrally Planned Economy: Lessons from China. Comments on Kamath." *Economic Development and Cultural Change* 43: 413–417.

Poston, Dudley L. 1992. "Fertility Trends in China." In *The Population of Modern China*, ed. Dudley L. Poston Jr. and David Yaukey. New York: Plenum Press.

Pothier, John T. 1982. "The Political Causes and Effects of Argentine Inflation." In *The Politics of Inflation: A Comparative Analysis*, ed. Richard Medley, pp. 186–224. New York: Pergamon Press.

Pourgerami, Abbas. 1992. "Authoritarian versus Nonauthoritarian Approaches to Economic Development: Update and Additional Evidence." *Public Choice* 74: 365–377.

Powell, G. Bingham, Jr. 1986. *Contemporary Democracies: Participation, Stability, and Violence*. Cambridge: Harvard University Press.

Powell, G. Bingham, Jr., and Guy D. Whitten. 1993. "A Cross-National Analysis of Economic Voting: Taking Account of the Political Context." *American Journal of Political Science* 37: 391–414.

Price, Simon, and David Sanders. 1993. "Modelling Government Popularity in Post-war Britain: A Methodological Example." *American Journal of Political Science* 37: 317–334.

Price, Simon. 1995. "Aggregate Uncertainty, Capacity Utilization, and Manufacturing Investment." *Applied Economics* 27: 147–154.

Protoparadakis, Aris A., and Jeremy J. Siegal. 1987. "Are Money Growth and Inflation Related to Government Deficits: Evidence from Ten Industrialized Economies." *Journal of International Money and Finance* 6: 31–48.

Przeworski, Adam. 1966. *Party Systems and Economic Development*. Ph.D. dissertation, Northwestern University.

Przeworski, Adam. 1991. *Democracy and the Market: Political and Economic Reforms in Eastern Europe and Latin America*. Cambridge: Cambridge University Press.

Przeworski, Adam, Mike Alvarez, José Antonio Cheibub, and Fernando Limongi. 2000. *Democracy and Development: Political Regimes and Economic Performance, 1950–1990*. Cambridge: Cambridge University Press.

Przeworski, Adam, and Fernando Limongi. 1993. "Political Regimes and Economic Growth." *Journal of Economic Perspectives* 7: 51–69.

Przeworski, Adam, and Fernando Limongi. 1997. "Modernization: Theories and Facts." *World Politics* 49: 155–183.

Psacharopoulos, George, and Ana Maria Ariagada. 1986a. "The Educational Composition of the Labor Force: An International Comparison." *International Labor Review* 125: 561–574.

Psacharopoulos, George, and Ana Maria Ariagada. 1986b. "The Educational Attainment of the Labor Force: An International Comparison." Report no. EDT 38. Washington, D.C.: Education and Training Department, World Bank.

Putnam, Robert D., with Robert Leonardi and Raffaella Y. Nanetti. 1993. *Making Democracy Work: Civic Traditions in Modern Italy*. Princeton: Princeton University Press.

Pye, Lucian. 1966. *Aspects of Political Development*. Boston: Little, Brown.

Quinn, D. P., and C. Inclan. 1997. "The Origins of Financial Openness: A Study of Current and Capital Account Liberalization." *American Journal of Political Science* 41: 771–813.

Radelet, S. 1999. "From Boom to Bust: Indonesia's Implosion." *Harvard Asia Pacific Review* 3: 62–66.

Radice, Hugo. 1995. "The Role of Foreign Direct Investment in the Transformation of Eastern Europe." In *The Transformation of the Communist Economics*, ed. Ha-joon Chang and Peter Nolan, pp. 282–307. New York: St. Martin's Press.

Ray, James L. 1995. *Democracies in International Conflict*. Columbia: University of South Carolina Press.

Remmer, Karen L. 1989. *Military Rule in Latin America*. Winchester, Mass.: Unwin Hyman.

Remmer, Karen L. 1990. "Democracy and Economic Crisis: The Latin American Experience." *World Politics* 42: 315–335.

Riker, William H., and David L. Weimer. 1993. "The Economic and Political Liberalization of Socialism: The Fundamental Problem of Property Rights." *Social Philosophy and Policy* 10: 79–102.

Roberts, K. W. S. 1977. "Voting over Income Tax Schedules." *Journal of Public Economics* 18: 329–340.

Robinson, Sherman. 1971. "Sources of Growth in Less Developed Countries: A Cross-Section Study." *Quarterly Journal of Economics* 55: 391–408.

Rodrik, Dani. 1991. "Policy Uncertainty and Private Investment in Developing Countries." *Journal of Development Economics* 36: 229–242.

Roemer, John. 1995. "On the Relationship between Economic Development and Political Democracy." In *Democracy and Development*, ed. Amiya Kumar Bagchi, pp. 28–55. New York: St. Martin's Press.

Romer, Paul M. 1986. "Increasing Returns and Long-Run Growth." *Journal of Political Economy* 94: 1002–1037.

Romer, Paul M. 1990. "Endogenous Technological Change." *Journal of Political Economy* 98: S71–S102.

Romer, Paul M. 1993. "Idea Gaps and Object Gaps in Economic Development." *Journal of Monetary Economics* 32: 543–573.

Romer, Thomas. 1975. "Individual Welfare, Majority Voting, and the Properties of a Linear Income Tax." *Journal of Public Economics* 14: 163–185.

Root, Hilton L. 1996. *Small Countries, Big Lessons: Governance, and the Rise of East Asia.* New York: Oxford University Press.

Roubini, Nouriel, and Jeffrey Sachs. 1989. "Political and Economic Determinants of Budget Deficits in Industrial Democracies." *European Economic Review* 33: 909–933.

Roubini, Nouriel. 1991. "Economic and Political Determinants of Budget Deficits in Developing Countries." *Journal of International Money and Finance* 10: 549–572.

Rouyer, A. 1987. "Political Capacity and the Decline of Fertility in India." *American Political Science Review* 81: 453–470.

Rubinson, Richard, and Dan Quinlan. 1977. "Democracy and Social Inequality: A Reanalysis." *American Sociological Review* 42: 611–623.

Russett, Bruce. 1995. "The Democratic Peace." *International Security* 19: 164–175.

Saint-Paul, G., and T. Verdier. 1993. "Education, Democracy, and Growth." *Journal of Development Economics* 42: 406–407.

Sandbrook, Richard. 1986. "The State and Economic Stagnation in Tropical Africa." *World Development* 14: 319–332.

Sanders, David. 1981. *Patterns of Political Instability.* New York: St. Martin's Press.

Sanders, David. 1995. "Forecasting Political Preferences and Election Outcomes in the U.K.: Experiences, Problems, and Prospects for the Next General Election." *Electoral Studies* 14: 251–272.

Sargent, Thomas J. 1976. "A Classic Macroeconometric Model for the United States." *Journal of Political Economy* 84: 207–237.

Sargent, Thomas J. 1982. "The Ends of Four Big Inflations." In *Inflation: Causes and Effects*, ed. Robert E. Hall, pp. 41–98. Chicago: University of Chicago Press.

Sartori, Giovanni. 1987. *The Theory of Democracy Revisited*. Chatham, N.J.: Chatham House Publishers.

Sarup, Madan. 1982. *Education, State, and Crisis*. London: Routledge and Kegan Paul.

SAS Institute. 1993. *SAS/ETS User's Guide*. Cary, N.C.: SAS Publications.

Sayrs, L. W. 1989. "Trade and Conflict Revisited: Do Politics Matter?" *International Interactions* 15: 155–175.

Schlossstein, Steven. 1991. *Asia's New Little Dragons: The Dynamic Emergence of Indonesia, Thailand, and Malaysia*. Chicago: Contemporary Books.

Schneider, Friedrick, and Bruno Frey. 1985. "Economic and Political Determinants of Foreign Direct Investment." *World Development* 13: 161–175.

Schumpeter, Joseph A. 1955. *Imperialism and Social Classes*. Cleveland: World Publishing Co.

Schumpeter, Joseph A. 1976. *Capitalism, Socialism, and Democracy*. London: Allen & Unwin.

Scully, Gerald W. 1988. "The Institutional Framework and Economic Development." *Journal of Political Economy* 98: 652–662.

Scully, Gerald W. 1992. *Constitutional Environments and Economic Growth*. Princeton: Princeton University Press.

Servén, Luis, and Solimano, Andrés. 1993. "Private Investment and Macroeconomic Adjustment: A Survey." In *Striving for Growth after Adjustment: The Role of Capital Formation*, ed. Luis Servén and Andrés Solimano, pp. 11–30. Washington, D.C.: International Bank for Reconstruction and Development.

Shirk, Susan. 1993. *The Political Logic of Economic Reform in China*. Berkeley: University of California Press.

Siermann, C. L. J. 1998. *Institutions and the Economic Performance of Nations*. Cheltenham: Edward Elgar Publishing.

Sims, Christopher A. 1972. "Money, Income, and Causality." *American Economic Review* 62: 540–552.

Sinding, S., J. Ross, and A. Rosenfield. 1994. "Seeking Common Ground: Unmet Need and the Demographic Goals." *International Family Planning Perspectives* 20: 23–28.

Singh, Harrier, and Dipak K. Gupta. 1997. "Role of Political Risk in Foreign Direct Investment." Working paper. San Diego State University.

Sirowy, Larry, and Alex Inkeles. 1990. "The Effects of Democracy on Economic Growth and Inequality: A Review." *Studies in Comparative International Development* 25: 126–157.

Siverson, Randolph M., and Juliann Emmons. 1991. "Birds of a Feather: Democratic Political Systems and Alliance Choices in the Twentieth Century." *Journal of Conflict Resolution* 35: 285–306.

Sloan, John, and Kent L. Tedin. 1987. "The Consequence of Regime Type for Public Policy Outputs." *Comparative Political Studies* 20: 98–124.

Smith, Adam. 1937. *An Inquiry into the Nature and Causes of the Wealth of Nations*. New York: Modern Library.

Smith, Michael R. 1992. *Power, Norms, and Inflation: A Skeptical Treatment*. New York: Aldine De Gruyter.

Smith, Stephen C. 1994. *Case Studies in Economic Development*. New York: Longman.

Snider, Lewis W. 1996. *Growth, Debt, and Politics: Economic Adjustment and the Political Performance of Developing Countries*. Boulder, Colo.: Westview Press.

Snow, Peter G. 1979. *Political Forces in Argentina*. New York: Praeger.

Snyder, David, and Edward L. Kick. 1979. "Structural Position in the World System and Economic Growth, 1950–1970: A Multiple-Network Analysis of Transnational Interactions." *American Journal of Sociology* 84: 1096–1126.

Solingen, Etel. 1996. "Democracy, Economic Reform, and Regional Cooperation." *Journal of Theoretical Politics* 8: 79–114.

Solow, Robert M. 1956. "A Contribution to the Theory of Economic Growth." *Quarterly Journal of Economics* 34: 65–94.

Stack, Steven. 1979. "The Effects of Political Participation and Socialist Party Strength on the Degree of Income Inequality." *American Sociological Review* 44: 168–181.

Stack, Steven. 1980. "The Political Economy of Income Inequality: A Comparative Analysis." *Canadian Journal of Political Science* 13: 273–286.

Starr, Harvey. 1992. "Democracy and War: Choice, Learning, and Security Commitment." *Journal of Peace Research* 29: 207–213.

Stephens, John. 1979. *The Transition from Capitalism to Socialism*. London: Macmillan.

Stockman, Alan. 1981. "Anticipated Inflation and the Capital Stock in a Cash-in-Advance Economy." *Journal of Monetary Economics* 8: 387–393.

Summers, Robert, and Alan Heston. 1995. *The Penn World Table (Mark 5.6)*. Cambridge, Mass.: National Bureau of Economic Research.

Summers, Robert, and Alan Heston. 2000. *The Penn World Table (Mark 5.7)*. Cambridge, Mass.: Center for International Comparisons at the University of Philadelphia.

Summers, Robert, and Alan Heston. 2001. *The Penn World Table (Mark 6.0)*. Cambridge, Mass.: Center for International Comparisons at the University of Philadelphia.

Szkudlarek, Tomasz. 1993. *The Problem of Freedom in Postmodern Education*. Westport, Conn.: Bergin and Garvey.

Tabellini, Guido, and Alberto Alesina. 1990. "Voting on the Budget Deficit." *American Economic Review* 80: 37–49.

Taiwan Provincial Government, Department of Budget, Accounting, and Statistics. 1994. *Statistical Yearbook of Taiwan Province*, no. 54. Taipei: Taiwan Provincial Government.

Tammen, Ronald L., Jacek Kugler, Douglas Lemke, Allan C. Stam III, Mark Abdollahian, Carole Alsharabati, Brian Efird, and A. F. K. Organski. 2000. *Power Transitions: Strategies for the 21st Century*. New York: Chatham House Publishers.

Taylor, Charles L. 1985. *World Handbook of Social and Political Indicators*. Ann Arbor, Mich.: Inter-university Consortium for Political and Social Research.

Taylor, Lance. 1988. *Varieties of Stabilization Experience*. Oxford: Clarendon Press.

Thompson, W. S. 1929. "Population." *American Journal of Sociology* 34: 959–975.

Thut, I. N., and Don Adams. 1964. *Educational Patterns in Contemporary Societies*. New York: McGraw-Hill.

Tocqueville, Alexis de. 1835. *Democracy in America*. Trans. Henry Reeve. London: Saunders & Otley.

Trebilock, Michael J. 1995. "What Makes Poor Countries Poor? The Role of Institutional Capital in Economic Development." Working paper no. WPS-38. Faculty of Law, University of Toronto.

Tyler, William G. 1981. "Growth and Export Expansion in Developing Countries: Some Empirical Evidence." *Journal of Development Economics* 9: 121–130.

Van Evera, Stephen. 1993. "Primed for Peace: Europe after the Cold War." In *The Cold War and After: Prospects for Peace*, ed. Sean Lynn-Jones, pp. 193–224. Cambridge: MIT Press.

Vanhanen, Tatu. 1990. *The Process of Democratization: A Comparative Study of 147 States, 1980–88*. New York: Crane, Russak.

Venieris, Yiannis P., and Dipak K. Gupta. 1983. "Sociopolitical and Economic Dimensions of Development: A Cross-Section Model." *Economic Development and Cultural Change* 31: 727–756.

Venieris, Yiannis P., and Dipak K. Gupta. 1986. "Income Distribution and Sociopolitical Instability as Determinants of Savings: A Cross-Sectional Model." *Journal of Political Economy* 96: 873–883.

Venieris, Yiannis P., and Douglas B. Stewart. 1987. "Sociopolitical Instability, Inequality, and Consumption Behavior." *Journal of Economic Development* 12: 7–16.

Venieris, Yiannis P., and Samuel M. Sperling. 1994. "Saving and Social Instability in Developed and Less Developed Nations." *Journal of Economic Development* 19: 209–252.

Venieris, Yiannis P., and Terrence Paupp. 1996. "The New Leviathans." Manuscript.

Verba, Sidney. 1991. "Threats to Democracy." In *The Transition to Democracy: Proceedings of a Workshop*, ed. Commission on Behavioral and Social Sciences and Education, National Research Council, pp. 74–83. Washington, D.C.: National Academy Press.

Wade, Robert. 1990. *Governing the Market: Economic Theory and the Role of Government in East Asian Industrialization*. Princeton: Princeton University Press.

Wade, Robert. 1993. "The Visible Hand: The State and East Asia's Economic Growth." *Current History* 92: 431–440.

Wallerstein, Immanuel. 1974. *The Modern World System.* New York: Academic Press.

Wallerstein, Immanuel. 1979. "The Present State of the Debate on World Inequality." In *The Capitalist World Economy: Essays,* ed. Immanuel Wallerstein, pp. 49–65. New York: Cambridge University Press.

Weede, Erich. 1980. "Beyond Misspecification in Sociological Analyses of Income Inequality." *American Sociological Review* 45: 497–501.

Weede, Erich. 1982. "The Effects of Democracy and Socialist Strength on the Size Distribution of Income: Some More Evidence." *International Journal of Comparative Sociology* 23: 151–165.

Weede, Erich. 1983. "The Impact of Democracy on Economic Growth." *Kyklos* 36: 21–39.

Weede, Erich. 1997. "Income Inequality, Democracy, and Growth Reconsidered." *European Journal of Political Economy* 13: 751–764.

Weede, Erich, and Horst Tiefenbach. 1981. "Some Recent Explanations of Income Inequality: An Evaluation and Critique." *International Studies Quarterly* 25: 255–282.

Wei, Shang-Jin. 1995. "Attracting Foreign Direct Investment: Has China Reached Its Potential?" *China Economic Review* 6: 187–199.

Wei, Shang-Jin. 1997a. "How Taxing Is Corruption on International Investors." Working paper. Kennedy School of Government, Harvard University.

Wei, Shang-Jin. 1997b. "Why Is Corruption So Much More Taxing Than Tax? Arbitrariness Kills." Working paper. Kennedy School of Government, Harvard University.

Weingast, Barry R. 1995. "The Economic Role of Political Institutions: Market-Preserving Federalism and Economic Development." *Journal of Law, Economics, and Organization* 11: 1–31.

Weingast, Barry R. 1997. "The Political Foundations of Democracy and the Rule of Law." *American Political Science Review* 91: 245–263.

Weintraub, Sidney. 1991. "What Is a Democracy? Economics." In *The Transition to Democracy: Proceedings of a Workshop,* ed. Commission on Behavioral and Social Sciences and Education, National Research Council, pp. 12–15. Washington, D.C.: National Academy Press.

Weitzman, Martin L. 1993. "Capitalism and Democracy: A Summing Up of the Arguments." In *Market and Democracy: Participation, Accountability, and Efficiency,* ed. Samuel Bowles, Hubert Gintis, and Bo Gustafsson, pp. 306–315. New York: Cambridge University Press.

Wheeler, David. 1984. "Sources of Stagnation in Sub-Saharan Africa." *World Development* 12: 1–23.

White, Herbert L. 1980. "A Heteroskedasticity-Consistent Covariance Matrix Estimator and a Direct Test for Heteroskedasticity." *Econometrica* 48: 817–838.

Whyte, Martin King, and William L. Parish. 1984. *Urban Life in Contemporary China.* Chicago: University of Chicago Press.

Wihlborg, C., and T. Willett. 1997. "Capital Account Liberalization and Policy Incentives: An Endogenous Policy View." In *Capital Controls in Emerging Economies*, ed. C. P. Ries and R. J. Sweeney, pp. 113–116. Boulder: Westview.

Willett, Thomas D., ed. 1988. *Political Business Cycles: The Political Economy of Money, Inflation, and Unemployment*. Durham: Duke University Press.

Willett, Thomas D., and Nancy Neiman Auerbach. 2002. "The Political Economy of Perverse Financial Liberalization: Examples from the Asian Crisis." Paper presented at the Western Economics Association Conference, Seattle, July 2–5.

Wittman, Donald. 1989. "Why Democracies Produce Efficient Results." *Journal of Political Economy* 97: 1395–1424.

Wittman, Donald. 1995. *The Myth of Democratic Failure: Why Political Institutions Are Efficient*. Chicago: University of Chicago Press.

Wolf, Arthur. 1986. "The Preeminent Role of Government Intervention in China's Family Revolution." *Population and Development Review* 12: 101–116.

Woodhall, Maureen. 1987. "Economics of Education: A Review." In *Economics of Education: Research and Studies*, ed. George Psacharopoulos, pp. 1–8. New York: Pergamon Press.

World Bank. 1985. *World Development Report*. New York: Oxford University Press.

World Bank. 1993a. *Sustaining Rapid Development in East Asia and the Pacific*. Washington, D.C.: World Bank.

World Bank. 1993b. *World Tables of Economic and Social Indicators, 1950–1992*. Ann Arbor, Mich.: Inter-university Consortium for Political and Social Research.

World Bank. 2000. *World Development Indicators*. New York: United Nations.

World Game Institute. 1997. *Global Data Manager 3.0: The Source of Global Statistics on Your Personal Computer*. Philadelphia: World Game Institute.

Yao, Xinwu, and Hua Yin. 1994. *Basic Data of China's Population*. Beijing: China Population Publishing House.

Young, Alwyn. 1992. "A Tale of Two Cities: Factor Accumulation and Technical Change in Hong Kong and Singapore." In *NBER Macroeconomics Annual, 1992*, ed. Olivier Jean Blanchard and Stanley Fischer, pp. 13–54. Cambridge: MIT Press.

Youngblood, Robert L. 1990. *Marcos against the Church*. Ithaca: Cornell University Press.

Zak, Paul J. 1997. "Institutions, Property Rights, and Growth." Working paper. Claremont Graduate University.

Zak, Paul J. 2000. "Socio-political Instability and the Problems of Development." In *Governing for Prosperity*, ed. Bruce Bueno de Mesquita and Hilton L. Root, pp. 153–171. New Haven: Yale University Press.

Zak, Paul J., and Yi Feng. 2003. "A Dynamic Theory of the Transition to Democracy." *Journal of Economic Organization and Behavior*. Forthcoming.

Zak, Paul J., Yi Feng, and Jacek Kugler. 2001. "Immigration, Fertility, and Growth." *Journal of Economic Dynamics and Control* 26: 547–576.

Zhang, Baohui. 1994. "Corporatism, Totalitarianism, and Transitions to Democracy." *Comparative Political Studies* 27: 108–136.

Zhao, Zhongwei. 1997. "Deliberate Birth Control under a High-Fertility Regime: Reproductive Behavior in China before 1970." *Population and Development Review* 23: 729–767.

Zheng, Xiaoying. 1995. *China's Female Population and Development*. Beijing: Beijing University Press.

Zou, Qingfeng. 1993. "China's Family Planning and the Chinese Culture." In *Asia 2000: Modern China in Transition*, ed. D. Bing, S. Lim, and M. Lin, pp. 92–107. New Zealand: University of Waikato Printery.

# Index